Interpreting America

The Vanderbilt Library of American Philosophy

offers interpretive perspectives on the historical roots of American philosophy and on present innovative developments in American thought, including studies of values, naturalism, social philosophy, cultural criticism, and applied ethics.

Other recently published titles in the series include

The Life and Thought of Josiah Royce
Revised and Expanded Edition
John Clendenning

His Glassy Essence: An Autobiography of Charles Sanders Peirce
Kenneth Laine Ketner

The Continuity of Peirce's Thought
Kelly A. Parker

Intensity: An Essay in Whiteheadian Ontology
Judith A. Jones

Transforming Experience: John Dewey's Cultural Instrumentalism
Michael Eldridge

The Thought and Character of William James
New Paperback Edition
Ralph Barton Perry

The Philosophy of Loyalty
New Paperback Edition
Josiah Royce

Rorty and Pragmatism: The Philosopher Responds to His Critics
edited by Herman J. Saatkamp, Jr.

Pragmatic Bioethics
edited by Glenn McGee

In Love with Life: Reflections on the Joy of Living and Why We Hate to Die
John Lachs

INTERPRETING AMERICA

Russian and Soviet Studies of the History of American Thought

John Ryder

VANDERBILT UNIVERSITY PRESS
Nashville and London

First Edition 1999

99 00 01 02 4 3 2 1

This publication is made from paper that meets the minimum requirements of ANSI/NISO Z39.48-1992 (R 1997)—Permanence of Paper for Printed Library Materials. ∞

Library of Congress Cataloging-in-Publication Data

Ryder, John, 1951-
Interpreting America : Russian and Soviet studies of the history of American thought / John Ryder. — 1st ed.
p. cm. — (The Vanderbilt library of American philosophy)
Includes bibliographical references and index.

ISBN 0-8265-1334-4 (alk. paper)
1. Philosophy, American—History. I. Title. II. Series.
B851 .R93 1998
191—dc21
98-58118
CIP

Published by Vanderbilt University Press
Printed in the United States of America

to Rita and Joseph Ryder
for all they have done

CONTENTS

FOREWORD

I first met John Ryder many years ago, in the early 1980s, while he was visiting Moscow State University as part of a research project he had undertaken on Soviet/Russian interpretations of American philosophy. Although all of us came to respect Professor Ryder as a competent scholar and a sympathetic friend, several of my colleagues initially regarded his research topic as rather exotic. Of course, all of us were flattered to have become the subject of interest of a visiting American scholar, but many of us kept wondering why a prominent scholar from the United States would spend so much time studying our modest efforts in understanding the history of American philosophy.

Partially, this question reflected a low level of academic self-esteem among Soviet historians of American philosophy, since many of them thought of their studies and interpretations as for "home use only." Few of them believed that Soviet/Russian studies of American philosophy could or should be "exported," since they were well aware that their interpretations were often spoiled by a militant Marxist stance aimed not only at contemporary American philosophers like Sidney Hook but also at historical figures such as Dewey, James, Peirce, Emerson, and Jefferson. In the eyes of many Soviet philosophers of that time, all American philosophers, historical or contemporary, by definition, were incorrect in their thinking unless they expressed Marxist or at least materialistic views in their work.

Consequently, in public Soviet philosophers adopted the line of an openly condescending form of criticism of American "bourgeois" philosophy. Indeed, this critical posturing was often imposed on scholars by Soviet ideological authorities as almost the only permissible condition under which research was conducted in the field of American philosophy. Nevertheless, in private many Soviet philosophers were well aware of the false nature of such an approach. Consequently, they were reluctant to have someone from outside the country witness this and analyze their personal opinions. Conflict such as this between the public and private discourse of scholars is an example of what has been described by sociologists as the "dual thinking" that was typical of the Soviet era. In this sense, the appearance of John Ryder in Moscow and the form of research he carried out there created feelings of contradiction and anxiety that were manifested as a peculiar combination of pride and fear among my colleagues.

Yet all Soviet historians of American philosophy, regardless of their possible ideological fears and scholarly "complexes," admitted that John Ryder's approach to his research was serious, thoughtful, and fundamentally important. During his stay, he met and interviewed almost every contemporary Soviet philosopher who had published anything on American philosophy. The hours he spent in our libraries were uncountable. As a result, his studies of the Soviet and Russian authors who have written in this area are simply unparalleled. Even today we can scan Ryder's bibliography and discover new sources and names in Soviet studies of American philosophy with whom we had not been familiar.

Professor Ryder's rigorous and exhaustive research has resulted in a book with a wide and panoramic view of the entire field. He has accomplished well the main objectives of providing a thorough interpretation of the texts he has studied and has clearly reconstructed the chain of core ideas in these sources. Ryder has, for example, dedicated a number of pages in his book to an analysis of my own writings on American philosophy, specifically on the Puritans, Jefferson, and the transcendentalists. In my view, his treatment is perfectly convincing.

Throughout the book, Ryder emphasizes the most essential concepts of each writer's work, and he also gives a multidimensional reconstruction of the arguments of each author. His quotations from the original sources are accurately representative of the authors he is discussing, and he offers very fine translations of each source. (In my opinion, Ryder's knowledge of written Russian is unquestionable.) His interpretations of the works of Bogomolov, Karimsky, Melvil, Sidorov, Yulina, and others are all excellent.

Ryder's own critical comments and judgments are usually hidden between the lines. Yet the modesty of his presentation never betrays his talents and scholarly identity. Always, one can tell which ideas Ryder likes (or dislikes), yet he never imposes his own views or personal biases upon the reader. Instead, Ryder artistically creates a diverse composition of analyzed sources and arranges them in a well-organized manner. His clear organization of a massive amount of material is the most admirable achievement of the book.

In the beginning sections of this book, Ryder gives his own interpretation of the role that American philosophy played in the Soviet Union. He is absolutely correct in saying that the principle "know your enemy" was a major argument for the justification of the study of American philosophy in the Soviet Union, especially among so-called ideological "hard-liners." Ryder offers Baskin as an example of the older Stalinist generation of scholars who followed this principle without question. Yet for many other mainstream Russian specialists in American philosophy—especially younger ones like Sidorov and myself but also, to some degree, the middle-aged and therefore more cautious Melvil, Bogomolov, Karimsky, and

Yulina—studying American philosophy was an effective way to represent and disseminate the principles of non-Marxist, liberal philosophical thinking in a country dominated by a totalitarian regime. By discussing in our publications and lecture courses the main figures in American philosophy, from the colonial age to the present, we were definitely and seriously trying to question the degenerating ideology of Soviet Marxism-Leninism. This was our main objective, whether we did it consciously or unconsciously. In brief, the spirit of American philosophy that affected us so deeply was incompatible with the Soviet system of thought. Thus by studying, lecturing, and writing about American philosophy, we stimulated discussions among the Russian public and intelligentsia on great American thinkers.

During the Soviet period, American philosophy was an elite area of research which provided selected scholars with access to the world of an "alternative," non-Marxist philosophy. Now it has lost that distinction and is scarcely more than one of many areas of research in the history of philosophy. It now lacks the elitism it once had and has far fewer special advantages to offer students. Personally, my own scholarly position has suffered under these new intellectual circumstances. Yet I do not regret it, since for me this is further evidence of the process of "normalization" in Russia's social and cultural life.

Today, American philosophy in Russia is no longer a "special subject" with many hidden political agendas. It is now an ordinary scholarly subject open to anyone who is interested in it. Although we, the specialists in this subject, are no longer treated as privileged gurus who know "the truth" that is inaccessible to others, I regard the process of demystification and desacralization of American philosophy for the Russian public as a positive step.

As Ryder writes in this book, "The time will come when American and Western European societies will also collapse, and we should like to believe that those looking back will not dismiss us simply because of our time and place." It is my own belief that the efforts of my colleagues who specialized in the study of American philosophy during the Soviet era have not been undermined or made irrelevant simply because the Soviet system has ceased to exist. John Ryder's book is an important historical record that concisely documents the fact that our scholarly efforts during the Soviet period were not quite in vain.

Nikita Pokrovsky
Moscow State University

ACKNOWLEDGMENTS

A work that takes years to complete, as this one has, invariably incurs a debt to many people. First among them in this case is Peter Hare. His early and sustained interest in Soviet studies of the history of American philosophy had a good deal to do with the origins of this project and with seeing it through. Many other people on this side of the ocean have also contributed in important ways, sometimes directly and sometimes by providing an intellectual environment that encourages inquiry. My colleagues and friends in the Society for the Advancement of American Philosophy deserve mention, specifically James Campbell, Armen Marsoobian, Richard Hart, and Herman Saatkamp. At SUNY, Cortland, special thanks go to John Marciano, Kathryn Russell, and Henry Steck. I am also grateful to SUNY, Cortland, for two sabbatical leaves over the years; the first of those, supported by a grant from the Faculty Research Program, allowed me to spend several months in Moscow conducting research.

This work would not have been possible without the help of many people in Moscow, both at Moscow State University and at the Institute of Philosophy, which at the time was part of the USSR Academy of Sciences. Those at the university that I particularly wish to thank are Alexander Panin, Nikita Pokrovsky, Valery Kuvakin, and Alexander Gryaznov. I also acknowledge the help I received from the late Yuri Melvil and Anyur Karimsky, debts that, sadly, I can now never repay. I am especially grateful to Nina Yulina at the Institute of Philosophy for her time and insights.

However, the greatest debt is to my wife Colleen, who was willing to accompany me half way around the world to undertake this work. Without her continued support the book would not have been written.

INTRODUCTION

Philosophers in the United States have been taking a closer look in recent years at the history of philosophy in America. The primary impetus for this may be the appearance of what is sometimes called neopragmatism, which rests to a large extent on aspects of John Dewey's thought. Whatever the reason, American philosophers are increasingly interested in what American philosophy has been, in its history, its prevalent themes, and its legacy. This book intends to join that stream of interest in American thought by focusing on the studies of and commentaries on the entire history of American philosophy by specialists in Russia and the Soviet Union. Interest in this or that aspect of the history of American philosophy has been evident in probably every society in which philosophy is done. But no society outside the United states has focused as much interest in the history of American thought as has Russia and the Soviet Union, especially since the end of the Second World War. Indeed, outside of English, the Russian language owns the largest body of literature on the history of American philosophy. By making some of that literature accessible, this work intends to contribute to the expanding concern with the history of American philosophy and with its understanding abroad.

There are actually three distinct themes here, the first of which concerns Russian and Soviet philosophy in general. As this is being written, it is less than ten years since the Soviet Union has ceased to exist, and the future development of Russia in particular, including its political and ideological directions, remains undetermined. Of course the changes in Russia since 1991, and even before, as the effects of *glasnost* and *perestroika* deepened and expanded, have been enormous, and those changes have naturally affected Russian philosophy. Only ten years ago it was safe to say that virtually all philosophers in that part of the world worked within the categories of Marxist or Marxist-Leninist thought. While many still do work and think in those terms, it is certainly no longer true that nearly all do. The Russian philosophical world has changed dramatically. The fact remains, though, that the majority of philosophers who were teaching and writing ten years ago are still teaching and writing today, and among their current ranks are younger ones who were their students. In other words, philosophy in Russia is not beginning from a *tabula rasa* but, on the contrary, rests to a considerable extent on its own past development. With respect to studies of the history of American philosophy, that means that the large body of literature that was produced during the Soviet period remains the primary source of information and secondary analysis of American philosophy available to Russian-speaking scholars and students. The works discussed in this book, then—though for the most part produced in the Soviet era and therefore under circumstances distinct from the present—remain highly relevant for both an understanding of the character of Russian philosophy and for a sense of how Russians have been and still are talking about American thought.

That these works were written largely after the Bolshevik Revolution and before 1991 means that to look at them closely is to look fairly closely at the world of Soviet philosophy. Despite recent and current developments, Soviet works that deal with the history of American philosophy in one way or another took seriously the conceptual framework of dialectical and historical materialism. Given the generally Marxist character of the material to be discussed here, a word is in order about the relation between this study of Soviet philosophy and what during the period of the cold war would have been called mainstream philosophical Sovietology. With some exceptions, Western European and American specialists in Soviet philosophy shared the view of J. M. Bochenski, the founder of Western philosophical Sovietology, who felt, in Richard T. DeGeorge's words, that "Marxism-Leninism . . . could not withstand philosophical scrutiny," or the view of Lewis S. Feuer, who wrote in 1964 of "how hard the Soviet ideological stance makes it for them to approach the history of ideas in an empirical spirit."[1] These are positions I did not share when I worked with this material while the Soviet Union still existed, and I do not share them now, at least not as assumptions or points of departure. This book is not an attempt to refute Soviet assessments of the history of American philosophy nor to expose any presupposed deficiencies in Soviet philosophical research. Of course, to the extent that there were deficiencies in a given analysis, one hopes that careful scrutiny and reflection will expose them, but then one hopes that careful scrutiny and reflection will reveal whatever virtues may present themselves, as well. As will become clear, my own view is that Soviet commentary on the history of American philosophy has its share of virtues and deficiencies. Though I occasionally indulge in commentary when it seems appropriate, my intention is to present the material as thoroughly and accurately as possible and to let the reader judge how it fares.

A second, and the most overt, theme is the history of philosophy in North America as it appears through the eyes of non-Americans. There is a long and valuable tradition of foreign, especially European, observation and commentary on American life and thought, from de Tocqueville to the contemporary Danish photographer Jacob Holdt's *American Pictures*, a searing and relentless exposure of poverty and racism in the United States.

Soviet analyses of American thought are components of that European tradition and deserve to be more widely known. We Americans have an unfortunate tendency to be somewhat provincial in our understanding of ourselves, and our self-conception can only be enriched through an encounter with the way others have understood and understand us, whether or not we find their observations and analyses acceptable in the end.

While all that is true, it is also the case that approaching the history of American philosophy through others' eyes presents both difficulties and advantages. The difficulties stem from the fact that the issues and concerns that dominate the book are those of the Russian and Soviet commentators, and they are occasionally different from those we might find in standard American discussions of the same material, or that I might have emphasized were I writing my own history of American philosophy. For example, for reasons that should become clear in chapter 2, Soviet commentators were interested in whether the American Revolution was primarily an anti-colonial rebellion or genuinely revolutionary, therefore belonging in the rank, especially, of the English and French bourgeois revolutions. Soviet discussions of the American Enlightenment, to give a related example, commonly included a concern with whether secular social contract theory, and by extension American constitutionalism, is grounded in Puritan covenant theory. In fact there is a more general interest in whether Puritanism and subsequent American thought and culture are more or less seamless or whether they are to be sharply distinguished. Some Soviet specialists expressed a concern with whether or not there is such a thing as "bourgeois philosophy"; with whether pragmatism is an imperialistically, or at least overtly capitalistically, oriented philosophy; and with whether this or that philosophical school accords sufficiently with the principles of dialectical materialism. These examples of prevalent themes all have an ideological air, but less ideologically charged issues can be defined that tended to interest Soviet commentators more than they might others—for example, whether Santayana was or was not genuinely a naturalist. These may not be immediately germane concerns, but because they were central in the Soviet literature they necessarily play a large role in the way any consideration of that literature will be organized.

The advantages of looking closely at the way another culture understands and evaluates our philosophical heritage, however, far outweigh the disadvantages. Looking at ourselves as others see us can bring into focus certain characteristics or useful questions that might otherwise go unnoticed. While we may disagree among ourselves as to what those traits and questions might be, there are several issues that appear prominently in Russia and Soviet works on the history of American philosophy that I think warrant serious consideration on our part. Soviet commentators, for example, have emphasized the role of what they call the Puritan "dissidents" in the eighteenth century transition from New England congregationalism to the Enlightenment. Along similar lines, they have wondered whether Enlightenment rights theory is *in principle* restricted to a ruling class, which in turn may help to explain the ongoing difficulty we Americans have in addressing social problems such as civil rights, women's rights, poverty, and other matters. In relation to the American Revolution, Soviets were interested in the sometimes sharp disagreements among members of the revolutionary leadership, the radicals and the moderates, and they have raised the question whether the Constitution sufficiently guarantees citizens their material rights and interests.

Interesting issues emerge in relation to other aspects of American philosophy as well. We might well wonder with our Russian colleagues about the extent to which transcendentalism, rather than looked at simply as a romantic reaction against the Enlightenment, can be better understood as the heir to Enlightenment revolutionary principles, or the degree to which the idealist self-reliance of Emersonian transcendentalism may well be an obstacle to the very sort of social progress that Emerson himself endorsed. Given the increasing interest in pragmatism, we might well ask after the possibility that pragmatism—with its voluntarism and its emphasis on human action rather than on the traits of the world in which we act—may turn out to be more debilitating than empowering. If we insist on ignoring the objectively determinate traits of the world, then our actions can be fruitful only by chance. And we might consider the related criticism that despite Peirce's, James's and Dewey's desire to avoid relativism and subjectivism, their own pragmatist principles force their ideas in that direction anyway. These and many other issues that bear reflection are raised in the Russian and Soviet commentary, occasionally in ways from which we might learn.

The third theme of this book reflects on the history of American philosophy. The opportunity presents itself to consider several of the central issues in American thought and culture. Many of the problems of the American philosophical tradition remain living, vital concerns, not simply because history conditions the present, which it certainly does, but because the themes that have characterized American thought for over three hundred years continue to be relevant and in crucial respects unresolved. Questions of the appropriate general conception of nature, of the relation of knowledge and action, of the possibility and character of metaphysical generalization, of the relation of religion and society, of the general traits of human nature, and of individuality and democracy are no less significant concerns today than in the past. Whether issues of technical ontology and epistemology or of social and political thought, neither philosophy nor American social relations have out-distanced them. The themes to be explored throughout these chapters are not merely of historical interest.

The temptation then is great to pursue them in more or less detail when they come up, and I have here and there given in to that temptation.

The chapters that follow will deal with a fairly wide range of figures, movements, and themes from the seventeenth century to recent years. There are, nevertheless, several topics that a study of Soviet analysis of American philosophy might well include but that will not be considered here. Among them are American religious thought, both historical and contemporary, the philosophy of education, the philosophy of science, American feminism, American phenomenology and existentialism, and contemporary American analytic philosophy. One of the reasons for the exclusion is that the emphasis of the study is historical. The more compelling reason, however, in fact that which necessitates the historical emphasis, is that with the exception of American feminism each of these topics has engendered such a mass of critical literature that Soviet studies of any one of them would itself be a legitimate topic of a separate book.

American religious thought has been the subject of a number of studies, including N. S. Yulina's *Theology and Philosophy in 20th Century American Religious Thought*, V. I. Dobren'kov's *Contemporary Protestant Modernism in the U.S.A.*, and a collection edited by A. S. Bogomolov titled *Contemporary Bourgeois Philosophy and Religion.* In addition to numerous articles on American religious thought, there have been several dissertations on the subject, including N. E. Sklaifer's "The Problem of Man in the Philosophy of American Protestantism," Yu. I. Mukovozov's "A Critique of the Ideological Foundations of the Protestant Theology of Reinhold Niebuhr," and L. P. Voronkova's "A Critical Analysis of R. Niebuhr's Theological Anthropology." Soviet literature on American education and pedagogical theory is extensive, examples of which are recent articles by T. V. Tz'rlina on values education in America and V. Ya. Pilipovsky on the technocratic character of contemporary Western pedagogy. Soviet analysis of American feminism, on the other hand, was only just beginning toward the later years of the Soviet period. Two significant discussions are N. S. Yulina's "The Question of Women: Philosophical Aspects" and T. A. Klimenkova's "Philosophical Problems of Neofeminism in the 1970s."

On existentialism, analytic philosophy and the philosophy of science, however, Soviet specialists produced volumes. On continental philosophy in the United States one might turn to E.Yu. Solov'ev's *Existentialism and Scientific Knowledge* and A.G. Grigoryan's *Existentialism in the U.S.A.*, written in 1966 and 1967 respectively. More recently there are D. Lukanov's "The Tradition of Existentialist Philosophy in the U.S.A.," L. A. Mirskaya's "The Relation of the Individual and the Social in America Existentialist Phenomenology," and articles by A. M. Rutkevich on existentialist psychology. Relevant dissertations include L. A. Mirskaya's

"American Existentialist Phenomenology" and I. V. Tzurina's "A Critical Analysis of Existentialism in the U.S.A."

Analytic philosophy had been the subject of Soviet scholarship for some time, and it continues to be interesting to Russian philosophers. Representative works include D. I. Dubrovsky's "From 'Scientific Materialism' to 'Emergent Materialism,'" N. S. Yulina's "Analytic Philosophy in the 20th Century," G. A. Brutyan's "Philosophy and Metaphilosophy," essays by Tregubova on Goodman, Blinov and Petrov on Davidson, and finally V. A. Lektorsky's "Analytic Philosophy Today." Examples of discussions of Quine in Soviet literature are an article by the Bulgarian philosopher E. Panova on "Quine and the Problem of Ontological Relativity" in the *Journal of Moscow University*, and an exchange in *Filosofskie Nauki* on Quine's "Logical Pragmatism" between the American James McClellan and the Russian specialist on British and American analytic philosophy A. F. Gryaznov. Among dissertations is G. V. Minitaite's "Current Tendencies in American Moral Philosophy," a study of John Rawls, and there is at present a lively interest among Russian philosophers and graduate students in the work of Hilary Putnam. The philosophy of science, however, has probably been the most widely discussed branch of contemporary American philosophy. One can refer to I. T. Kasavin's study of Feyerabend, *The Theory of Knowledge as the Captive of Anarchy*, V. M. Legostaev's "Thomas Kuhn's Philosophical Interpretation of the Development of Science," V. N. Porus's "*The Structure of Scientific Revolutions* and the Dialectic of the Development of Science," and V. S. Shvyrev's "The Problem of the Relation of Science and Metaphysics in Contemporary English and American Philosophy of Science."

Our study is limited to the history of American philosophy not because there is no substantial and interesting Soviet material on more contemporary topics, but because there is far too much. Another principle of delimitation that will serve to exclude what would otherwise be relevant and interesting material is that with very few exceptions the discussion will be limited to works produced by Soviet and Russian philosophers. Philosophy in all places and times intersects with other disciplines and fields, and this is particularly true of certain periods of American philosophy. The American Enlightenment interests historians as much as philosophers, and transcendentalism is no less a literary movement than a philosophical one. The significance of these periods in American thought was not lost on Soviet historians and literary specialists. There are, for example, numerous works by Soviet historians that deal with various aspects of the American Enlightenment, including G. N. Sevost'yanov and A. I. Utkin's *Thomas Jefferson*, V. O. Pechatnov's *Hamilton and Jefferson*, B. M. Shpotov's *The Agrarian Movement in the U.S.A.*, and the prominent Soviet scholar V. V. Sogrin's *The Founders of the U.S.A.: Historical Portraits.* Soviet specialists in American literature were no less active, as is clear, for example, in a collection of articles edited by Ya. N. Zasursky titled *The Sources and Formation of American National Literature: XVII-XVIII Centuries*, which contains a number of articles of both philosophical and literary interest. An example of a more contemporary philosophically pertinent discussion of American literature is O. O. Nesmelova's "The Influence of Existentialism on American Literature," a study primarily of Norman Mailer. Thus again, our attention is confined to the work of Soviet and Russian philosophers not because of any paucity of valuable material by those in other fields, but because there is enough outside of philosophy to merit several additional books like this one.

There is, finally, a limiting principle that concerns language. The works studied here are, with very few exceptions, written in Russian, and the exceptions are works that for one reason or other are available in English. Many other languages, however, are spoken and written in what was the Soviet Union, and occasionally a book or article on the history of American philosophy appeared in one of them. Since I do not read any Soviet language other than Russian, those works are closed to me. Thus I have no access, for example, to V. G. Gogoberishvili's *The Philosophy of Pragmatism* because it is in Georgian and as far as I know not translated into Russian or English. While one could also mention works in Ukrainian and other Soviet languages, it is nevertheless the case that the vast majority of Soviet research on the history of American philosophy was written in Russian and falls within the purview of this study.

This, then, is an analysis of works that for the most part are written in Russian by professional Soviet and post-Soviet philosophers and that deal with various aspects of the history of American philosophy. In addition to recently deceased thinkers like Yu. K. Melvil and A. M. Karimsky, these authors are for the most part currently working at differing stages in their respective careers and tend to be affiliated with either the Philosophy Faculties of prominent Russian universities or the Institute of Philosophy, within what is now the Russian Academy of Sciences. This means that their perspectives on the history of American philosophy have represented the views of the mainstream of the Soviet philosophical community as it developed over the past several decades. An analysis of these perspectives can, it is hoped, provide insight into the world of Soviet philosophy generally, the nature of Soviet and Russian perceptions of American thought, and finally into the depth, richness, and problems of our own philosophical heritage.

Why Soviet Commentary?

The question of why at this point we would be interested in Soviet commentary on the history of American philosophy has already been raised and will likely come up repeatedly. To approach the answer, consider the fuller version of the question: Because the Soviet Union ceased to exist some time ago already, why should we now turn to a study of Soviet discussions of the history of American philosophy? Put slightly differently, does not the demise of the Soviet Union render the commentary by Soviet philosophers on the history of American philosophy no longer relevant or interesting?

One can answer the question in its initial formulation simply and directly: We publish now a study of Soviet commentary on the history of American philosophy because the study has only just now been completed. While simple and true, this answer is unsatisfying because it does not address the purpose of the question. The latter formulation of the question hints at the real point, since underlying the question is the assumption that when the Soviet Union ceased to exist so also did any good purpose for studying the philosophical works produced in Russia during the Soviet period. Several arguments reject this assumption.

First, the idea that with the end of the Soviet Union also came the end of any good reason to study things Soviet rests on yet another assumption, that there was not nor could there have been anything intrinsically interesting produced by mainstream Soviet intellectuals or about Soviet intellectual life. We have thoroughly believed our own Cold War propaganda—that only the dissidents could have imagined something of cultural or intellectual value, that the very idea of valuable work done by mainstream writers is virtually unthinkable. This assumption is false, in my opinion, as much of this book's discussion will indicate. But even if this were defensible, it is still the case that Soviet intellectual life offers historical interest. The body of commentary studied in this book represents a significant slice of Soviet intellectual work, and so it reveals a good bit about the character of academic work produced during the Soviet period.

A second, and the most common, approach to Soviet affairs requiring argument is more complex. The assumption is that there was nothing of interest in Soviet academic life, that absent the Soviet Union, studying the work of Soviet philosophers is pointless. And this assumption conceals yet another presumption: Though Soviet commentary is intrinsically insignificant, it would nevertheless have been worth studying during the Soviet Union's existence in order to know what the other side was thinking. Notice, however, that this presumption is a variant of the "know your enemy" approach characteristic of so much of the worst of Soviet era philosophical commentary. Soviet studies of American philosophy, especially during the late 1940s and through the 1950s, usually took as given that the cultural products of American society, including its philosophy, were nothing more than expressions of the dominant traits of American society. Since American society was exploitive and militantly imperialistic, it follows that American philosophy was nothing more than a dressed up expression of the same unjust values and ends. Therefore, the only reason to study American philosophy was to expose its inadequacies.

This kind of approach to the study of American philosophy is clearly indefensible to us; yet, interestingly enough, we tend to take much the same approach to the study of Soviet philosophy. During the Cold War era American philosophers tended to regard the Soviet system in its most characteristic traits as an unjust order and anyone not explicitly critical of that order necessarily an accomplice to injustice. It followed that mainstream Soviet philosophical works had to be little more than apologies for an overtly unjust and oppressive society. Consequently, the only reason to study Soviet philosophy was to expose its inadequacies.

This is a tidy view, but to regard Soviet philosophy in this way is as weak an argument as that used by Soviet philosophers for regarding us. It was the worst of Soviet commentary on American philosophy that took it to be merely an expression of American shortcomings, just as it has been the worst of American and Western commentary on Soviet thought that took it to be nothing but an apology for the authority and power of the Soviet Communist Party. The best of Soviet commentators on American philosophy took their subject matter seriously and treated it as worthy of careful consideration in its own right. We should do the same.

Third, the assumption that absent the Soviet Union studying Soviet philosophical work is no longer worthwhile is a particularly egregious instance of "poisoning the well." Any given analysis covered in this book may or may not be sound, but its adequacy or lack thereof has nothing to do with its author's philosophical commitments, or the economic theory he holds, or in which country he holds citizenship. We are, presumably, more philosophically advanced than to reject out of hand an analysis because its author is a Marxist or a Republican or a Frenchman or a Soviet. The work studied in this book is grouped together because it is all a product of a single society, from more or less the same epoch, and written in the same language. This is not to say, however, that its criteria of adequacy are to be found in its social origin, its epoch, or its language. The time will come when American and Western European societies will also collapse, and we should like to believe that those looking back will not dismiss us simply because of our time and place. Their obligation would be to judge our work on its merits and let it stand or fall on philosophical grounds. Our obligation with respect to Soviet commentators on American philosophy is the same.

Furthermore, while the Soviet Union may be gone, a Marxist critique of many aspects of American society and culture is not. The claim that without the Soviet Union is no good reason exists to study Soviet era philosophy may be an imprecise way of stating a different point, namely, that the collapse of the Soviet Union indicates the failure of Marxism and that, therefore, nothing requires us to look seriously at what Marxists have had to say. Of course, if one has no interest in or curiousity about or if informed by an overt distaste for Marxist criticism, one is unlikely to undertake such a study or, for that matter, to read this book. The fact is that I feel that way about the work of quite a few philosophers of various stripes, so I am sympathetic. But I cannot dress up that distaste as a philosophically defensible judgment. Judgment requires understanding and understanding requires study. In the absence such study there is no good reason simply to dismiss as unworthy Soviet commentary on American philosophy.

But more is involved here than just one's taste. It has become a common and virtually unchallenged view that the end of the Soviet Union and the accompanying end of socialism in Central and Eastern Europe is sufficient evidence to conclude that Marxism and socialism are dead and that a "free market" economy and liberal democracy have emerged as more or less the natural order of things. I would point out, though, that it is not obvious that liberal, capitalist society will prevail indefinitely, and to assume that it will is to engage in a good bit of wishful thinking on the part of its proponents. Consider these two historical analogies. (1) One of the first great experiments in an early version of a "republic" was the English Revolution and the subsequent Commonwealth. The latter quickly turned into an authoritarian dictatorship, and a brutal one at that, and collapsed after a short while, leading to the restoration of the monarchy. No doubt this looked to the Stuarts and their supporters like clear evidence that a society cannot survive without a monarchy and that the more or less republican experiment of parliamentary rule was a pipe dream that could lead only to disaster. (2) At the end of the eighteenth century the explicitly republican experiment in France also devolved first to the Terror and then to a dictatorship. With the ultimate defeat of Napoleon came the restoration of the monarchy and another clear lesson in the folly of republicanism and the historical inevitability of monarchical rule. The point I assume is obvious. Both the English and the French revolutions failed, but their failure in the short run did not prevent their basic republican and liberal principles, or later versions of them, from coming to dominate the modern world. Those who today comfortably announce the end of history should take another look. What follows from this is not that Marxism represents the inevitable future but simply that the acceptability or not of any given Marxist analysis has nothing to do with the fact that the Soviet Union has ceased to exist. Again, the adequacy of any analysis should be judged on other grounds.

Finally, the simple fact is that for a whole host of reasons, some of them discussed in the following section, a huge body of literature on virtually all periods of the history of American philosophy was produced in the

Soviet Union. Because it was written in Russian, virtually no one in the United States or elsewhere who has an interest in the history of American philosophy has been able to read or study this material. My assumption is that those interested in the history of American philosophy can be expected to extend that interest to a previously largely unknown body of critical literature. Its source ought to be irrelevant. If it were a body of literature produced in French or German or Chinese, my assumption would be the same, that people interested in the subject matter would want to know what is contained in the critical literature. I can think of no good reason not to make this assumption about Russian and Soviet literature. We may or may not benefit from Soviet commentary, but we will need to have a look at it to find out.

Why the Russian Interest in American Philosophy?

I have already made the point that outside the United States no country has a more extensive literature on the history of American philosophy than Russia and that there are more books, dissertations, and articles about American thought written in Russian than in any language other than English. Why, one might wonder, have Soviet and Russian philosophers been so interested in American philosophy?

A full answer to that question is likely to be fairly involved, but it would certainly include at least three factors. First, Soviet philosophers were inclined, for reasons we can specify, to take history and the history of philosophy seriously, perhaps more seriously than philosophers elsewhere have been inclined to take them. Second, there is a social answer in the sense that the social and political circumstances in which the Soviet Union found itself after the Second World War contributed to the interest of its philosophers and ideologists in American philosophy. Third, several aspects of American thought intrigued Soviet philosophers on philosophic grounds.

Concerning the first point, Marxists are likely to hold that to understand ideas requires that one understand their history, as well as their relations with other ideas and with their social and cultural contexts. The meaning of the idea of freedom, for example, is different if its context is a struggle on the part of developing bourgeois forces for private property rights against an entrenched aristocracy, than if its context is the attempt by wage workers to protect their incomes and their families' material well-being. The meaning in each context is not absolutely different, but it is significantly different. In the first case, the freedom of the merchant from domination by the aristocrat suggests his ability to do as he pleases with his property. In the second case, the freedom of the worker from the economic power of the owner suggests restraint on the owner's ability to do as he pleases with his property. Given the flexibility of the concept of freedom, both merchant and worker can legitimately appeal to it, though for exactly opposite ends. Consequently, if one is to understand what such an idea means it is necessary to study it in context. An abstract analysis of the concept, as is common among English language philosophers, can reveal common traits of the concept throughout its history and its cultural relations, and there is a good deal of value in that. But an abstract analysis will not reveal the full breadth of meaning, since so much of that meaning is a consequence of factors that lie outside the concept itself. The same point can be made about ideas that do not deal as explicitly with social matters as does the idea of freedom. What we mean by inquiry itself may change from time to time and from place to place, not to mention the changes over time in the familiar battery of philosophical concepts such as knowledge, truth, reality, being, substance, attribute, thing, relation, and so on. That social and historical context is central to philosophical inquiry was taken for granted by Soviet era philosophers in Russia, and it colored their whole approach to the study of philosophy.

One effect of the historicist point of departure is that if one is to understand the contemporary intellectual and ideological world, it becomes necessary to study its development, its *whole* development. So, for example, the Soviet philosophical system included specialists in the philosophic traditions of all the regions of the world, both contemporary and historical. The study of Asian philosophy was far more respectable there than it is even now in the United States, and there were also specialists in British, German, and French philosophic traditions, as well as in Latin American and African philosophy. The study of the history of American philosophy was a quite natural component of an intellectual system that took seriously conceptual history. But still, one might ask why the Soviets exhibited as much interest in American thought as they did?

One answer has to do with the social and political context of the Soviet Union in world affairs, especially after the Second World War, and in the place of philosophy in that society. From the social and political perspective, the primary motivation for the study of American intellectual life and history was in order to know the other world power. In times of the sharpest hostility, that became a desire to know the enemy, though most of the time it was more an interest simply in understanding the most important and influential other. The Soviet intelligentsia desired to understand the American, and for Soviet philosophers that meant to understand American philosophy.

As we have mentioned, the explosion of Soviet studies of the history of American philosophy began after the Second World War, as the Soviet Union and the United States emerged as the two great world powers. Those in positions of authority and influence in the Soviet Union naturally felt the need to know and understand as much as they could about American history, society, and culture. For many of the intellectuals, that meant understanding American culture's philosophic expression. Soviet specialists took the not unreasonable view that a society's characteristics are related to its philosophy. Just what those relations are might be very difficult to spell out, but they nonetheless assumed that American philosophy provided insight into America. The most obvious illustration of this concerns pragmatism. Soviet commentators tended to argue that there is something distinctly American about pragmatism. If that is so, then it had to be examined carefully. The American character could be read off the pages of pragmatist philosophical works, and thus a clearer understanding of American society, culture, and even politics and foreign policy might be gleaned. Whether Soviet or Russian policy makers ever made use of such analyses I do not know, but the work was certainly available to them. In many cases the most prominent intellectuals working in the area of American philosophy were well known to party and government officials and may have been influential in party affairs. In any case, whether or not policy makers appealed to these studies, Soviet and Russian intellectuals certainly have made use of them, and they continue to do so to the extent that they remain interested in American philosophy.

This presumption, we should notice, indicates a difference between Russian and American cultures. It has been a commonplace to point out the deep strain of anti-intellectualism in American society and culture. Although many individual Americans are interested in intellectual matters, the culture as a whole does not tend to value such activity. As a result, we tend to pay little attention to intellectual issues, whether pursued in the U.S. or abroad. For the Russians, by contrast, intellectual work is an important affair and to be taken quite seriously. This I take it is one of the reasons that the philosophical establishment was as well supported as it was during the Soviet period. Soviet society took its own intellectuals seriously, and on the same grounds it assumed that the intelligentsia in other societies were also to be taken seriously. The fact that the Soviet Union and the United States were the dominant contending forces in the world clearly meant for the Soviets that American intellectual life should be studied. When this is coupled with the previous point that the historical development of ideas is also to be taken seriously, we can begin to see why for the Soviet specialist it was important not only to study contemporary intellectual life but also its history. Consequently, both the contemporary American philosophical scene and its entire history were important subjects of study for Soviet specialists in "philosophical Americanistics."

While a social and political basis of explanation for Soviet interest in American philosophy has merit, I would contend that the philosophic answer is more important. As it turns out, many aspects of the history of

American philosophy spoke to Soviet concerns, and it is not without interest to notice that many aspects of American philosophy continue to speak to contemporary Russian concerns. It is worth looking at several examples in some detail to help make the point. Specifically, let us consider here the American revolutionary period, American romanticism, pragmatism, and naturalism.

The Soviet Union and the United States were born through revolutions. For both societies their revolutions were great historical leaps forward and embodied new and profound commitments to human freedom and development. The Soviets, on historical materialist grounds, regarded theirs superior because the Bolshevik Revolution—through the system of soviets and on Leninist grounds through the leadership of the party—for the first time in world history extended sovereignty, self-determination, and most importantly economic power to the whole of the adult population. But on the same historical materialist grounds, the Bolshevik Revolution was not a repudiation of the French and American revolutions, but an extension of them. The American Revolution was part of the historical background of October 1917, and American revolutionary theory was critical for the Soviets. They wanted to understand both how it underlay their own revolution and how theirs advanced and extended the American theory. American revolutionary theory, in other words, was directly relevant to Soviet concerns, both theoretical and practical.

This sense of relevance encouraged among Soviet specialists an interest in a wide range of issues concerning the American Enlightenment: its relation to the religious society that preceded it; the role of the religious dissenters in the development of Enlightenment principles; the character of philosophic materialism; the Enlightenment's humanism; its conception of rights; the whole issue of religious freedom and freedom of conscience; the disagreements between the moderate and radical wings of the American Enlightenment; the treatment of property and property rights; and the Enlightenment's philosophical anthropology.

While these make up the subject matter of chapter 2 and are discussed at length there, some points are worth making now, however. For example, the fact that Soviet society was officially secular, though it succeeded an overtly theological society and polity, raised for the Soviets many of the same issues that faced, and continue to face, American society and culture. All the difficult questions that concern the place of religion in a secular society, and the related issues of freedom of and from religion, had important practical and theoretical implications for Soviet society; therefore, the study of how these issues were handled in the history of American philosophy was of some moment. We should notice, too, that in the post-Soviet Russia, the question of the relation of religion to the public is no less important and no less difficult than it was before. To the extent that studying those issues in their American context has a value to philosophy, the American experience remains as useful to Russian intellectuals today as it was during the Soviet period. Comparable points may be made about the other aspects of American Enlightenment thought that interested Soviet philosophers. The question of how best to understand rights is no less serious now than in the past, and as Russia moves toward capitalism, to whatever length that movement eventually extends, the question of property rights rears its head in what for Russians are fairly new forms, though with many of the same problems and complications that have been faced by American thinkers and policy makers since the eighteenth century.

A second area that Soviet philosophers tended to find interesting for philosophical reasons is American romanticism. There were several reasons for this. On the one hand, romanticism was a reaction against the rationalism of the Enlightenment. One might expect a dogmatically minded materialist simply to reject romanticism, transcendentalism in its American guise, as a retreat into objective idealism. Fortunately, treatment by the best of the Soviet and Russian commentators was and is far better than that. Romanticism on their view was a dialectical rejection of the preceding rationalism, in the sense that rather than simply rejecting the earlier ideas, it recast them into new concepts. If the Enlightenment was the antithesis to the theologically oriented philosophical conceptions that preceded it, then romanticism was its *aufhebung*. The clearest illustration of this feature of American romanticism, and that Soviet specialists found this feature interesting, is in the prevalence of the judgment by Soviet commentators that American transcendentalism was the bearer in the first half of the nineteenth century of the humanistic spirit of the Enlightenment. On the basis of this point, Soviet specialists tended to distinguish American from European romanticism, arguing that its American version was more socially progressive. This feature of transcendentalism resonated with the Soviet commentators' own humanist point of view, and it inclined them to look closely at what Emerson, Thoreau, and their less prominent contemporaries had to say. They did not always approve of what they have found, but to a large extent the philosophic humanism of transcendentalism, rather than extraneous considerations, prompted Soviet interest.

In addition to its humanism, other features of American romanticism also attracted Soviet commentators' interest. Among them is the fact that Emerson can well be seen as crucial a figure in the development of an American philosophy of action that reached its most profound development in pragmatism. Emerson, then, and by extension the romantic spirit he embodied, becomes interesting by virtue of his place in the ongoing story of American intellectual life. We might also note of romanticism in particular that it had certain features in common with prominent strains of nineteenth century Russian philosophy, such as slavophilism, that bear distinctly romantic traits. It was not purely by accident that Tolstoy valued Thoreau as much as he did.

While Soviet commentators had a good deal to say about the American Enlightenment and transcendentalism, they were probably interested in pragmatism more than in any other trend in American thought, judging by the amount of literature devoted to it. As we will see in the introduction to part 2 and in chapter 4, the Soviet treatment of pragmatism tended to be quite hostile, especially in commentaries written between 1945 and the early 1960s. But for all the hostility, especially against Dewey, there are many points of contact between pragmatism, again especially Dewey's, and Soviet Marxism. It was important to the Soviets, on intellectual grounds, to sort it all out. Among the more obvious similarities between pragmatism and Soviet historical and dialectical materialism are the rejection of intellectualism and an emphasis on activity; an emphasis on the social as opposed to the atomistic individual; and the close relation that both philosophies assert to exist between theory and practice.

It was not enough, however, simply to note the similarities between the two schools of thought. There are also extensive differences between them, and the differences demanded a close look at the similarities to determine what to make of them. For example, Soviet Marxists always emphasized their philosophical materialism, which, following Lenin, they defined, with respect to ontology, simply as acknowledging the objectivity of the world's traits; with respect to epistemology they regarded knowledge to be the reflection in consciousness of nature's or the world's objective traits. No pragmatist ever so baldly asserted either of these ideas; in fact they have always tended to reject them both. Among the classical figures, Peirce defined truth as whatever is agreed to by the community of inquirers; James interpreted both matter and mind as second-order entities constructed from pure experience, and he famously defined truth as usefulness; Dewey in turn developed much of his ontological conception in terms of the problematic situation, which is to say that the traits of the world are determined in part by their relation to the human element of the situation, and his epistemology revolved around an understanding of inquiry as the solving of problems. Clearly, for Peirce, James, and Dewey, the truth was more complex and subtle than these remarks suggest, but in each figure there is this strain of anti-objectivism, and it is that strain with which Soviet commentators were determined to come to terms.

There is one other area of American philosophy in which Soviet and Russian specialists have had a genuine philosophical interest, and that is American naturalism. Of all the prominent strains of American philosophy, naturalism in various of its forms, comes closest to Soviet thought, that is, to dialectical materialism; and as one would expect, for that reason it appealed to Soviet philosophers. They tended to react differently to naturalism than to pragmatism. For all its similarities to Soviet Marxism, pragmatism nonetheless flirted, sometimes overtly and sometimes by default, with subjective idealism, and to that extent was rejected by Soviet philosophers. Naturalism, by contrast, has tended toward materialism in some of its versions, and in all its manifestations it tries to avoid the subjectivism that can arguably be attributed to pragmatism. In addition to this ontological point, one might also, as some Soviet commentators did, regard naturalism as a prominent contemporary expression of the humanism and secularism that so dominated the Enlightenment. In one book, for example, naturalists are described as "the successors to the humanistic, materialistic and democratic traditions in philosophy and social thought in the United States" (Karimsky 1972, 35–36). Another commentator expressed the point by saying that "the quest of American naturalism, its basic scientific and humanist position, cannot but elicit a deep sympathy" (Bogomolov 1974, 308).

There are many reasons for the sympathy with which Soviet and some contemporary Russian specialists regard naturalism, and they will be discussed in some detail in chapter 5. At the risk of excessive anticipation, we might briefly discuss some of them here. First, some American naturalist philosophers were friendly to or at least respectful of Marxist thought, including its Soviet versions. Roy Wood Sellars was sympathetic to dialectical materialism, as was Marvin Farber, and other prominent naturalist philosophers such as Abraham Edel have been sensitive to Marxist considerations. More important, though, is the fact that philosophic naturalism often intersects on general points with dialectical materialism. We saw in the brief discussion of pragmatism above that Soviet philosophers were invariably materialist, which meant in their case that they insisted on the objectivity of the world. This in turn means that whatever traits the world has, it has them independently of spirit and consciousness, whether individual or absolute. Of course no materialist of any kind is going to accept the existence of absolute spirit, so for the dialectical materialist the critical question concerned the relation of individual consciousness to the world. On this point, as we have said, Soviet philosophers tended to hold that the world has its traits objectively and that knowledge is a "reflection" of those traits in consciousness. Along with the affinity many naturalists have had with the methods and the results of the natural sciences, this objectivism is the aspect of naturalism that Soviets found most congenial.

This issue is in fact more complex, and more interesting, than just this joint sympathy for objectivism. This point will be discussed again in the Introduction to part 2, though by way of preview we may point out that the objectivism of dialectical materialism was not and is not the more simple objectivism of pre-Kantian modernism, where the mind from its "God's eye" vantage point either rationally or empirically surveys the traits of the world. On the contrary, Marxists are far more likely to be committed to the view that knowledge is always perspectival and conditional. This view comes as a result of Marxism's emphasis on the role played by material conditions in the formation of any society and its members. There are two relevant points here. First, on historical materialist principles the dominant ideas of any society arise and are sustained in so far as they are consistent with the interests of the dominant economic class of the society. For example, the idea of a right to private property could not have prevailed in a feudal society, since a feudal aristocracy could not have endorsed consistently the rights of all to property and at the same time maintained its own dominance in the society. It is only with the rise to power of a bourgeois class that the concept of universal property rights could become prevalent. This, Marx argued, was true of all dominant ideas, including political, religious, ethical, as well as more technical philosophical concepts. The basic conceptual principles to which the members of a society are likely to subscribe, then, are not grasped purely by reason or experience but are conditioned by the economic structures of the society. Second, a related point applies to individuals as well. Individuals' ideas are no less conditioned by social and other factors, and are therefore no less perspectival, than are the ideas that prevail in the society as a whole. An individual's class and general social conditioning are critical factors in that individual's consciousness and conception of the world. With respect both to the society in general and to the individual, the precise relation between economic and social factors, on the one hand, and concepts, ideas, and knowledge, on the other, is likely to be fairly complex and to require careful study in any given case. The general point, though, is that we should expect that the development of ideas, that is, the acquisition of knowledge, is a conditioned and perspectival process, and so our ontology and our epistemology must take that into account.

In some respects these points have a decidedly postmodernist ring to them, since postmodernism in its various manifestations also denies the "God's eye view" conception of knowledge. Postmodernists, however, tend to join this epistemological concept with an ontological claim that either there are no objective traits of the world to seek anyway, or that given the perspectival character of knowledge it would be impossible to know them if there were any. Either way, the postmodernist associates the perspectival conception of consciousness and knowledge with a rejection of an objectivist ontology. On this point the dialectical materialist disagrees. The objectivity of the world, he argues, is fully consistent with the fact that knowledge is conditioned and perspectival. A search is contextual in many ways; for example, it has a purpose, it has a point of departure, and it has a particular method. But the contextual nature of the search is not inconsistent with the claim that the result of the search, what is found or known, has its character independent of the search. In other words, the fact that knowledge is perspectival in no way implies that *what* is known is a function of its being known. By virtue of becoming known, it becomes a trait of the object that it *is* known, but that it is something known does not exhaust its traits. It is likely to have whatever other traits it has quite independent of its being an object of knowledge. As a result, the dialectical materialist would assert simultaneously the perspectival character of knowledge and the objectivity of the object of knowledge, and he would therefore be able to hold that knowledge, despite its conditioned nature, is able to "reflect" the objective world.

Pragmatism—with its interpretation of knowledge in terms of the problems, needs, or "doubts" of the knower—tended toward what we may now call a postmodernist view. This is precisely the reason Soviet critics of pragmatism found it objectionable in the end and described it as a strain of subjective idealism. Naturalism, on the other hand, often came much closer to the dialectical materialist view, and was therefore intriguing to Soviet philosophers. The "reformed materialism" of Roy Wood Sellars is an example, as is the functionalist naturalism of John Herman Randall Jr., to mention just two examples. As we will see, Soviet commentators had problems with both of these philosophers' ideas and theories, but in reading the criticisms one has the distinct impression that these are family disagreements. It is almost as if the critics are saying that naturalism is to be admired because it at least tries to get it right, even if in the end it fails for one reason or another. The failure is that for various reasons naturalists have not been able to reconcile the objectivity of the world with the conditioned, creative activity of the subject. In some cases naturalism is accused of flirting with the voluntarism and subjective idealism of pragmatism, or in other cases of collapsing into positivism or scientism. In some of the most recent Russian discussion of American naturalism, it is suggested that contemporary naturalism, particularly Justus Buchler's ordinal naturalism, has some promise in that it simultaneously proposes both the conditionality of the individual and the objective determination of nature's traits. It may well turn out that ordinal naturalism can avoid the confusion of contemporary postmodernism in a way that resembles the dialectical materialist view of Soviet commentators, and thereby sustain the perspective that they find lacking in earlier versions of American philosophic naturalism.

These are among the general social and philosophical factors that have motivated Soviet and Russian interest in the history of American philosophy since the October Revolution of 1917. There are no doubt other factors as well. Some of them, one would assume, must be individual, in the sense that different individuals find themselves attracted to one period or school of thought. One suspects, for example, that transcendentalism, particularly the work of Thoreau, has a special appeal to Nikita E. Pokrovsky, who has written extensively on this theme, because he finds its ideas attractive. His books and essays certainly give that impression. A fuller sense of what interests Russian and Soviet thinkers about American philosophy may be gained by looking closely at their work, to which we now turn.

Part I
Early American Philosophy

Preamble

Soviet studies of the history of American philosophy tended to focus on philosophic trends and schools of the late nineteenth and twentieth centuries, on what is sometimes referred to as the "Golden Age" of American philosophy. The earliest study to appear in the Soviet period, P. P. Blonsky's two volume *Contemporary Philosophy*, the first volume of which appeared in 1918 and the second in 1922, addresses two of the then most prominent American philosophic schools, pragmatism and neorealism. Other work in the earlier Soviet period dealt with these same subjects. Most notable among them are V. F. Asmus's 1927 article on William James and M. Shirvindt's 1930 article on neorealism. From the end of the Second World War to the 1990s the bulk of Soviet commentary and analysis concerned pragmatism and other twentieth century developments in American thought.

Despite the predominant interest in recent and contemporary American philosophy, studies began to appear in the decades following World War II that dealt with earlier stages in the development of American thought. M. P. Baskin's pamphlet *The Philosophy of the American Enlightenment*, based on lectures delivered in the Faculty of Philosophy at Moscow State University, appeared in 1955. N. M. Goldberg's *Freethinking and Atheism in the USA (17th-18th Cts.)* appeared in 1965, and in 1969 a two volume collection of primary sources from the American Enlightenment in Russian translation was published with an introductory essay by B. E. Bykhovsky. Interest in early American philosophy began to deepen in the mid-1970s with the work of A. M. Karimsky, in particular his 1976 article on the Declaration of Independence, explicitly dedicated to the bicentennial of that document and the American Revolution, and more importantly his 1976 book *The Revolution of 1776 and the Formation of American Philosophy*, the first detailed study of the early development of American thought by a Soviet philosopher. The breadth of Soviet analysis of early American philosophy expanded significantly with the appearance in 1983 of N. E. Pokrovsky's *Henry Thoreau*, and throughout the 1980s an increasing number of articles and books appeared on all aspects of the topic. One stimulus was the bicentennial of the U.S. Constitution, which was the occasion for several studies of American social and political thought in the eighteenth century. At the same time interest in American transcendentalism continued, evidenced, for example, by the appearance in 1986 of a volume that includes Russian translations of Emerson's *Nature*, "The American Scholar," "The Young American," the First and Second Series of Essays, and Thoreau's *Walden*. The volume also includes Pokrovsky's introductory essay "America Lost and Found." More recently still, Emerson's philosophic views are the subject of technical analysis in I. N. Sidorov's 1989 book *The Philosophy of Action in the U.S.A.: From Emerson to Dewey* and in Pokrovsky's 1995 study *Ralph Waldo Emerson: In Search of His Universe*.

Soviet analyses of the early periods of American thought reached still fuller maturity with Pokrovsky's *Early American Philosophy*, which appeared in 1989 and deals exclusively with Puritanism and early eighteenth century idealism. Pokrovsky begins by considering two issues: first, whether there is in fact anything in American thought before pragmatism that can be legitimately called philosophy and, second, in what consists its value?

It is not uncommon, Pokrovsky says, to take the view that little genuine philosophy existed in America prior to Peirce. There was, to be sure, political, literary, and religious thought, but virtually nothing one would regard as philosophy. Such a view was expressed by de Tocqueville, and even by Charles Dickens. Pokrovsky disagrees. Though early American philosophy, he says, "did not give the world any geniuses of abstract philosophizing," it nevertheless "gave rise to a number of remarkable thinkers, who combined an encyclopedic education and a thorough familiarity with contemporary movements in European philosophy with a sober and practical view of reality and a hope in the possibility of embodying truth . . . in the concrete life of the developing American nation" (Pokrovsky 1989b, 6).

Pokrovsky offers two reasons for regarding early American intellectual life as philosophically significant. The first is simply that even if it was only with Peirce that American thought broke into the ranks of technical European philosophy, it is nevertheless necessary that the stage had been set for this development by previous philosophically pertinent activity. The second reason rests on the fact that the very conception of what philosophy is changes over time. For the Puritans, Pokrovsky points out, philosophy included logic, grammar, rhetoric, mathematics, physics and theology. In the eighteenth century, especially with the influence of the Scottish Common Sense school, it meant primarily moral philosophy, and even included economics. In the nineteenth century it was fairly common to conflate philosophy with psychology. It is inappropriate, he concludes, to apply our current conceptions of what philosophy is or should be to earlier periods generally, and certainly it is inappropriate to apply them to the extraordinary richness and complex intellectual life of that period in

American history. Two points, he feels, must be borne in mind. While there were no professional philosophers in the early periods of American culture, the task of developing philosophical thought was fulfilled by Protestant preachers, political activists, writers, economists, natural scientists and social reformers. We must also remember that early American thinkers saw themselves as doing philosophy. The historical phenomenon of early American philosophy, while having its own unique characteristics and conditions, is nonetheless philosophy. In fact, Pokrovsky says, if we are to call American philosophy of the late nineteenth and early twentieth centuries the "Golden Age" of American thought, we would do well to regard the earlier periods as its "Bronze Age." (Pokrovsky 1989b, 11)

That early American thought is genuine philosophy is the first of four theses of Pokrovsky's study. The second thesis is that early American philosophy has three distinct periods which, though they overlap and converge in a variety of ways, nevertheless represent differing philosophic approaches and cultural problematics. The first distinct period is Puritanism, which is characterized by the subordination of philosophic methods and categories to the commitments of Calvinism. The second period is the Enlightenment, which saw the spread of anticlerical free thought and the influence of the philosophy of Locke, the scientific theories of Newton, the ideas of English Deism and the French Enlightenment. The philosophic developments of the Enlightenment were worked out, Pokrovsky suggests, primarily in connection with the socioeconomic and political ends of humanism, anticlericalism, free thought and democratism. The third period of early American philosophy is Romanticism, a reaction against the absolute value of reason. In the hands of American philosophers, Pokrovsky says, romantic pessimism was combined with a faith in the creative potential of people, in the unlimited possibilities of the moral perfection of the individual and the purifying significance of the interaction of human beings and nature.

Pokrovsky's third thesis is that the historical development of early American philosophy reflects the sharp ideological and sociopolitical conflicts of its time. This is a common point in Soviet philosophic study in that it reflects the general Marxist view that philosophic products can never be adequately understood if abstracted entirely from the broad cultural contexts in which they are produced. The details of the relation between philosophy and culture are likely to be complex, and a given philosophic work may be related to cultural issues and problems in any number of ways. It may be an expression of some of the dominant general ideas of a given time or a given society, as Aristotle for example reflects many of the cultural and social commitments of ancient Athenian and Greek society, or as Spinoza represents the broad intellectual trust in the cognitive power of mathematics which so dominated the seventeenth century in Europe. The relation may, on the other hand, express not the dominant ideas of a culture but alternatives to them. Josiah Royce's treatment of the concepts of community, individual, and interpretation, for example, presents a striking contrast to the atomistic and mechanistic understanding of individuals and their social relations which dominates in American culture. The likelihood, however, is that a philosophy will embody a complex of cultural factors, both those that dominate a culture and their alternatives. One of the reasons for this is that any given culture is itself a complex of various forces and themes many of which conflict more or less sharply at various stages of a culture's historical development. The first two centuries of American history, from Puritanism through the height of New England Transcendentalism, exhibit precisely such conflicting, sometimes contradictory, forces, and it is natural that we would find those conflicts reflected in early American philosophical development.

The point is evident, Pokrovsky says, from the clearly public and polemical character of philosophy in America from the seventeenth through the first half of the nineteenth centuries. Even abstract documents from the period, he suggests, have a direct or indirect concern with ideological struggles over the problems of freedom, democracy and human rights. As for the forms of philosophizing in early America, especially significant is the close relation between philosophy and religion. Pokrovsky cites the suggestion made by Elizabeth Flower and Murry Murphy that in early America philosophy in fact mediated between religion and science.[1] While he finds this claim to be disputable, the close relation between philosophy and religion, he says, is not. In its earliest period religious concerns were the context of American philosophy, and philosophic thought took the form of sermons and commentaries on Biblical texts, both of which, Pokrovsky emphasizes, were an integral part of public life. With the Enlightenment came new forms of philosophic work, equally public and no less concerned with the timely issues of developing American society: philosophy in the Enlightenment tended to take the form of political documents, pamphlets, and topical essays. The *Federalist Papers* were primarily a defense of the proposed federal Constitution, but they were also a consideration of the psychology and philosophy of human nature as developed by Locke and Hume, and Thomas Paine's pamphlets were not only political manifestos but also attempts to ground his political views in more general philosophic conceptions.[2] The public and topical, polemical character of philosophy in America is no less evident in the nineteenth century, in which philosophy tended to take the form of essays and lectures. Whether it was Emerson exhorting the graduates of Harvard Divinity School to reject orthodoxy and strike out on their own, or Thoreau pleading with us repeatedly not to overlook the most fundamental natural, moral, and aesthetic aspects of human being, American romanticism continued the tendency of American philosophy to be tied closely with American social life. In Pokrovsky's view, early American philosophy is itself a "melting pot," a blending of European influences with "ingredients" from indigenous American experience. Ultimately, he claims, an adequate understanding of early American philosophy requires the often difficult task of sorting out these strains.

Pokrovsky's fourth thesis, and an intriguing one in that it enables a clearer understanding of the motivations of Soviet scholars, is that a careful familiarity with early American philosophy contributes to an understanding of twentieth century American ideology. The ideology of any given time, he feels, reflects not only current sociopolitical movements and conditions but also its own historical development. Contemporary American social and ideological life, for better and worse, embodies themes, values, and commitments that have been with us since the seventeenth and eighteenth centuries, and we cannot understand ourselves today unless we understand our past and our appropriation of the past in the present.

The relation of early American thought to contemporary American society is also the subtext of A. M. Karimsky's studies, written from the late 1960s through his death in the early 1990s. In his view the study of early American philosophy is important for three reasons. First, he regards previous Soviet studies of the period (he specifically mentions the work of Goldberg and Bykhovsky) to be insufficient. Second, early American thought is significant in that it is, as he puts it, the "awakening of American self-consciousness." Primarily, though, an understanding of early American philosophy is important because of the ways it is interpreted and appropriated by contemporary American social, political, and economic historians and historians of philosophy. He noted a sharp increase over the last few decades in interest on the part of bourgeois (that is, contemporary American) scholars in early American thought. That interest is motivated, he feels, more than anything else by a desire to undercut revolutionary American ideas and traditions. This is done, he suggests, by attempting to ground the American Revolution in Puritan thought, which by implication deprecates the significance and influence of the philosophic materialism and democratic conceptions of the American Enlightenment. Karimsky will argue that precisely those two aspects of eighteenth century American thought played a decisive role in the birth of the nation and the development of American society, but that they also directly contradict the dominant ideological and social traits of contemporary American life. Thus, modern apologists of American society are constrained to reject what in Karimsky's opinion are the most progressive and valuable components of the American philosophical legacy. His task, ironically enough, is to rescue what on his view is the best of early American philosophy from contemporary misinterpretation and to illustrate its inconsistency with modern American ideology.

I

THE COLONIAL PERIOD

Puritanism and Eighteenth Century Idealism

Puritanism

Soviets, like Americans, tended to study Puritan thought in light of the subsequent development of American culture. The features of Puritan philosophy judged to be the most significant, which most clearly require investigation and explanation, are those that have had the greatest impact on American life. Consequently, while they discussed technical traits of Puritan philosophy such as its use of scholastic Aristotelianism and the Platonism inherited through Ramus, the Soviets dealt with those matters not so much because they are philosophically significant in their own right, but more because they shed light on those aspects of Puritan thought that are important by virtue of their relation to the more enduring characteristics of American society and ideology. In the case of Puritanism the themes that received special emphasis have to do in one way or another with social and political matters. Particularly important in Soviet commentary are the issues of the role of religion in American society, Puritan messianism, the relation between Puritanism and democracy, and finally the fact that New England Puritanism, unlike its English parent, developed in the absence of feudal social relations and institutions. An additional theme, especially significant for Karimsky, is the criticism of contemporary American—that is, bourgeois—appropriation of elements of Puritan social thought.

The Background of Puritan Thought

As it is the first thorough Soviet treatment of early American thought in general, Pokrovsky's *Early American Philosophy* (1989) is the first detailed consideration of Puritan philosophy by a Soviet scholar. In it he explores the characteristics of Puritan thought, its philosophical, religious, cultural, and material backgrounds, and its relation to the subsequent development of American philosophy.

In Pokrovsky's view three general factors are important for understanding the development of Puritan thought: its European backgrounds, the reasons for the emigration to New England, and the material and cultural conditions of the Puritan colonies. Concerning the European intellectual context of Puritan thought, Pokrovsky emphasizes (1) medieval theocracy, scholasticism, and Augustinianism, (2) Francis Bacon's work in philosophy and science, and (3) Calvinist rigorism.

With respect to the reasons for the emigration of Congregationalist groups, including not only the Puritan Bay Colony but also the Pilgrim settlement at Plymouth, Pokrovsky suggests both material and spiritual factors. The emigration was, among other things, economically motivated. The development of English Capitalism was, he suggests, constrained by political Absolutism, and North America represented the wider and more open opportunities it needed. Despite this economic context, though, Pokrovsky feels that among the many reasons for the early emigration from England to North America, the most important for the development of early American philosophy was the desire of the Congregationalists to find a place to exercise their religious ideas freely.

The third general factor or context of Puritan thought concerned the material and cultural conditions in which the settlers found themselves. While the influence of European ideas and conditions was crucial for Puritan philosophy, so too were the ways those influences were transformed under new conditions. The New England colonies were so far removed from the centers of intellectual life that they suffered an unenviable spiritual poverty. However, Pokrovsky says, "the secret of New England and the other British colonies of North America is the speed with which they developed their own unique economic, political, and cultural conditions" (Pokrovsky 1989b, 53). The point can be illustrated by the characteristic messianism of Puritan and subsequent American self-consciousness. The Puritans brought with them from Europe the Augustinian view of the world as a great drama in which God's plan is unfolded, and of history as the progressive struggle between good and evil. It was precisely the isolation of North America, however, that made it an appropriate place to live the struggle and to advance the historical progress of good. Augustinian eschatology and North American isolation combined, in other words, to make New England the "City on a Hill," a distinctive theme not only of Puritan ideology but of subsequent American self-perception. The Puritan self-image of constructing God's kingdom on earth, its messianism, can be seen, Pokrovsky says, in the concepts of exceptionalism and uniqueness, which are still a part of American ideology and, to use his expression, civil religion.

Puritan Social Thought

From the point of view of Soviet commentators, the most significant issue in the study of Puritan social thought is the extent of its influence on the course of American philosophy and society, and most directly on the

American Enlightenment and revolutionary thought. Of the many aspects of Puritan social and political ideas, relations, and institutions, the place of religion in and the class character of Puritan society emerge as its dominant features. Pokrovsky, for example, discusses in considerable detail the religious character not only of the Puritans' messianism but also of their conception of the social covenant, political institutions, rights, freedom, and democracy. Karimsky, too, in his analysis of the relation between the Puritan covenant and later social contract theory, takes the uniqueness of the covenant to be its religious grounding. For him, furthermore, one of the most distinctive features of Puritan society and social thought, one which sharply distinguishes Puritanism from the Enlightenment and revolutionary ideals, is its religious intolerance. Other Soviet scholars, too, emphasize religion in their remarks on Puritanism. In an article on the general character of the American Enlightenment, for example, T. L. Morozova regards Puritanism as the basis of the unique role of religion in American society. Specifically, in her view, the Puritan expression of the "Protestant ethic" has profoundly affected American culture, and she makes the interesting observation that in the late colonial and revolutionary periods religion played a crucial role, in that Puritan clergy tended to support the revolutionary movement and did so in terms easy for the congregations to understand. Also in relation to the Enlightenment, E. A. Stetzenko in an article on Thomas Paine suggests that the social optimism of the Enlightenment was an extension of Puritan religious messianism. And in a study of the U. S. Constitution and civil rights, A. A. Mishin and others again emphasize the religious character of the Puritan predecessors of later American social and political principles, specifically, popular sovereignty, natural rights, and the social contract.

The class character of Puritan society, and consequently Puritan social thought, is emphasized by some Soviet scholars more than others and in fact receives different interpretations in different hands. Pokrovsky, as we have already seen, regards economic interests as among the motivating factors in the Puritan emigration to North America. Karimsky sees bourgeois class interests as permeating Puritan theoretical and social development, specifically in its notion of "paradise," in its sanctification of material prosperity, in its institutionalization and justification of material inequality, indeed, in every aspect of Puritan theocracy.

A somewhat different approach to the class character of Puritanism is suggested by M. P. Baskin in his 1955 lectures on the American Enlightenment. For him Puritanism represents not so much an early stage of bourgeois development, but more a late holdout of feudal social relations. The context is his approach to the American revolution, an event he takes to be as important a factor in bourgeois development as was the French Revolution a decade later. Baskin's interpretation is in fact a direct application of the historical materialist categories of the historical process. According to the Marxist view, the feudal mode of production ultimately collapsed as a result of the class antagonism between the feudal nobility determined to preserve the material and social base of its power and the emerging commercial class, for which feudal structures proved an impediment to their class interests. The commercial class was ultimately victorious in that struggle, though its victory required both the complete overthrow of feudal economic, social, political, and ideological conditions and a revolutionary transformation to a bourgeois, that is, capitalist, mode of production. The English Revolution of the seventeenth century and the French Revolution of the eighteenth are generally regarded as the major social revolutions in this process, in that they secured bourgeois interests by the direct overthrow of absolute monarchy, itself a transitional form in the historical movement from feudalism to capitalism. One might argue that it is more problematic to interpret the American Revolution in the same way since it was directed neither against an absolute monarch nor against the dominant economic and social relations of bourgeois England. Baskin, however, wishes to place the American Revolution fully on a par with the English and the French, in part because he correctly sees the extraordinary impact of the American Revolution on the *subsequent* development of world capitalism with respect to economic relations and practices, social and political institutions, and theoretical principles and ideals. To make his case, though, he thinks it necessary to show that the American Revolution was as much a direct reaction against semifeudal obstructions as were the English and French. To that end he insists that there were indeed feudal elements in the North American colonies in the seventeenth and eighteenth centuries, examples of which were the general character of property relations in the southern colonies in the seventeenth century, the existence of slavery and indentured servitude throughout the colonial period, and, finally, New England Puritanism. The "rigid fanaticism" of seventeenth century Puritanism was, Baskin suggests, comparable to the more or less feudal Catholic fanaticism that the Puritans had fled and was certainly comparable to medieval Catholic social domination.

In Baskin's analysis ideology gets the better of scholarship. In his attempt to place the American Revolution squarely in the process of the revolutionary transformation of feudal into bourgeois society, Baskin forces the facts where they simply will not go and need not go to make his general point. Slavery and indentured servitude, for example, might be better seen as ways to enhance the accumulation of capital necessary for the development of early capitalist economic and social relations rather than as medieval holdovers. Those forms of labor were useful for capitalism, at least until technology, the economy, and social relations developed more fully, at which point wage labor became more suitable. Similarly, to equate

"Puritan fanaticism" with the Christian domination of the feudal period too easily misses the extent to which Puritan thought expressed distinctly modern, one might argue bourgeois, ideals of work and prosperity, and expressed the modern tension between the individual and the community. As we will see, these latter points were clearer to other Soviet commentators than they were to Baskin.

The most prevalent aspects of Puritan social practice and thought are theocracy and covenant theory, and it is these features of Puritanism that have received the most detailed treatment by Soviet specialists. In Karimsky's opinion, Puritan theocracy was a theoretical and political expression of the material and social relations required by early capitalist society: "Puritanism, as a form of early bourgeois ideology, frankly and rather crudely expressed the instinctive intention of a new class to replace one inequality with another" (Karimsky 1976c, 36). In New England, he goes on to say, this inequality was secured in law and received its theoretical justification in theocracy. The inequality Karimsky has in mind was essentially material, and it was defended on theological grounds: prosperity is not, indeed cannot be, a common, universal expectation since it reflects God's will, his selection of those to be so blessed. Material inequality, furthermore, received a political expression in the theocratic grounding of political power in religious conceptions and the consequent intolerance of religious and social dissent.

Karimsky's reading of Puritan theocracy serving social and political ends has some justification. Two of the most influential early theoreticians of Puritan theocracy were John Eliot and John Cotton. Cotton's primary contribution was the conception of the unity of the visible and invisible churches. His concern was to provide a theological grounding of New England communities, to establish social and political cohesion of the varying churches and sects in the colony. The "visible" churches, that is, the distinct communities in the colony, all had a single "invisible" basis, which is to say that as earthly organizations the churches represent God's will and power. The single transcendent ground of Puritan communities required a political structure that enabled social unity and that embodied divine will. Social cohesion required a theocracy, and as an expression of God's will political power was necessarily intolerant. There was no place for opposition and protest in Puritan social and political thought because to oppose political authority was equivalent to opposing God, and since God is the "invisible" ground of social unity and order, dissent, whether specifically religious or overtly political, was a fundamental threat to the very possibility of social organization. And in any case, in the Puritan view, the human condition after the Fall necessitated strict and precise guidance from authority, which in the nature of things must at once be social, political, and religious.

The nature of Puritan theocracy, in particular its intolerance, directly suggests questions concerning general social and political ideals, among the most prominent of which is the ideal of freedom. Given the general tendency to understand and interpret Puritanism in its relation to later developments in American thought, it is particularly important to see how the Puritans understood human freedom and how they incorporated that understanding within a general defense of theocracy. As both Karimsky and Pokrovsky point out, the nature of freedom received its most direct and sustained treatment from John Winthrop. In his *History of New England* Winthrop distinguishes two kinds of freedom, natural and what he called civil or moral freedom. On the one hand, natural freedom is the ability to do what one "has a mind to do," or what one is inclined to do, and humans have this freedom in common with the rest of creation. With respect specifically to human beings, it is, Pokrovsky suggests, Hobbes's "war of all against all." Civil or moral freedom, on the other hand, is peculiar to human beings, and it sets the limits to the exercise of natural freedom, the limits to be determined in accordance with scripture and divine law. Winthrop's treatment of freedom, Karimsky says, conveys a clear notion of the Puritan view of human nature. Prior to the Fall, Adam and Eve had no limits to the exercise of their freedom, which is to say that for them natural and moral freedom coincided. With the advent of sin, however, moral freedom becomes the observance of moral law, and natural freedom is equivalent to the ability to sin. Thus understood, natural freedom as a result of the Fall becomes the instrument of the Devil. Civil or moral freedom, unlike natural freedom, is law bound and grounded in the covenant between God and man.

The covenant is, for both Karimsky and Pokrovsky, the single most important component of Puritan social thought. It grounds not only an understanding of civil freedom but also the Puritan assessment of natural rights and democracy, social and political concepts that were gaining increasing importance in Europe in the seventeenth century and that by the eighteenth century would dominate American thought. Ultimately the most important question concerning the covenant, again for both Karimsky and Pokrovsky, is its relation to social contract theory. On the face of it a relation is not difficult to draw. The very terms Pokrovsky uses to describe Winthrop's distinction between natural and civil freedom seem to imply a connection. For Hobbes, the social contract is the mechanism that enables the construction of civil society from the inevitable chaos of the state of nature. If Winthrop's natural freedom is comparable to the Hobbesian state of nature, and if the covenant is the ground of civil freedom much like the social contract grounds civil society, then the relation is fairly obvious. The question becomes, then, whether the relation between the covenant and social contract theory is as close as it appears to be.

Karimsky regards this question as particularly important because of its treatments by modern American commentators, treatments closely related to the contemporary concerns of dominant American ideology. It is popular in bourgeois historiography, he says, to view Puritanism as a stage in the development of American democracy. Herbert Schneider, Ralph Barton Perry, Perry Miller, and others are inclined to understand covenant theory as an ecclesiastical version of social contract theory and to hold that "the relation between Puritanism and the Enlightenment is so close that the development of the former into the latter was easy, and for the most part unconscious." (Karimsky 1976c, 44)[1] In a more recent essay Karimsky added Clinton Rossiter, W. S. Hudson and Richard Hofstadter to the list of Americans who attempt to identify religious covenantism with the theory of natural rights and the social contract and who treat the Enlightenment as but a modification of Protestant social doctrines. Such interpretations of the covenant and its relation to the social contract, Karimsky suggests, amount to the view that

> Puritan social philosophy contains within itself the principles that the tradition attributes to the Enlightenment . . . and holds that these same principles are at the foundation of the program of the American Revolution. . . . The Puritan covenant has been understood as the source of the theory of natural rights, and even as anticipating the realization of such rights in the constituting acts of the American Revolution. (Karimsky 1976c, 44–45)

Karimsky argues that such an understanding of the theory of the covenant is without sufficient justification. He suggests that while there is some basis for this interpretation, it is a mistake to emphasize it as much as many Americans have. Religious life at the time did introduce, he says, "unique principles of republicanism: the election and rotation of clergy, autonomous congregations, pluralism of sects, and others." But, he continues, it is a mistake to idealize these components of Puritan social and political theory. They were important features of the social mechanism of the realization of the power of the bourgeois leadership and the new clergy, but "about real power and the 'natural' equality of rights they say nothing at all" (Karimsky 1989b, 28). Karimsky's objection rests on the point that there is a fundamental difference between covenant and social contract theories, specifically, that while the latter implies an agreement among people (men, for the most part), the former is never reducible to such an agreement. The power and authority possessed by a social contract is derived from the mutual agreement of the parties to it, while the authority of a covenant is a result of the signatories having individually made a compact with God. John Cotton had written that there are three forms of covenant—a general covenant of grace, the church covenant, and the civil covenant—all of which consist of agreements with God. Such compacts with God were common among the ancient Jews, Karimsky says, and he suggests that the historical and ethnographic evidence indicates that agreements of this kind, where the authority of the agreement derives from God, were equally common among ancient Africans, Asians, and Germans. The theoretical basis of covenant theory, then, is related to ancient religious conceptions rather than to the revolutionary social and political theories of the seventeenth and eighteenth centuries.

For Karimsky, this distinction between an agreement deriving its authority from the parties to it and one deriving its authority from God is crucial in that it bears on the Puritan assessment of rights. In social contract theory, particularly its eighteenth century versions, civil society and the authority of government are grounded in the consent of the governed, which is itself an acknowledgment of certain natural human rights. An agreement between individuals and God, however, involves no such acknowledgment. In the former case the source of civil society and political authority is natural rights, while in covenant theory "the source of government and law turned out to be the Scriptures themselves" (Karimsky 1988b, 27). Karimsky is saying, in other words, that one of the most characteristic and significant features of social contract theory in general, and specifically of the theoretical underpinnings of the social and political ideas of the American Enlightenment, plays no role at all in the Puritan covenant. Orthodox Puritan thought of the seventeenth century, in fact, never endorsed the notion of natural rights. Winthrop, Karimsky says, explicitly rejected the view that power derives from the consent of the governed, and he cites Bradford's *History of Plymouth Plantation* to the effect that one of the reasons a compact among the Mayflower colonists was necessary in the first place was that too many of them were insisting on acting as they individually saw fit. To suggest a close relation between the social contract and the covenant, then, "not only misinterprets the contract theory of the origins of government, but it also gives a false picture of the premises and components of American constitutionalism" (Karimsky 1988b, 29).

Other Soviet commentators were less critical than Karimsky of the view that there is a fairly close relation between the Puritan covenant and social contract theory. In a collectively written study of the U. S. Constitution and Enlightenment natural rights theory, for example, the authors suggest that "the fundamental traits of the American conception of rights and civil freedom were already formed in the colonial period" (Geevsky et al. 1987, 7). Even in the seventeenth century, they say, there were in North America the ideas of popular sovereignty, natural rights, the social contract, and the right of people to rebel and resist tyranny. While they emphasize the religious grounding of the early forms of these ideas in

North America, they suggest that it was the very defense of religious rights that led Americans to the defense of rights and freedom in general. They offer two examples of this point: (1) the way freedom of religious thought gradually led to a commitment to freedom of thought in a wider sense of the term; (2) the covenant, which they refer to as an "early social contract." That the covenant involved a relation to God indicates simply the religious character of early American contract theory rather than a sharp distinction between the covenant and the social contract. This approach differs from Karimsky's not only concerning the interpretation of the covenant but also with respect to the view that later American notions of rights and freedoms have Puritanism as a precursor. As we will see further on, Karimsky argues that the only expressions of rights and freedoms in any way consistent with the Enlightenment's understanding of them came from Puritan dissidents, never from Puritan orthodoxy. The authors of the collective study implicitly acknowledge the role of the dissidents, Roger Williams in particular, in the early formation of ideas that blossomed in the revolutionary period and in American constitutionalism. Even here, though, the important differences between orthodox Puritans and dissidents do not preclude an equally significant continuity.

Another detailed consideration of the relation between the covenant and the social contract is found in Pokrovsky's work. Like Karimsky, Pokrovsky emphasizes the difference between a covenant with God and an agreement among citizens, but unlike Karimsky he nevertheless regards the relation between the covenant and later American concepts and ideals to be relatively close. Many Americans, he says, see the Mayflower Compact as the first document expressing distinctly American principles of self-governance, voluntary association, and the spirit of democracy. Citing Commager, however, Pokrovsky thinks it more appropriate to regard the Mayflower Compact as an expression of the widely held view at the time of a religious covenant concerning social relations. It is not simply a religious document, however, since it also involves political and economic concerns. The community is formed in the name of God, its Calvinist principles commit it to self-governance, and it is concerned to enable the well-being of all its members. Despite its religious character, Pokrovsky says, the Mayflower Compact expresses the general commitment to civil equality consonant with the epoch of bourgeois revolutions soon to unfold. "In this sense," he continues, "the compact genuinely anticipates the development of republican-democratic institutions born in the course of the American Revolution of 1776" (Pokrovsky 1989b, 46).

The distinctive characteristic of Pokrovsky's treatment of the Puritan covenant is his emphasis both on the religious, Calvinist character that distinguishes it from later conceptual developments, and on those of its specific social and political components that connect it with secular contract theory. The covenant, in other words, is an inherently contradictory concept that reflects the general contradictions of Puritan society. The covenant arose, he suggests, from the need to hold congregations and communities together, in other words as a check on the Puritans' own tendency to separatism and isolation. In crucial respects, the covenant, in addition to its grounding in Scriptural sources, was distinctly antidemocratic:

> The transformation of the conception of the covenant of blessings into the centerpiece of the Puritan world view reflected the unique nature of the motives of New England intellectuals, dictating their will to the whole of Colonial society. Balancing between a fanatical blind faith and a sober contract with God, determining the full range of the subtleties of the interrelationship between the other worldly and the secular, the Puritans keenly grasped the psychological nuances of the historical situation unfolding in the North American colonies in the seventeenth century. The general economic expansion of colonial society required disciplined regulation, the highest sanction of which proceeded from God as set out in the covenant. However, the covenant would have had little social effect had it not been imbued with an irrational immersion in faith, following the ideals of Calvinism. Precisely this outward contradictory combination of two factors was embodied in the conception of the social covenant, which accents the regulation of New England society. (Pokrovsky 1989b, 70–71)

The covenant expresses a sobriety and a fanaticism that combine in the rigid control of thought and social relations. Puritan social and political thought provided no place for opposition and protest, since to oppose political authority was equivalent to opposing God. The Puritans in fact argued explicitly against democracy on the grounds that the Bible nowhere provides any such model and that it contradicts Biblical injunctions concerning treatment of one's elders, among which Winthrop and the other theoreticians of theocracy included themselves and the entire civil magistry.

The antidemocratic characteristics of the covenant are explicit, but that, for Pokrovsky, is not the whole of the story, and it is in this context that he explicitly raises the question of the relation of the covenant and the social contract. The tension in this relation is noticed, he points out, by some American commentators. Herbert Schneider, for example, notes both the democratic and the antidemocratic traits of the covenant. The covenant is democratic, Schneider says, in so far as it endorses the election of magistrates and church leaders by the citizens, while it is undemocratic in that it rejects the responsibility of elected officials to those who elect them, and in that it maintains that law and power stem only from God. In general, however, Schneider's view is that the covenant is a religious expression of the social contract and a step on the way from feudalism to a commercial conception of power and government.[2] Pokrovsky remarks that by attributing to the covenant a generally democratic character, and by emphasizing its close relation to the social contract, Schneider and other American thinkers are attempting to establish a direct link between the social philosophy of Puritanism and the Enlightenment as the basis of the political and legal ideals and documents of the American Revolution. Is there, he asks, in fact such a relation?

Pokrovsky notes Karimsky's objection that the covenant is not a direct relation or agreement among citizens. He also points out another important difference between the covenant and the social contract, specifically that the covenant establishes inequality as a reflection of God's will and wisdom, while the social contract, at least in its more democratic interpretations, posited natural and social equality. Pokrovsky agrees with Karimsky that a fairly wide gap opens between the covenant and the social contract, though for him it is significant that the distance between them was covered in a relatively short period of time, which suggests to him that the gap was not as wide in practice as it appears in theory. Despite the covenant's undemocratic character, he says, it was transformed within a century into a democratic and revolutionary weapon: "In this sense we have an example of the fact that the Puritans thoroughly worked out the familiar covenant-contract schema, which crystallized in the eighteenth century into an umbrella for Enlightenment social thought. . . . Puritan covenantism laid the first stone in the foundation of lawful government and made possible an affirmation of respect for law and jurisprudence." (Pokrovsky 1989b, 77–78)

Pokrovsky's assessment of Puritanism is grounded in his appreciation of its inherently contradictory character. Although the covenant's religious character represents one of the crucial distinctions between the covenant and the social contract, Puritanism was clearly at its most democratic in its religious relations. By the same token, in its secular relations, that is, in those respects in which Enlightenment thought was most revolutionary, Puritanism was at its least democratic. "Could it be," he asks, "that one of the most fundamental traits of New England Puritanism was its unique combination of religious democracy and clerical hierarchy, of equality through God with a basic impossibility of equality among each other?" (Pokrovsky 1989b, 83)

The Puritan Dissidents

We have to this point considered the nature of seventeenth century Puritan orthodoxy and its relation to later American thought, which leaves still the issue of the Puritan dissidents and the development of Puritan orthodoxy at the turn of the eighteenth century. For both Karimsky and Pokrovsky, the most significant opponents of one or another aspect of Puritan orthodoxy were Ann Hutchinson (1591–1643), Thomas Hooker

(1586–1647), Roger Williams (1603–1683), John Wise (1652–1725), and Jonathan Mayhew (1720–1766). These dissidents were, they argue, pivotal figures in the development of American thought. In Karimsky's opinion they represent the antithesis of orthodoxy and the genuine root of the American Enlightenment. In Pokrovsky's view, however, they are both a reaction against and a development of orthodoxy. They are rooted in the orthodox tradition, in that for the most part they were concerned with religious and church matters and in that, with some notable exceptions, their thinking and arguments were wholly within a theological context and utilized theological concepts and categories. At the same time they were a reaction against the tradition to the extent that their ideas were increasingly democratic and hostile to orthodox theocracy.

Taken together, the theoretical and practical ideas of the Puritan dissidents were the core of the conceptual foundation of the revolutionary movement of the second half of the eighteenth century. They include in different ways and in varying degrees the advocacy of natural rights, secular social-contract theory, democratic social and political organization, popular sovereignty, a conception of the proper end of government as the safety and happiness of citizens, the right to rebellion and revolution, religious tolerance, the separation of church and state, the abolition of slavery, the rights of native populations, limitations on the amount of private holdings in land, and the abolition of property and religious qualifications for political participation. Equally important was the gradual replacement of theological by secular arguments that appeal to natural law to ground religious, social, and political theory.

In Pokrovsky's view, whether their concern was exclusively with church organization or with the general character of social and political life, the Antinomians and Independents of seventeenth century New England represented a new stage in the struggle for bourgeois democracy. Citing the Soviet historian L. Slezkin, he points out that in England this function had been served by mainstream Puritanism itself, specifically through the revolution and Commonwealth. In New England, however, mainstream Puritanism represented the social and political status quo, and new, more democratic ideas appeared largely in reaction to it. And the Massachusetts colony was quite young when the first dissident ideas arose. The earliest opponents of Puritan orthodoxy appeared within a few years of the founding of the Massachusetts Bay Colony. The first of them were Ann Hutchinson and Thomas Hooker who, along with John Wise at the turn of the eighteenth century, were concerned almost exclusively with the principles of church organization and structure.

Like Hutchinson and Hooker before him, John Wise was an ardent advocate of Congregationalist principles and, for both Karimsky and Pokrovsky, a pivotal figure in the development of early American social philosophy. At the turn of the eighteenth century Congregationalism was under attack from two sources. From one side, members of the Puritan oligarchy were attempting to unite Massachusetts' congregations under the rule of a single synod of elders, as a way of exercising greater control. At the same time there was an attempt on the part of the English church, and the English government, to establish more extensive domination over the religious and political structures of the colonies. Wise defended Congregationalism against both of these threats and in the process advanced ideas and arguments that went far beyond the issue of congregational self-control. In opposing the subordination of the colony's churches to the English, for example, he argued against the infringement by the crown of the colonists' rights in general. In the opinion of both Karimsky and Pokrovsky, Wise's overt theological concerns were merely the context of much more significant general social ideas. Karimsky says, for example, that "church issues were for Wise merely the form of his argument about social affairs. This is evident from the fact that both of his books appeared at a time when the 'debate over the churches' was already effectively concluded" (Karimsky 1976c, 62). In Pokrovsky's words, "Though Wise's polemics did not go beyond the theological sphere, they included no small degree of purely secular philosophy, and much of Wise's work is imbued with rationalism, Enlightenment criticism, and a tendency toward natural scientific analysis" (Pokrovsky 1989b, 144).

Both Karimsky and Pokrovsky emphasize the theoretical underpinnings of Wise's arguments, specifically his appeal to the natural freedom and sociality of humankind. He defended Congregationalist principles on the grounds that they are rooted in the "original condition and freedom of humanity" and that they reflect the "light of nature," and he saw a democratic and communitarian structure as fulfilling this "natural freedom." Wise further defends democracy by arguing that it is grounded in the inherent sociality of human beings, a condition that itself is related to the natural necessity of self-preservation. In an argument that Pokrovsky says sounds much like Dewey, Wise advocates a principle of the general interest rather than egoism as the heart of social and political organization. Human beings are by nature free and equal, and their "sociable disposition" allows them to develop political structures the function of which is to protect their freedom and equality. Though Wise used a covenant rather than a contract theory to ground the transition from a natural condition to civil society, he does so without presuming divine providence, which is to say, he advances an unusually secular covenant theory. For this reason Karimsky and Pokrovsky both refer to Wise as a "sociological Deist," for whom, as Pokrovsky puts it, "God is not the ground of society, but its adjunct. Human beings are fully situated in the jurisdiction of natural laws" (Pokrovsky 1989b, 146). Wise is especially important, then, because of the extent to which he approaches the principles and methodology of the Enlightenment. It is probably not appropriate to identify him as a source of American Enlightenment thought, but, Pokrovsky says, though the natural law philosophy of Franklin, Samuel Adams, and Jefferson is more an outgrowth of the legacy of Locke and Bollingbroke, "this does not detract from the merit of John Wise" (Pokrovsky 1989b, 147).

As important as Karimsky and Pokrovsky took Wise to be, they and other Soviet writers were inclined to regard Roger Williams as the most significant representatives of democratic Puritan thought. I. A. Geevsky, A. A. Mishin, and their colleagues, for example, say that Williams was "one of the leading progressive philosophers and religious thinkers of the English speaking world in the seventeenth century" and that he had a significant influence on the development of the ideas of American constitutionalism (Geevsky et al. 1987, 8–9). One of the reasons for this kind of assessment of Williams is that his overt concerns were much broader than those of Hooker and even Wise. While Hooker and Wise appealed to contract theory and natural law in defense of Congregationalism, Williams went much further in his overt rejection of the divine origin of government and in his advocacy of inalienable natural rights, freedom of religious belief, and the rights of native peoples and blacks.

The orthodox Puritan theocracy justified itself by appeal to Scripture, more specifically to Old Testament moral and social principles. According to Williams's reading, however, no Old Testament principles can be understood as adequate in themselves because they are essentially anticipations of the New Testament. This view provided Williams with the grounds on which to criticize the Massachusetts oligarchy. It is illegitimate, he argued, to base a social order on Mosaic law, since Old Testament principles can only rightly be understood through their New Testament fulfillment. As Pokrovsky puts it, "The theocratic Mosaic laws lost their force and were reduced simply to symbolic anticipations of the moral code of Jesus. From this it quickly follows that the oligarchical order in Massachusetts did not possess an absolutely divine justification, as its apologists did not correctly understand the Bible" (Pokrovsky 1989b, 129). Pokrovsky discusses three basic theses of Williams's principles of spiritual and civil freedom: a rejection of the divine origin of the state, superiority of social contract over covenant theory, and the necessity of developing the principles and mechanisms of a democratic social structure. With respect to the origin of the state, Williams argues that the Bible nowhere sanctions oligarchy. He argues further that sacred law is based on natural law, not, as Puritan orthodoxy had it, the other way around. Thus the state can have a divine character only to the extent that it corresponds with natural law and human nature, which when extended to social relations means, according to Williams, a peaceful, democratic community. If the state cannot have a directly divine origin and ground, then one of the necessary conditions of covenant theory is missing. Society can issue not from a compact with God but only from the consent of the people. Williams argued that popular consent, and not Christianity in itself, is conducive to the common good. And as corollaries of his principle of popular sovereignty Williams argues for the general equality of people and that the social contract, hence all political power, proceeds from the people's inalienable rights and freedoms.

In Pokrovsky's opinion Williams's ideas are also related to later developments in American thought through his conception of the most appropriate social structure. Williams's model of a democratic society was the medieval corporation of artisans and traders. Such a vision of small, independent, self-organizing, and self-governing social units was influential, Pokrovsky notes, on the principles of Jeffersonian democracy and, he adds, on American utopian socialists and anarcho-communists. The similarity with Jefferson is more striking still when one notes Williams's advocacy of religious tolerance and the separation of church and state, positions that made him one of the most advanced freethinkers of his century. Pokrovsky illustrates the progressive character of Williams's principles by suggesting a comparison between his ideas and formulations and those that appear in Jefferson's Declaration of Independence. The main difference between them, he says, is that Williams does not advocate the right to revolution. In most other respects, however, Williams is taken to be an outstanding forerunner not only of Jefferson but of the American Enlightenment as a whole. The fact that Williams was something of a mystic, as Perry Miller has said, and that before long many of his principles were abandoned in the Rhode Island colony, does not in Karimsky's and Pokrovsky's opinion detract from his standing as a prominent democratic thinker. It remains the case that under his leadership Rhode Island developed new juridical norms of administration, established liberal criminal and civil codes, prohibited slavery and servitude, avoided overt expropriation of land from native populations, prohibited the concentration of land in the hands of large landlords, and effected an advanced though limited freedom of conscience and religion. The influence of Williams's thought on subsequent developments may or may not have been direct, but the likeness is too striking to overlook:

> And though there has been no documentary confirmation of a continuity of the social and philosophical views of Roger Williams and Thomas Jefferson, there can be no doubt that Williams's independence and separatism, requiring and grounding the separation of the state from the church, especially the English Church, created certain intellectual presuppositions for the left revolutionary radicalism of the epoch of the War of Independence of Great Britain's North American colonies. (Pokrovsky 1989b, 137)

The last of the Puritan dissident reformers Karimsky and Pokrovsky discuss is Jonathan Mayhew. In Mayhew Puritanism came as close to Enlightenment thought as it ever did, due in part to the fact that he lived during the central decades of the eighteenth century, dying only ten years before the Declaration of Independence. Mayhew is significant for having united in a single social vision the ideas of the separation of church and state, popular sovereignty, government as grounded in the consent of the governed, and the fundamental end of government being to secure the safety and happiness of the people. For Karimsky and Pokrovsky, Mayhew's most important contribution, and the one which marks him as the most radical of the Puritan reformers, was his advocacy of the right to revolution. His initial argument for the right to rebel has a theological underpinning, though he also advances a more secular defense. Church leadership, he argues, has an obligation to God to conduct its affairs in certain ways. If the leadership violates that obligation, it is a duty to rebel against it. In a more secular vein, Mayhew argues that no one is obligated to subordinate himself to any government that does not fulfill its fundamental commitment to security and the general good.

The importance of regarding revolution as a right was a theme common to Soviet commentators on early American thought. The fact that Mayhew advocated it indicates in their view the progressive character of his thought. Furthermore, as we will see in the next chapter, the fact that the Declaration of Independence asserts the right to revolution while the Constitution does not raised for Soviet specialists the question whether the Constitution is in some respects a reactionary document, a retreat from the advanced bourgeois democratic principles of the revolutionary Enlightenment. However that issue is decided, Soviet commentators, in particular Karimsky and Pokrovsky, regard the thought of the Puritan dissidents as the conceptual link between Puritanism and the Enlightenment. However, as has been noted, a difference arises in their respective assessments. Karimsky regards the differences between orthodox and dissident Puritans as exceptionally sharp, in which orthodoxy is a reactionary force and dissident thought progressive. For Pokrovsky, though, the content and especially the methodology of dissident Puritan ideas and arguments were not always as progressive and radical as they have sometimes been understood, and at the same time orthodoxy was not as thoroughly reactionary as it might appear. While reformist and dissident thought moved in the direction of deism and the Enlightenment, prominent orthodox thinkers, in particular Cotton Mather and, later, Jonathan Edwards, attempted to reconcile traditional Puritan Calvinism with contemporary developments in philosophy and science.

Later Puritan Orthodoxy and Cotton Mather

Dissidents and reformers were not the only challenges to orthodox Puritanism in the late seventeenth century and the turn of the eighteenth. At the conceptual level, Puritan thinkers had to contend with the expanding impact of contemporary developments in philosophy and the natural sciences, in which fields the most influential figures were John Locke and Isaac Newton. Newton's physics and Locke's epistemology posed challenges to Ramist Calvinism that orthodoxy could not ignore. In addition to such theoretical matters, in the final two decades of the seventeenth century Massachusetts theocracy was beset by a barrage of social, political, and economic problems. In 1684 the British government annulled the Massachusetts Charter, and in 1691 it appointed a colonial governor, measures that overtly usurped the oligarchy's political power. In addition, the Puritans felt themselves increasingly threatened by the immigration of Catholics into New Hampshire and Maine and by the Catholic domination of French Quebec. The growing Catholic presence around them worried the Puritan leaders because in the context of the Counter-Reformation, Catholicism was a direct threat to the New Canaan, to the future of the City on a Hill. The problem of the Catholics was compounded by the disastrous result of an armed force sent by Massachusetts against Quebec in 1690. The detachment returned decimated not by battle but by disease. And in the economic sphere, in 1690 Massachusetts was suffering a recession that affected a significant portion of the colony's farmers. All of these factors combined and genuinely endangered the stability of the Puritan theocracy. Karimsky and Pokrovsky interpret late Puritan orthodox thought in light of this set of theoretical and practical problems.

Karimsky actually pays very little attention to late Puritan orthodoxy, primarily because according to his view it is irrelevant to the process of the development of American philosophy. "The two fundamental aspects of its formation," he says, "were the decay of Puritan theology and the development of a secular philosophic thought that took on the characteristics of the ideology of the Enlightenment" (Karimsky 1976c, 52). For Karimsky, then, it is pre-Enlightenment secular thought, that is, the ideas of the Puritan dissidents to the extent that they were secular, that is significant, and for the development of those ideas Puritan orthodoxy served as little more than the foil. Traditional Puritan theology in the hands of Cotton Mather, and even of Jonathan Edwards, is interesting to Karimsky only negatively, as the inadequate conceptual system against which American philosophy arose. Unlike Karimsky, Pokrovsky understands late Puritan orthodox thought as playing a more positive role in the Colonial intellectual atmosphere, and as a result he pays greater attention to its details. Nevertheless, he agrees with Karimsky that late orthodox theology was primarily an attempt to stem the tide of modern social, political, and conceptual processes.

Among the prominent figures in the oligarchy's response to the social, political, and economic problems of the Massachusetts colony were Increase Mather (1639–1723) and Cotton Mather (1662–1728). Together they and others tried to consolidate theocratic power and social control. One of the strategies they employed was to attempt to unite all of Massachusetts' churches under a single structure and leadership, a procedure that contradicted the Congregationalist principles on which early Puritanism was grounded. Concrete conditions, however, had rendered Congregationalism inconsistent with theocratic power, though it is doubtful whether the two had actually ever been consistent. Hutchinson and Hooker had challenged theocracy in the name of Congregationalism as early as the 1630s and 1640s, and at the turn of the century John Wise and others continued the struggle for Congregationalism. By the end of the seventeenth century Congregationalism had become the structural context of the growing influence of democracy and freethinking, both of which the orthodox "lights" could not tolerate. Thus the more or less Presbyterian attempt to bring the churches together under one synod was intended to repress the threat of Congregationalist democracy, independence, and freethinking.

A superficial view of orthodox concerns at the end of the century might give the impression that the leaders of the theocracy were motivated by little more than a desire to retain power for its own sake. Pokrovsky, however, finds it preferable to try to understand orthodoxy's perception of the situation from within its own principles. One can imagine how the Puritan leaders felt. From the point of view of the Mathers and their colleagues, the Puritan settlements were still the New Canaan, with all the eschatological meaning that view entails. The defense of Puritanism was the defense of righteousness, and challenges to its success were not simply threats to a social and political status quo but represented a danger to the most important of all causes. In this context, the sources of the colony's many problems—the abrogation of its charter, the new governor, the proximity of the Counter-Reformation, and the economic situation—took on a cosmic significance. Orthodox Puritanism felt besieged by the forces of evil itself, and the very survival of its holy cause was at stake. The Puritans were pinned in an ideological corner, and their response was one that had happened before and that has happened since: repression.

The attempt to unify the churches was one aspect of the defense of theocracy, but the Puritan leaders were in need, Pokrovsky argues, of still more effective means of social control. They found what they needed, he suggests, in the appearance of witches. His view suggests that the hysteria of the witch-hunt was an attempt to galvanize public support behind the power of the theocracy. Massachusetts was already surrounded by evil, and the witches represented the presence of Satan's forces inside the colony, an absolutely intolerable situation. Orthodoxy's response, then, to its social, political, and economic problems was to contradict its own traditional Congregationalist principles and at the same time to effect an atmosphere of repression and terror.

Such an understanding of late orthodox Puritanism is not new. Pokrovsky cites V. L. Parrington as one who regarded the activity of the Mathers, especially Cotton Mather, as an indication of the degenerate condition of Puritan culture at the time. While there is no doubt a good deal of truth in this assessment, Pokrovsky suggests that "the evaluation of the intellectual legacy of both father and son should not be one-sided. . . . The evaluation should be supplemented by the recognition that Cotton Mather enabled the diffusion in the colonies of Newtonian philosophy and physics and was himself an outstanding naturalist" (Pokrovsky 1989b, 153–154). Cotton Mather was a genuine though limited advocate of contemporary advances in scientific theory and in medicine, and it is in this respect that Pokrovsky thinks that a negative assessment needs to be tempered. In both abstract and practical respects, Mather tried to incorporate new knowledge into Puritan thought and life. At the practical level, Pokrovsky mentions, as does T. L. Morozova, that it was Cotton Mather who introduced small pox vaccination into the colony. And at the philosophical level, Mather again was the most outstanding figure in the attempt to reconcile Newtonian natural philosophy with traditional Puritanism.

Mather's most important work in this respect was *The Christian Philosopher*, which appeared in 1721 and in which Mather attempts to absorb contemporary scientific knowledge into a traditional Calvinist context. Pokrovsky points out that though Mather in this work does accept much of the Newtonian view of the natural world, he remained committed to a "religious-dogmatic" perspective in that he never accepted the experimental methods of contemporary science. Mather effected the combination of Newtonianism and Puritanism by grafting onto Newton's principles several components of the Ramist "technologia": (1) any ordered process is rational; (2) rational ordering is a means toward an end; (3) consequences invariably resemble causes; and (4) the laws of nature are reflections of divine creativity. By availing himself of these features of traditional Puritan thought Mather was able to turn Newtonianism into a more rationalist and teleological construct, thus squaring it with his religious convictions. In one sense this was not difficult to do, since Newtonianism lends itself to a religious interpretation. Though Pokrovsky does not make the point, it is worth noticing that a mechanistic conception of nature incorporates no principles of development and thus leaves unanswered the question of how nature came to be the way it is. For Newton himself, and for many in the eighteenth century, the mechanism of nature implied a creator. To that extent, Mather's treatment of Newtonianism is not unusual. Its uniqueness is not in reading Newtonianism theologically but in its specific conception of the nature of the creator and the relation between the creator and its product. Rather than understand the creator and creation in an increasingly common deistic way, Mather's treatment of the ground of nature's mechanism is fully Calvinist.

Despite the availability of Newtonianism to a theological rendering, however, Mather's attempt to reconcile science and Puritanism was severely limited, and it had implications that were not consistent with central features of Ramist thought. Any reading of Newtonianism undermined what for the Puritans had been a comfortable Aristotelian—Ptolemaic cosmology, leaving them with a picture of the universe devoid of any clear "higher" and "lower," "greater" and "lesser," without any center. Without a cosmology that places the earth and its human inhabitants at the center, sustaining a traditional Christian conception of history becomes increasingly difficult. And a conception of nature's processes as governed by natural law is ultimately inconsistent with central Calvinist principles. Mather interpreted the Newtonian principles of gravity and thermodynamics as proceeding from God's design. Otherwise, he argued, they could not be explained. Nature, furthermore, is understood as a symbol of the divine. Thus Mather also interprets unusual or exceptional natural events such as eclipses and floods as symbolic acts of God. God used natural law, he thought, to effect these acts, a view that is consistent with Calvinist predetermination. On the one hand, though, he regarded these acts as divine responses to human behavior, but if they are the result of natural laws, then human behavior is irrelevant. In a similar vein, Calvinism is not capable of incorporating one of the most significant features of the new science, which is that it allows for more widespread prediction. A view of nature as symbolic of the divine and of natural laws as the means of divine action is not consistent with the predictability of events that natural laws enable.

According to Pokrovsky's fairly generous reading, Cotton Mather is significant for his attempt to modernize Puritanism and to see it through the difficulties of a rapidly changing intellectual and social environment. This was, however, an aspiration doomed to failure. By the early eighteenth century Puritanism's time had come and gone, and in the opinion of a number of Soviet commentators its death knell was struck by the Great Awakening, a wave of popular, enthusiastic revivalism that swept the congregations of New England between 1720 and 1750. As Pokrovsky describes it, the Great Awakening was not a return to conservatism but an attempt on the part of "perfectly ordinary people" to move beyond orthodox dogmatic clerics and create a heartfelt sense of God and religious community. Karimsky in his description sees the Great Awakening as an inherently contradictory event. On the one hand, he says, it was characterized by the activism of a democratically minded clergy, by a mass expression against intolerance, and by radical sociopolitical demands. On the other hand, he feels, it represented an intensification of the struggle by one strain of traditional Protestantism against the increasingly widespread and influential deistic, secular world view. In the end, however, both Karimsky and Pokrovsky think that the progressive nature of the Great Awakening was its most important aspect. As a popular and cross-Colonial movement, Karimsky feels, it was a significant pre-revolutionary development. And Pokrovsky notes that "The 'Great Awakening'—and this was its fundamental historical result—destroyed the dominance of earlier church institutions, above all those of the Puritan-Congregationalists" (Pokrovsky 1989b, 178).

As its social and political position unraveled, and as European science and philosophy became more influential, Puritan orthodoxy lost its hold on New England Colonial life, giving way ultimately to the Enlightenment. First, however, the philosophic and religious issues generated by the work of Newton, Locke, and Berkeley commanded the attention of the two most prominent eighteenth century pre-Enlightenment American philosophers—Samuel Johnson and Jonathan Edwards.

Eighteenth Century Idealism

Both Karimsky and Pokrovsky discuss Johnson and Edwards, though Pokrovsky examines their specific philosophic conceptions and the meaning of their work for the development of American philosophy in much greater detail. In Karimsky's view, however much the details of their ideas differ, Johnson and Edwards both represent a conservatism that arose in direct reaction to early eighteenth century developments in North America. In the intellectual sphere, the new physics of Newton and the philosophic writings of Locke and Berkeley, which challenged Puritan orthodoxy, were accompanied by the growing strength of materialism and deism. In America, John Wise was already advocating a form of deism in the first two decades of the eighteenth century, and the early works of Benjamin Franklin, themselves expressing deistic and materialist views, were appearing in the 1720s. At the same time, the social and political crises that would lead before long to revolutionary theory and practice were intensifying in the first several decades of the century. Karimsky interprets Johnson and Edwards against this conceptual and social backdrop. Their idealism, he argues, was a philosophic defense of ideological and social conservatism, and thus they represent the forces of reaction in an increasingly revolutionary time:

> The rehabilitation of religion and Christian social and ethical values, and through them the neutralization of social activism and its political radicalism, was the fundamental social function of the idealism of Johnson and Edwards, which was an ideological expression of the aspirations of those conservative bourgeois forces whose interests were represented by tradition and by the prevailing social order. (Karimsky 1976c, 73)

The conceptual presumption underlying Karimsky's assessment of Johnson and Edwards is the general view that certain philosophic conceptions are conducive to progressive social development and others are essentially conservative. Specifically, and here again we see the general Marxist flavor of Karimsky's assessment, religious and overtly idealist philosophic positions have historically buttressed prevailing social conditions and consequently have been impediments to social progress. Philosophic materialism, on the other hand, has in Karimsky's opinion corresponded with forward-looking, often revolutionary social and political ideas. This is the same view that informs his emphasis on the Puritan dissidents as the genuine precursors of the most valuable aspects of the American Enlightenment, and it is the same view that inclines him, as we will see in the next chapter, to associate philosophic materialism with the most radical forces of the American revolutionary movement. The source of this view, of course, is Marx, for whom religion was at the same time the "sigh of the oppressed" and the "opium of the people" and for whom philosophic materialism was a necessary condition of social progress. Pokrovsky by contrast is less inclined than Karimsky to read idealism and materialism in as sharply opposed a fashion.

Samuel Johnson and Jonathan Edwards were contemporaries, both educated at Yale in traditional Ramist philosophy. Both of them seriously engaged contemporary philosophic trends, their respective major works appearing in the 1750s, and each played a prominent role in American academic life. Johnson was one of the founders and the first president of King's College, later Columbia University, and Edwards was president of Princeton College. While their lives were in these respects similar, their philosophic views differed considerably. Though they were both raised in the traditional milieu of Puritan New England, Johnson rejected Calvinism early in his life, spending most of his career as a Colonial representative of Anglicanism. Edwards, on the other hand, embraced traditional Puritanism and spent most of his life as an active clergyman. Johnson was an opponent of the fundamentalism that characterized the Great Awakening, while Edwards became one of the movement's leaders. And philosophically, Johnson's primary interest was in a Berkeleyan immaterialism, while Edwards' most fundamental task was to put Locke and Newton in the service of Puritanism.

Samuel Johnson

Though he broke with his Calvinist background, Johnson never fully abandoned its Christianized Platonist ontology and Ramist epistemology. Thus he was a transitional figure, on the one hand genuinely post-Puritan, even approaching Enlightenment views, especially in his ethics, while on the other hand remaining in a philosophic context formed by the Puritan roots of American intellectual culture.

Johnson's primary contemporary philosophic stimulus was Berkeley. After reading Berkeley's *Treatise on the Principles of Human Knowledge*, and after meeting him in 1729, Johnson became a staunch advocate of Berkeleyan idealism, which he pursued in his central work *Elementa Philosophica* (1752). His interest in Berkeley notwithstanding, Johnson did not simply duplicate Berkeley's views. Johnson's own Puritan background and the intellectual and social situation in Colonial America required something else. Consistent with seventeenth century American traditions, Johnson was most impressed by the Christian Platonist side of Berkeleyanism, which Berkeley himself overtly developed only later in his life. There is an irony here, Pokrovsky thinks, in that while it was Johnson who advised Berkeley to pursue a more explicit Platonism, "The fact that Berkeley accomplished this exceptionally well in his own later *Siris* (1747) essentially undermined the influence of the *Elementa Philosophica* as an innovative philosophical work" (Pokrovsky 1989b, 196).

Berkeley's thought as it is expressed in the *Treatise* and in *Three Dialogues Between Hylas and Philonous* contains a central tension between subjective and objective, or Platonist, idealism. To the extent that the existence of the objects of perception derives from their being perceived by human minds, and Berkeley argued precisely this, he advances a subjective idealist position. To sustain this view, however, he was forced to argue also that the existence of both the objects of perception and perceiving finite minds require God's "perception," that is, that they exist in God's "mind." To the extent that existence requires divine conception, Berkeley's is an objective idealist position. His subjective and objective idealism, however, are not consistent. If, on the one hand, the objects of perception exist in God's mind, then they do not require finite perception in order to be. On the other hand, an emphasis on the subjective idealist side of Berkeley verges on solipsism. Johnson was sensitive to this problem, and he took it as his main task to prevent Berkeleyan idealism from sliding over the edge of solipsism, which is to say, to preserve immaterialism while avoiding nihilism. He chose to do this by emphasizing the Platonist, objective idealist strain in Berkeley, and his analysis of the problems of substance, space, time, and perception are directed to this end.

Johnson interpreted the problem in terms of traditional Ramist epistemology. Ramist theory provides for three sources of knowledge: (1) archetypal-divine forms as prototypes of all existing things; (2) entypal-created embodiments of these forms; and (3) ectypal-human representations of the created world. In Ramist terms, the Berkeleyan dilemma is whether the existence of objects is archetypal or ectypal. Johnson understood Berkeley to be saying that there are actually two sources of the existence of objects of perception: archetypes, or divine forms, and ectypes, or human perceptions. Archetypes, he thought, were the cause both of objects of perception and our perceptions of them. This was, however, a misreading of Berkeley who, though he agreed with the existence of archetypal forms, did not agree that they were the causes of things, a point he made explicit in a letter to Johnson. But to say this leaves the inconsistency between objective and subjective idealism unresolved.

To resolve the inconsistency, Johnson comes down on the Platonist side of Berkeleyan immaterialism. One of the disagreements he had with Berkeley's subjective idealism was that in his view it treated spirit, or mind, as essentially active, as a necessarily perceiving thing. But mind, he thought, must be to some degree passive since it can and does exist without perceiving. Johnson's commitment to the theological principle of the immortality of the soul did not permit him to rest the soul's existence on its own activity of perception. Thus, spirit is to some degree passive and owes its existence to God. Of course Berkeley himself took much the same view in *Three Dialogues Between Hylas and Philonous* when he introduces the notion of existence in God's perception, but it is precisely here that Berkeley breaks with his own principle that to be is to be perceived. Johnson avoids the discrepancy by never fully accepting the subjectivist principle.

Johnson's conception of mind or spirit, Pokrovsky says, is an idiosyncratic mixture of Platonist absolutism, Augustinian intuitivism, and the principle of Descartes' *cogito.* This view of mind, Pokrovsky continues, had a single general goal: "to ground the hierarchy of similar rational forms, 'descending' from God to man, from divine reason to human reason, while preserving the Berkeleyan necessity of the activity and autonomy of the individual self" (Pokrovsky 1989b, 197–198). The crucial issue here is the relation of divine forms to human perception, of divine reason to human reason. Concerning this question Johnson argued that all impressions in consciousness of any possible objects directly depend on God through their relation to archetypes. Archetypes are divine ideas, and they have a higher, divine, character and a lower, human, one. The relation between archetypes as divine ideas and human sensation is that archetypes unite the "realm of ideas" with human consciousness. In Johnson's view, then, both the existence of objects of perception and perception itself are grounded in divine forms. This Platonist attempt to resolve Berkeley's dilemma reflects Johnson's own Puritan philosophical background, which is also apparent in his further claim that archetypes themselves are not accessible to human knowledge. Rather, they enter consciousness through intellectual intuition, something akin to Descartes's Augustinian "light of reason." Pokrovsky notes that in Johnson's view this intellectual intuition is possessed by all people without exception, which, he says, is a tribute to Johnson's philosophical democratism in that it breaks from both classical Platonist and orthodox Puritan elitism.

Johnson's position is a Platonist Berkeleyanism in that Johnson agrees with Berkeley that real things have a sensibly perceived character, but then he grounds the nature of perception in divine forms. This resolves the threat of solipsism in Berkeley's subjective idealism, but it also results in a marked disagreement between Johnson and Berkeley over certain fundamental ontological issues. Pokrovsky illustrates this in a consideration of Johnson's treatment of space. Berkeley argued explicitly that primary as well as secondary qualities were dependent on perception. Consequently he disagreed with Newton over the independent existence of space. And Berkeley's view is clearly not an objective idealist one: primary qualities depend on human perception. Johnson could not follow Berkeley on this point, his disagreement being rooted, Pokrovsky says, "deep in his own distinct practical, theological, and philosophical conditions" (Pokrovsky 1989, 190–191). One of the aspects of Berkeley's arguments that Johnson found attractive was his appeal to common sense, and for Johnson the objective existence of space was fairly obvious to common sense. Furthermore, on traditional theological grounds such a thoroughgoing subjectivism was unacceptable. Nevertheless, Johnson could not ignore Berkeley's compelling arguments for the dependence of primary qualities on perception. He was able, however, to find a resolution to this problem in his Platonism, reconciling Newton and Berkeley through his conception of archetypes. Primary qualities, he argued, are "faint reflections" of divine attributes, and thus Newton was right to attribute objective existence to space. At the same time, Berkeley was right to relate primary qualities to perception in that they are related to consciousness through ectypes. They are nevertheless objective because human ideas and perception are grounded in divine archetypes. Thus as Pokrovsky puts it, "Johnson tried to transform the philosophical conflict between Berkeley and Newton into a simple epistemological matter, and thus resolve it" (Pokrovsky 1989b, 193).

Johnson developed his metaphysical and epistemological views in part 1 of *Elementa Philosophica*, which he titled "Noetica." Part 2, "Ethica," which had first appeared as an independent essay in 1746, contained his moral theory. In his ethics, just as in his metaphysics and epistemology, Johnson has one foot in traditional Puritan theology and the other in more contemporary philosophic ideas. The most significant modern feature of Johnson's moral theory is his understanding of the foundations of ethics as inquiry into the "highest happiness." Johnson was, Pokrovsky says, an unexpected advocate of the hedonistic tradition in the heart of Puritan New England. The emphasis on happiness reflects the influence of Wollaston, and in his association of ethics with "natural religion" Johnson came close to Wollaston's deism. Pokrovsky notes that his understanding of happiness in terms of nature and natural law anticipates to a certain extent the idea of natural rights as it was expressed in Jefferson's accent in the Declaration of Independence on the "pursuit of happiness" as an inalienable right. In the end, however, Johnson's interpretation of happiness and moral virtue had less of an Enlightenment and rationalist character than did Wollaston's deism. For Johnson, natural religion required not only reason but also revelation, and to that extent he was not quite a forerunner of the Enlightenment.

Pokrovsky's assessment of Johnson is as a significant transitional figure between early American Puritanism and the American Enlightenment. "The conceptual legacy and creative biography of Samuel Johnson," he says, "is highly instructive, above all in that this American philosopher embodied the complex collisions of his time, standing as he was on the threshold of great historical events—revolutions, wars of independence, and the formation of new states in America" (Pokrovsky 1989b, 207). To the extent that Johnson relied as much as he did on Puritan and Platonic conceptual tools, it might appear that he had little to offer the Enlightenment. To see Johnson in this way, Pokrovsky thinks, would be a mistake:

> Even such transitional figures as this American part-Berkeleyan, part-Puritan, and part-Newtonian played a role of no small importance in their society—they gradually shook loose people's minds, enabling them to perceive the truly revolutionary ideas of the "Age of Reason." This ferment seized the whole of society, and attempts to suppress it with the help of old or renovated theological schemes merely accelerated the process. (Pokrovsky 1989b, 208)

Jonathan Edwards

The intellectual ferment of which Pokrovsky speaks was equally significant for the life and thought of Jonathan Edwards, Johnson's slightly younger contemporary. Edwards was, in Pokrovsky's words, "one of those who through the force of philosophical conviction, theological strategy, and clerical activity attempted to transform the intellectual ferment engendered by the disintegration of orthodox Puritanism into a stimulus for the strengthening and renewal of faith" (Pokrovsky 1989b, 209). The picture of Edwards that emerges from Pokrovsky's reading is of a singularly interesting figure who embraced at the same time traditional Puritan philosophic and religious thought, contemporary epistemological and scientific conceptions, and indigenous American cultural forms. He is significant further in that some of his views anticipated if not paved a way for later distinctly American philosophic developments, in particular the religious and moral optimism of New England transcendentalism, and later still William James's emphasis on the phenomenological value of religious feeling.

As early as his university years, Pokrovsky says, Edwards was working to synthesize Ramism, Cartesianism, Lockean empiricism, and Newtonian physics. His major works were not written until late in his life, in part because soon after leaving Yale, Edwards, as a young preacher in Northampton, Massachusetts, found himself in the heart of the religious enthusiasm and pietism of the Great Awakening. Edwards quickly became one of the leaders of the movement, the spirit of which sunk deep roots in his consciousness, to emerge later in his theoretical interest in religious feeling as the foundation of faith.

Like Cotton Mather before him, Edwards adapted much of current thought to suit his Calvinist conceptual scheme. He accepted, for example, the Lockean concepts of simple, complex, and abstract ideas, though not without some development of his own. That he was not simply a follower of Locke is not surprising since, as Pokrovsky puts it, "to adapt Lockean empiricism to Puritan theology without a corresponding 'revision' of it was in any case impossible" (Pokrovsky 1989b, 213). Pokrovsky illustrates the sort of revision to which Edwards subjected Locke through a discussion of his treatment of atomism. On the one hand, Edwards agreed that every body is either an atom or is constituted of atoms, but he does not regard an atom simply as the smallest bit of matter. He defines it rather as having the trait of indivisibility, which he in turn equates with density and materiality. Matter, in the end, is whatever has the property of resistance. As Pokrovsky points out, however, in Edwards's analysis resistance turns out to be a complex idea, which is to say that to a certain extent he transformed Locke into Berkeley. By understanding the material world in terms of ideas, that is, in terms of perception, Edwards provides the link to Puritanism. The world is the result of the creative acts of God and particular subjects, and knowledge of the world is in the end knowledge of God.

While there were some features of contemporary thought that Edwards adapted to his purposes, there were others that he was compelled to argue directly against. In particular, he could not accept the Lockean and Newtonian conception of the void. Locke had argued that the concepts of matter and empty space require each other, but in Edwards's view an "absolute nothing" is impossible. His hostility to a void stemmed from his concern that it would limit God's omnipotence, since God is absolute being. The only sense, he thought, which could be given to nonbeing is as something relative to consciousness rather than absolute, though by arguing this way he moved to a more clearly objective idealist position.

Edwards's treatment of contemporary thought never left the parameters of Puritan theology, which is to say that his philosophic life was fully consistent with his religious life and thought. Just as his philosophy was to some extent modernized by incorporating and adapting new insights and discoveries, so too, Pokrovsky wants to say, was his religious thought and practice:

> When speaking of Edwards's evangelical fundamentalism, one must note that the general emotional tenor of Puritanism was becoming decidedly warmer. In place of the strict rigorism of the early American Calvinists there developed a more humane, life-loving view, full of an internal optimism which later, in the beginning of the nineteenth century, was transformed in New England into Unitarianism and Transcendentalism. (Pokrovsky 1989b, 220)

The Jonathan Edwards Pokrovsky describes is a man who writes eloquently about people's love of life, about the experience of beauty, and of the soul's relation to nature and God, and he makes a point of contrasting Edwards's tone, if not his doctrine itself, with that of Cotton Mather. If Mather is the stern, rigid orthodox dogmatist, Edwards is the brilliant, more gentle enthusiast and pietist, prefiguring an Emersonian sensitivity to nature as expression and symbol of the divine.

This point bears reflection. Pokrovsky offers a striking portrait, largely because it contrasts so sharply with the more common image of Edwards. For most Americans who know anything about Edwards at all, philosophers and non-philosophers alike, Edwards is the very paradigm of the hellfire and brimstone preacher. Probably the most well-known single sermon of this style is Edwards's own "Sinners in the Hands of an Angry God," in which he terrifies his congregation with hideous images of their being dangled from a slender thread over the consuming fires of hell by a God able and willing to let go at any second; and if God chooses not to let them perish, it is not because of anything they have done or could do. Who, then, was Jonathan Edwards? Was he a precursor of American religious romanticism, of the Emerson who in the Divinity School Address urged his audience to abandon religious dogma? Or was he an early American fundamentalist, concerned, as many of his descendants still are, to frighten his congregation into complete submission?

The probable answer is that he was both, which makes his place in the development of American culture all the more interesting. If in philosophy he found room for both Ramus and Newton, Calvin and Locke, it should not be surprising that in religion he was at once the thunderous messenger of an angry God and the sensitive commentator on the character of religious experience and the divinity of nature. American religious experience has always had both of these strains, vacillating in relative importance and influence over time. In Edwards, too, we find them both. In practice he was a fundamentalist preacher and a leader of a movement grounded in heartfelt religious enthusiasm. In theory he in one work defends Calvinist predetermination and in another argues for religious feeling as the basis of faith.

One of the theoretical issues with which Edwards was most concerned was the question of free will. In the context of his struggle against Arminianism, which defended free will as a necessary condition of individual human responsibility, Edwards developed an intricate philosophic defense of determinism. Pokrovsky points out that his arguments against free will rest on three theses: the dominance over behavior of the strongest motivation at any given time, the recognition of the cause-effect relation, and the distinction between natural and moral necessity. Behavior, Edwards argued, results not from choice but from our strongest impulse, which in general he said is our desire to achieve happiness. And every act of will, he thought, is a link in a causal chain. Edwards grounded his view in what he took to be "common sense," arguing, unlike Locke, that the intuitive belief in universal causality is an innate idea, one which he represents as the idea of God as the source of all earthly harmony and beauty. There is, then, a moral necessity with which free will would be inconsistent. With respect to physical necessity there is, he thought, some room for human freedom. We can choose whether to go left or right, whether to stand or sit, but moral choice is impossible. In the end Edwards defends moral necessity on purely theological grounds, specifically that God predetermines every event and every detail. Pokrovsky makes a point, though, of noting that in his arguments Edwards does not simply appeal to Scripture, but attempts to ground his view philosophically. To the extent, for example, that his argument rests on the ubiquity of the cause-effect relation, Edwards was, Pokrovsky says, the first Protestant theologian to depart from a purely providential treatment of determinism. That Edwards was concerned to provide a rational justification of his position indicates the extent to which "American culture began more and more to reflect European culture, and even to generate its own unique Enlightenment consciousness; it stood on the threshold of the Age of Reason" (Pokrovsky 1989b, 226).

Nevertheless, despite Edwards's commitment to rational argument, there remained his other, pietist side, the side that Pokrovsky takes to have anticipated Unitarianism and transcendentalism. Just as early nineteenth century romanticism was in part a reaction against the rationalism and materialism that dominated the Enlightenment, Edwards's pietism was a response to what was then the growing influence of rationalistic deism as well as to the increasingly rationalist character of religious orthodoxy. The ground of religious faith and truth, he argued, is feeling, affection. It is here that Pokrovsky sees the background not only of romanticism but also of William James's later emphasis on the importance of religious feeling. Furthermore, he says, we find here an approach to religious experience uniquely related to American culture and consciousness:

> The significance of Edwards's psychological views was not simply that they anticipated the theories of James but that Edwards was the first to attempt to provide an analysis of religious feeling, to find the psychological sources of religion. This was extraordinarily important for a country in which Protestantism became one of the fundamental formative factors of national culture. (Pokrovsky 1989b, 228)

* * *

For all his attempts to reconcile it with contemporary philosophical, scientific, and religious developments, Edwards was the last great representative of New England Puritanism. As Pokrovsky puts it, it had lost its monopoly on the American mind. The questions that interested Soviet commentators, and their American counterparts as well, concern the role of Puritanism in the formation of American thought and culture and, more explicitly, the relation of Puritanism to later trends in American philosophy.

From the point of view of some Soviets, the Enlightenment was the antithesis of Puritanism. In the Enlightenment's advocacy of democracy, the separation of church and state, natural rights, and in its grounding in contract theory rather than covenant theory, Karimsky sees the Enlightenment as abandoning Puritanism for something nearly wholly different. And though it was certainly true that, as Stetzenko puts it, the Enlightenment "shook the foundations of Puritan ideology" and, as Morozova argues, that it was the final blow to Puritan theocracy, Pokrovsky, Mishin, and others see a great deal more continuity in the relation between Puritanism and the Enlightenment than does Karimsky. They regard covenant theory as an early form of contract theory, and they tend to see Puritanism as paving the way for later developments, specifically in the attempts by its later spokesmen to take account of contemporary thought. And Pokrovsky also sees a relation, both positive and negative, between Puritanism and romanticism. In his essay "America Lost and Found," for example, he sees American romanticism as arising in part as a reaction against Puritanism's pessimism and its failure to create the New Canaan. On the other hand, as we have already seen, he regards Puritanism in the hands of Edwards as already beginning to take on the optimism and conception of nature that characterized transcendentalism.

However one interprets the relation between Puritanism and later schools of thought, there is no question but that it was a significant period in the development of American thought and culture. Pokrovsky takes it to have left distinctive marks on subsequent American history, as "a fundamental stage in the formation of American culture and national self-consciousness, determining in no small degree the characteristics of contemporary American society" (Pokrovsky 1989b, 230). But Pokrovsky also sees the negative role of Puritanism. In retrospect, he says, the strength of the American people was not in Puritanism or Puritan philosophy but in the fact that they were able to overcome it when it became a hindrance to social development. The next stage, of course, was the Enlightenment, certainly among the most prominent periods of American thought and easily its most influential.

2

THE AMERICAN ENLIGHTENMENT

Nature and Knowledge, Revolutionary Social Thought, and Political Theory

LIKE their American counterparts, Soviet specialists in American thought have in recent years paid increasing attention to philosophy in the American Enlightenment. With the exception of M. P. Baskin's 1955 booklet, *The Philosophy of the American Enlightenment*, the most significant Soviet studies of the period have been written since the mid-1970s. This scholarship was assisted by the appearance in 1968 of *Figures of the American Enlightenment*, a two volume selection of primary works from the period in Russian translation. The most direct stimulus, however, was the bicentennial of the Declaration of Independence in 1976. This was the occasion for A. M. Karimsky's *The Revolution of 1776 and the Formation of American Philosophy*, for his article "The Problem of Man in the 'Declaration of Independence' and the Contemporary Ideological Struggle in the U.S.," dedicated explicitly to the two hundredth anniversary of the American Revolution, and for his article "Pedagogical Ideas of the American Revolution." More recently, the bicentennial of the drafting of the U.S. Constitution has stimulated additional works by philosophers, historians, and political theorists. Among them is the collectively authored *USA: The Constitution and Rights of Citizens*, and several articles on the conceptual issues associated with the Constitution, including A. A. Mishin's "The U.S. Constitution: The First Written Bourgeois Constitution," and two articles by Karimsky, "The Problem of Man and Society in the Philosophy of the American Enlightenment," and "The U.S. Constitution and the Problem of Human Rights." The Constitution's bicentennial was also the occasion for essays by Mishin, "Thoughts on the U.S. Constitution," Yu. N. Rogulev, "The Nationalization of Socio-Economic Doctrine in Contemporary Constitutional Law," and V. A. Nikonov, "The Adoption of the U.S. Constitution as Viewed by Soviet Historians." And in the early and mid-1980s several other articles appeared, including N. E. Pokrovsky's "Jefferson and the Federalists: A Conflict of Philosophic Views," E. B. Gaidadymov's "On the Question of the Genesis of the Bourgeois Conception of 'Human Rights' in the Social

Philosophy of the U.S.A.," T. L. Morozova's "On the National Uniqueness of the American Enlightenment," and E. A. Stetzenko's "Thomas Paine and the Problems of the Enlightenment."

Each of these authors emphasizes in one way or another the significance of the American Enlightenment for subsequent conceptual and social development in the United States and internationally. American thought in the eighteenth century developed in distinctive conditions, exhibited uniquely American philosophic traits, and was characterized, as Morozova says, by the "immense role it played in the formation of the American nation and the development of national self-consciousness" (Morozova 1985, 162). Both Baskin and Karimsky note as one feature of the role of American thought in national self-consciousness the conceptual underpinnings of the continuing democratic struggles that have characterized all of American history. The principles of freedom and equality advocated by the American revolutionaries have nourished popular movements ever since, from abolition to suffrage to civil rights. In Baskin's words, "The philosophers of the American Enlightenment played a great and positive role in the struggle against theology and medieval obscurantism. . . . Imbued with humanism and a deep faith in the power of human reason, the ideas of the American Enlightenment continue to be utilized by progressive scholars and cultural figures in the U.S." (Baskin 1955, 1). The faith in reason of which Baskin speaks also characterized European thought in the eighteenth century, and it was one feature of the social optimism of the Enlightenment in general. The American situation was somewhat unique, however, in that the North American colonies already had a history of social experimentation. As Stetzenko puts it, "It was characteristic of the Enlightenment generally to view the present as a springboard for building the future, and in America this had an especially long tradition connected with the Puritan messianic world view" (Stetzenko 1985, 240).

Perhaps the most distinctive characteristic of American philosophy in the eighteenth century was the degree to which it integrated theory and practice. Pokrovsky notes that it has been common among American commentators to regard the influential figures of eighteenth century American thought as significant social and political leaders, and to a certain degree as social and political theorists, but not as philosophers of any particular merit, with the possible exception of Benjamin Franklin. This assessment has been due in part, he says, to the fact that they functioned outside the mainstream of technical modern philosophy. While their thought was certainly influenced by the mainstream—Locke, Hume, Rousseau, Montesquieu, the Scottish Intuitionists and others—they made no original contributions to the development of modern philosophic thought. Pokrovsky mentions that Kant was a contemporary of the American Enlightenment thinkers and that it was Kant's legacy that influenced subsequent philosophic development, not anything done by the Americans.

The validity of this point depends in part on what is accepted as the "mainstream." If European thought of the nineteenth and twentieth centuries is regarded as the mainstream, which has been the case among historians of philosophy, then it is true that eighteenth century American thinkers contributed very little. But if, as is beginning to happen, our conception of the mainstream is broadened to include, for example, Emerson and Thoreau, Peirce and Dewey, then American Enlightenment thought becomes far more influential. Pokrovsky's point is that even without such an expansion of what is to count as the mainstream, it is a mistake to limit our attention to such a narrow range. To regard philosophy as occurring only in the mainstream, he says, is to miss the "complexity of the historical philosophical process." There is much more to philosophy than its primary directions:

> In the course of its formation and development, philosophy invariably attracts the "near-philosophical," adapting elements of knowledge from other disciplines, not only influencing them but also being enriched from contact with them. Furthermore, far from the main course of the formation of philosophy there invariably arise self-developed, though of course not isolated, centers of philosophic thought which, flaring up from the sparks of philosophical classics, find among themselves their own peculiar form of philosophic expression corresponding to the time and place of their appearance, i.e. the historical conditions which engendered them. (Pokrovsky 1983a, 270)

This point is particularly applicable, Prokovsky says, to eighteenth century American philosophy. European philosophers of the seventeenth and eighteenth centuries had certainly not been immune to social developments around them. Consider the possible influence of the Thirty Years War on Descartes, Locke's role in the English Revolution of 1689, and Kant's admiration for the French Revolution of 1789.[1] But the American situation was different. As Karimsky puts it, "The uniqueness of the American Enlightenment is that the course of events compelled it to be oriented to the armed struggle as the inevitable way to express the principles of reason and justice, and its leading theoreticians were compelled to become not merely ideologues but also political leaders of the bourgeois revolution" (Karimsky 1988b, 32–33). The fact that the leading American thinkers were not tangentially but inextricably involved in the most profound social processes of their time gives this period of American philosophy a special cast. It indicates, for one thing, that philosophy need not be, if indeed it ever really is, a purely intellectual affair. With human concerns as its basic problem, Pokrovsky says, American philosophy in the Enlightenment "demonstrates again that philosophy is not merely a theoretical exercise of the intellect, but brings to people concrete answers to the sharp problems of real life" (Pokrovsky 1983a, 288). Furthermore, the integration of theory and practice in American Enlightenment thought prefigures a characteristic that distinguishes indigenous American philosophy to this day. From Emerson and Thoreau through Peirce, James, Royce and Dewey to the contemporary reappropriation of the tradition by Richard Rorty, Cornel West, and others, American philosophy has never accepted a sharp distinction between theory and practice, between the intellect and life as lived.[2] Even in its most technical and abstract moments—Emerson's ruminations on Nature, Royce's mathematical articulation of the Absolute, Santayana's speculations on the realms of being, or Dewey's logic—American thought has been a philosophy of praxis and action. In this regard, American Enlightenment thought is fully a stage, and an influential one, in the development of distinctly American philosophy.

Soviet assessments of American philosophy in the Enlightenment, while on the whole appreciative, are not without their critical moments. The criticisms stem from two central features of the American Enlightenment that Soviet specialists tend to emphasize. First, sharp divisions existed within Enlightenment thought itself, one strain fairly conservative philosophically and politically, the other far more radical. While the Soviets are attracted to the more radical camp, they see even there debilitating conceptual and social limitations, and this is the second reason for their criticisms.

Karimsky grants the difficulties in any attempt to develop a clear topology of American Enlightenment thought. Specific conceptions of nature and knowledge, social and political foundations, and structure crisscrossed in complex ways. First, while for the most part those who tended to be most radical in their social and political ideas also tended to embrace a more or less materialistic and deistic world view, there was no direct or necessary correlation between a philosophic commitment to materialism, deism, or atheism, on the one hand, and social and political radicalism on the other. Karimsky mentions Cadwallader Colden as a case in point: "A prominent representative of free thought and the materialist line in American philosophy, C. Colden to the end of his life (he died in the year American independence was declared) never accepted separation (let alone by revolutionary means) from England" (Karimsky 1988b, 33). Second, there is no clear way to demarcate the influences of European theoretical sources on American thinkers. More moderate liberals, Karimsky says, tended to be oriented toward Grotius, Shaftsbury, Hutcheson, and Bollingbroke, while the more radical circle had a greater sympathy for Milton, Mandeville, and the English and French materialists. Nevertheless, all of them were influenced by certain key European thinkers, including

Montesquieu, Pufendorf and Locke, and Pokrovsky points out that Jefferson, generally taken to be the leading figure of the more radical group, himself gravitated toward the intuitionism of Shaftsbury and Hutcheson. Finally, Karimsky says, the situation is further complicated by the fact that the theoretical views and political positions of some Enlightenment figures changed over time, in particular from the period of the struggle to win independence to the period of the struggle to consolidate it.

All of this indicates the impossibility of providing a strict and formal topology of Enlightenment thought, but Karimsky and his colleagues nevertheless accept the general distinction between moderates or conservatives and radicals. The former group had among its leaders John Adams, Alexander Hamilton, John Jay, in certain respects James Madison, and others, while the latter was dominated by Thomas Jefferson, Thomas Paine, Benjamin Franklin, and a number of less influential figures such as Ethan Allen and Benjamin Rush.

In general, moderates and radicals differed in their philosophic conceptions of nature and human nature, in their understanding of rights, in the character and extent of their commitment to equality and democracy, and in their ideas of appropriate political structures. The moderates favored a minimal degree of social transformation and for the most part represented the interests of large Northern finance—industrial and commercial capital—as well as those of Southern plantation owners, while the radicals advocated more thoroughgoing social and political changes and represented the interests of small farmers, traders, and workers. The radicals tended to endorse materialism and deism and were to a considerable degree hostile to religion, both theoretically and as a social institution. The moderates, on the other hand, were more likely to reject materialism and were deeply suspicious of freethinking. The radicals held a fairly optimistic view of human nature as implying sociality and cooperation and as morally sound. The moderates had a much dimmer, Hobbesian view of human nature and its potential. The radicals advocated fairly democratic forms of republican political structures, while the moderates rejected the possibility and abhorred the likely consequences of democracy. There is a relation, Karimsky and others feel, between the specific philosophical, social, and political views of the two camps and the class interests that each represented. The moderates representing the more wealthy elite were conservative in their views while the representatives of broader mass interests were more radical. Karimsky claims, in fact, that the material interests of these figures were causally related to their philosophic positions: "The development of Enlightenment social philosophy occurred under conditions of sharp political struggle, and its ideological stances to a significant degree determined the character of its theoretical argumentation. . . . That which from the point of view of Enlightenment figures derived from 'human nature' in fact objectively determined the interpretation of human nature itself" (Karimsky 1988b, 35).

The specific differences between the moderate and radical camps of the American Enlightenment will be developed in much more detail, but the general distinction is important at this point to account for the approach Soviet and Russian specialists take. These interpreters are attracted to the American Enlightenment as much as they are because they tend to find the views of the radicals particularly congenial. However, the historical fact is that in the dispute between moderates and radicals, which became the dispute between the Federalists and the Jeffersonians, the former prevailed. In the end conservatism dominated, and the upshot of the American Revolution and the social and political structures it engendered was that the radical commitment to freedom, equality, and democracy of the Jeffersonians was consigned a subordinate, at times overtly repressed, role in American ideological, social, and political life. It is this feature of the American Enlightenment that receives at times severe criticism from Soviet commentators.

Even had the Federalist position not prevailed, however, there would still have been much to criticize, from the Soviets' point of view, primarily because the positions of the radicals themselves contained debilitating contradictions and limits. To approach their criticisms, however, we must first understand that the virtues of the radicals' views were many. In their cosmological ideas they cleansed philosophy of much of its traditional reliance on theology, and as a result their conception of nature developed along materialist lines. A similar secularization characterized the approach to knowledge, replacing theological dogma and revelation with an emphasis on experience and reason as the appropriate methods of obtaining knowledge of the world, one result of which was a blossoming of theoretical and applied science. In the social sphere, secular thought took the form of humanism, in the context of which the Enlightenment radicals developed conceptions of human nature and social relations that emphasized human development and happiness as fundamental values. Social relations were no longer grounded in God's will, or divine right, or *noblesse oblige*, but in the equality of natural, human rights. And the political form most consistent with human dignity and equality, and therefore the one defended by the most persistent of the radicals, was democracy. All of these conceptions, however, bore the stamp of their time and are consequently inadequate as live theoretical options.

To understand the critical approach Soviet commentators have tended to take, one must bear in mind Marxist historiography and social theory. Marx had argued that the historical process is driven by the contradictory interests of the more significant economic classes in any given social epoch. In each such epoch one class dominates by virtue of its control of the productive forces that characterize the society. In an agricultural society, the ruling class is that group in control of the land and the dominant form of labor, in some cases slaves, in other cases serfs. In a society characterized more by trade or industry, the ruling class is that group in control of the means of industrial production and/or the means of transportation and distribution of goods. In any society in which the means of the dominant forms of production and distribution are controlled privately, there are invariably different classes with contradictory interests—slave owners and slaves, nobility and serfs, independent producers and merchants, owners of industrial capital and wage workers, and so on. The divergent and conflicting interests of these classes are constantly being expressed in one way or another, and periodically the class that dominates the society can no longer sustain its position, and control passes to one of the others. These are periods of thoroughgoing revolutionary change.

For Marx, one such period was the demise of feudalism and the corresponding rise of bourgeois, capitalist society, a process characterized first by the preeminence of the interests of commercial capital, later by the dominance of large industrial capital, and throughout by the gradual creation of a class of wage workers, "free" in the sense of no longer being confined by law and tradition to the land, but not free in so far as they were subject to a new master—private capital. Marx's developmental principles of the historical process were coupled with structural principles of social relations. Every society is characterized not only by forces and relations of production but also by distinct institutions and ideas. The latter, which Marx called the society's "superstructure," consists of political, legal, religious, kinship, and educational systems, along with the most prominent philosophical, religious, ethical, legal, social and political ideas. Marx's central point is that the specific forms that the dominant systems and ideas of any society take will always be consistent with the material interests of the dominant class of that society. Thus as the feudal economic structure collapsed, so too did its institutional and conceptual superstructure. Its economic structure was replaced over time by capitalist, that is, bourgeois relations of production, and its institutions and ideas were replaced by a new set of systems and concepts, which reflected the interests neither of the feudal nobility nor the working majority, but those of the new dominant class—the bourgeoisie.

The process of the transition from feudalism to capitalism occurred at different rates in different places, and in general spanned several centuries. It was in full swing in some areas by the early sixteenth century, at which point it took the form of an alliance between merchants and certain aristocratic families, the result of which was the rise of absolute monarchies and a corresponding extension of commercial activity. Such alliances were relatively short lived, however, and by the seventeenth and eighteenth centuries the bourgeoisie began the process of ridding itself of absolute monarchical power, replacing it with the economic, social, political, and conceptual structures and systems that characterize capitalist societies to this day. This broad historical process is the context of American Enlightenment thought.

Even if one accepts the Marxist theories of history and social structure, as Soviet scholars traditionally had, there remains a good deal of room for disagreement over how to interpret specific aspects of any phenomena in light of them. With respect to the American Enlightenment, several controversial issues arise, such as whether the revolution was a directly anti-feudal struggle and thus on a par with the English and French Revolutions, or whether it was essentially anticolonial, in which case it would have been less central to the overall historical process. At the conceptual level there is the question of the specific ways and extent to which American thought in the Enlightenment reflects bourgeois commitments and interests. From the Soviets' point of view, however, there is no question that the ideas of even the most radical of the American thinkers are bourgeois in nature, and in this is to be found their contradictions and essential limitations. On the one hand, from the Marxist point of view, bourgeois ideas are valuable and admirable ones in that they represent advances over feudal ideas. On the other hand, however, since bourgeois ideas ultimately reflect primarily bourgeois material interests, and since there remain contradictions between the interests of capitalists and the wage-earning majority in a capitalist society, even the most advanced bourgeois ideas cannot adequately reflect, embody, or aspire to the genuine material interests of working people.

From the point of view of Soviet commentators, virtually every aspect of American Enlightenment thought took a bourgeois form. In their cosmology, for example, while the most radical thinkers held a more or less materialist understanding of nature, it was an atomistic and mechanical materialism. In its mechanism it was ahistorical, which is to say, its principles did not conceive nature as consisting of processes of development, and in its atomism it could not appreciate the complex, constitutive relations of phenomena. To say that an ahistoric and atomistic conception of nature has a bourgeois tint is not to say that it was developed *in order to* provide a bourgeois social conception writ large, but that it achieved its prominence when it did in part because it was fully consistent with the ahistorical and atomistic bourgeois conceptions of social relations. The fact that Newton and Adam Smith paint analogous pictures of their respective subject matters is not merely a curiosity of intellectual history. The case is similar with respect to the Enlightenment's philosophical anthropology and sociopolitical thought. Even the most radical of the Americans had an ahistorical, naturalistic conception of human nature, one that does not appreciate the extent to which the prevailing form of social relations conditions the human character and one which is conducive to the bourgeois ideological justification of its social order as embodying the eternal nature of things. Despite their conception of equality and human rights, the Americans for the most part were unable to extend them in practice to all people, or for that matter even to most, and the same is true of the political structures they advocated. From a Marxist point of view, one cannot expect bourgeois society to be characterized by genuine social equality and political democracy because such a condition would threaten bourgeois interests. As a result, its social and political ideas and ideals will invariably be of limited applicability and inherently contradictory. Thus the most progressive features of the philosophy of the American radicals can be consistently developed and applied in the interests of the majority only once they are stripped of their bourgeois character, and this, Soviets have traditionally argued, requires Marxist theory and practice. The genuine heirs of the radical wing of the American Enlightenment, then, are dialectical and historical materialism and socialism.

This suggests a final point by way of introduction to the Soviet analysis of the American Enlightenment. In the process of discussing the development of eighteenth century American thought, several Soviet specialists are equally concerned with the ways contemporary American commentators interpret our own conceptual history. They argue that to a large extent American intellectual historians distort or misuse a good deal of eighteenth century thought in order to support contemporary American reality which, from the Soviet perspective, is inconsistent with the best and most progressive features of the Enlightenment. With the defeat of the aspirations, ideals, and programs of its radical wing, American ideological, social, and political reality took an overtly bourgeois, antidemocratic form, and from the perspective of Soviet commentators it became increasingly oppressive over time. The United States was expansionist from its inception, and this process took a more virulent, imperialist form after the resolution of the country's most crucial material contradiction—the incompatibility of the economies of the capitalist north and the plantation based agricultural south—and with the industrial development that followed. By the late nineteenth century, the United States was a full-fledged colonial power, flexing its muscle in the interest of capital abroad against national liberation movements and at home against workers' movements and organizations. Emerging from the Second World War relatively unscathed, the United States assumed the role of the leader of world capitalism.

From the Soviet point of view, America had by the middle of the twentieth century come a long, long way from the early Jeffersonian ideals of equality, human dignity, and democracy, and this created a serious ideological problem. On the one hand, Americans continue to celebrate their revolutionary roots, while on the other hand the reality of American social relations and the country's domestic and international policy were overtly contradicting many of the central principles of the American Enlightenment. One solution to this problem is to distort and deprecate the more radical, progressive character of American revolutionary thought, and several Soviet commentators find precisely this process at work in the analyses of our social, political, and intellectual history by many contemporary American scholars. Writing in 1955, a time of sharp Cold War antagonism between the Soviet Union and the United States, Baskin, in the context of a discussion of the general character of the American Revolution, says that though many American historians appeal to the War of Independence to justify American virtue and by extension its "contemporary, unjust imperialist wars," there is in fact a considerable difference between them. The American Revolution, he says, was a just war, while contemporary imperialist wars are not. The revolution was a struggle to free people from the fetters of feudal institutions and domination, while current wars waged by the United States are attempts to dominate other people (Baskin 1955, 5). Baskin also raises another point that has interested and concerned Soviets, and that is the concept of American "exceptionalism." With our messianic roots in seventeenth century Puritanism, Americans are to this day inclined to see ourselves as having a special role in history, a view that is at times still expressed in theological language. But, Baskin says, the fact that the ideas of the American Enlightenment have had such an extensive influence on world culture and history indicates that they are fully a part of a broad, worldwide historical process, which in turn shows how false is the common view among American historians that there is something exclusive or unique about the development of American capitalism and American society generally (Baskin 1955, 1).

It is Karimsky who discusses in greatest detail the current approach to American Enlightenment philosophy. In his opinion the Declaration is most important as a statement of profound and valuable social principles: "The Declaration of Independence is the ideological justification for one of the most important progressive social transformations of modern times, and in a theoretical respect it enriched the foremost social thought by cultivating the ideas of popular sovereignty and national self-determination, and 'lawfulness' of revolution." He feels that the contrast between American reality and the Declaration is so great that "the social system in the U.S. constantly violates, fails to fulfill, or is unable to realize those principles and demands with which its own formation was related." He continues by suggesting that "the norms of bourgeois democracy, and even more so the principles of revolution, have become so dangerous to monopoly capital that the neutralization of their influence is one of the fundamental tasks of contemporary bourgeois ideologues in the U.S." (Karimsky 1976b, 57–58; also 1976a, 117–119). In general, he thinks, a good deal of

American commentary on the Declaration and Enlightenment thought is designed to minimize what in his view are the most valuable aspects of revolutionary thought: "In most cases, sociological reflection on the Declaration is combined with a direct rejection of the Jeffersonian treatment of nature and the historical destiny of human beings, which specifically concerns the hope of social progress, taking the form of a celebration of reason, the realization of happiness, and a faith in the social equality of rights based on the natural equality of people" (Karimsky 1976b, 59–60).

Whatever the character of contemporary commentary, Soviet and American specialists do agree about the significance of American Enlightenment thought. Its most influential aspects have undoubtedly been social and political, but from the perspective of many of the Soviets, the more general philosophic views and contributions of the American Enlightenment are important in their own right and are the conceptual if not material foundations of revolutionary social and political thought. We will begin, accordingly, with Soviet discussions of Americans' treatment of nature and knowledge.

Nature and Knowledge

Frederick Engels thought that the fundamental question of philosophy focuses on the struggle between materialism and idealism, whether "what there is" is to be understood as based in some way on matter and material processes or on spirit in some sense or other. Philosophers in the West have rarely accepted Engels's claim, either ignoring it altogether or holding that the distinction itself needs to be overcome, or more recently arguing that philosophy should not be an attempt to understand "what there is" at all. Soviet philosophers, however, traditionally accepted Engels's point of view, and for them it served as an organizing principle in the study of the history of philosophy, which helps to explain the emphasis in Soviet literature on the philosophic materialism of the American Enlightenment. Thus Karimsky, for example, says that in America in the eighteenth century the conflict between materialism and idealism took the form of a struggle between Puritanism and religious world views, on the one hand, and freethinking and deism on the other. Though deism itself need not be a materialist philosophic perspective, Karimsky and others argue that in the American Enlightenment it was the general perspective in which philosophic materialism was developed and that ultimately the more interesting feature of American philosophy of the period is not its deism but its materialism. There are three specific respects, Karimsky says, in which American Enlightenment materialism engaged the struggle with idealism. First, and most important, its suggestion and in some cases elaboration of the ideas of the eternality, indestructibility, and essential activity of matter were ways of overcoming religious idealism and its creationism. Second, the rejection of spiritual substance and the advocacy of materialist monism undermined all forms of objective idealism, including theism as well as the Platonism and vitalism then widespread in America. Third, he says, American materialists struggled against subjective idealism by working out their views of the nature of consciousness, in their materialist epistemology, and in the direct critique of Berkeley and his American followers (Karimsky 1976c, 139).

If religion was the foil against which Enlightenment cosmology developed, it was no less so for American epistemology. Stetzenko describes reason as "the organizing principle" of the Enlightenment, though like European thought at the time, rationalism in America was in an unstable marriage with empiricism. The alternative to reason and experience as the appropriate avenues to knowledge was religion. Earlier religious, rationalist, and mystical views, Stetzenko says, appeared absurd in light of logic and empirical observation, and they "could not reasonably explain the existence of evil, the imperfections of human relations, and the discord of natural and social laws" (Stetzenko 1985, 232). Thus, he continues, for the majority of Enlightenment figures, God was relegated to the role of originating nature and then removing himself from it.

The criticism and rejection of theology in American cosmology and epistemology is a prevalent theme in Soviet analysis. Morozova, for example, describes the struggle against religion and the church as "one of the most fundamental characteristics of the Enlightenment." There were, she says, two principle factors involved in the attack on religion, one social and the other theoretical. First, Enlightenment figures were hostile to the church because it was one of the bulwarks of the feudal order against which Enlightenment theory and practice were directed, and second, their interests in developing science required the rejection of a theological, revelatory foundation of knowledge (Morozova 1985, 165). Morozova, Baskin, Stetzenko, and Karimsky all point out that religion and even the Bible itself were criticized by several influential Americans, most notably Benjamin Franklin, Thomas Paine, Ethan Allen, and Thomas Cooper. In his *Reason, The Only Oracle of Man* Allen criticized the irrationality of orthodox religion, Cooper came fairly close to atheism in his philosophic materialism, Franklin felt that faith was inconsistent with reason, and Paine attacked religion as mystical and superstitious, violating both common sense and reason, and he refers to the Bible as a "fraud and a forgery." For most Enlightenment figures religion continued to play a role, primarily in ethics, but from the Soviet point of view the most significant philosophic achievements of the period came in an overtly antireligious context.

Franklin's philosophic development is especially illustrative of the character of eighteenth century American thought, moving as it did from rationalism to a vacillation between sensationalist empiricism and materialism. It was Franklin, Karimsky feels, who "felt the pulse" of his time better than anyone (Karimsky 1976c, 93). He describes Franklin's "Dissertation," "despite its immaturity," as a "fundamental work in the history of American philosophy," both because of what it contained and because Franklin later rejected its basic ideas. The "Dissertation" developed a philosophical view of the world based on rationalist principles, one of which is that all suffering is balanced by pleasure. The rationalism of Franklin's work is significant, in Karimsky's opinion, because it is an attempt to explore fundamental questions independently of religious dogma. Franklin's subsequent rejection of the ideas of the "Dissertation" was a result of his sense of the contradictions between rationalism and empiricism, the latter of which impressed him with its demonstration of the failure of the theory of innate ideas and the possibility of accounting for a diverse and varied world. The rejection of the "Dissertation" was a step toward a more full-blown Enlightenment philosophy, Karimsky feels, in that it constituted a rejection of a rationally grounded determinism in favor of human freedom and efficacy. But Franklin was never a consistent advocate of sensationalist empiricism either, combining it as he did with both deism and a materialist approach to nature and spirit (Karimsky 1976c, 115–117).

Despite the complexities of and differences among the Americans' general philosophic views, they all reflected an approach that took "nature" as its central philosophic concern. Nature was granted its own "harmony," as Stetzenko puts it, and that which was "natural" came to be regarded as "ideal." The elevation of nature to the role of final court of appeal for virtually all theoretical questions was fully part of a process that had been underway at least since the middle of the seventeenth century. For all its positive accomplishments, Cartesianism managed to reinforce a sharp distinction between the natural and the eternal and between nature and the human spirit, as a result of which nature could not be the source of human aspirations and relations. To that extent Cartesianism continued the Platonist and Christian traditions of treating nature and the "ideal" as antithetical. However, an alternative conception of the character of nature and the relation of nature to human life was being approached from at least three sources. Spinoza tried to overcome the Cartesian dichotomy by equating nature with the eternal and by treating both matter and mind as attributes that constitute the essence of nature. At the same time, the development of social contract theory made it possible to regard social relations as arising for discernible reasons from natural human conditions, and it became reasonable to posit the source of the principles of social relations either in the natural human condition itself or in a necessary modification of it. Finally, nature came to be taken more and more seriously, as the progress of natural science rendered its fundamental traits and processes more accessible and familiar. The great achievement in this respect was Newton's, and by the middle of the eighteenth century the "ideal" no longer resided in Platonic Forms or Ramist archetypes, but in a Newtonian universe.

Neither Newton nor most of his European and American followers, however, could embrace a thoroughgoing naturalism, primarily because the Newtonian universe did not contain the principles of its own generation: Paley's watch required a watch maker. Furthermore, it was widely held that the principles of natural and social philosophy were incapable of providing an account of value and meaning, thus these most important aspects of human life must have another explanation. God was a theoretical necessity, invoked as the ground of nature's mechanisms and of ethics, but once created, nature was the primary source of explanatory principle. God and nature thus understood were combined in deism, which was the overarching context of American Enlightenment thought. Jefferson, Franklin, Paine, Cooper, and others all embraced deism to one degree or another.

Despite their criticisms of orthodox religion and theology, the Americans retained God in deistic form. One of the questions Soviet commentators are inclined to ask is why atheism was not more prevalent at the time? It would appear that the rejection of religious orthodoxy combined with philosophic materialism would lead naturally to atheism, yet this rarely occurred. Karimsky suggests that one reason atheism was not more widespread in the American Enlightenment is that in America religion did not represent a united reactionary force, as it did, for example, in France. More generally, eighteenth century natural philosophy led to deism rather than atheism, Karimsky and others argue, as a result of the inherent limits of Enlightenment thought. Though philosophic materialism was common, it was for the most part a mechanistic materialism, in which change is understood as a rearrangement of the external relations of otherwise essentially immutable particles. According to such a view natural *development* is incomprehensible, and nature itself requires a nonnatural source. In the Marxist view, natural philosophy is able to jettison its theological legacy only once it consists of a materialism that does not require mechanistic principles. Thoroughgoing materialism, in other words, must be dialectical rather than mechanical. This possibility, however, had to wait until Marx. In the meantime, philosophic materialism adopted a deistic umbrella.

Virtually all the more prominent figures in the radical wing of the American Enlightenment were materialists in some significant degree—Thomas Jefferson, Benjamin Franklin, Thomas Paine, Ethan Allen, and Benjamin Rush. Materialism was also advocated by Cadwallader Colden, not himself a revolutionary, by Joseph Priestly and Thomas Cooper, relative latecomers to America, and by Joseph Buchanan, an early nineteenth century Jeffersonian radical and follower of Rush. Karimsky locates the most important materialist philosophic developments in the theories of matter and motion suggested by Colden, Allen, Rush, and Cooper, in discussions of the nature of mind by Colden, Jefferson, Allen, Rush, Buchanan, and Cooper, and in the philosophies of science of Colden, Franklin, and Cooper.

The mechanistic conception of matter that dominated eighteenth century conceptions of nature treated matter as temporal, which is to say, created, and as passive, not containing inherent principles of motion and change. In American hands, however, both conceptions of matter were challenged. Karimsky points out, for example, that in arguments against idealism, and in particular against Berkeley, Colden argued for both the essential activity and eternality of matter. Ethan Allen held a similar position, arguing that nature is material, eternal, indestructible, governed by natural law, and invariably active. The conception of matter as temporal and passive was one of the features of eighteenth century natural philosophy that inclined it toward deism. Another such feature was the apparent difficulty of accounting for animate nature. If matter is essentially passive, no way immediately appears to account for the origin of life on natural principles. If matter is understood as inherently active, however, this becomes at least a possibility. It is not surprising, then, that as American philosophers explored the possibility that matter is eternal and active, some of them also suggested a more naturalist account of animate nature. Benjamin Rush, for example, discussed life as a fully natural phenomenon, holding that the traits of both animal and human life were determined in part by the environment. And on the question of the origin of animate nature, Cooper went so far as to suggest the possibility of the self-generation of life, though it seemed to him impossible to demonstrate. As Colden, Allen, Rush, and Cooper abandoned those aspects of natural philosophy according to which a supernatural source appeared to be required, they also relied less and less on deism. Karimsky says, for example, that Colden's materialism was practically free of deism. Allen for his part retained the notion of God, though in Karimsky's view his God was less a creator of nature than a symbol of eternal natural activity, and Cooper, with his advocacy of the activity of matter and the possible natural generation of life, came fairly close to atheism.

While Cooper, Allen, and Colden were, in Karimsky's opinion, among the most advanced of the American philosophers with respect to their treatment of matter and the consequent overcoming of aspects of deism, the views of more traditional deists were also influenced by materialism. Franklin, Karimsky notes, while never embracing atheism, held that God is material on the grounds that an immaterial God would be a violation of the general principle that "nothing comes from nothing." Jefferson had a similar view, thinking that God, indeed anything at all, must be material. Late in their lives John Adams wrote a letter to Jefferson in which Adams advanced a number of idealist views. In his letter of August 1820, Jefferson responded unequivocally:

> On the basis of sensation, of matter and motion, we may erect the fabric of all the certainties we can have or need. I can conceive *thought* to be an action of a particular organization of matter. . . . To talk of *immaterial* existences, is to talk of *nothing*. To say that the human soul, angels, God are immaterial, is to say, they are nothings, or that there is no God, no angels, no soul.[3]

In addition to the question of the nature of matter, and its implications for deism and the understanding of God, Americans were also interested in the nature of mind, and this issue, too, they approached in a materialist spirit. Despite some theoretical weaknesses, Karimsky says, "American materialist thought was fairly fruitful in this complex area" (Karimsky 1976c, 130). Rejecting the existence of mental substance, American materialist philosophers attempted to understand the nature of thought and consciousness by emphasizing their relation either to the brain and nervous system or to the external environment. In both cases thought is regarded as arising from material conditions, and in this lies the materialist character of their treatment of the problem of mind. Karimsky is interested in the approaches to the issue taken by Colden, Jefferson, Allen, Rush, Buchanan, and Cooper. Though their understanding of the functioning of the brain and nervous system was limited, both Colden and Jefferson were convinced that mental activity could be understood only as the result of the human individual's material processes. Cooper also argued explicitly that all forms of psychological activity are a function of the complex material organism. Others addressed the problem more in terms of the relation between the individual and the environment. Allen held that consciousness is ultimately the capacity of the human organism to respond to the demands of the dynamic, changing conditions of its surroundings. Rush had a similar view, though his treatment of the nature of mental activity in general was an aspect of his concern with the more specific problem of the origin of moral consciousness. Rush rejected the view widespread at the time that ethical activity was grounded in innate moral ideas, arguing instead that moral consciousness derived from the individual's interaction with environing conditions. Buchanan, influenced by Rush's work in psychology and medicine, was particularly interested in the role of perception in the development of consciousness. Karimsky regards all of these attempts to understand mind, despite their many limitations and weaknesses, as valuable philosophic contributions in that they were a stage in the process of freeing inquiry into nature and "human being" from the fetters of subjective idealism in either its secular or religious forms. Notwithstanding the inadequacies of the mechanical form in which American Enlightenment philosophers couched their materialism, it provided for important advances in the understanding of the natural factors which conditioned human life.

Revolutionary Social Philosophy

Enlightenment social thought was dominated by the problems of the relation of nature and the individual, nature and society, and the individual and society. The general concept in terms of which the individual and society were understood was natural law. In Karimsky's words,

> The essence of the idea of natural law is not reducible to the recognition of the natural equality of people. It is above all a specific sort of answer to the question of the sources of political power and written law. Natural law is taken to be the eternal and immutable laws of nature, manifesting the permanent properties of the human being, the first of which is the law of self-preservation. Each person from birth possesses full natural rights, the most fundamental of which are the right to life and individual freedom. (Karimsky 1988b, 36)

From the concept of nature and natural law issued the full range of distinctive Enlightenment social principles: its philosophical anthropology, natural rights, and the significance of freedom and property.

Human Nature and Natural Rights

Enlightenment social thinkers had a naturalistic philosophical anthropology. Human nature, they thought, was the product of the mechanical processes of nature in general and the biological condition of human beings. Two significant aspects of this approach were the conception of the essential traits of human nature as ahistorical and the tendency to regard human beings as essentially asocial. The traits of human beings are formed by their natural condition, and social relations and structures are later constructs which, if done correctly, derive their principles from the pre-social nature of people. In Karimsky's opinion a serious problem arises with a naturalistic philosophical anthropology of this kind. While naturalism is generally correct, he thinks, in taking the human condition as a fully natural process rather than as requiring supernatural traits or explanations, it fails in both the eighteenth century and, as he argues elsewhere, in the twentieth century as well to understand the relations of nature, the individual, and society. Not only are human beings fully natural, he would argue, but so too is society. Social relations are not "extra-natural" human conditions, but rather are components of the very processes of nature that condition the character of human beings. The failure of Enlightenment thought to understand that human nature and society constitute each other in the historical process led to the "vicious circle." On the one hand, since society and nature are sharply distinguished and since the essential traits of human beings are products of nature, human nature is ahistorical and asocial. On the other hand, the general philosophic alternatives concerning human nature available to eighteenth century thinkers emphasized either reason or experience as the central formative influence on the human character. Given these alternatives, to characterize human beings as essentially natural rather than spiritual is to emphasize experience over reason. But if experience is a crucial formative feature of human being, then individuals are formed by their social environment. The vicious circle, then, as Karimsky puts it, is that "human beings are formed by the social environment, while the basic traits of that environment are determined by the characteristics of human beings," which themselves are essentially asocial (Karimsky 1976c, 183).

In ideological and political respects, the materialist view of human nature was the context for one of the most significant products of American Enlightenment social thought: natural rights theory. The view that by virtue of their natural condition human beings have certain entitlements was a central component of American social and political theory in general and of democratic thought in particular. As I. A. Geevsky and his coauthors put it, of all the English legal and political ideas and charters to which the colonists appealed to defend their own rights and interests, the most important was the conception of natural rights, and they note that Thomas Paine deserves special mention for contributing to a distinctly American democratic ideology through his firm insistence that human rights and freedom belong to people by nature (Geevsky et. al. 1987, 11–12). The significance of the concept of natural rights is clear from its central role in the argument in defense of revolution contained in the Declaration of Independence, and Gaidadymov refers to it as "the theoretical expression of a new conception of the relation between the individual and society" in general (Gaidadymov 1986, 3).

The specific content of the Enlightenment theory of natural rights was related to both the conception of human nature and to the material conditions and class interests of the revolutionary leadership. In a philosophic respect, the conception of natural rights derived, as Geevsky and his colleagues put it, from the understanding of human being as isolated, having its essential nature outside of society and government, a state of nature in which each individual pursues his or her own interests in a more or less sharp struggle with others (Geevsky et. al. 1987, 12). It is precisely in this feature of natural rights theory that Soviet commentators find the relation to prevailing material conditions and class interests. Geevsky and his coauthors say, for example, that the conception of natural rights was related to capitalist economic activity, so that one of the central natural rights frequently, though not always, acknowledged was a right to acquire and develop property.

From a Soviet point of view, the class content of the Enlightenment's conception of natural rights is evident in at least two ways. One is the fact that despite its appeal to the universality of rights, few revolutionary leaders attempted in a systematic way, and many actively tried to forestall, an extension of rights to what amounts to the vast majority of the population—women, workers, slaves, native Americans, and other such groups. The theoretical conception of natural rights, in other words, was never intended to underwrite a universal system of social rights. The relation between natural or human rights and social or civil rights is crucial here. In theory, the human rights that derive from the natural human condition provide the principles on which social structures are based, but which precise social rights are implied by natural rights is an open question. If the *material* interests of the entire population are equally significant, then one would expect a system of social rights and structures that would secure a general equality of *material* opportunities. If, however, an influential group is inclined to regard its own material interests as more significant than those of others, then the social rights and structures derived from natural rights, even when natural rights are considered universally applicable, are likely to be restricted to the interests of that group. This, in the Soviet view, is precisely what happened. Thus not only was the majority of the population in the late eighteenth century excluded from the material benefits of universal human rights, but throughout American history social rights and material opportunities have been extended to broader segments of the population only as a result of continuous struggles waged from below. The fact that even today the acquiring of civil rights continues to require mass struggle is additional evidence that the conception of natural rights informing American ideological and social traditions was and is in practice class specific.

In so far as the revolutionary leadership in general represented a specific class, or more accurately a coalition of differing ruling class interests, it was necessary to endorse at the same time universally applicable natural rights and social rights of restricted applicability. This is accomplished by treating the social expression of natural rights in a purely legal fashion. In Karimsky's opinion this way of treating the relation between natural and social rights is both valuable and unacceptable. On the one hand, he says, the universalization of legal norms "was undoubtedly progress in relation to feudal and colonial inequality. In this respect the United States was a pioneer in legal equality." On the other hand, he suggests that social rights must extend not only to legal equality but also to the guarantee and protection of such material conditions of social life as work, leisure, education, housing, and health. American society, he notes, has not yet realized anything even remotely resembling equality in these respects even to a minimal degree, and while this fact does not contradict the formal, legal interpretation of rights developed in the eighteenth century, it does betray the spirit and broad social potential of the Enlightenment's conception of natural rights (Karimsky 1988a, 248–253).

Inadequacies like these notwithstanding, the theory of natural rights of the American Enlightenment contained a number of profoundly important elements, not the least of which was the emphasis on freedom. Karimsky expresses what he takes to be the value of the Enlightenment's treatment of freedom:

> The understanding of human freedom developed by American thinkers was in the mainstream of the best traditions of bourgeois philosophy in the seventeenth and eighteenth centuries. It presupposed the overcoming of external constraints, as well as the tying of needs and ideals to adequate means for their satisfaction and realization. . . . [T]o this traditional understanding of freedom the Americans were able to add a new meaning, that it applied to all people. To the credit of the Americans, they tried to construct a democratic program for the practical realization of human freedom. (Karimsky 1976c, 186–187)

Like the general theory of natural rights, the conception of freedom was both admirable and severely flawed. As a central principle of Enlightenment social thought, the emphasis on freedom brought to the fore the importance of individual interests and development, and by understanding freedom as a natural condition American thinkers broke through the constraints of feudal social relations and colonial policies. At the same time, the American conception of freedom was and is, in the Soviet view, essentially bourgeois. Gaidadymov, for example, says that in practice the right to freedom meant primarily the right to property, and in Baskin's opinion even for Jefferson freedom meant above all the freedom of private property. Baskin suggests that in practice the implementation of this understanding of freedom meant that older feudal relations were replaced by bourgeois class relations, that is by social structures and institutions that protect bourgeois class interests rather than guarantee genuine freedom to the entire population. Marx's remark about Rousseau, he thinks, applies equally to Jefferson, and by extension to the dominant strains of Enlightenment social thought generally: "The rule of reason was nothing other than the idealized rule of the bourgeoisie" (Baskin 1955, 8–9).

Radicals vs. Moderates: Human Nature and Ethics

The demands of the postwar period to create the structures and institutions of the new nation brought to the surface and in some cases exacerbated the often deep disagreements in the revolutionary coalition. In the Soviet perspective, two distinct camps emerged, even if on some issues the line dividing them was sometimes blurred. One wing was the radicals, or Jeffersonians, and the other is variously referred to as the moderates, conservatives, or Federalists. The most prominent figures among the radicals included Jefferson, Franklin, Paine, Allen, and Rush, while the outstanding representatives of the moderate or conservative wing were Adams, Hamilton, and Madison, though on many issues Madison had more in common with the radicals than with the conservatives. The disagreements between the two camps over both general and philosophical principles and specific social policies often ran very deep and spanned the full range of Enlightenment concerns. Most central for social thought were their differing approaches to human nature, ethics, history, natural and civil rights, freedom, equality, property, economics, and religion.

In general, the radicals had an optimistic view of human beings and of the possibilities for fairly thoroughgoing, rational transformations of the social order. For them, the War for Independence was but the first step of a much broader revolutionary process. In Benjamin Rush's words from a letter dated May 1787, "We have completed only the first act of a great drama." The moderates, on the other hand, were likely to be pessimistic about the inherent, natural characteristics of human beings, and they tended to advocate at most rather minimal revisions of traditional social relations and institutions. In the 1780s and 1790s the moderates, several Soviet commentators suggest, were concerned above all to put the brakes on the process of revolutionary change.

Revolution, even if its ultimate end is essentially to overcome colonial status, is an inherently radical process, and not surprisingly the language and principles in which the aspirations of the revolutionaries were expressed were those of the radicals. In its appeal to natural equality, freedom, inalienable rights, and self-determination, the Declaration of Independence embodied ideals that the conservatives were later either to reject outright or to modify significantly. It was the radical camp, in other words, that set the early revolutionary agenda by asserting the principles to which the colonists appealed to justify the revolution and to which Americans continue to look as expressions of the moral foundation of American society. In various Soviet analyses, however, it was the moderate wing of the revolution that had a much clearer sense of objective social and historical processes and of the limits of any attempted social transformations. Thus the principles of the radicals, in so far as they were ideals that clashed with the constraints imposed by material reality, had a utopian character, but by expressing the commitments of the entire revolutionary coalition in the struggle for independence, they have come to represent, in the words of Eduard Batalov, an *official* American utopia.

In his book *The American Utopia*, a study of the history of utopian theory and practice in the United States, Batalov distinguishes three general types of utopian thought in American cultural and political history: the official utopia, the folk utopia, and the literary and sociotheoretical utopia. Through the course of American history the latter two categories have included the utopia of farmers' America, the romantic utopia, the socialist utopia, the technocratic utopia, and other forms in more recent years. The official American utopia, he says, arose with American statehood.

Batalov understands a utopia as a set of social ideals that are at variance with the objective tendencies and processes of the social and historical epoch in which they arise. As ideals they express the aspirations of some part of the population, but they are utopian in so far as they conflict with objective possibilities. The official American utopia of the late eighteenth century was a set of just such ideals, "official" because it was a "system of social ideals advanced by the authorities," and its first clear expression was in the Declaration of Independence. Batalov does not describe the Declaration itself as a utopian document, since several of its "provisions reflected objective trends in America's political and social development and identified certain abilities and intentions of the young American bourgeoisie to remove obstacles to free enterprise, individualism, and freedom from tutelage by the state." But the Declaration, as Karimsky too emphasizes, is not simply or even primarily a political document; it is as much an expression of social ideals. "The authors of the Declaration," Batalov says, "had a vision of a free society whose citizens enjoyed political sovereignty and had a right and ability to liberate themselves—through revolution—from any government incapable of ensuring self-evident civil rights. It was a society based on the recognition of human equality" (Batalov 1985, 53).

The clash between social ideal and social reality was expressed in the American context in the struggle between Jeffersonian radicals and Federalist conservatives. The Jeffersonians had the vision capable of mobilizing society into revolutionary action, while the Federalists had the understanding of objective social reality necessary to institutionalize American independence. The principles of radical Enlightenment thought were forced ultimately to give way to objective necessity and to the program of the Federalists. That the ideals of the radicals were inconsistent with reality and ultimately with bourgeois interests accounts for what Soviets regard, as we have seen, as the frequent reinterpretation and disparagement of the ideas of Enlightenment radicals by contemporary American commentators. In Stetzenko's opinion, Paine, as one of the most progressive visionaries of the period, has been especially victimized in this way: "His radicalism was and remains unacceptable for the official ideology of America to such a degree that even today bourgeois historians speak of him sparingly and with hostility, his works are rarely reprinted, and from time to time he receives still new slander and attacks." The fate of Paine's ideas is representative of the fate of the most valuable features of Enlightenment social thought. Paine's tragedy, Stetzenko says, "is the tragedy of the entire Enlightenment, which, distinguished by its rationalism and activism, was not able to overcome the discrepancy between the ideal and the real, between absolute freedom and equality and historically concrete bourgeois democracy, between the abstract civil individual and the social individual, between philosophy and power, between theory and practice" (Stetzenko 1985, 260).

In his essay on Jefferson and the Federalists, Pokrovsky also sees a discrepancy between radical social ideals and the material realities of historical development. Despite the many contradictions in Jefferson's ideas, he writes, and the fact that history has shown some of the Federalists' ideas to have been correct (for example, the importance of industry), Jefferson's thought remains an example of democracy and humanism, laying the foundation of the tradition of progressive philosophical and sociopolitical thought in the United States (Pokrovsky 1983, 285). Batalov, Stetzenko, and Pokrovsky develop the common theme that American radical thought of the eighteenth century was wrong—that is, it misunderstood the nature of real social development and possibilities—but for all its mistakes it is the most admirable strain of Enlightenment social thought.

To appreciate this feature of the Soviet evaluation of the American Enlightenment it is important to realize that from the Soviet point of view such figures as Jefferson and Paine were wrong not in general but *for their time*. The radical commitment to freedom, individual development, and social equality did not and could not conform to the material interests of the bourgeois class, but the objective historical reality of the eighteenth century was such that the only social force that *could* prevail was the bourgeoisie. A successful revolution in the eighteenth century could not be anything other than a bourgeois revolution that established the conditions for capitalist development and the power of the capitalist class. For *that* purpose the ideology and policies of the Federalists were far more appropriate than the radicalism of a Jefferson or a Paine. The radicals looked beyond the conditions and character of capitalist society, and that is precisely why Soviet commentators have been inclined to find many of their views so congenial.

At the level of theory, the most fundamental disagreement between radicals and moderates concerned their respective conceptions of human nature. Both groups accepted the distinction then common between nature and society, and they both held that the essential traits of human nature were forged by humanity's natural condition rather than by its social relations. In that respect they agreed that human nature is inherently asocial, or at least pre-social. The differences between them arose from their respective understanding of the specific character of this asocial or pre-social nature and its implications for human behavior after the construction of civil society. The radical view was that though human nature is determined outside of social relations, it nevertheless has characteristics that predispose it toward social organization. This conception was the source of the radicals' optimism concerning the possibilities for positive, constructive social relations. The conservatives, on the other hand, tended to think that human nature was not only formed outside society, but also that it was to a large degree hostile to social organization. Human nature, in other words, is both asocial and antisocial. As a result, the conservatives were likely to be pessimistic about the possibilities for constructive social organization. For the radicals, the natural predisposition to sociality implied the possibility of social structures that would provide the conditions for the free development of all individuals. For the conservatives, the natural hostility to sociality implied the necessity of social structures that at the same time allowed for and impeded human selfishness.

Karimsky describes the conservatives' view of human nature as a direct revision of Enlightenment philosophy and as a secular variant of the Puritan idea of the innate depravity of human beings. They interpreted human dispositions, he says, by "accenting aggression, rivalry, competition, and hostility," terms that Pokrovsky also uses in his description of the conservative, Federalist view. Given this position, Karimsky continues, these traits preclude the possibility of social and economic equality, threaten the inalienable human rights to individual freedom, security and property, and at the same time necessitate a civil structure that is able to restrain and stifle such things as egalitarian aspirations that destabilize the social world (Karimsky 1988b, 38–29).

In contrast to the conservatives' views the radicals tended to hold that human nature is essentially virtuous and predisposed toward collective, social life. Paine, Karimsky points out, argued that people are naturally equal and that people's relative physical weakness is the basis of their inclination toward a collective form of life, a description echoed by Stetzenko when he says that the radicals acknowledged humanity to have an inherent virtue and morality that is distorted by the amorality of hierarchical social structures. However, the most distinctive terms in which the inherent virtue and sociality of human nature are expressed were the concepts of an innate moral sense and the moral sentiments, the most notable advocate of which was Jefferson. In Pokrovsky's opinion, Jefferson's theory of moral sentiments is the foundation of his belief in the natural equality of people, in natural rights, and in the possibility of democracy. Since all people equally possess the moral sense of justice and injustice, it follows that all people are by nature morally equal. Since there is no "natural moral aristocracy," Jefferson inferred that no individual or class is morally superior to any others, and thus the rights possessed by some are necessarily possessed by all. Furthermore, Pokrovsky points out that Jefferson sees the moral sense as largely social in nature, suggesting that an altruism and benevolence toward the members of one's community are at the ethical core of human nature (Pokrovsky 1983a, 277–278). The evidence for this reading of Jefferson's view of the moral sense is in a letter to Thomas Law, written in 1814, in which he discusses his views on the subject. In a passage criticizing Helvetius' view that individual self-interest is the fundamental motivating force of morality, Jefferson remarks that "nature hath implanted in our breasts a love of others, a sense of duty to them, a moral instinct, in short, which prompts us irresistibly to feel and to succor their distresses. . . ."[4]

Karimsky agrees with Pokrovsky that Jefferson's theory of moral sentiments or instincts is fundamentally important, though they have disagreed about just how he understood the character of the moral sense. Pokrovsky sees Jefferson as holding a view of innate moral ideas, gravitating, as he puts it, toward the views of the Scottish Intuitionists Shaftsbury and Hutcheson. Karimsky, while he acknowledges in one of his recent essays that "many American Enlightenment thinkers recognized an innate moral sense that indicated the disposition toward social life," nevertheless argues in his earlier book that Jefferson did not take the moral instincts to be a set of innate ideas (Karimsky 1988b, 36; 1976c, 189–190). There is at least prima facie evidence for each of these views. In the same letter to Thomas Law, Jefferson says that the evidence "shows how necessary was the care of the Creator in making the moral principle so much a part of our constitution as that no errors of reasoning or of speculation might lead us astray from its observance in practice." If people are endowed with moral principles specific enough to be observed in practice, it would appear that such principles are indeed innate ideas. But such a view, Karimsky suggests, is inconsistent both with remarks made later in the same letter and also with positions expressed by others with whom Jefferson was in general philosophic agreement. Karimsky cites the following passage from the letter to Law in which Jefferson attempts to account for the fact that in different times and places, different ethical principles have prevailed:

> The answer is, that nature has constituted *utility* to man, the standard and test of virtue. Men living in different countries, under different circumstances, different habits and regimens, may have different utilities; the same act, therefore, may be useful, and consequently virtuous in one country which is injurious and vicious in another differently circumstanced.

A remark such as this seems to indicate that the moral sense is not a set of innate ideas but rather describes a potentiality—one which is actualized or not, and in this way or that—by different people in different times and places. This understanding of Jefferson's position makes it easier, Karimsky says, to reconcile Jefferson's views with those of others among the radicals. We have already seen that Benjamin Rush, for example, criticized the "antinaturalist" interpretation of the moral sense offered by Shaftsbury and Hutcheson, suggesting instead that the moral sense is an acquired trait, and that Thomas Cooper held that the concept of innate ideas contradicted the principles of science. Jefferson's close philosophic association with these and other colleagues, and his inclination to share their general materialist sensationalism, makes it likely that he would have been disinclined to endorse the concept of innate ideas, especially with respect to a matter as important as the moral sense.

Whether Jefferson regarded the moral sense as a set of innate ideas or as a natural potentiality, it is clear enough that for him the distinctive traits of human nature are to be expressed in ethical categories, a procedure not uncommon among American Enlightenment figures. The Jeffersonian view that human beings are by nature altruistic and benevolent criss-crossed with rational egoism, the other prominent Enlightenment conception of the ethical character of human nature. Whatever the specific views of humanity's moral nature, ethics played a central role in Enlightenment social theory. Stetzenko explains the centrality of ethical theory as a result of the general break from religious orthodoxy. The deistic view of God as relegated to the role of originating nature and then removing himself from it "led to ethical views that placed on humanity not only the blame for injustice but also the responsibility for its own future, opening the possibility for a transformation of reality and for building a free, humane society" (Stetzenko 1985, 233). Ironically enough, however, others emphasize the fact that for many Enlightenment figures ethics was in fact grounded in religion. Karimsky points out that in Jefferson's view ethics could not be derived from scientific sources, and that Franklin referred to religion as a "means" to the "end" of morality. Even Paine, who was among the most overt antitheists of the Enlightenment radicals, saw a practical relation between faith and morals.

Agreement on the religious grounding of ethics, however, did not translate into a corresponding agreement concerning a specific ethical theory, nor, for that matter, were the dominant trends themselves applied in a uniform way. Rational egoism, for example, found a variety of expressions. Among many of the conservatives it produced a more or less Hobbesian picture of individuals each seeking whatever is judged to be in his own self-interest, if need be at the expense of others. This kind of description of the character of ethical judgments convinced the conservatives of the necessity of political and social structures that would prevent egoistic human beings from violating one another's natural rights in the pursuit of their own interests. One of the rights the conservatives were most eager to protect was the right to property, a concern that gives their ethical, social, and political philosophy its bourgeois character. The ethics of rational egoism and bourgeois values also found expression, though with somewhat different emphases, in Franklin.

Franklin, in the eyes of Soviet commentators, was a somewhat contradictory figure. Like the conservatives, his ethical views embodied the principles of bourgeois economic and social relations, but unlike the conservatives he was wary of some of the consequences of those principles. Baskin, citing Franklin's "Advice to Young Merchants," describes his rational, utilitarian conception of ethics as contributing to the "American cult of capitalist 'business,'" and he says that Franklin "has become the 'evangelist' of modern American businessmen, proclaiming as the highest principle of ethics the pursuit of maximum capitalist profit" (Baskin 1955, 18–19). Franklin's ethical individualism, however, had its progressive side. Despite the fact that, as Baskin suggests, he regarded belief in God and the immortality of the soul as the "best guarantee of moral behavior," in its rationalism his ethical views are a break from the more traditional theological context of ethical theory. This allowed Franklin, as Morozova puts it, to take from the past, in particular from Puritanism, ethical conceptions that were consistent with bourgeois values while rejecting its antirational and antidemocratic features. Morozova takes as evidence of a close relation between Puritanism and the Enlightenment the fact that Franklin could express in rational and egoistic terms the Puritan values of love of work, persistence, tireless industriousness, and earthly prosperity. Such values as these express the behavioral foundations of bourgeois society, though Morozova suggests that they already "contained the kernel of the contradictions that led to the new American masters, the Mellons and DuPonts, who proclaimed Franklin their spiritual father" (Morozova 1985, 177–178). One of the interesting features of Franklin's ethics, and by extension his social philosophy generally, is that unlike the conservatives he did not regard individualistic and egoistic values as providing a justification of the social power that accompanied large concentrations of wealth. Franklin's ideal of the "self-made man" and the ethical values that underscored it were in his eyes expressions of the significance of labor. On the basis of the fundamental value of labor, Baskin writes, Franklin criticized parasitism, condemned the "excessive property" of the larger magnates of capital, and warned that excessive wealth could be transformed into a new "feudalism" and could overturn the principles of bourgeois democracy (Baskin 1955, 19).

If Franklin's rational egoism differed from the conservatives', in Jefferson's hands it was further away still. Though the dominant strain in Jefferson's ethical views was a moral intuitionism, egoism also makes its appearance, most noticeably in the emphasis on the pursuit of happiness in the Declaration of Independence. Karimsky points out that a conception of human happiness as a factor of and a stimulus to the unity of people in political association was not new in social thought, having already been developed in the rationalist and egoist tradition in Europe in the seventeenth and eighteenth centuries. And, as we have already seen, happiness as an ethical ideal was prominent in Samuel Johnson's moral theory. While Johnson never broke from a theological basis of an understanding of happiness, in that for him its possibility required revelation, Karimsky reads Jefferson's appeal to happiness as an emphasis on the satisfaction of secular and worldly needs, and thus, like for Franklin, it was essentially antitheological in character (Karimsky 1976b, 57). For Jefferson, however, the coexistence of happiness as a moral ideal and inherent moral virtues produced social conceptions that differed sharply from those of the more conservative Federalists, in the understanding of history, for example, and for the possibilities of social organization.

Radicals vs. Moderates: Freedom and Equality

The distance between radicals and conservatives in their understanding of human nature and its most overt ethical traits led to distinctly different conceptions of natural, moral rights, which in turn affected a range of social issues. One of the more significant for both theory and policy concerned religion and freedom of conscience. Though natural religion was regarded by Jefferson, Franklin, Paine, and others as a necessary ground of ethical principle and behavior, and as an expression of humanity's moral nature, there was nevertheless a social struggle over the power of religious establishment and the social role and implications of religious belief.

The American Enlightenment's treatment of religion both as a social institution and as a matter of personal belief, particularly in the 1780s, reflected both continuity with and a break from religion, as it had functioned in Colonial American society. The move for disestablishment, which was directed primarily against the entrenched power of Anglicanism in many of the states of the newly independent nation, had its most powerful expression in the Virginia Statute for Religious Freedom and soon after in the disestablishment clause of the First Amendment to the U. S. Constitution. By breaking the social and political power of the Anglican Church and its clerical hierarchy, disestablishment represented a turn to greater individual and congregational autonomy. This was a significant development, though some Soviet commentators make a point of saying that disestablishment and related developments were not as sharp a break from the past as one might suppose. Congregational autonomy, they point out, had always been a prevalent theme in New England Puritanism, and even individual autonomy in matters of religious belief had had its advocates since Roger Williams. And both themes had figured prominently in the social phenomenon of the Great Awakening only a few short decades before the revolution. In Morozova's opinion, even this degree of continuity suggests that Puritanism had far more democratically significant features than is often acknowledged (Morozova 1985, 168–170).

Without denying such continuity, it is clear that the disestablishment of the Anglican Church and the legal sanction of freedom of individual belief was something new, progressive, and very much a central component of the radicals' approach to social principles. Soviet commentators are unanimous in their praise of the Enlightenment's commitment to disestablishment and its advocacy of freedom of conscience. Baskin refers to the Virginia Statute for Religious Freedom as one of Jefferson's most important contributions, and Karimsky echoes that sentiment when he says that the Virginia Statute inspired republicans in the struggle for democratic additions to the Constitution, one of the more valuable results of which was the First Amendment's disestablishment clause. Both Karimsky and Pokrovsky praise Jefferson for his lifelong commitment to religious toleration as a fundamental aspect of democratic civil rights. Such admiration, however, is tempered by the suspicion, especially for Karimsky and Pokrovsky, that in practice the Enlightenment understanding of freedom of conscience did not extend as far as it should have. Freedom of conscience, Karimsky thinks, was reduced merely to the right of religious freedom, in other words, to the right to hold whatever religious view one sees fit rather than to the right to hold any view at all, including atheism. "And though Franklin, Jefferson, and Paine," Karimsky says, "spoke of the human right not to believe, in the interpretation of the majority of Enlightenment figures freedom of conscience amounted to the secularization of social life and the privatization of religion" (Karimsky 1988b, 43).

In his article on Jefferson and the Federalists, Pokrovsky is even less confident than Karimsky that Jefferson held the right not to believe. Pokrovsky argues in reference to Jefferson's Bill for the Establishment of Religious Freedom that while it was an important progressive document, it suffers from limitations imposed by its author's own time and place. He cites another Soviet author, N. Goldberg, to the effect that religious freedom stopped short of freedom of conscience:

> despite the progressive character of Jefferson's Bill, it bears bourgeois limitations. While professing freedom of inquiry and freedom of thought, it was not genuine freedom of conscience, which must include the recognition not only of the right to profess any religion, but also the right not to believe in God, the right to be an atheist and profess atheism. (Pokrovsky 1983a, 287)

This in an intriguing issue, and one worthy of consideration. Pokrovsky and Goldberg may have overstated their case here. While there is no question that Jefferson himself did not embrace atheism, and that the arguments he offered in favor of religious freedom tend to be framed in theistic or at least deistic language, the more significant documents of the period that deal with religious freedom do not explicitly preclude atheism. The Virginia Statute for Religious Freedom, for example, requires that no one can be compelled to attend or support any form of religious worship or ministry, that no one can be made to suffer in any way for religious opinions and beliefs, that all people are to be free to express and maintain "their opinion in matters of religion" and that people's religious views "shall in no way diminish, enlarge, or affect their civil capacities."

While the Virginia Statute appears to include the right not to believe, there may still be grounds for the suspicion both Karimsky and Pokrovsky express that at the time it was a hollow right, one that was not at all taken seriously in practice. Despite the Virginia Statute and the First Amendment, in the eighteenth and nineteenth centuries there were numerous circumstances that attest to the fact that the legal documents did not achieve religious disestablishment throughout the country and that people continued to suffer in their civil capacities as a consequence of their opinions in matters of religion. In Massachusetts, for example, Congregationalist churches held a privileged religious, social, and political position under its 1780 State Constitution and several other contemporary legislative acts. The Constitution required a loyalty oath that essentially excluded Catholics from holding public office, and the State also required an oath to be taken by the governor, lieutenant governor, and all state legislators that they "believed the Christian religion." Both requirements were in effect until 1820. Massachusetts also had a tax to support religion, and Maryland and North Carolina both had religious requirements for public office well into the nineteenth century. As for repercussions over individuals' religious opinions, there was the case of an editor of a Boston newspaper who in 1833 was prosecuted and convicted for his sarcastic attacks on Unitarian theology.[5] And ironically enough, Jefferson himself had to deal on more than one occasion with the consequences of his opinions on religion, or what some people took to be his opinions. In the presidential campaign of 1800, for example, Jefferson was repeatedly charged with irreligion and even atheism. One of the most overt instances of an individual suffering as a result of a distaste for religion concerned the prominent scientist and philosopher Thomas Cooper. When Jefferson proposed that Cooper be the first president of the newly founded University of Virginia, the outcry against Cooper because of his flirtation with atheism was so great that he was never able to accept Jefferson's offer.

The fact that disestablishment, freedom of religion, and freedom of conscience failed to take hold as thoroughly as its advocates may have intended might be explained in part by the lack of agreement among leading Enlightenment figures concerning religious tolerance. Pokrovsky suggests that there was a fairly clear difference between the radical and

Federalist approaches to the issue. In his opinion, the Federalists faced something of a dilemma with respect to the question of religious freedom. Their choices were either actively to encourage freedom of conscience or to reject it. On the one hand, if they chose the former they would have been in a position of encouraging democracy, and they would have had to grant some degree of natural equality among the populace. On the other hand, had they actively rejected freedom of conscience they would have been committed to a clericalism that would have been equally inconsistent with their general social requirements. Thus, Pokrovsky suggests, their only choice was virtually to ignore the question. The notable exception to this was Madison, who on the question of religious freedom was a thoroughgoing Jeffersonian. It was Madison who steered Jefferson's Statute through the Virginia legislature while Jefferson was in France, and Madison was the architect of the First Amendment's disestablishment clause. At the theoretical level Madison had made his opposition to religious establishment clear in both his "Detached Memoranda" and his "Memorial and Remonstrance against Religious Assessments." Pokrovsky points out that Madison assumes the freedom of religious beliefs in his remarks in "Federalist 52." However, he continues, the Federalists' disinclination to deal in any detailed way with the question of freedom of conscience is illustrated by the fact that the *Federalist Papers* contain no sustained analysis of the matter. And on the question of religious views generally, Pokrovsky argues that the Federalists rejected even the least radical views of the deists: "It would not be an exaggeration to say that the very thought of atheism, as well as deism, appeared to the Federalists as a hostile influence of France and French free-thinking" (Pokrovsky 1983a, 288).

The complexities of the Enlightenment's treatment of religious rights, and the disagreements between radicals and conservatives over them, are mirrored in the approaches to the other fundamental rights that characterized American Enlightenment social thought. Perhaps the two most influential statements of an Enlightenment conception of rights which receive a good bit of attention from Soviet scholars are the Declaration of Independence and Thomas Paine's *Common Sense*. Both documents asserted as either fundamental social values or rights equality, life, liberty, the pursuit of happiness, and resistance to oppression. The right to revolution as advocated by Jefferson, Paine, and others represents from a Soviet perspective a profound achievement of the Enlightenment, and its treatment before and after the War for Independence illustrates from that point of view a central difference between a radical and a conservative understanding of rights.

Soviet commentators write with unanimity on the significance of the right to revolution. As it is expressed in the Declaration of Independence and the Virginia Bill of Rights, the right to revolution is a logical extension of the equality of inalienable rights, of the commitment to the pursuit of happiness as a fundamental individual and social ideal, and of the principle of popular sovereignty. If people really do possess a rough equality in inalienable rights, and if popular sovereignty is necessary to guarantee that government protect those rights, then they would be little more than hollow slogans without the further entitlement to depose a government that does not fulfill its function. The right to revolution was such a crucial feature of natural, inalienable rights theory that Jefferson, Karimsky says, held it to be a universal principle, going so far as to suggest in a letter in 1787 that a revolution in every generation might well be a desirable state of affairs. Based on a principle similar to Rousseau's that the will of the majority embodies natural law, periodic revolution by the citizenry is a way of instantiating in social structures natural human rights. The right to revolution, one Soviet study asserts, was one of "the fundamental traits of the American conception of rights and civil freedom" (Geevsky et. al. 1987, 7)

That the right to revolution was a valuable and progressive feature of natural rights theory is accompanied in Soviet literature by the suggestion that it reflects the view only of the more radical social theorists and that it came under attack immediately after the War for Independence and is still rejected today. Baskin notes that it is opposed by contemporary bourgeois theorists, and in their joint study of the U. S. Constitution the authors say, "The proclamation and insistence on the right of people to the revolutionary overthrow of their government if it prevents the realization of their natural and inalienable rights have been treated by reactionaries of all times with indignance and continues to be so treated today" (Baskin 1955, 9–10; Geevsky et. al. 1987, 17). The suggestion is that although the right to rebel as expressed in the Declaration of Independence was endorsed nearly unanimously by the Continental Congress, for the more moderate and conservative wing of the revolutionary leadership it was less a matter of principle than a matter of political expediency. By the middle of the 1780s, while Jefferson was expressing the universality of the right to revolution, the Federalists were busy attempting to put a stop to the revolutionary spirit. The clearest evidence of this, Baskin and others suggest, is that the right to revolution, understood by the radicals as necessary to natural rights theory, is absent from the Constitution drafted in 1787, suggesting the antidemocratic character of Federalist thought. As Mishin puts it, "The 'Founding Fathers,' then, followed the precepts of the Declaration of Independence, though the right of the people proclaimed in the Declaration to overthrow a government unacceptable to them was nevertheless consigned to oblivion, which once again shows their 'dread of the people'" (Mishin 1988a, 71). By rejecting the right to revolution, Mishin says elsewhere, the Constitution was in that respect "a step backward in the democratic development of the United States" (Mishin 1988b, 3).

Radicals vs. Moderates: Property and Economic Theory

The pursuit of happiness, as we have already seen, was significant as a secularization of ethical ideals, in part as an expression of rationalist and egoistic principles. Nevertheless, it is in Karimsky's words the most "hazy and intriguing" of the Enlightenment's natural rights. The confusion over the meaning of the pursuit of happiness, he thinks, stems in part from the question of its relation to earlier statements of rights, specifically Locke's "trinity" of life, liberty, and property. Some commentators regard Jefferson's inclusion of the pursuit of happiness among the natural rights as a rejection of the Lockean position, but this interpretation, Karimsky says, is an unjustified simplification. Jefferson, along with Franklin, Paine and others, Karimsky argues, agreed with Locke that a right to property arises in the very nature of laboring activity. On the Jeffersonian interpretation, the fundamental natural right is the unfettered exercise of labor, from which the right to property derives as a secondary right. This understanding of the nature of property rights is different from Locke's, but it is not wholly incompatible with it, and thus Jefferson's rights to "life, liberty and the pursuit of happiness" are not simply a rejection of Locke's "life, liberty and property." This is not to say, Karimsky continues, that there was not disagreement among the American revolutionaries over the nature of property rights, but the argument about property in the American Enlightenment, he suggests, was on a different plane altogether. The important issue that separated the radicals and conservatives, according to Karimsky, was not over whether property was a fundamental right but rather over the legitimate extent of property accumulation. The representatives of the radical group, he says, argued against the excessive concentration of property because it creates the danger of a polarization of poverty and wealth, while the Federalists believed that an unqualified guarantee of property accumulation is a condition and expression of freedom. If the crucial disagreement was over property accumulation and if the right to property derives from the activity of labor, then the pursuit of happiness, Karimsky concludes, in no way excludes but rather implies the right to property (Karimsky 1976b, 55–56; 1976c, 221).

Read in this way, Jefferson appears to have understood the right to property as a derivative but nonetheless natural right. Soviet commentators share no general agreement on this point, and Karimsky himself suggests otherwise elsewhere in the same work. In addition to the issue of the legitimate extent of property accumulation, Karimsky points out, there was also clear disagreement among Enlightenment social theorists over the question of whether property is a natural or a civil right. The Federalists held that property was a natural right in the Lockean tradition, while the radicals with some exceptions thought property to be a secondary, civil right. The distinction is a crucial one because each view has differing implications for the question of the legitimate extent of property accumulation and for political theory and practice.

That there is a natural right to property was a widely held view in the eighteenth century, one with clear material foundations and explicit theoretical justifications. The centrality of property had been a crucial component of what by then had already been a centuries-long struggle by the European merchant classes first against feudalism itself and later against the power of absolute monarchs. And it is not surprising that the same opinion would be expressed by Americans, themselves engaged in a revolution directed in part against a British mercantilism that involved policies restricting the exercise of property on the part of the colonists. The theoretical justification of the natural right to property was developed in the context of this broad historical process. The same John Locke who participated in the revolution that finally subordinated the British monarch to Parliament also provided the first explicit defense of property as a natural right in his *Second Treatise of Government*. To regard property as a natural right was the rule by the late eighteenth century, and in the American context this position was represented by the Federalists.

The radicals, however, thought otherwise. Morozova, probably overstating the case, cites the Declaration of Independence as evidence that property as a natural right was the minority view: "A fundamental characteristic of the social views of a majority of American Enlightenment figures was that they did not include a right to property as among the natural rights of people, regarding it as a derivative institution subject to the authority of civil power" (Morozova 1985, 184). Others are more circumspect. Pokrovsky says that Jefferson did not regard property as a natural right but as a right granted by government, grounded only in laws established in a given society at a particular stage of its development (Pokrovsky 1983a, 283). This approach differs from Karimsky's reading of Jefferson, although Karimsky himself at another point in the same book says explicitly that for Jefferson property was not a natural right but a secondary civil right, a view which would account, he suggests, for the willingness on the part of revolutionaries to expropriate loyalist property during and after the war (Karimsky 1976c, 248). One of the significant exceptions to a radical tendency to see property as a civil right was Paine, who regarded property as a natural right. Stetzenko points out, however, that Paine's view nevertheless differed from the Federalist approach in that "he did not regard property as an absolute but as a historically fluid and contradictory concept, distinguishing its private and social, just and unjust forms" (Stetzenko 1985, 255–256).

There was, then, disagreement over the nature of the right to property, though Karimsky is right to say that there was even more extensive dispute over the question of property accumulation and the problem of disequality in property. On the one hand, the Federalists, again following Locke, held that there is a natural right not only to the pursuit and acquisition of property but also to its unlimited accumulation. The radicals, on the other hand, tended to be suspicious of property accumulation and its social implications. In general, Karimsky says, Enlightenment democrats were hostile towards the polarization of property and poverty, to any attempt to overlook inequality in property, and, like Franklin, were concerned with the relation between wealth and political power. The Federalist view, he continues, was the direct opposite: since property is a natural right, any encroachment on it is inappropriate. The Federalists held, furthermore, that disequality in property is a direct consequence of natural differences among people and that the value of freedom implies the legitimacy of inequality in property (Karimsky 1976c, 221–222). In "Federalist 10," for example, Madison says,

> The diversity in the faculties of men, from which the rights of property originate, is not less an insuperable obstacle to a uniformity of interests. The protection of these faculties is the first object of government. From the protection of different and unequal faculties of acquiring property, the possession of different degrees and kinds of property immediately results.[6]

Hamilton made a similar point, according to Madison's notes, on the floor of the Constitutional Convention: "it was certainly true: that nothing like an equality of property existed: that an inequality would exist as long as liberty existed, and that it would unavoidably result from that very liberty itself."[7]

Several Soviet commentators emphasize the radicals' alternative conceptions. We have already seen, for example, that Baskin describes Franklin as having warned of the danger of excessive wealth for democratic principles. In a similar vein, Stetzenko says of Enlightenment thinkers that they "recognized that the cause of oppression is the inequality of property" (Stetzenko 1985, 233). And Batalov sees the same concerns in Jefferson:

> While not rejecting private property, Jefferson wanted America to steer clear of the contradictions arising from the logical development of private property relations and bourgeois individualism, ultimately leading to concentration of property, proletarianization of farmers and moral crisis, and eroding those popular democracy [*sic*] institutions that Jefferson had always upheld sincerely. In other words, he wanted to build, by following the classical logic of utopian thinking, a society which would make the best of the advantages of capitalism while protecting itself securely against the disadvantages. (Batalov 1985, 76)

Jefferson's understanding of the nature of property rights and its accumulation differed so much, in fact, from the Federalist approach that Jefferson even entertained the possibility that property accumulation could reach such an extent that it might contradict more fundamental natural rights. That Jefferson took this view is made clear in a letter to Madison sent from France in 1785, in which he calls for legislative measures for "subdividing property" and for a progressive income tax as "another means of silently lessening the inequality of property." He goes on to suggest that unlimited property accumulation may well lead to the violation of others' rights: "Whenever there is in any country, uncultured lands and unemployed poor, it is clear that the laws of property have been so far extended as to violate natural right."[8]

The differing approaches among Enlightenment figures to the question of the nature and source of property rights had implications for both economic theory and the more general philosophic problems of the relation of property to equality and freedom. With respect to economic thought, however, the profound differences are not simply reflections of disagreements over the nature of property rights. Representatives of both the radical and conservative camps supported the development of industry, for example, and the most profound contributions to liberal economic theory were made not by conservative Federalists but by radicals. Arguably the most significant feature of eighteenth century economic theory was its articulation of some of the fundamental features of a labor theory of value. Though the labor theory of value was not more fully explored until Ricardo and Marx in the nineteenth century, its underpinnings had been suggested as early as Locke's argument for property rights in the *Second Treatise* and more clearly still in Adam Smith's *Wealth of Nations*. By arguing that the source of rights in property is the relation of human beings to nature, specifically the transformation and appropriation of nature through labor, Locke offered the basis of the view to be developed later that the value of commodities is a function of the labor necessary to produce them. One of the ultimate consequences of the emphasis on labor in economic theory was the expression later in the eighteenth century of liberal, *laissez-faire* economic and political policy, which in the American context was embraced implicitly by the Federalists. Nevertheless, at the theoretical level the significance of labor was noticed most explicitly by radicals. Karimsky notes that Cooper saw the centrality of the interaction of human beings and nature through labor as fundamental in the development of human nature, as did Franklin in his definition of human beings as toolmaking animals. In fact, he says, Franklin's understanding of the interrelation of social and natural factors led him eventually to a more or less explicit labor theory of value, where wealth is the result of the productive use of nature (Karimsky 1976C, 199–202; 1988b, 35).

Some of the more outstanding members of the radical camp also shared the liberal, Federalist faith in industry. Franklin, to a degree, was one of them, as was, somewhat surprisingly, Thomas Paine. Stetzenko points out that unlike Rousseau, and of course one might add Jefferson, Paine was not suspicious of the development of industry. Though he was aware, Stetzenko says, that the accumulation of wealth in industry was the result of paying workers as little as possible and of the essentially conservative nature of property interests in general, he never endorsed either Jefferson's agrarianism or his ideal of an equal distribution of land. Paine's proposal for eliminating social injustice was not to avoid industry but to create through taxation a national fund to compensate the poor (Stetzenko 1985, 256).

Despite Franklin's and Cooper's endorsement of the liberal understanding of the role of labor, and Paine's faith in industry, it is nevertheless Jefferson's agrarianism and egalitarianism which has come to characterize most clearly a distinctly radical Enlightenment economic perspective. Jefferson's concern over the unjust consequence of the accumulation of property, and his sense that industrial labor was, to use a later term, essentially alienating, drove him to the view that a just society must be agrarian and must be one in which all have access to the morally uplifting activity of agricultural labor. The Jeffersonian vision of a society of small, private farms has survived in American consciousness and ideology as what Batalov calls the "utopia of a farmers' America" (Batalov 1985, 70–83).

In the course of its historical development, American society in its mainstream bypassed Jefferson's agrarian democracy and took the path of increasing industrial development. To that extent, as we have already seen, the liberal Federalist view turned out to be more astute with respect to the future than the radical Jeffersonian agrarianism. From a Soviet perspective, however, both views had virtues and shortcomings. While the Federalists had the clearer sense of historical processes and the necessity of the development of industry, it was to the credit of the radicals that they did not lose sight of the material aspects of social and economic justice. Both approaches, however, make in Karimsky's view two critical mistakes: they do not take sufficient account of the historical development of both human nature and the process of material production, and they do not appreciate the centrality of the relations of production in the economic life of a society and the social consequences of its productive process. The radical, Jeffersonian treatment of property, the problem of property accumulation and economic theory, is grounded in a conception of the moral character of human nature, while the more conservative, Federalist approach appeals to natural rights. Both the moral sense and natural rights, however, are asocial and ahistorical, which, Karimsky suggests, prevented either side from realizing that production is a special sort of relation between human beings and nature and among human beings themselves. The social and economic theory of neither the radicals nor the conservatives could see that the character of a society is a function largely of the essentially social and historically changing nature of the relations people enter into with one another in the productive process of the transformation of nature (Karimsky 1976c, 188–189).

The conceptions of property and property rights were inextricably linked in Enlightenment thought with the general principles of equality and freedom. All of the outstanding figures of the American Enlightenment endorsed equality and freedom as central principles of social theory, structure and policy. Liberty was among the Declaration's inalienable natural rights, and equality was implied by the understanding of rights as natural. As Karimsky puts it, the idea of the equality of all people was concretized by the assertion of their possession of inalienable rights, and in Gaidadymov's opinion, the view that people are naturally equal was based on the inviolability of natural, human rights.

The Enlightenment's general appeal to equality and freedom appears somewhat disingenuous, however, in light of the fact that for the most part neither equality nor freedom were taken to apply to the majority of the population. The social and political structures derived from Enlightenment thought institutionalized the disequality of slaves, native Americans, women, and the unpropertied, as well as the continued subjugation of slaves to their masters and women to men. There were several reasons for this, including cultural traditions and the necessity of political compromise necessary to secure the economic, social, and political gains won by the revolution. With respect to slavery, for example, Karimsky suggests that Jefferson's approach to the question was due not so much to the fact that he held some racist assumptions about the incompatibility of blacks and whites but more to the fact that all the Virginia leaders were connected to plantation agriculture. In general, he says, "The attitude to slavery reflected the real alignment of forces among social leaders and the compromise that secured the unity of the national patriotic forces" (Karimsky 1988b, 42).

While political compromise was no doubt crucial, there were also differences of principle among Enlightenment thinkers. Among those who objected to slavery, for example, the differences are evident. Karimsky puts it this way:

> Many Enlightenment figures spoke out against slavery, but only Franklin, Rush, Samuel Adams, and several others were theoretically and politically consistent in their demands. . . . They proceeded from what to them was the evident scientific fact of the full intellectual value of nonwhite Americans and the necessity to extend the principles of natural and legal equality to all races. The criticism that Hamilton, John Adams, and other Federalists aimed at slavery attacked it primarily as an

> archaic system of agriculture hindering capitalist enterprise and the economic integration of the country. Jefferson, Washington, and Madison condemned slavery, but even Jefferson did not display his characteristic persistence in the attempt to abolish it. (Karimsky 1988b, 42)

The radicals, in other words, were opposed to slavery on the grounds of its inconsistency with the principles of equality and freedom, while the conservative opposition was essentially material in its motivation. That both groups ultimately accepted the political compromise tolerating slavery should not obscure the fact that their differing objections to it reflected different interpretations of equality and freedom.

Political Theory

"The central problems of the American Enlightenment," Karimsky writes, "were political," a view he supports elsewhere by the view that the main results of the War of Independence that circumscribed American thought were political (Karimsky 1976b, 112). The propertied class had abolished a colonial regime that inhibited its development, and it had won for itself full political power, the final consolidation of which was the ratification of the 1787 Constitution that "secured the fundamental social results of the American Revolution" (Karimsky 1988b, 27).

The Soviet assessment of the relation of postwar political developments to the general character of American Enlightenment thought is double-edged. On the one hand, the new political structures and institutions were expressions in practice of general American Enlightenment social principles. "One of the fundamental national characteristics of the American Enlightenment," Morozova says, "was the immense role it played in the formation of the American nation and the development of national self-consciousness" (Morozova 1985, 162). Karimsky expresses much the same point when he says that in America "the revolutionary transformations anticipated and stimulated the basic constitutional ideas and principles that ripened in the context of Enlightenment ideology" (Karimsky 1988b, 27). And in Stetzenko's words, "Enlightenment thought played its role in American history in the period of the formation of the nation and its self-consciousness: it helped ground the necessity of political independence; it raised the people to a struggle against tyranny; it indicated the fundamental points in the construction of a new society, shaking the foundations of Puritan ideology" (Stetzenko 1985, 258). On the other hand, the class character of Enlightenment social thought, together with the fact that it consisted of wide and deep disagreements, conflicts, and contradictions, inevitably colored both its political theory and practice. Karimsky says, for example, that while the American Revolution was one of the most successful of the bourgeois revolutions, it could not realize its own fundamental first principle of the equality of social, political, and legal rights (Karimsky 1976c, 252–253).

Enlightenment political thought was a product of both general philosophic commitments and urgent practical problems. The conceptual characteristics of American thought, from its mechanistic conception of nature to its fundamental social principles, were so irreconcilably different from what preceded it, Karimsky suggests, that American thinking gave rise necessarily to novel political conceptions, among the more significant of which were democracy, the separation of church and state, and its understanding of the ground and function of government. These political ideas were embodied, Karimsky notes, in the Declaration of Independence, in the Constitution, and in the Bill of Rights. Of all the components of Enlightenment thought in general, the most significant for political theory were its ethical principles. American Enlightenment political theory, Soviets tend to feel, was grounded in ethics. Stetzenko makes the point in a general way: Enlightenment naturalism and its philosophical anthropology led to the ethical principle of natural equality and to the view that with people lay the responsibility to transform social reality and to create a more free society. "On a belief in the natural equality of all people," he says, "is based Enlightenment democratism, the theory of the social contract, and the idea of popular control over the execution of established laws" (Stetzenko 1985, 233). More specifically, Baskin notes that Franklin's criticism of the power of Colonial government was made in ethical terms, in particular its violation of natural rights. "Franklin's Enlightenment, individualistic ethics," Baskin says, "were inseparably linked to his political views. It is as if the political requirements of the entire progressive segment of the American bourgeoisie were translated into the language of ethics" (Baskin 1955, 17). And Pokrovsky makes a similar point about Jefferson, for whom, he says, the very possibility of democratic political organization is grounded in the moral intuitions that provide us all with the sense of justice and injustice (Pokrovsky 1983a, 277).

The Necessity of Central Government

If the central concepts of American political thought—including popular sovereignty, the social contract, and democracy—received much of their content from Enlightenment ethics, they were no less the results of pressing practical problems that emerged in the postwar years. A number of factors converged in the 1780s to create a crisis of the Articles of Confederation, which in turn forced American thinkers and political leaders to confront directly the task of nation building. Soviet historians, if not philosophers, have been interested in the specific characteristics of postwar conditions that precipitated the Constitutional Convention of

1787. V. A. Nikonov describes Soviet historical interpretation from the early 1960s as seeing a complex relation between class interests and the virtues of a more centralized government. Soviet historians also recognized powerful economic and foreign policy problems in the period of the Articles of Confederation. Separate state legislatures, for example, often pursued conflicting financial and economic policies that continually threatened economic chaos. It was thus in the interest of the wealthy classes to establish a government that had the power to regulate commerce, deal with the deepening recession, and oversee the process of settling Western lands. Furthermore, Soviet historians point out that the Confederation did not have sufficient power to conduct foreign policy effectively, which left the country weak with respect to international relations. However, Soviet historians also make the point that these conditions were equally damaging to the interests of the masses. Economic chaos, for example, was not only a threat to the wealthy but was dangerous for the entire country. Thus calls for a strong central government came both from the ruling classes as well as from a large segment of the masses, especially urban workers and artisans interested in defending national industry and combating inflation. Furthermore, a strong federal government was supported not only by conservative Federalists but also by more radical political leaders such as Paine, Samuel Adams, and Thomas Jefferson, who took stronger government as a way to defend the democratic achievements of the revolution. In this analysis, then, both conservatives and radicals had their own reasons for opposing the Confederation and advocating more centralized government. The interests of the wealthy classes were threatened by economic and political problems as well as by manifestations of popular unrest, such as Shays's Rebellion. At the same time, radicals saw the uncoordinated activities of relatively independent states as threats to the democratic interests of the majority of the population. The political problematic, then, was complex and perhaps contradictory: a strong central government was necessary both to serve elite interests and to defend democratic institutions (Nikonov 1988, 3–11).

This complexity in the relation of the differing material interests of various segments of the population to the political structures that were eventually erected is a reflection of the theoretical relation of the social principles of the revolution to postwar political principles. Just as the conceptual underpinnings of postwar political documents in some respects embody revolutionary principles while in other respects they betray them, so too does the form of the new federal government institutionalize democratic structures while at the same time it consolidates specifically ruling class power. The contradictory character of the theoretical and practical situation is expressed in the Soviet commentaries. Writing of Thomas Paine, Stetzenko says that "together with Franklin and Jefferson, he developed the basis and explained the principles of the governmental structure of the United States, making the American experience accessible to Europe. Serving America, Paine served the general cause of freedom" (Stetzenko 1985, 246). A few pages later he suggests the class commitment of the same governmental structure: "America was the first experimental stage to test the vitality of Enlightenment ideas. The theories of the Federalists became the ideological foundation and reflection of the requirements of a bourgeois republic with its inherent clashes of class and property interests, the stabilization of which was in the interest of the power of the elite" (Stetzenko 1985, 258).

A similar dual assessment emerges in Karimsky's analysis. While American political documents embody revolutionary principles, certain features of the political structures they created were incompatible with those same principles. For example, the division of power in government, in his opinion, does not coincide with revolutionary principles in that the division of power, and here he cites Hofstadter, was intended to regulate not governmental organs but rather social strength. "Formal democracy," he says, "is not consistent with popular power," a point of which some contemporary radicals were aware. "The inability of a system of formal democratic elections (progressive for its own time) to protect in governmental organs the influence of the lower and middle strata puzzled Jefferson." Even the Bill of Rights, Karimsky suggests, does not abolish social inequality, legal chicanery, and the manipulation of democratic procedures. His call for periodic rebellion, in Karimsky's opinion, reflects Jefferson's lack of faith in the mechanisms of bourgeois democracy to protect and embody popular sovereignty (Karimsky 1976c, 235–236). The contradiction at the heart of the Enlightenment political project lends the entire process, from some Soviets' point of view, its utopian character.

Popular Sovereignty, the Social Contract, and Democracy

Of the general political principles characterizing the American Enlightenment, perhaps the most significant was popular sovereignty. As Karimsky points out, the commitment to political self-determination had been a crucial component of pre-revolutionary debates and theoretical analysis. In that context it took the form of an insistence that since the ground of government is natural right, no government could legitimately infringe on those rights without the consent of the governed. In the period immediately preceding the revolution there was general agreement on this point among the Colonial intellectual and political leadership, and it was precisely the principle of popular sovereignty to which it appealed in its theoretical justification of the rejection of British political authority. Even then, however, deep differences in the understanding and extent of popular sovereignty were emerging among Enlightenment thinkers.

One of the first sustained theoretical expressions of the centrality of popular sovereignty appeared in Paine's *Common Sense*, published in 1776. In Stetzenko's view, Paine, working wholly with distinctly Enlightenment categories, articulated the absolute priority of political self-determination. Applying the Enlightenment dichotomy of harmony or disharmony with the laws of nature, for example, Paine contrasted two sets of concepts, "man, society, popular control and natural rights," and "state, government, monarchy and despotism." The first set of concepts is positive, in Paine's view, while the second is negative. Society, for example, Paine thought to arise from our natural needs, while government has its source in our defects. To that extent he agreed with the prominent Enlightenment political thinkers, who believed that we are incapable of living in our natural condition and, thus, that our own natures require political organization. Paine breaks from the mainstream of Enlightenment political theory, however, in his assessment of the relation of government to natural human rights. For most Enlightenment figures, and Stetzenko specifically mentions Locke, Montesquieu, and Rousseau, government is called upon not to suppress human freedom but to serve the interests of justice. Paine, however, regarded even the new forms of government such as constitutional monarchy as forms of tyranny. Political self-determination is so central a value that the only kind of state that has any right at all to exist is one arising from the free choice and agreement of its members, and the only state that could arise in this way is a democratic republic.

Paine, in Stetzenko's evaluation, was "one of the most consistent champions of democratic and republican ideas," and with respect to such principles as popular sovereignty, he "was in the forefront of the left wing circle in the American Revolution" (Stetzenko 1985, 236–237). Like Jefferson, Samuel Adams, and other radicals, Paine held that popular sovereignty was a necessary condition of a just social order and with Jefferson went so far as to suggest that with respect to social relations, popular sovereignty presupposes a genuine securing of the appropriate conditions of the satisfaction of basic human needs. The radical interpretation and defense of popular sovereignty, however, contrasts sharply with the approach taken by the conservative wing. Karimsky points out that Madison, who in many other respects was much more a radical, disagreed with Paine and Jefferson about both the nature and significance of popular sovereignty. Madison did not think, for example, that the people are the guarantor of social order; on the contrary, he believed that the popular will is a sustained threat to social health and the capacity of government to effect justice. John Adams, too, did not accept popular sovereignty as a central political principle. Karimsky says, for example, that in his *Thoughts on Government*, written in response to *Common Sense*, Adams advocates not the sovereignty of the people but the sovereignty of the government.

The contrast between the radical and conservative approaches to the principle of popular sovereignty is reflected in a comparable dispute over the nature and implications of the social contract. The conception of a social contract arises from the more fundamental principles of popular sovereignty, natural rights, and the distinction between the state of nature and civil society. If the natural human condition is logically prior to social relations and institutions, and if in their natural condition people possess rights—one of which is the right to determine so far as is possible the character of their lives—then specific forms of social interaction and institutions must in some way be determined by agreement of the members of an emerging society and by an ongoing, if implicit, agreement by citizens of a society already in place. Though Karimsky feels that the role of the concept of a social contract has been "greatly overemphasized," he acknowledges that to the extent that American political theory took seriously the existence of natural rights, despite disagreements over precisely what they are, Enlightenment political leaders were compelled to understand the emergence of political institutions as involving a contract of some kind. Karimsky suggests that reliance on social contract theory led to two theoretical problems: first was the question of among whom the contract is concluded, and the second involved the problem of what happens to innate natural rights under the conditions of the contract. The ways these questions were answered, he suggests, indicates the deep discrepancy between radical and conservative members of the political leadership (Karimsky 1976c, 207–208, 215).

The fundamental difference between the two camps was that for the conservative Federalists the contract was concluded between the government and the citizenry, between the rulers and the ruled, while for the more radical democrats the contract was an agreement among the populace. This distinction embodies two very different conceptions of government. If the contract is an agreement between the government and the citizenry, then it is the means by which the rulers legitimate their power and authority while still acknowledging some degree of popular sovereignty: the ruled agree to accept the power of the rulers. If, however, the contract is an agreement among the populace, then government is more fully answerable to the popular will. Karimsky uses the views of Paine and Hamilton to make the contrast. Hamilton, he says, did not think that the social contract was grounded on all people's natural rights, but rather took it for granted that it was an agreement between the rulers and the ruled, establishing a partnership between government and citizenry that in turn allowed the rulers to limit or contest the right of democratic control. Paine, on the other hand, argued that government could not be a party to the social contract because it was itself a product of the contract (Karimsky 1976c, 215).

The divergent conceptions of the nature of the social contract suggest the central questions of the function of government and its relation to the rights of the populace. While both sides held that it is government's function to protect rights, their differences over the character of natural and civil rights implied a dispute over those rights which it is government's function to protect. In Hamilton's view, and here Madison and the other Federalists agreed, the agreement between government and the governed empowers the government to protect the natural rights to life, liberty, and property, primarily the latter. The practical implication of this approach is that it becomes government's responsibility to defend the rights to life, liberty, and property against any threat to them that might emerge from the population. The possibility of such a threat—or, given the Federalist conception of human nature, one should say its likelihood—accounts for the suspicion and fear of democratic control that Hamilton, Madison, and their colleagues so often expressed. The radical advocates of popular power, however, rejected this conception of government's function. Once the distinction is drawn between natural and civil rights, and if property is understood not as an absolute natural right but either as a historically conditioned right, as in Paine's case, or as a civil right arising from the social contract, as Jefferson believed, then the threat to natural rights is likely to come not from the populace but from government itself. In that case it is essential not that government be empowered to constrain democracy but that democratic control be deepened to constrain the power of government. As Karimsky puts the point, "The disagreement between the Federalists and democrats over human nature and civil society was above all a dispute over the lawfulness or unlawfulness of democratic control over the activity of government, and correspondingly over the character of human rights arising from 'natural law'" (Karimsky 1988b, 41).

Karimsky acknowledges, however, that the radical defense of democratic control does not automatically resolve the issue of the relation between government and natural rights, because the question remains whether or not the very existence of government requires the "alienation" of some natural rights. The radical position, Karimsky says, generated something of a contradiction. Despite their essentially atomized character, human beings nevertheless possess a natural propensity toward sociality. This "social nature," however, can be realized only in an "unnatural" civil society, and people's natural rights can be guaranteed only by a government possessing some degree of compulsory power, which necessarily assumes the limitation of natural rights. The very possibility of governmental power requires the alienability of some rights (Karimsky 1976c, 216). What Karimsky here calls a contradiction in radical Enlightenment political theory is a uniquely late eighteenth century expression of a problem that has been central to modern political theory and policy. It is the issue of the relation between the individual and society with which J. S. Mill grappled in the middle of the nineteenth century and which continues to lurk beneath many contemporary political and social controversies. In the radical Enlightenment camp, Karimsky notes a disagreement in the assessment of this problem. Paine, he says, was more frank than Jefferson in recognizing that given the very nature of government citizens cannot retain all their rights. That Jefferson did not see it this way accounts for his optimistic expectation of a civil, political society that could secure individual rights and in which people could develop and flourish. That Paine did see it this way accounts for his general suspicion of government.

Regardless of such problems, radical American leaders agreed on the necessity of a democratic form of political organization, and in this respect they differed sharply from the Federalists. An emphasis on the differences among Enlightenment leaders on the issue of democracy pervades Soviet discussions. The distinction is clear with respect to the issue of the function of government: for the democratic republicans, Karimsky says, state power was to protect popular interests from the oligarchic pursuits of the propertied elite, while the Federalists saw the danger of tyranny in the people and in democratic government. Stetzenko makes a similar point:

> The ideology of the followers of Jefferson operated on a faith in people, in the possibility of carrying a democratic transformation through to its end, in a continuous renewal of social institutions, in continuous progress and in the victory of the new over the obsolete. . . . The Federalists took a different position, representing the interests of the large bourgeoisie, securing the benefits of their position and striving to restrain revolutionary progress. Urging the establishment of order and equilibrium, they demanded a strong government, strict controls, and a centralized state, justifying the curtailment of democracy by the necessity to suppress with the help of "rational" power the spontaneous instincts of the ignorant mob. (Stetzenko 1985, 257)

The radical, Jeffersonian support of popular power is contrasted over and over again with a Federalist fear of democracy. The characteristic trait of Federalism, Karimsky says, was an apologetic for the strength of government to guard against real control from below, and Pokrovsky suggests that a fear of democratic "anarchy" is like a bugbear pervading the pages of the *Federalist Papers* (Pokrovsky 1983a, 282). Hamilton certainly thought that popular rule led to anarchy, and Madison asserted the inevitability of a conflict between the advantaged and the disadvantaged, in which it is government's role to protect property from an unstable majority. In its hostility to popular power, the Federalist position is in the Soviet view a retreat from the revolutionary if limited democracy of the radicals. A Jeffersonian bourgeois democracy—"bourgeois" largely due to its commitment to private property and to the willingness of many of its proponents to exclude the bulk of the population from access to political power—embodies the most valuable principles and aspirations of the Enlightenment.

The Constitution

The theoretical issues of popular sovereignty, the contract, and democracy converged with the practical problem of constructing the political institutions of a new nation in the Constitutional Convention of 1787, where representatives primarily from conservative Federalist circles met to produce one of the most significant documents in all political history. The U. S. Constitution has been the most stable, in many respects the most effective, and probably the most influential expression of fundamental national law in modern political experience, and as a result attracted a good deal of attention from Soviet philosophers, historians, political scientists, and legal theorists. Taken together, their studies of the document deal with the theoretical principles implicit in the Constitution, the historical influences on its framers, the interests of the delegates to the Convention, the character of the arguments during the process of ratification, the reasons for its longevity, the relation of the Constitution to the revolutionary process as a whole, a general assessment of its virtues and shortcomings, and the role of the Constitution in contemporary American ideology.

As with the Declaration of Independence, some Soviet scholars argue that contemporary American commentary on the Constitution and its significance is in several ways a distortion of its principles and its current application in American domestic life and foreign policy. There is, according to some, a "cult of the Constitution" serving as "a basis of official American propaganda" (Geevsky et. al. 1987, 4). Americans display a tendency to regard the Constitution with a reverence that obscures its complex character and the fact that it is a product of distinctly late eighteenth century principles, problems, and priorities. Despite the claims of its defenders and propagandists, the same authors suggest, the Constitution does not provide equality: "Carefully concealed is the fact that the class, social, and material inequality of Americans predetermines a corresponding inequality of their laws." The cult of the Constitution fails to acknowledge that history has not stood still for two hundred years. Specifically, the range of legitimate human rights has broadened, and the constitutionally grounded bourgeois democracy in America resists the incorporation of these developments. The reference here is to the ever-increasing significance of material rights, about which the Constitution has virtually nothing to say. The Constitution and Bill of Rights speak only about political and individual liberties and nearly completely ignore social and economic rights and freedoms. In the Soviet view, whatever virtues the Constitution had in its own day, and as we will see Soviet commentators thought there were many, it serves today an essentially reactionary and antidemocratic role in American domestic and foreign affairs. In the ongoing effort to broaden and institutionalize social and economic rights, for example, Americans must overcome the inertia of Constitutional traditions: "The history of bourgeois democracy in the United States is the history of a political struggle of the masses for freedom" (Geevsky et. al. 1987, 5). And with respect to the influence and role of the Constitution abroad, Mishin said that it now "occupies a special place in the arsenal of weapons of the ideological expansion of American imperialism. . . . In foisting on the developing countries their own constitutional model, American ideologues want not so much that these countries embody in their governmental and political systems the democratic ideals of the American Revolution, but more that everywhere should be propagated the capitalist principles of private property, the spirit of which saturates the U. S. Constitution" (Mishin 1988a, 85).

Karimsky has a similar perspective on the contemporary appropriation and function of the Constitution. Like Mishin, he feels that in current conditions, to take rights seriously at all is to include social and economic rights, and he sees precisely this process at work in contemporary American social activism: "Wide sectors of the population have associated the equality of rights with the hope for an improvement of material conditions and the possibility of general prosperity. And in as far as the actualization of real civil equality of rights favors the struggle for the social and economic interests of working people, progressive American thinkers and social activists gradually turned to traditional ideas of human rights and their democratic understanding" (Karimsky 1988a, 242). In this process, Karimsky thinks, the Constitution's role is less than salutary. The rights expressed or implicit in the Constitution are bourgeois rights, primarily the right to be free of governmental interference, while there is nothing in it to guarantee material, social rights. The Constitution is, in other words, inherently disassociated from the democratic requirements of contemporary social development. The relation between the Constitution and current processes is obscured, however, by a good deal of prominent American commentary on the Constitution. There is a genuinely progressive character to the Constitution, but it is distorted by scholarship that overlooks its more revolutionary foundations. The Constitution can fulfill contemporary democratic ends only if the content and substance of its principles are fully and correctly understood.

One of the more significant ways in which the Constitution's revolutionary principles are circumvented, Karimsky argues, is by interpreting it as a product not of the progressive features of Enlightenment thought but of Colonial religious traditions. As we saw in the previous chapter, Karimsky notes that as early as the nineteenth century European and American intellectual historians began to argue that the conceptual source of American democratic institutions and the revolution itself was not the Enlightenment, but New England Puritanism, and contemporary commentators continue to offer this interpretation. The association most often emphasized is between the Puritan covenant and the social contract, a relation that Karimsky thinks was never really there. The crucial difference between the two is that the covenant was an agreement between members of the community and God, while the social contract was an agreement either among citizens or between citizens and their government. In both its radical and moderate versions, social contract theory rests on a conception of natural rights, while the Puritan covenant is grounded in the authority of God's will. Thus the covenant is missing the very feature that marks the progressive, revolutionary character of the Enlightenment social contract, and to link the two as closely as Americans do is to obscure the revolutionary substance of Enlightenment political thought and of the Constitution itself. Karimsky does acknowledge, however, that Puritan social and political practice did incorporate certain "principles of republicanism," including the election of clergy and the autonomy of congregations. But it is a mistake, he thinks, to idealize such features of Puritan political structure, primarily because they in no way rested on a recognition of the rights of individuals or communities, but rather they were "important components of the social mechanism of the realization of the power of the bourgeois leadership and the new clergy." Karimsky's general point is that an emphasis on Puritanism as the forerunner of Enlightenment political theory and practice "not only misinterprets the contract theory of the origins of government, but it also gives a false picture of the premises and factors of American constitutionalism" (Karimsky 1988b, 29).

The other common distortion of American constitutionalism is, Karimsky claims, characteristic of contemporary neoconservatism. As a concrete example he cites Orrin Hatch, who said several years ago that a celebration of the bicentennial of the Constitution is important because the document embodies the permanent principles of human life—the separation of powers, federalism, a system of checks and balances, and the limits of government's power. In Hatch's opinion, these principles are as vital today as they were two centuries ago. Karimsky agrees with Hatch that such principles really are essential for an understanding of the organization and ideological foundations of the American state, but it is a mistake, he thinks, to treat the Constitution as if it can be reduced to them. These principles are not "eternal" features of the human condition on which the Constitution is based, but rather they are products of a political process and theory that are themselves grounded in a naturalist understanding of human nature. To regard the products of the Constitution as if they were its source is to bypass the real sources. In this case, Karimsky feels, two significant characteristics of the conception of human nature that informs the Constitution are obscured. The first is the crucial role of the idea of the complete protection of human rights as a fundamental constitutional principle. The second is the social and political significance of the contribution of the radical circle of the Enlightenment in the formation of American constitutionalism, which is to say, that component of the democratic legacy which is especially meaningful in the contemporary struggle for civil rights and freedom. By overemphasizing the role of religious tradition and underemphasizing specific components of the Enlightenment's philosophical anthropology, Americans deprive the Constitution of its most revolutionary features and disarm it as a potential weapon in contemporary democratic struggles (Karimsky 1988b, 24–30).

In the Soviet view, the dominant forms of the appropriation of the Constitution by contemporary American scholars, then, tend to make a virtue out of what are actually its shortcomings and in the process obscure what are actually its virtues. The Constitution's virtues are those respects in which, as Karimsky said, it "secured the fundamental social results of the American Revolution": political freedom, the separation of church and state, and the centrality of human rights (Karimsky 1988b, 27). Its failures are expressed in its contradiction with principles expressed in the Declaration of Independence and in its inability to embody the spirit of the revolution. In the view of both Karimsky and Mishin, the revolution was more than anything else an attempt to establish the conditions necessary for the free and full development of human potential, which in their interpretation means to effect social well-being. Thus the "spirit of the revolution" is above all the struggle to institutionalize and protect social rights, and it is precisely this that the Constitution fails to do. "The failure to secure social rights," Karimsky argues, "on the one hand inevitably leads to a failure to observe the principles of equal protection even of equal opportunity, and on the other hand it encourages a direct revision of the principle of equal rights" (Karimsky 1988a, 253). There is evidence of both tendencies, he thinks, in American life. The superficiality in practice of the general legal commitment to equality of opportunity is evident in the effects of widespread illiteracy, for example, and in gender inequality. Furthermore, he argues, the absence of social rights and equality creates a climate suitable for the influence of conceptions that deny even the general principle of natural equality. For example, a sociobiological reinterpretation of the meaning of happiness as property, material security, and ultimately as survival and reproduction implies that happiness cannot universally be achieved because individuals inevitably conflict in their pursuit of happiness. What Jefferson asserted as a natural right held equally by all becomes in sociobiological theory an impossibility. Other examples are also possible. Karimsky suggests that it has become increasingly common to argue on the basis of studies of animal behavior that hierarchy rather than equality is the "natural" condition. And there is a tendency, which Karimsky finds in the work of Toffler and others, to argue that in conditions of postindustrial society democratic principles are superseded (Karimsky 1988a, 254–259). Batalov finds the same rejection of the possibility of equality and democracy in what he describes as the American intellectual tradition of the "technocratic utopia" (Batalov 1985, 102–109).

In failing to embody the "spirit of the revolution" as a struggle for social rights, the Constitution contradicts the principles of the Declaration of Independence, which was the voice of that spirit. The contradiction arises from the very nature of bourgeois democracy and the specific characteristics of the political problematic of late eighteenth century America: "The contradiction between the principles of the Declaration of Independence and the U. S. Constitution (including the Bill of Rights) testified to the inconsistent democratism of bourgeois revolutionary ideology and the inevitable gap between abstract principles of human rights and social and political programs" (Karimsky 1988b, 42–43). The general principles of Enlightenment political thought and their practical realization were constrained by the historically conditioned requirement that they be interpreted and structured to embody and protect bourgeois property interests. Thus the process of the development of the Constitution and the meaning of its provisions are inextricably related to distinct class interests and problems, and any adequate interpretation of the Constitution must take its class nature into account.

The factors that influenced American constitutionalism were both theoretical and practical. Theoretically, the founders drew on American Colonial experience, British law, and the leading political scholars of the time. Karimsky and others note the influence of the Puritan dissidents, in particular Hooker and Williams. The seventeenth century settlements in Connecticut and Rhode Island were characterized by a notable democratization of social life, by the relaxation and even abolition of religious and property qualification for political participation, and in Rhode Island in particular by such radical measures as the separation of the church from civil power and the abolition of slavery (Karimsky 1988b, 31–32). Geevsky and his coauthors note that the founding documents of Rhode Island speak not of a covenant with God but of a secular, civil social contract, and they provide a precedent for the limitation of governmental power and for the centrality of civil rights and freedoms (Geevsky et. al. 1987, 9). More generally, Mishin suggests that the founders were able to draw on the wide experience of Colonial constitutionalism and the experience of the constitutional development of the independent states (Mishin 1988a, 69). British legal traditions were also influential in a variety of ways, in particular in that they enabled on the part of Americans a defense of individual freedom and local self government. In the revolutionary period colonists had argued that their rights under British law were being violated by colonial rule, and they ultimately appealed to what they took to be the principles of British law to justify political separation from England. Karimsky cites both Jefferson and Samuel Adams to the effect that British law derives from the law of nature and reason; "Thus the appeal to English law by the leaders of the American Enlightenment was in the end a tool for their own interpretation of natural rights" (Karimsky 1988b, 30–31). Of the English charters and political documents, one which exerted a particular influence on Americans was the Magna Carta, which is regarded even today as an early piece in the American political tradition. This is particularly instructive in that the Magna Carta was very much a product of its own time, limited by the prevailing class relations of feudal England. It granted liberty only to the barons, who were themselves tyrants. This "double standard" of laws, rights, and freedoms with respect to different social strata and class antagonisms continues to characterize American bourgeois constitutionalism (Geevsky et. al. 1987, 10). In addition, finally, to colonial experiences and British law, the founders were influenced by prominent political philosophers, most notably Locke and Montesquieu, each of whom had developed a theory of the separation of governmental powers. All the theoretical factors and colonial experience that formed the background of American constitutionalism were, however, filtered through distinct practical concerns. When the representatives of the various states met in Philadelphia in 1787 to draft the Constitution, Mishin says, "the strongest determining factors were the economic and political interests of the propertied" (Mishin 1988a, 69).

There were, Mishin feels, three primary tasks for the drafters of the Constitution. They were concerned to halt the further development of the revolution, to create "a more perfect union," and to guarantee the right to property. All three of these tasks conformed directly to the interests of the Colonial economic elite (Mishin 1988a, 68–69). The radical revolutionary camp endorsed principles and policies that would threaten the economic and political power of the propertied elite, for example its advocacy of democracy, so that it was essential that the revolutionary process be stopped. The economic problems of the 1780s and the political insufficiencies of the Articles of Confederation were also threats to the interests of the elite, who required greater stability and political effectiveness. Thus, their interests could be met only by a more stable, powerful, and centralized government, "a more perfect union." And the defense and institutionalization of property rights was an absolute necessity for the security of elite interests.

Mishin interprets virtually all of the fundamental political principles that governed the drafters of the Constitution in light of propertied class interests. The commitment to republicanism was a rejection of monarchy as a form of tyranny, but it was also a rejection of democracy in that it was predicated on the belief that the masses should not have a direct role in governmental affairs. The founders were ardent advocates of freedom and property because they believed that all people had equal, inalienable rights to life, liberty, and property. However, Mishin notes, this belief did not prevent them from consenting to slavery and to the actual inequality that existed in the American states. In the founders' view, inherent inequality was a natural manifestation of human diversity in so far as people could not be identical in intelligence, talent, capabilities, virtue, and so on. "In short," Mishin says, "the Convention delegates had a purely bourgeois understanding of freedom and equality," and he adds that "they did not think that their views on property could be directly and openly expressed in the Constitution" (Mishin 1988a, 71). Mishin is well aware, in other words, of the fact that property is not mentioned at all in the main body of the Constitution and that the first appearance of the term is in the Due Process Clause of the Fifth Amendment. This does not, however, obviate the centrality of the concern with property on the founders' part, Mishin thinks, because their commitment to it is apparent in the substance of the principles and governmental structures that they do overtly endorse. One might add here that Madison himself stated explicitly in his *Notes of Debates in the Federal Convention of 1787* that with only one exception the delegates agreed that the protection of property was the central concern of government. The sole dissenting voice was James Wilson of Pennsylvania who, according to Madison, "could not agree that property was the sole or the primary object of Government and society. The cultivation and improvement of the human mind was the most noble object."[9]

Other principles that the founders endorsed were also imbued, Mishin argues, with a bourgeois spirit. With respect to the social contract, the founders' view was that political power is based on an agreement between the people and the government, wherein the government is obliged to protect people's natural rights and the people are obliged to be faithful and obedient to the government. A feature of this understanding of the social contract is that it eliminates what Mishin takes to be one of the most democratic principles of the revolutionary period—the people's right to revolution: "The 'Founding Fathers,' then, followed the precepts of the Declaration of Independence, though the right of the people proclaimed in the Declaration to overthrow a government that was unacceptable to them was nevertheless consigned to oblivion, which once again shows their 'dread of the people'" (Mishin 1988a, 71). In a similar vein, constitutional bicameralism incorporates the Senate as the power of the elite to check any overly democratic actions of the lower house. And of the founders' federalism, Mishin says, "The federal form of governmental structure fixed by the Constitution was a result of the class compromise between the bourgeoisie and slave owners, who were frightened by popular agitation and the confusion of the Confederation" (Mishin 1988a, 73–74).

The centrality of property interests in the Constitution reflects both the personal class position of the founders and the specific nature of their underlying theoretical principles. Mishin points out that the representatives to the Philadelphia Convention were themselves all propertied, wealthy people—planters, slave owners, landowners, bankers, businessmen. In the context of a reference to Charles Beard's analysis of the economic motivations of the founders, Mishin says, "They all were representatives of the economic ruling class, and their constitutional proposals expressed absolutely determinate interests" (Mishin 1988a, 68).[10] Given the criticisms made of Beard's position, the obvious question arises whether Soviet commentators, in their assessment of the Constitution as a mechanism for effecting ruling-class interests, are themselves committed to an indefensible economic determinism, that is, whether they are interpreting the Constitution by assuming that its drafters were interested solely or primarily in lining their own pockets?

In his overview of the interpretation of the Constitution by Soviet historians, Nikonov acknowledges the influence of Beard's analysis. Soviet specialists were making use of Beard's position as early as the 1930s, but Nikonov points out that his ideas had also been sharply criticized in the USSR. One criticism has been that while Beard correctly saw some of the evils of bourgeois government, he incorrectly attributed responsibility to the founders for failures and shortcomings which only arose much later, in the era of monopoly capitalism. A second problem with Beard's approach, Nikonov suggests, is that "while stressing the role of financial capital, Beard neglected the interests of Southern slave owners, who also played an important role in the creation of the new constitutional order." Finally, and perhaps most importantly, Beard's analysis does not give sufficient weight to the theoretical principles that the founders endorsed: "In his commitment to an economic interpretation Beard did not pay attention to the political ideology of the Founding Fathers, who absorbed many principles of the European Enlightenment, principles which were progressive for the eighteenth century" (Nikonov 1988, 5–6).

The Soviet analysis of the U.S. Constitution, then, rests primarily on two issues: the direct class interests of its drafters and the substance of the theoretical principles they advocated. As men of property, the founders had personal material interests that differed from and often conflicted with the material interests of other segments of the population, and those general interests influenced policies and proposals that they might endorse. None of them, for example, could endorse a federal economic policy that would have eliminated debts owed to them by small farmers, which had been one of the demands of the participants in the Shays affair. They would, however, endorse a policy transforming the debts of individual states into a federal obligation, thus relieving more direct, local pressure. In more purely political respects, to the extent that people of property regard their own material interests to be distinct from those of other social groups, they are likely to wish to protect those interests through the creation of political structures that deposit power primarily in their hands. The picture is complicated, however, by the fact that property interests themselves are not uniform. The centralized regulation of commerce, for example, was in the interest of merchants and manufacturers but was viewed with suspicion by large agricultural interests. Soviet commentators have been inclined to read the Constitution as a whole as reflecting property interests in general and to interpret many of the specific disagreements and debates that arose during the course of the Convention as reflections of the differing interests of the various forms of property.

At the same time, there were also general theoretical principles involved. The founders really did think that some form of popular sovereignty was a political virtue and not simply a practical necessity. They really did believe that the legitimacy of government derives in some way and to some degree from the consent of the governed and that civil power ought to be separated from religious affiliation. And they were firmly convinced that property was not simply something that they happened to own, but that it was in fact a *natural right* and that virtue demanded government acknowledge that right and protect it from any threats. Soviet analysis recognizes the reality of these principles and their influences on the founders' thinking, but it adds the observation that the substance and application of the general theoretical commitments were perfectly consistent with the founders' specific material interests. As Nikonov puts it, "The fact that the Constitution embodied some principles of the Enlightenment does not indicate that it was free from class bias. The Enlightenment was not a non-class ideology; it was the creed of the progressive bourgeoisie of that time. Furthermore, the authors of the Constitution rejected the radical principles of that ideology and accepted only its moderate doctrines" (Nikonov 1988, 17).

The prevalent Soviet view that bourgeois theoretical principles converged with propertied material interests to produce the U.S. Constitution generates a picture of the government created by the Constitution that differs markedly from the more common and popular interpretation among Americans. Americans are more inclined to take a "pluralist" reading of the Constitution. Thus, it is argued, because the founders were committed to popular sovereignty and because they recognized that their society consisted of individuals and groups with differing interests on a range of issues, they constructed a government that could serve as an arena for the competition among those varying interests while remaining neutral with respect to any of them. The separation of powers, according to this view, is one of the more significant structural characteristics that enable government to guarantee access to political power by all interests. The question arises whether any evidence exists for the Soviet class interpretation over the pluralist reading. One answer emerges in a suggestive though undeveloped remark by Pokrovsky in his article on Jefferson and the Federalists. The Federalists, he says, were indeed pluralists, though some more than others, in that they recognized the plurality of interests, factions, in society. They did not, however, hold that all social issues were equally important, nor did they hold that all factions are equally legitimate. He refers specifically to John Adams, to whom he attributes the view that the legitimate factions in society are different groups of property holders, the various interests of which government must "restrain and counterbalance" (Pokrovsky 1983a, 283). If this attribution is correct, then the government created by the Federalists was not structured to acknowledge balance and protect all competing social interests but only or primarily those of the various forms of property, and it is precisely this that reflects its essentially bourgeois character.

This reading can be rendered plausible by an analysis of Madison's discussion of the question of factions in "Federalist 10."[11] Madison acknowledges that there are many features of a society that generate different, often opposing interests. There are, for example, conflicts that arise from religious or from regional causes. But he also knew that not all causes of factions present equally serious political problems, and he knew that some were more fundamental in the character of a society than others. Of all the causes of divergent and conflicting interests, Madison said that "the most common and durable source of factions has been the various and unequal distribution of property. Those who hold and those who are without property have ever formed distinct interests in society."[12] On the Convention floor he made much the same point: "In all civilized countries the people fall into different classes having a real or supported difference of interests. These will be creditors and debtors, farmers, merchants and manufacturers. There will particularly be the distinction of rich and poor."[13] The first point to notice in these remarks is that the factions arising from the kinds and unequal distribution of property are not simply some among many social conflicts but are "the most common and durable." The second point to note is that property generates two different kinds of divergent interests. There is first the conflict between "those who hold and those who are without property," and there is second the conflicts that arise from the different forms of property, among which are "farmers, merchants and manufacturers." Property, then, is a central, fundamental issue, and it has two distinct forms, the problem generated by the conflicting interests between the propertied and the unpropertied, and the problem created by the differing interests of the various forms of property.

Madison and his Federalist colleagues endorsed four propositions that taken together frame the political problem of property and their necessary solution of it. First, they held that some form of representative, republican government is the only legitimate and justifiable political structure; second, they held that there is a natural, absolute right to the acquisition and accumulation of property; third, they understood the sole or primary function of government to be the protection of the natural right to property; and, finally, they recognized conflicts of interest between the propertied and the unpropertied, and among those with differing forms of property. Given all four of these commitments, it is impossible for the founders to have held that government should be so constructed that it could be a neutral arena for all competing interests, because to do so would be to acknowledge the equal legitimacy of all factions. But in the common and durable conflict between the propertied and the unpropertied, to ascribe equal legitimacy to both sides would be to give up the second and third propositions. On the basis of the second proposition, those with property have their interests as a matter of natural right, which implies that the interests of the unpropertied, in so far as they conflict with those of the propertied, are threats to citizens' rights. Thus the interests of the unpropertied are of necessity socially dangerous and morally unjust. Furthermore, if according to the third proposition it is government's responsibility to protect natural rights in general and property rights in particular, then government by necessity must prevent access to power by unjust and dangerous social forces, the most serious of which is the unpropertied. Government, then, must be so ordered that it functions in the interests of the propertied *against* those of the unpropertied, and it must do so while remaining representative and republican. During the Convention Madison made the point this way:

> In framing a system which we wish to last for ages, we should not lose sight of the changes which ages will produce. An increase of population will of necessity increase the proportion of those who will labor under all the hardships of life, and secretly sigh for a more equal distribution of its blessings. These may in time outnumber those who are placed above the feelings of indigence. According to the equal laws of suffrage, the power will slide into the hands of the former. No agrarian attempts have yet been made in this country, but symptoms, of a leveling spirit, as we have understood, have sufficiently appeared in certain quarters to give notice of the future danger. How is this danger to be guarded against on republican principles?[14]

Government, in the interests of "those who are placed above the feelings of indigence," must through republican structures prevent the access to power of the unpropertied, even or especially if and when they become a majority. The founders accomplished this end through several Constitutional provisions, including the role of the Senate and the manner of its election, the Constitution's toleration of the various property qualifications on suffrage in differing states, and above all through the very size of the nation. Madison argued that a geographically extensive nation would "consist in the greater obstacle opposed to the concert and accomplishments of the secret wishes of an unjust and interested majority." The reason it will so function is that "a rage for paper money, for an abolition of debts, for an equal division of property, or for any other improper or wicked project, will be less apt to pervade the whole body of the Union than a particular member of it."[15]

These considerations imply the first part of Pokrovsky's point, that the only legitimate factions for which government must be a neutral arena are those that arise from property interests. But the fact that the various forms of property generate distinct and at times conflicting interests indicates the founders' second political problem. In the factious competition that arises from the various forms of property, all of the competitors have their interests as a matter of natural right; thus this problem cannot be solved as the conflict between the propertied and the unpropertied had been, that is, by the de facto exclusion of one set of interests from political power. It would have been illegitimate on general principle to structure the government so that manufacturers could dominate commercial interests or so that Northern financial concerns could exclude from power representatives of Southern agriculture. Yet Madison and many of his colleagues knew that if given the opportunity any one of these interests might well attempt to use the power of government to dominate the others:

> Shall domestic manufacturers be encouraged, and in what degree, by restrictions on foreign manufacturers? are questions which would be differently decided by the landed and the manufacturing classes, and probably by neither with a sole regard to justice and the public good. The apportionment of taxes on the various descriptions of property is an act which seems to require the most exact impartiality; yet there is, perhaps, no legislative act in which greater opportunity and temptation are given to a predominant party to trample on the rules of justice. Every shilling with which they overburden the inferior number is a shilling saved to their own pockets.[16]

Government must be so structured that all factions grounded in various forms of property have access to political power to effect their interests but also so that none can use political power to infringe unjustly on the natural property rights of the rest. This is the second part of Pokrovsky's point, that it is the function of government to "restrain and counterbalance" the various interests of groups of property holders. This end was accomplished through the separation of powers, wherein the processes of drafting and executing legislation and of adjudicating disputes is so fractured that no one legitimate, propertied faction is likely to control them sufficiently to repress other equally legitimate, propertied factions. This function of the separation of powers is what leads Karimsky to say that it is not essentially a democratic principle. Its role was not to regulate governmental organs in the democratic interests of the people but to regulate the social strength of those factions among the citizenry whose interests are grounded in natural and absolute property rights (Karimsky 1976c, 234).

Madison made these arguments concerning the nature and, in his view, the virtues of the Constitution in the context of the debates throughout the country over its ratification. This process interested Soviet historians, who over the years offered varying interpretations of the grounds and character of the disputes between Federalists and anti-Federalists. In works written in the 1930s and early 1940s, according to Nikonov, the distinction between Federalists and anti-Federalists was understood to have reflected fairly clear class divisions: representatives of large commercial and financial capital and wealthy farmers and planters supported the Constitution, while "the majority of the population—debtors, poor farmers, inhabitants of the frontier and average urban dwellers" opposed it. In works from the late 1940s through the early 1960s Soviet historians tended to have a somewhat more complex interpretation. They too saw the Federalist camp as composed of wealthy bourgeoisie, planters, and intellectuals, but they included among the anti-Federalists, in addition to the majority of the rural and urban population, some Southern planters who were anxious about the power of Northern capitalists and some Northern bourgeoisie who preferred to protect the privileges they already had in their home states. In these works, too, Soviet historians included the radical democrats among the anti-Federalists. Interpretations offered in more recent works, however, differ considerably from the earlier approaches. Nikonov says that in writings from the 1970s and 1980s, Soviet historians have rejected a number of previously common claims. It is an oversimplification of the process, they argue, to regard the disputes over ratification as representing two clearly discernible camps; that attitudes towards the Constitution did not reflect simply class concerns but also involved regional, ideological, and political contradictions; that anti-Federalism was not necessarily more democratic than Federalism; and that it is a mistake to regard the Federalists as a small group of elite and the anti-Federalists as representing the broad masses. They argue that in addition to wealthy property holders who favored a strong central government, the Federalists also included people from the urban lower class, mechanics, artisans, sailors, and many small eastern farmers who "hoped that the centralized authority would animate interstate and foreign commerce, put an end to the economic turmoil, and impose some protectionist measures." Recent and contemporary Soviet historians also include among the Federalists representatives of the radical wing of the revolutionary coalition such as Paine, Franklin, and Rush. Jefferson too, they note, supported a stronger federal government, although his "consistently democratic" criticism of the proposed Constitution for its design of executive power and the absence of a Bill of Rights makes it impossible to describe him neatly as belonging to one camp or the other (Nikonov 1988, 18–22).

The interpretation by Soviet historians of the Federalist camp as including both conservative and radical forces accords with Soviet philosophers' and legal theorists' inclination to regard the Constitution as both a profound step forward and at the same time a mechanism for consolidating ruling class power. The overall assessment of the U.S. Constitution by Soviet specialists invariably includes both of these traits. In considering the Constitution's general character and historical role, Soviet commentators note several points. One of them is its influence abroad. Mishin points out that the U.S. Constitution, along with the Declaration of Independence and other documents, had a profound influence on the first French Constitution of 1791 and that it has exerted a continuing influence elsewhere in the world, especially in Latin America (Mishin 1988a, 84–85). Another outstanding feature of the U.S. Constitution noted by Soviet commentators is its extraordinary longevity. Not only is it the oldest functioning constitution, but it has been amended relatively few times in its two hundred years. "This," Mishin observes, "is remarkable stability for a constitutional text!" (Mishin 1988b, 6). Such stability has been enabled, it is argued, by the interaction between the written and the "living" constitutions. Y. N. Rogulev, a specialist in twentieth century American history, suggests that "the most important stages of American society's development were clearly recorded in the history of the 'Living Constitution' when, on the basis of socioeconomic changes a fundamental restructuring of the mechanism of state power occurred, and new sociopolitical doctrines appeared, intended to substantiate the necessity of the changes" (Rogulev 1988, 1). Mishin makes the same point:

> But we must remember that in the United States there are two existing and functioning Constitutions—the "Sacred Charter" of 1787, and the Living Constitution, or the "Real Operational" Constitution. The Living Constitution bears some similarity to the British unwritten Constitution. It has no form. It consists rather of a great number of interpretations, commentaries, court decisions, statutes, customs, traditions, political behavior, etc. The written Constitution is a very rigid document, to be amended with great difficulty. The Living Constitution is incredibly flexible. It reflects the real social, political, economic, and legal life of American society. We can say, then, that the only reason for the stability of the U.S. Constitution is the flexibility of the Living Constitution. (Mishin 1988b, 6)

These points notwithstanding, the common context for a general assessment of the U.S. Constitution by Soviet specialists was the question whether at bottom it is essentially conservative and reactionary or democratic and progressive. The answer, as a rule, has been that it is both. This conclusion is reached in part through the methodological assumption that any reasonable evaluation of the Constitution demands that its historical context be taken into account. "An adequate assessment of the Constitution," Mishin says, "requires that we move beyond theoretical issues alone and take into consideration all the historical circumstances that define the essential character of the Constitution and the process of its development" (Mishin 1988b, 1–2). In the late eighteenth century Europe was still under absolutist rule, and in this period the conditions for bourgeois democracy existed in only a few countries. "We cannot forget," he says, "that the U.S. Constitution was adopted in an age when, with some exceptions, people lived under the tyranny of absolute monarchy," and Nikonov points out that "in Russia the czarist regime of Catherine the Great spread servitude on the Ukrainian lands just five years prior to the Constitutional Convention in the U.S." (Mishin 1988b, 2; Nikonov 1988, 26). It is impossible in Nikonov's view "to say that the document which was adopted at a time when the monarchical and colonial order reigned in the rest of the world was reactionary." Mishin echoes the point: "given the conditions of the epoch, the American Constitution should be evaluated, beyond any doubt, as a democratic document even before the acceptance of the Bill of Rights" (Mishin 1988a, 70). He lends substance to the point by saying that "even without a Bill of Rights, the Constitution astonished its contemporaries, primarily in Europe, with its republicanism, federalism, separation of powers, and its secularism" (Mishin 1988b, 2). The most significant respects in which the Constitution was a democratic and progressive document were its destruction of feudal social and political relations, its institutionalization of the rule of law, its secularization of government and the degree to which it is grounded on human rights. By establishing a republican order, outlawing noble titles, eliminating religious requirements, embodying such legal principles as habeas corpus, and by taking seriously natural rights and popular sovereignty, the U.S. Constitution effectively undercut the grounds and traditions of European monarchical absolutism.

There are, however, several respects in which the Constitution must be judged conservative and even reactionary. One of the more obvious of such features is its toleration of slavery, though interestingly enough Mishin thinks it unreasonable to fault the founders for their acceptance of slavery. The Constitution, he and others point out, was a compromise between the Northern bourgeoisie and the Southern slave owners. Without an agreement between these two social forces there would have been no Constitution, and thus their compromise was a necessary condition for the realization of the document's democratic and progressive features. The compromise most central to the process was over slavery, so that in

Mishin's view it was the toleration of slavery that enabled the Constitution's progressivism (Mishin 1988b, 2). Leaving aside the question of slavery, however, all Soviet commentators have agreed that the Constitution's conservative and reactionary features are those of its provisions that embody the antidemocratic side of bourgeois interests and power. Several Soviet historians refer to it as "a small Thermidor" in the American Revolution in that it was a retreat from the principles particularly of the Declaration of Independence and the Virginia Bill of Rights. The latter two documents were, Mishin feels, the most democratic of the period in their proclamation of the inalienable rights to life, liberty, and the pursuit of happiness and also of the natural right of people to overthrow a despotic government. By rejecting the right to revolution and by positing the right to property as the fundamental political concern, the Constitution, from this viewpoint, derailed the most democratic features of the revolution. Nikonov makes the point more softly when he says that the Constitution "did not fully incarnate the enormous democratic potential of the American Revolution, and in that sense it was a revision of these ideals toward a more moderate conservatism" (Nikonov 1988, 26). Mishin also finds a conservative, antidemocratic element in the way the Constitution articulates the separation of powers. While the French model of the separation of powers is based on the equality of the branches of government, and the British model on the supremacy of Parliament, the American model was based on the supremacy of the executive branch, and in practice on the judiciary as well: "The Constitution strictly defined the Legislative powers of Congress (article 1, sec 8), but it did not define the powers of the other branches of government. By so doing, the Constitution places the judicial and executive branches of government in a more preferable position than the legislative branch." In this, Mishin suggests, "we find signs of the founders' mistrust of Congress" and their determination to avoid what they took to be the evils of democracy. And, finally, the fact that the Constitution does not embody social and economic rights indicates its role as a mechanism for institutionalizing bourgeois power at the expense of the interests of the majority (Mishin 1988b, 4–5).

The ambiguities and contradictions of the U.S. Constitution and the inconsistency of new American political structures with revolutionary principles is a reflection, Karimsky thinks, of the inadequacy of Enlightenment social and political principles generally. At its most advanced, the Enlightenment's principles represented a "timid egalitarianism," which for several reasons was incapable of realization. The most progressive American thinkers did not for the most part understand the natural historical development of society through industrialization. Furthermore, the most democratically minded of the American leadership did not understand the class nature of government. Many sincere democrats, Karimsky suggests, saw its role as a constitutional guarantor of justice and underestimated the political and social significance of economic inequality (Karimsky 1976c, 256–258). The most serious problem of all, however, was the contradiction, built into the very heart of Enlightenment thought, between egalitarian principles and bourgeois interests: "The crisis of the Enlightenment was not theoretical, but social: Enlightenment ideas became 'antiquated' because they ceased to satisfy the bourgeoisie as ideological tools. More than that, they developed into potentially dangerous weapons for the criticism of the bourgeois order from the position of a more forward looking democratism" (Karimsky 1976c, 260). The contradictions between the Enlightenment's conservatism and radicalism indicate, in Karimsky's opinion, that its most progressive and democratic principles can be realized only when they shed their bourgeois substance and when freed from the constraints of a bourgeois political order:

> The accomplishments of the American Revolution and their philosophical and theoretical foundations, having achieved legal status and having been deposited in the traditions of American progressive culture, are vital and genuine factors of the contemporary struggle for democracy and socialism. The limits of constitutional democracy indicate that the bourgeois order is incapable of fully realizing genuine equality—this task is achieved by the proletarian revolution. (Karimsky 1976c, 286)

* * *

The threat of democratic principles to the newly established bourgeois order led to a general reaction against Enlightenment thought by the end of the eighteenth and beginning of the nineteenth centuries. The American experience clearly indicates, Karimsky feels, that the "historic mission of the Enlightenment" was to lay the conceptual groundwork for the revolution and not to provide an apologetic for capitalism (Karimsky 1976c, 269). Consequently, as capitalist economic and social relations became entrenched in the new American nation, and as the political power of the economic ruling class was consolidated through the Constitution, it became imperative that the revolutionary philosophical principles of the Enlightenment be abandoned. The most progressive features of Enlightenment thought had been its democratic commitment to equality and the pursuit of happiness, its deism and its materialism. Karimsky sees the post-Enlightenment reaction as the revision or rejection of each of these philosophic positions.

A revision of the principles of equality and the pursuit of happiness had already taken shape in the Federalists' rejection of democracy and in their arguments in support of the Constitution. The revolutionary, democratic notion that it is government's responsibility to protect the natural equality and right to the pursuit of happiness of the citizenry was replaced by the conviction that there is a natural inequality and that government's function is to secure the economic and social consequences of that condition. At the same time, the Enlightenment's deism, which had had a revolutionary significance in that it had helped free American thought from the traditionalist and authoritarian character of Colonial religious experience, was overshadowed by a resurgence of religious ideas and practice. The commitment to freedom of conscience, which in Karimsky's opinion was most revolutionary to the extent that it meant freedom *from* religion, was gradually being transformed into freedom *of* religion, thus undermining one of the central manifestations of the Enlightenment's secularism. Furthermore, there was in the waning years of the century a resurgence of revivalism, especially on the frontier and in the West generally. The growth of religion, Karimsky argues, served both to offset Enlightenment secular ideas and to provide a mechanism, as religion so often has in history, for the protection of ruling class interests. The bourgeoisie, he suggests, realized the importance of churches and religion for the mitigation of the protest of the working and poorer classes and for the suppression of democratic ideology. And finally, there was by the turn of the century a resurgence in the universities of philosophic idealism. There was a glimmer, Karimsky remarks, of the Berkeleyan ideas that had been so central in pre-Enlightenment American philosophy, and there was also a widening influence of Scottish realism. The former is of course a direct challenge to the philosophic materialism that Karimsky had argued was a definitive feature of the most advanced forms of American Enlightenment thought, and the latter two involved conceptions which in practice served bourgeois interests. In particular, he says, while Jefferson had understood the moral sense as a human social disposition, as the natural ground of the possibility of democratic social organization, the Scottish realists understood it to be an organ that generates the ideals of duty and responsibility (Karimsky 1976c, 260–268).

Until the later decades of the nineteenth century, objective idealism and religion were to be the general rubrics within which American philosophy developed. In this respect American philosophy conformed with contemporary European intellectual trends. European thought too reacted against the materialism and mechanism of the Enlightenment, and the romanticism that developed there had its American counterpart. Centered in New England, as pre-Enlightenment American philosophy had been, transcendentalism proved to be the richest and most influential form of early nineteenth century American thought. In its romanticism it was clearly a rejection of eighteenth century materialism, but it was also much more than that. In the interpretation suggested by Soviet commentators, American transcendentalism both translated the Enlightenment's social ideals into new philosophic terms and established a conceptual problematic that to this day continues to influence the development of philosophy in America.

3

TRANSCENDENTALISM

The Romantic Worldview, Emerson, and Thoreau

IF it is fair to judge on the basis of publication dates, American transcendentalism first enjoyed some popularity among Russian speaking readers in the late nineteenth and early twentieth centuries. There are several prerevolutionary editions in Russian translation of some of the writings of Emerson and Thoreau, including a two volume edition of Emerson's *Works* that appeared in 1902, and Thoreau's "Civil Disobedience" (1898), a collection of selected works (1903), "Life without Principles" (1907), and *Walden* (1910). Precisely why interest in transcendentalism developed during these years is difficult to say. Several factors likely combined to explain both the delay in interest in the Americans' ideas and the fact that interest developed when it did. The predominance of Slavophilism among the nineteenth century Russian intelligentsia and the exigencies of Tzarist censorship no doubt contributed. That works began to appear in the late nineteenth century may well have been motivated by Tolstoy's well-known appreciation of Thoreau. Whatever the influences may have been, it is intriguing to note that the transcendentalists' works began to appear in precisely those years in which the Russian Empire was experiencing growing revolutionary tensions. Perhaps the spirituality of Emerson and Thoreau offered a refuge for some Russian intellectuals from the increasingly dangerous social ferment, and it is equally possible that American transcendentalism served as a fresh, original source of revolutionary ideas.

Whatever its prerevolutionary role, interest in American transcendentalism all but disappeared in the postrevolutionary period, to reemerge only in 1962 with a new Russian edition of *Walden.* A third edition appeared in 1979, and translations of "Civil Disobedience" and "Slavery in Massachusetts" were published in 1977 in a volume also including a selection of Emerson's essays. The most recent edition of transcendentalist writings appeared in 1986 in a single volume that includes Emerson's *Nature,* "The American Scholar," "The Young American," the First and Second Series of Essays, and Thoreau's *Walden*. Scholarly discussion of the philosophy of American transcendentalism by Soviet specialists was also of later date. Commentaries by Soviet philosophers, in fact, appeared first in the 1980s. The first detailed philosophic study of Thoreau was N. E.

Pokrovsky's *Henry Thoreau*, published in 1983. Since then, utopianism in transcendentalist thought has been explored in Batalov's *The American Utopia* and Karimsky's "The American Romantic Utopia." Pokrovsky returned to a discussion of transcendentalism in "America Lost and Found," which is the introduction to the 1986 edition of primary works, and he explores the Romantic conception of the relation between the aesthetic and the ethical in his paper "Through the Beautiful to the Human." E. P. Zykova considers the impact of Oriental thought on American Romanticism in her essay "The East in the Works of the American Transcendentalists," and I. N. Sidorov analyzes aspects of Emerson's thought in *The Philosophy of Action in the U.S.A.: From Emerson to Dewey*. The most recent study to date is Pokrovsky's 1995 book *Ralph Waldo Emerson: In Search of His Universe*, an exegesis of Emerson's thought in relation to his time and contemporaries.

As a result of its unique history, American culture from the beginning has had a dual character. It is, on the one hand, a product of European historical and cultural development, invariably absorbing European material and theoretical trends. On the other hand, the American and European situations differ fundamentally. America's geography, history, economic development, and social and political relations, together with Americans' ideological expressions, presented conditions not to be found in Europe. Both of these factors influenced the development of American philosophy in the Colonial period and during the American Revolution, and they were no less central to early nineteenth century American thought. Transcendentalism was the expression on American soil of European Romanticism, and its character was a result of the features of philosophic and literary Romanticism in general and of the distinctive conditions of nineteenth century America in which it developed. In their interpretation of transcendentalist thought, Soviet philosophers attempted to identify those respects in which it reflects the Romantic temper in general and those in which it constitutes a uniquely American philosophic frame of mind. This sense of the generic and the particular in transcendentalism is also reflected in Soviet evaluations of its definitive characteristics and of its philosophic and cultural impact. On the whole, Soviet commentators have located the inadequacies of transcendentalism in its philosophic idealism and found its virtues in the very respects in which it is distinctively American. Unlike European Romanticism, they tend to argue, transcendentalism was the early nineteenth century philosophic vehicle of the more revolutionary democratic ideals of the Enlightenment, attempting to effect in its own way what Enlightenment thought had engendered but failed to realize; and in technical respects the transcendentalists, Emerson in particular, established a framework that was to blossom later into a new and distinctly American philosophic direction and vision.

The interpretation and evaluation of American transcendentalism as an expression of Romanticism and as a philosophic product of unique national circumstances are the parameters within which Soviet commentators raise a range of issues. Among the more salient are transcendentalism's conceptual and historical backgrounds, the philosophic traits that define it as a distinct world view, its social and political components and implications, and the subsequent impact and influences of transcendentalist thought. With respect to its theoretical backgrounds, Soviets are interested in the philosophic traditions it absorbed and those against which it reacted. Classical culture in general and Platonism in particular had their effects on transcendentalism, as did Kant, German idealism, and English and German literary Romanticism. While absorbing these influences, however, the American Romantics were also reacting against aspects of their philosophic heritage, most notably Cartesian and Lockean epistemology and the materialism and rationalism of the Enlightenment. As a product of American culture, transcendentalism also both absorbed and reacted against the heritage of Puritanism, the American Enlightenment and the Unitarianism that dominated the religious atmosphere of early nineteenth century New England. The metaphysical and epistemological characteristics of transcendentalism that most interested Soviet commentators include the role of mysticism and spirituality; the conception of nature; the relations of nature to human being, of nature to society, of the individual to society, and of nature to spirit; the moral significance of nature and the Romantic conception of the relation between the aesthetic and the ethical; the transcendentalist conception of the world as dynamic, mutable, incomplete, and "in the making"; and the understanding of knowledge as an inherently active process. Not surprisingly, Soviets were particularly interested in the social and political characteristics of transcendentalism, specifically its assessment of industrialism and capitalism, its theoretical treatment of individualism and democracy, and the role of solitude and escapism in transcendentalist theory and practice. And finally, from the Soviet point of view, one of the more significant indications of the meaning and value of transcendentalism has been its impact and influence on later thinkers and social movements from Tolstoy, Gandhi, and Martin Luther King to the American counter-culture and the contemporary ecological movement.

The Romantic World View

Although Romanticism arose as a reaction against a specific philosophic heritage and against certain prevailing material conditions, it was not, in the Soviet view, primarily reactionary. The immediate philosophic context against which Romanticism reacted was Enlightenment thought, and its material stimulus was the consequences of industrialization and capitalist development. The Romantics rejected the materialism and deism, the mechanism and rationalism of the Enlightenment, and they opposed the new principles and relations that were quickly coming to dominate social life as a result of industrial capitalism. But this rejection, especially in the case of American Romanticism, was neither wholesale nor backward looking. While abandoning the Enlightenment's conception of nature and its understanding and commitment to reason, the American Romantics endorsed and embodied the democratic and revolutionary vision of the late eighteenth century, which in turn gave substance to the Romantic criticism of prevailing social conditions.

Heir to the Enlightenment

Pokrovsky suggests that the primary cause of the Romantic response to the Enlightenment was a loss of faith in the ability of reason to establish a just social order (Pokrovsky 1989a, 97). In the eyes of many Europeans and Americans in the early nineteenth century, it had become clear that the Enlightenment social project was a failure. The process of industrialization and capitalist accumulation was exacerbating the inequality in the distribution of wealth and deepening the material desperation of the poor. Furthermore, the processes unleashed by the theory and practice of the revolutionary period had engendered a spiritual poverty that was reflected in the self-aggrandizing principles of a commercial culture. The evident lack of social justice and the deterioration of moral values suggested to many that the theoretical principles on which the Enlightenment project was based were themselves flawed. If adequate social relations and values were not being realized on the basis of a materialist, mechanical conception of nature and the ability of reason to comprehend nature and effect justice, it was because that the understanding of nature and knowledge was mistaken. Romantic metaphysics and epistemology are defined by the alternatives that developed to the Enlightenment's conception of nature and reason.

Thus, from a Soviet point of view, the distinctive features of the Romantic world view had a social grounding. The precise character of this social concern, however, is one of the features that distinguishes American from European Romanticism. Karimsky argues that while Romanticism was qualitatively distinct from the Enlightenment, there was also a kinship between them, specifically in the case of the American Romantics, who, he suggests, retained a greater continuity with the Enlightenment than did their European counterparts. European Romanticism opposed bourgeois society in large part by idealizing the feudal past, while Americans, not having such feudal roots, remained socially more progressive. "Many American Romantics," Karimsky says, "strove to express and convey the heroic spirit of the struggle for independence. The human rights to freedom, equality, and the pursuit of happiness remained for them permanent values, and loyalty to democratic ideals among the Romantics was in the very order of things" (Karimsky 1986, 282). This theme is repeated throughout Soviet commentaries. Batalov puts it this way: "Having appeared as a reaction to the social consequences of industrialization (the restructuring of the lifestyle, the collapse of the traditional patriarchal relations, and the destruction of the old values), the American Romantic movement was also a legitimate search—this was its salient sociohistorical feature—for ways to realize the promises of the American Revolution" (Batalov 1985, 84–85). As Sidorov puts it, Romanticism generally strove to "retain and further develop a fundamental theoretical achievement of the bourgeois revolutions—the conception of human beings as the active subjects of history," which in the American case meant to effect a practical realization of the ideas of the Declaration of Independence, to transform that document from a political manifesto into "a basis of the cultural process" (Sidorov 1989, 4, 8).

The transcendentalist commitment to American revolutionary and democratic principles indicates a problem inherent in its world view. In acknowledging the failure of the Enlightenment to realize its social ends, Sidorov suggests, the Romantics rejected the rationality of social relations, recognizing in its stead the reality of conflicting interests and social conditions, which in turn had both beneficial and detrimental consequences. Romanticism, Soviet commentators argued, ultimately replaced one inadequate conception of social relations with another. They were right to abandon the Enlightenment view that reason alone, or primarily, is capable of effecting social justice and to recognize the reality and importance of social contradictions. However, the argument goes, the Romantics did not understand the material causes of those contradictions, and they translated their suspicion of the omnipotence of reason into an equally powerful but mistaken suspicion of order and lawfulness in the historical process. Thus, on the one hand, as Sidorov puts it, "though they were extraordinarily far from realizing the actual sources and essence of the contradictions, their position nevertheless allowed the possibility of social protest and engendered utopian hopes for the establishment of justice" (Sidorov 1989, 5). On the other hand, the failure to understand the material ground of social contradictions—which according the Marxist view explains why the democratic vision of the American Enlightenment had not been realized in the nineteenth century—and the corresponding suspicion of determinate and lawful processes in history meant that Romanticism could produce no concrete social programs and indicated the ultimate failure of its social vision.

Nature and Reason

The social context of American transcendentalism is, according to several Soviet readings, the ultimate source of its entire philosophy and conditions both its contributions and its shortcomings. That it embodied revolutionary principles identifies it as the bearer of the democratic and progressive line in American social thought in the first half of the nineteenth century, though its own bourgeois grounding marked the ultimate inadequacy of its social and political views. With respect to its metaphysics and epistemology, the transcendentalist rejection of the Enlightenment's deterministic and mechanistic conception of nature and human nature conditioned the development of its own approach, one that has had profound implications for the subsequent development of American philosophy. Karimsky directly expresses the character of the transcendentalist alternative to the Enlightenment understanding of nature, while also making it clear that he finds it problematic:

> The failure of the rational, Enlightenment scheme of social progress strengthened the tendency toward irrationalization of social being, life, and human activity. The transcendentalist perception of the world included principles of dynamism, mutability, activity, and the incompleteness of the world, but the foundation of this activity was a spiritual, substantial origin: Emerson's "oversoul," Thoreau's "reason," and the abstract God of the transcendentalist Unitarians. (Karimsky 1986, 279–280)

Whether or not Karimsky's judgment of the transcendentalist world view as an "irrationalization" is justified, its conception of nature as dynamic, mutable, and incomplete prefigures a theme that is to run through much of American philosophy, from James's open universe and Dewey's rejection of the fixed and final in nature, to Justus Buchler's contemporary ordinal conception of the indefinitely ramifiable character of nature's complexes and his rejection of a final "Order" of nature. Furthermore, the transcendentalist conception of nature, as Karmisky also points out, incorporated the inherent efficacy of human action. That which is unrealized, potential, and in the process of becoming, he remarks, points to the unlimited possibilities of life and creativity; there was a philosophic emphasis on the indeterminate and the novel, which is to say, on everything that can be actualized by, in transcendentalist terms, a thinker's intuition and creative imagination. This is an expression of a "meliorism" that has been a central theme in American philosophy, and it points as well to a distinctively American "active" epistemology. In pragmatism's operationalism and instrumentalism, Santayana's animal faith, Royce's active relation of the individual to the absolute, and Buchler's articulation of the active mode of judgment, American philosophy has in a variety of ways constituted an alternative to the more passive epistemological conceptions of rationalism and empiricism. And finally, with its emphasis on human action and the mutability of the world, transcendentalism is located in the strain of American philosophy which, as we have already seen Pokrovsky applaud, blends theory and practice, which reads theory in terms of practice, and which is implicitly concerned with lived experience and urgent human problems.

The consequence of the "Invisible Hand" in the marketplace had been, in the transcendentalist view, a commercial, business culture that reduced human beings to atomized economic units, each functioning on the basis of its own internally determined principles on the basis of individual self-interest; and whatever Adam Smith's own understanding of moral philosophy and the relation of individual economic activity and moral values may have been, the commercial principle of individual profit was quickly becoming the criterion of ethical activity, itself the preeminent moral value. Human beings were losing their souls, were becoming alienated from the spiritual spark that provided the meaning and the most significant values of distinctively human life. The parallel between Smith's mechanistic understanding of economic life and the Newtonian, Enlightenment conception of nature was not lost on the transcendentalists. Just as human activity understood through Smith's principles had been stripped of its spirit, so too had the mechanical and atomistic understanding of a physical world so brilliantly described by Newton deprived nature itself of its inherent spirituality. If human beings are not soulless, meaningless machines, neither is nature. To approach nature as a machine that functions through the mechanical interaction of its parts is to miss its essential character and to lose sight of its inherent meaning and value. Nature no less than human being is an organism imbued with soul, from which derives its own meaning, value, and significance for human life. The transcendentalist alternative to the Enlightenment was inherently a turn to spirituality.

By rethinking nature in terms of spirit, the transcendentalists placed themselves in the Platonist, objective idealist strain of Western philosophy, and they confronted in one way or another the many permutations of idealist thought available to them: Platonism itself, recent German idealism, English and German literary Romanticism, and the newly discovered texts of ancient India and China. Transcendentalism shares with Plato the fundamental distinction between the physical and "metaphysical," and the elevation of the ideal or spiritual to some kind of superiority over nature. The same conception was being expressed in late eighteenth and early nineteenth century German idealism, which the transcendentalists absorbed in some cases directly but for the most part, Pokrovsky suggests, through the writings of Coleridge, Carlyle, de Stael, and others. From the German idealist philosophers, primarily Schelling but also Hegel, came both a contemporary rendering of the priority of the spiritual over the material, and also a newly invigorated conception of nature as symbol and of the symbolic character of philosophic cognition and insight. And it was from Kant that transcendentalism took its name, though only by ignoring, as Pokrovsky notes, Kant's distinction between *transcendental* and *transcendent*. Despite its affinity with Platonism, however, transcendentalism, and Romanticism generally, is distinguished by a distinctly non-Platonic reverence for nature. In this respect, English and German literary Romanticism from Wordsworth to Goethe had a profound impact in New England, though Pokrovsky will argue that the specific traits of American geography and landscape ultimately would lend the transcendentalist conception of nature a unique character. Into the mix of philosophic sources and influences is added the transcendentalists' interest in classical Hinduism and, especially in Thoreau's case, Confucianism. This unique blend of ideas in the background of transcendentalism inclines Karimsky to describe it as idealism augmented by "pantheistic and mystical moments" (Karimsky 1986, 279).

The role of Oriental thought in American Romanticism had been explored in some Soviet discussions in part because, as E. P. Zykova puts it, the transcendentalists were "the first American thinkers to have a serious and sustained interest in the East: its culture, literature, and philosophy," or more generally, in Pokrovsky's words, "For the first time in the history of the U.S.A and possibly of Europe, the philosophical ideas of India, China, and Persia became widely known in these countries" (Zykova 1988, 86; Pokrovsky 1989a, 76). Zykova notes that classical Oriental thought has a good deal in common with Romanticism generally, including a suspicion of rationality, a concern with society as a factor in human alienation from spirit, an emphasis on a direct relation between human being and "the macrocosm," and mysticism. She suggests, however, that Eastern thought had a much greater impact on American Romanticism than it did elsewhere. The transcendentalists were, as Thoreau himself had said, far less Eurocentric than were the European Romantics, which enabled them to look beyond the confines of European traditions for congenial ideas. Furthermore, the American Romantics found themselves in an ideological struggle with orthodox Unitarianism, and they found an ally and philosophic support in Oriental ideas. In Zykova's opinion, however, the primary reason Indian and Chinese philosophy was as significant as it was for the transcendentalists was that the failure of the American revolutionary attempt to create a new kind of society inclined them to look elsewhere for alternatives (Zykova 1988, 89). Batalov makes a similar point while discussing the concept of the "natural man" in American Romantic philosophy and literature. Emerson's "self-reliant" individual, the Thoreau who retreats to Walden Pond, and Melville's Typee all have something in common, and "the only reason why Melville is looking for this man in the Marquesas and Thoreau and especially Emerson in the Orient and not in America is that they are convinced that this man does not and, given the then social conditions, simply cannot exist in America." Batalov qualifies the point in a footnote: "Naturally, the Orient to which American Romanticists turned so often was not the geographical region with all its actual cultures and histories but a myth, the antithesis of Western dehumanization" (Batalov 1985, 86).

Oriental thought was not, however, simply an ideal alternative but was a source of specific concepts that resonated with transcendentalist ideas. While both Emerson and Thoreau were interested especially in the Eastern conception of human spiritual perfection by contrast with the materialist principles of contemporary society, Zykova suggests several ways in which Emerson in particular attempted a synthesis of Eastern and Western ideas. The Emersonian concept of the oversoul is analogous to the Brahman of the Upanishads and Vedantism, and the Hindu atman has its correlative in the transcendentalist understanding of the individual spirit. In Pokrovsky's words:

> Just as the Brahman, the transcendentalist oversoul is a living, dynamic spirit, the source and receptacle of the infinitely varied phenomenal forms of being. It is infinite not in the sense of excluding everything finite but in the sense of being the inner basis of all things finite. Just as the Brahman, the oversoul is not reducible to thought, to the thinking spirit; it is a living unity of essence and existence, of the ideal and the real-of knowledge, love, and beauty. (Pokrovsky 1989a, 77)

Zykova suggests that in his Second Series of Essays, Emerson combined the Western conception of human perfection with the Eastern conception of salvation, of escape from the limits of the individual, of the transition from partial to universal consciousness. In general, Emerson interpreted the otherwordly ideas of Hinduism in terms of the ethical dimension of human life. He treats karma, for example, as an ancient ethical myth, and he employs the concept of maya to illustrate the distinction between false and genuine values, especially the false values of bourgeois society and the genuine values of spiritual and ethical development (Zykova 1988, 98–106).

To these Pokrovsky adds two more specific parallels between Hinduism and transcendentalism, specifically Thoreau. "The idea of the involvement of the individual soul with the cosmic spirit," he says, "became a fundamental one for Thoreau and the transcendentalists," specifically through a common conception of nature. Nature as it is conceived in the Upanishads is an expression of Brahman, and it is the realm that provides access for the individual spirit to the universal, in which atman and Brahman converge. And with respect to epistemology, Thoreau shares with the Upanishads the conviction that "intuitive cognition is higher than all other rational modes of assimilation of being" (Pokrovsky 1989a, 77). This may have been Emerson's view as well, for whom "a foolish consistency is the hobgoblin of little minds."[1]

That there is a relation between transcendentalism and Oriental thought is beyond question; precisely what that relation was is more controversial. For her part Zykova regards Oriental philosophy as exerting an influence on the transcendentalists, while Pokrovsky, speaking specifically of Thoreau, holds that "the role of (Oriental philosophy) in the formation of his worldview need not be exaggerated." By the time Thoreau read and wrote about Indian and Chinese ideas, his own fundamental philosophic conceptions had already been worked out. In fact, Pokrovsky feels, it was precisely because Thoreau's views were already fairly well formed that he was so taken by Oriental thought when he did encounter it: "This discovery confirmed one of Thoreau's most important assumptions: true knowledge is eternal and absolute, it does not become obsolete, neither is it invented, it can only be rediscovered. The East became a symbol of eternal and immutable wisdom for Thoreau" (Pokrovsky 1989a, 76– 77).

Whether Oriental thought actually influenced or simply corresponded with the ideas of the transcendentalists, their approach to and appropriation of Indian and Chinese ideas bore the stamp of their own understanding of spirituality. For Emerson and Thoreau, Zykova suggests, the East represents "passivity and contemplativeness," while the West expresses activity and practicality. This distinction had a symbolic significance for Thoreau, who said that the struggle between East and West goes on in each nation, and for Emerson, who saw the same struggle in the individual consciousness of every person. Just as Emerson and Thoreau rejected the incessant commercial activity of their own culture, they also rejected the passivity and contemplative otherworldliness of the East. Oriental thought could contribute to the West an understanding of the spirituality of nature and human being, but in transcendentalist hands that spirituality was transformed from a metaphysical to a practical moral principle. Spirit is embodied in nature, and nature is the source of moral and aesthetic values. The task of all societies and individuals is to avoid the extremes of passive spiritualism and active commercialism by understanding the spiritual ground of action and the active role of spirit.

The pervasive expression of spirit is nature. For the transcendentalists nature was a central concept, though it emerges through a range of meanings not all of which were always consistent. Minimally, nature means, as Karimsky describes it, both the material, sensible world by contrast with the social, cultural world, and a universal mind, spirit, that embodies the creative activity of the soul. Nature as the material world is secondary to nature as informed by spirit in that it is nature in the latter sense that gives nature in the former sense meaning. But these are only minimal descriptions, since both nature as the material world and nature as the embodiment of spirit are susceptible to additional interpretations. A question arises, for example, concerning whether material nature is in itself significant or whether it is in the end an obstacle to human access to spirit. In varying degrees both views find expression in transcendentalist writings. And if the material world is significant, there are various ways to understand in what its significance lies. The two most prominent conceptions of the significance of material nature in trancendentalist writings are, first, that the material world is a symbol of spirit and, thus, that it reveals spirit symbolically; and, second, that in its materiality nature expresses ethical and aesthetic values and enobles the human individual. One might say that Emerson embraces the former view of material nature as symbolic of spirit, while the virtue of materiality, of landscape, is more pronounced in Thoreau. In the end, however, there is a tension between the two approaches of the authors.

What if nature is significant only in so far as it reflects spirit? Here too several questions emerge. One concerns the way in which nature and spirit are related and another the character of spirit itself. With respect to the relation between nature and spirit, one possibility is conveyed in Karimsky's definition of nature and universal mind as spirit, for here nature is not an expression or embodiment of spirit as much as it *is* spirit. Karimsky, Pokrovsky, Sidorov, and others all find this pantheistic conception of nature in transcendentalism, but they are also aware that in many respects spirit and nature are more sharply distinguished. Emerson's oversoul is not so much nature proper as it is a spiritual principle that renders nature significant and is the ultimate source of the values nature makes available to humanity. And of spirit itself, whatever its relation to nature and however vaguely it is described in many respects, there is one crucial respect in which the transcendentalist understanding of spirit is distinct from other idealist conceptions. The spirit or oversoul of Emerson, Thoreau, and their colleagues is not the finished, fully determined absolute pushing and pulling nature, history, and humanity through the lawful necessity of its own inherent character, as Hegel saw it. Nor does the transcendentalist conception of spirit represent the fixed, final, and "closed universe" that would so bother William James several decades later. On the contrary, the spirit Emerson and Thoreau were interested in was the principle of creativity itself, the very factor that precluded determinacy and provided nature and knowledge with open possibilities. The transcendentalist spirit is what lends intuition and imagination their power and human action its efficacy. If neither Emerson nor Thoreau was concerned to develop a systematic characterization of spirit, or to clarify precisely its relation to nature, that was because those conceptual details were at worst irrelevant and at best unimportant. What *was* important was to understand that nature is infused with spiritual significance and that it is only through nature that fundamental human values can be understood and human potential can be actualized.

The transcendentalists approached nature through the Romantic conception of nature and knowledge as symbol. Ontologically, "nature is the symbol of spirit," as Emerson said, and in Thoreau too we find natural phenomena, from Walden Pond to the traditional basic material elements of earth, fire, air, and water, functioning as symbols of spirit. Equally significant is the pervasive reliance in transcendentalism on symbolic knowledge. Sidorov describes the essential character of symbolic knowledge as the view that the comprehension of the spiritual harmony of the universe is accomplished not in a theoretical and conceptually systematic form, but in a freely symbolic form. "Not objectivity," Sidorov says, "but morality is the goal of such comprehension" (Sidorov 1989, 38). The senses reveal the material traits of nature, and rationality offers access to whatever characteristics of the world are deductively available, but neither sensation nor reason, and by implication empiricism, rationalism, or the practice of natural science that combines them, can provide an entrée to the spiritual, moral, and aesthetic dimension of nature. Spirit is accessible only through the free play of creative imagination, which is to say, through symbolic form. The conceptions of nature and knowledge that the modern European and American tradition had made available all miss the essential traits of nature, those of its characteristics that are most humanly significant. It is in nature as symbol that we locate moral and aesthetic principles, and it is those principles in which "wisdom" and the activity that constitutes the "philosophical life" are grounded. "According to Emerson's methodological schema," Pokrovsky writes, "the transcendental symbolism of nature resulted in a description of nature becoming in fact a description of the states of individual consciousness in its relation to the absolute idea, to the oversoul" (Pokrovsky 1989a, 95–96). Human activity is rooted in the symbolic understanding of nature.

Perhaps the most profound of nature's traits are the aesthetic and moral principles it provides. As the bearer of spirit and in its materiality, nature is the seat of beauty and the good, and it is through direct interaction with and intuition of nature that human beings are ennobled aesthetically and ethically. Emerson, as Sidorov and Pokrovsky both note, develops this view in his essay *Nature*, and it runs throughout much of Thoreau's writings, receiving its most sustained expression in *Walden*. Nature in this sense is a contrast with society, and it represents a purifying and humanizing power that offsets the degradation and dehumanization of social life: "Following Thoreau," Pokrovsky says, "we penetrate into the infinite world of virginal, primordial nature, represented, according to Romantic philosophy, as the aesthetic and ethical antipode of the capitalist town" (Pokrovsky 1986, 19).

"Both Emerson and Thoreau maintained," as Pokrovsky says elsewhere, "that by exerting a profound aesthetic influence on man, virgin nature ennobles him ethically, raises him above the humdrum life of the industrial city and makes him feel more a product of nature than of society" (Pokrovsky 1988, 2–3). The Romantic conception was not simply that nature expresses aesthetic and moral value but that through the interaction with the aesthetic dimension of nature an individual is ethically enriched. This sense of the moral power of nature is present in European and American Romanticism, though Pokrovsky suggests that it takes different forms in each, due largely to differences in the conception of nature. For the European Romantics, he argues, nature is a moral power only as an idealization, while for the Americans, Thoreau in particular, it is the landscape itself that teaches. The difference is a result of the unique conditions in Europe and in North America:

> The infinite and majestic nature passionately worshipped by Novalis, Coleridge, or Schelling was ideal (metaphysical or transcendent) nature. Even given the relatively virginal quality of the West European landscape in those days, it was delineated, discrete, and finite. The Romantics were tragically sensitive to all this. The borders of the dwarflike states, the numerous waterways and roads seemed to crush and fragment the world of nature. The headlong pace of urbanization and growth of industry, the encroachment of civilization on forest, rivers, and mountains—all of this taken together imparted a feeling of fatal division and doom hanging over the Romantic passion for nature. (Pokrovsky 1989a, 117–118)

The consequence for the European Romantics of the constraints on nature was an idealization of the very conception of nature, but the contrast between the idealization and the reality surrounding them produced an inevitable sense of despair:

> It was only with the aid of their famous fertile imagination that philosophers and poets overcame the horizon of immediate sensuous givenness and immersed themselves in images of ideal nature—the product of the absolute spirit's unconscious creativity. But creation of an ideal world did not rid them of burning dissatisfaction with the real world, and their worshipping of nature suffered from the incurable disease of chronic pessimism. (Pokrovsky 1989a, 118)

The American situation was quite different. By virtue of geographical extent and the relatively limited degree of economic expansion, the natural landscape of North America was still relatively untouched and did not require the idealization of the Europeans. The Americans were able to appreciate directly the wild beauty of their natural surroundings and to regard the landscape itself as the source of wisdom:

> The nature that surrounded Thoreau and served as the source of creative inspiration did not yet carry any traces of civilization's active encroachment and appeared to him

to be infinite and inexhaustible. The forests surrounding Concord flowed in a broad stream westward, giving way to the prairies and the ridges of the Rockies bordering on the Pacific Coast. . . . Unlike the European Romantics, Thoreau drew such a fine line between nature and Nature that it virtually vanished. The fact that Thoreau turned to pristine landscape for inspiration was of decisive significance for his whole artistic-philosophical creativity. In the world of nature, Thoreau found infinitely more than a mere living collection of biological entities. He saw the untouched nature of North America above all as an embodiment of the Romantic ideal. (Pokrovsky 1989a, 118–120)

The transcendentalist sense of the moral and aesthetic value of nature was an American rendering of a more generally Romantic conception, and it suffers, Pokrovsky thinks, from the shortcomings of Romanticism. One of the problems is that the Romantic approach describes the relation between the human individual and the edifying traits of nature through a "mysterious 'correspondence' between man and the absolute," an ideal employed by Emerson, Thoreau, and, Pokrovsky notes, the contemporary German naturalist Alexander von Humboldt. Furthermore, the transcendentalist understanding of the way in which nature "teaches" human beings is, in Pokrovsky's view, excessively individualistic in that it does not take into account that the interaction of an individual with nature is itself mediated by social practice. Despite such problems, however, Pokrovsky argues that Emerson and Thoreau "proceeded from an essentially correct precept" that the aesthetic contemplation and experience of landscape has an ethically salutary effect on people. If this conception is developed in ways that overcome its Romantic drawbacks, its significance can be seen all the more clearly. He suggests that much the same position is expressed by the Soviet specialist in education Vasily Sukhomlinsky, who took a special interest in the notion of "education by nature" or a development "through the beautiful to the human" (Pokrovsky 1988, 3–8; 1989a, 146–150).

The transcendentalist approach to experience begins with the rejection of Cartesian rationalism, which had "cut off the voice of poetry," and Lockean sensationalism, which restricted the given in experience to sensation, thereby precluding access to nature's spirit, and which construed sensation and therefore knowledge as a passive relation between subject and object. While they abandoned the empiricist grounding of knowledge in material sensation, the transcendentalists did not reject what Sidorov calls the classical methodological conception of empiricism—the possibility of immediate knowledge. Cognition is indeed immediate, not primarily through sensation but through intuition. Parker, Sidorov notes, held that God is immediately given in consciousness, and Brownson accepted a distinction between objective and subjective reason in which objective reason, the impersonal Logos, and subjective reason, our individual cognitive ability, are related by an "internal light." Along similar lines, Ripley held that there are truths that surpass the immediately sensed and that everyone has the same ability to grasp this spiritual truth, an ability made possible by intuition, by Jonathan Edwards's "feeling of the heart." To the extent that they accepted the reality of a direct intuition of spiritual truth, the transcendentalists could be located on a long line of religious, primarily mystical, thinkers. The uniqueness of their view, however, derives in part from the conviction that the truth revealed by intuitive experience is largely ethical, and it is this, Sidorov suggests, that connects intuition with concrete action (Sidorov 1989, 5, 11–17).

The transcendentalist conception of the relation between knowledge and action is complex. On the one hand, human activity is located in and rendered meaningful by a pervasive spiritual reality from which the individual derives life's values and purposes. On the other hand, the openness and mutability of the world means that human activity, both cognitive and practical, is a creative power. The individual achieves knowledge through the creative activity of intuition and the imagination, and in the exercise of rational and practical activity is engaged in a process of "world-making," which Pokrovsky identifies as the centerpiece of the humanism that the transcendentalists developed to replace Puritan rigorism (Pokrovsky 1986, 11). This humanism—which is expressed in the role of creative activity in knowledge and the efficacy of action in remaking the world and which frees individual insight and development from revealed dogma and clerical authority—is one of the features of transcendentalism that the Soviet commentators have found most attractive. They are, however, quick to suggest that the transcendentalists' humanism, whatever virtues it may have had, suffered from its essentially religious grounding. Pokrovsky remarks, for example, that "their manifestly humanistic tendency was fundamentally constrained by their equally evident philosophic idealism, teetering on the verge of theosophy and pantheism" (Pokrovsky 1986, 11).And Sidorov says that by grounding the principles and ends of knowledge and practice in spirit and consciousness rather than in the processes of material development and social relations the transcendentalists rendered their own activity futile (Sidorov 1989, 20).

Individual and Society

The spiritual, ideal source of action, however, did not prevent the transcendentalists themselves from being concerned with matters of social theory and practice, and the humanism that permeated their metaphysics and epistemology also conditioned their approach to society. Batalov says of transcendentalism that "its central principle is the *natural* condition and its central value, the *free man*. The American Romanticist," he continues, citing the Soviet specialist in American literature Yu. V. Kovalev, "is above all a *humanist* proclaiming 'man's supremacy over the law, the state and the church'" (Batalov 1985, 85). This remark suggests a preeminent issue in transcendentalist social thought—the relations among the individual, nature, and society.

The development of the individual was the primary value for the transcendentalists. Batalov notes Margaret Fuller's remark that "man is not made for society, but society is made for man," and adds on his own part that "the Romantic ideal is a society in which the individual can follow his inner motivations, in which he is free from any external coercion or imposition by others, from the dictates of the state" (Batalov 1985, 85). Their dissatisfaction with prevailing social conditions created in the transcendentalists a distrust of society in general and led them to suspect that the influence of society on an individual is most likely detrimental. Karimsky makes the point through a contrast between Romantic and Enlightenment conceptions:

> The Enlightenment and Romanticism had essentially different approaches to the problem of man and society. The first saw the conflict between the individual and society as caused by an irrational social structure, which needed to be changed to correspond with human nature. The second, analyzing the contradictions between man and society, accented not only social transformation but also changing the aims and behavior of man himself, who through unity with the natural world will find life's meaning and freedom from the enslaving aspects of civilization. (Karimsky 1986, 289–290)

"The Romanticist sees nature as the only true source of moral purity, wisdom, and power," Batalov says, so that "to become a natural man, one had to *break with society*—organizationally (like Thoreau and the inhabitants of Brook Farm) or spiritually (like Emerson and Margaret Fuller) and to establish, or rather restore, *unity with nature* (in Emerson's words, 'harmony' of man and nature)" (Batalov 1985, 86).

The "break with society" and return to a natural condition expresses the asocial character of the Romantic conception of the individual, but it does not necessarily imply a rejection of the possibility of morally defensible social relations and structures. While Romanticism's "natural man," Batalov notes, looks much like the ideal of the noble savage, especially in such of its personifications as Melville's Typee, it actually means simply to live a natural life, in or out of society. In fact, the point of the return to nature is not to avoid society but rather to achieve the individual moral development that is a necessary condition of adequate social life. Though it is not groundless to associate escapism with transcendentalism, Pokrovsky remarks, the Romantic idea of "escape" was more a symbol than a concrete program. "Furthermore," he continues, "this escape inevitably implied a return to people, to society, strengthened and spiritually renewed for the struggle to realize the (Romantic) ideal" (Pokrovsky 1986, 17–18). In a discussion of several of James Fenimore Cooper's literary characters, Karimsky remarks that "the author intends to show the better sides of civilization and of the natural condition," which is to say that he does not advocate returning to a condition outside of civilization. And both Karimsky and Pokrovsky find the clearest expression of the inherent return of the "natural man" in what might otherwise be taken as the most overt example of Romantic escapism, Thoreau's retreat to Walden Pond. "Thoreau's seclusion," Karimsky says, "was not a flight from civilization, but a stage in the search for social ideals and a general world view" (Karimsky 1986, 292). Pokrovsky, for his part, argues that for Thoreau, man and society, and society and nature, were in opposition "only in the external course of events," and that in his own life Thoreau was neither a hermit nor a nihilistic escapist. "His withdrawal into the woods was dictated in the end by an attempt to find a point of moral bearing," which inherently entails his return. From life at Walden, Pokrovsky points out, Thoreau entered the stormy political battles over slavery, and "without any hesitation he emerged on the side of the popular masses" (Pokrovsky 1986, 19).

The social ideal of American Romanticism embodies a commitment to democracy and individualism. Its advocacy of democracy represents its link to the progressive wing of American revolutionary social thought, while its individualism indicates its ultimately utopian character. The transcendentalists' approach to democracy—what they rejected and what they endorsed—is significant in part because it rests on a distinction often submerged in American conceptions of what democracy is. As a strictly political category, democracy implies a faith in people to rule themselves and the necessary mechanisms for the will of the majority to prevail. Under the conditions and to the extent to which a political system of popular sovereignty was practiced in America in the early nineteenth century, the transcendentalists were not democrats in this formal sense—thus Thoreau could say that "any man more right than his neighbors constitutes a majority of one already."[2] Thoreau and Emerson both had a deep distrust of American political democracy, perhaps because they thought that the ethical and economic values of a commercial society corrupt individuals to such a degree that a formal political system of majority rule is rendered useless, and perhaps even dangerous. Thoreau expresses this concern in many places, from his attack on a business culture in "Life without Principle" to his angry condemnation of the electorate of his home state in "Slavery in Massachusetts," and Batalov cites a passage in which Emerson voices similar misgivings: "When I . . . speak of the democratic element I do not mean that ill thing, vain and loud, which writes lying newspapers, spouts at caucuses, and sells its lies for gold. . . . There is nothing of the true democratic element in what is called Democracy; it must fall, being wholly commercial" (Batalov 1985, 87).[3]

However, one can identify a much different substantial rather than merely formal sense of "democracy," one that found expression in the Jeffersonian circle of American revolutionaries. In this sense, a formal system of self-rule requires material conditions that enable the individual development of all members of a society. Democracy in the Jeffersonian tradition is much more an egalitarian matter, such that a society is undemocratic to the degree that it fosters and defends social and economic inequality, regardless of the extent to which its political decisions and policies are determined by the majority. This is why Jefferson's rejection of a right to an unlimited private accumulation of property is an expression of a democratic tendency. To the degree that privately owned property generates unemployment and poverty it is undemocratic and loses it legitimacy. Democracy in this more substantial sense, "ethical democracy" as Batalov calls it, is what the transcendentalists endorsed. Emerson and Thoreau rejected the formal democracy of their day in favor of an ethical democracy that would encourage the moral and material development of the citizenry. This is the reason Pokrovsky, for example, describes Thoreau as a "sincere democrat," and why Soviet commentary in general reads transcendentalism as the heir to Enlightenment social thought (Pokrovsky 1989a, 172).

The transcendentalists' distrust of the American political process did not preclude their advocacy of the democratic principle of self-government. On the contrary, their conception of democracy was predicated on a thoroughgoing individualism. Democracy as Emerson and Thoreau understood it is a social condition in which individual development is so far advanced that *self*-government can be realized literally. Democracy is a condition in which individuals govern themselves and in which a government formed by majority decision is wholly superfluous. In Emerson's case, the ground of democracy is the principle of self-reliance. Batalov cites Emerson to this effect: "the root and seed of democracy is the doctrine. Judge for yourself. Reverence thyself. It is the inevitable effect of the doctrine, where it has any effect (which is rare), to insulate the partisan, to make each man a state. At the same time it replaces the dead with a living check in a true, delicate reverence for superior, congenial minds" (Batalov 1985, 87).[4] Thoreau expressed the same point in the well known passage in "Civil Disobedience":

> I heartily accept the motto,—"That government is best which governs least"; and I should like to see it acted up to more rapidly and systematically. Carried out, it finally amounts to this, which also I believe,—"That government is best which governs not at all"; and when men are prepared for it, that will be the kind of government which they will have.[5]

Transcendentalist democracy implies not a form of political organization but what Batalov describes as "a *nonpolitical* (*depoliticized*) *society* in which there is neither the state nor parties nor classes nor power struggle—a society ruled by custom, where one's own conscience is the highest authority" (Batalov 1985, 88).

Its individualism is, in the various Soviet perspectives, at the same time the most distinctly "American" feature of transcendentalism and the trait that most vividly conveys its essential utopianism. Zykova remarks, for example, that with his concept of self-reliance Emerson, ironically, became a voice of the very "American form of life," which she associates with the principle "every man for himself", against which he struggled through most of his life and work (Zykova 1988, 105). Batalov has a more complex reading of transcendentalist individualism in which he distinguishes it from the form of individualism that Emerson, Thoreau, and their colleagues opposed. Romantic individualism, he says, is not the "entrepreneurial individualism" of American self-consciousness. The latter is "based on the fetish of petty private property and the pursuit of wealth and social success." By contrast, while the Romantic individualist "does not in principle reject private property, he does not make a fetish out of it either, seeing it merely as a condition for the normal existence of man and society." The transcendentalist, Batalov continues, "is revolted by the mercenary spirit of greed and breathless pursuit of profit as something that denigrates man. The individualism of the Romanticist is *ethical individualism*" (Batalov 1985, 86). There is a Jeffersonian spirit in this reading of transcendentalist individualism and its approach to property, in that Jefferson, too, regarded property as a necessary condition of social life and as a means to a greater ethical end rather than an end in itself. While Batalov sees a fairly clear distinction between the "ethical" and "entrepreneurial" individualists' conception of property, Pokrovsky finds the relation to be more problematic. The issue of property, he feels, is the "stumbling block" of the whole philosophy, in that by accepting private property transcendentalism criticized bourgeois society without attempting to break from it. "Emerson," he says, "harbored the illusion that a 'moderate' development and protection of private property . . . could secure the self-development and freedom of the individual," while Thoreau's view, though he was more aware of the relation of "the general institution of private property to the more unsavory aspects of the economic and spiritual life of the United States of his time," took the form not of a critique of private property but "of a moral repudiation of the well-to-do classes" (Pokrovsky 1986, 11–12).

The transcendentalists' ambiguous treatment of property and more generally their ideal of an ethical individualism produced a social conception "not organically connected with existing being," a phrase Karimsky uses to describe the central trait of utopianism. Romanticism in general, he says, "above all expresses a concern with the fate of the individual in the conditions of capitalist development, and attempts in one form or another to work out an abstract social model with which reality should conform, or at least be compared" (Karimsky 1986, 277–278). A utopian conception is characterized by social ideals that themselves are determined in abstraction from the objectively determinate traits of prevailing social conditions, and one of the themes of Karimsky's discussion is that the whole of the Romantic world view was conducive to just such an approach. For the Romantic consciousness, he says, the idea of an objective, lawful historical process is an imposition, a constraint on individuality and the creative imagination. If the world is open, malleable, and replete with infinite possibilities, as the Romantic understands it to be, then there is little point in looking to actual conditions to judge what is or is not possible. When this is combined with the equally characteristic Romantic conception that prevailing conditions are the product of human imaginative, creative, and practical activity, and that whatever has been done can just as well be done differently, then there is even less of an impulse to ground one's ideals in "existing being." The result of the Romantic cosmology and of the "world-making" capacity of human activity was the generation of vague social ideals without specific plans for realizing them and, Karimsky notes, the appearance of more than a few utopian communities that had no hope of having an impact on the broader society. The Romantic rejects existing conditions, he says, but does not see in them the basis for achieving his own ideal, "Thus it is not surprising that there is an absence of a social and political program, or of the technical details of the ideal situation" (Karimsky 1986, 288).

That the social ideals of transcendentalism were dissociated from prevailing social conditions may be a reason they have never achieved broad realization, but Batalov suggests that that very trait may also explain why the "Romantic utopian tradition . . . has always remained a living source of American culture and national social awareness." As the rapid development of industrialization and corporatism of the post-Civil War period and the emergence of the United States as a world power with the turn of the twentieth century pushed the society farther and farther away from the radical social ideals of the American tradition, the transcendentalist vision became all the more vivid and occasionally attractive as an alternative. This vision is rarely far beneath the surface, Batalov feels, of American utopian literature, experiments in utopian communities, American socialist theory, and at times even broad social movements, the most recent example of which was the counter-culture of the 1960s. The disconnection of transcendentalist social thought from the existing conditions of its own time is precisely what makes it continuously available: "The social ideals of Romantic utopia of the first half of the nineteenth century were so highly transcendental and so far from actual social reality that to this day they remain unrealized and inexhaustible (hence the topicality of Thoreau's ideas). At best, they could be reproduced, but not surpassed" (Batalov 1985, 90).

Emerson

Though in the end several Soviet commentators found Thoreau's naturalism far more congenial than Emerson's spiritualism, they nevertheless recognized that it was Emerson who first gave voice to the distinct philosophic perspectives of American transcendentalism and who throughout his long career extended and applied them in often creative and forceful ways. It is to Emerson's *Nature* that Karimsky turns to locate the fundamental characteristics of the transcendentalist understanding of the world: that nature is to be contrasted with culture and civilization and expresses universal mind. It is the same work, Pokrovsky notes, that describes nature as the symbol of spirit and that develops the symbolic approach to nature and knowledge so characteristic of transcendentalism. And it is *Nature* that expounds the theme that the aesthetic dimension of nature is ethically ennobling, which Pokrovsky regards as the most valuable of all the transcendentalist ideas.

It is Emerson, too, who embodies the democratic traditions of American thought, though, Pokrovsky suggests, not always consistently. We have already seen that Batalov emphasized Emerson's account of "ethical democracy" in terms of self-reliance, and Pokrovsky also reads the call to self-reliance as an expression of a democratic spirit. Emerson's injunction, he says, was an attempt to encourage self-development and the liberation from clerical and ecclesiastical dogma. Emerson regarded a faith in oneself as necessary to plumb the depths of culture, history, and nature, as a necessary condition, in other words, of the enrichment of the human community. Emerson here is responding to the conditions of his own society and attempting to articulate an alternative. The concern with self-reliance came, Pokrovsky suggests, at a time of increasing ideological and political regimentation in bourgeois society, "gradually but inexorably dominating Americans' spiritual and civil freedom." In this context, the principle of self-reliance was a call to escape from routine and to develop a distinctly American culture "'relying' on its own people, its own democratic and revolutionary traditions. . . ." Emerson's conception, however abstractly and speculatively expressed, had its implications in his own social activity: "At times Emerson, as if a Brahmin, gazed impassionately at the collision of human passions. However, this was not always the case. Sometimes the writer and philosopher spoke his weighty words on the most burning issues of the day." Pokrovsky mentions in particular

Emerson's involvement in the abolitionist movement and his sympathy with attempts to organize communes, "in which a genuine 'self-reliance' might be achieved through cooperative labor and the collective upbringing and education of all their members" (Pokrovsky 1986, 16–17).

Of all the uniquely Emersonian concepts, self-reliance, for Soviet commentators, most clearly expresses the virtues and shortcomings of Emerson's transcendentalism. If for Batalov and Pokrovsky it gives shape to Emerson's understanding of democracy, it also, Karimsky says, embodies the anti-historicism of Romantic thought. And even for Pokrovsky, the virtues of Emersonian democratism are offset by its individualism:

> Emerson's "self-reliance" also signifies a closing in on oneself, plunging headlong into the delightful and magnetic labyrinth of the "soul's" self-knowledge. It implies a priori that the internal world of the individual has no comparison in its universal significance with that which is found outside, including society. (Pokrovsky 1986, 17)

The same "self-reliance" in terms of which Emerson strove to articulate his democratic vision also led him later, in a more conservative state of mind, Pokrovsky says, to criticize sharply and unjustly utopian socialism, "the principles and practical achievements of which stood taller than any abstract notion of 'self-reliance'" (Pokrovsky 1986, 17). The fact is, as T. L. Morozova suggests, the concept of self-reliance itself embodies the contradictions of Emerson's thought and, for that matter, of his whole culture: "Thus while on the one hand the principle of 'self-reliance' expresses a beautiful humanistic faith in human power, reason, will, and abilities, it also reflects the law of capitalist competition with its motto 'every man for himself'" (Morozova 1982b, 110).

There is another side of Emersonian thought in which, as Sidorov develops it, Emerson stands at the beginning of a distinctively American "philosophy of action." The history of philosophy in North America, he argues, is characterized above all by an epistemological conception that places action at the heart of the cognitive process, and by so doing it has produced a philosophic approach that is distinct from other prominent historical and contemporary trends and that remains a live philosophic option, meaningful for "the topical concerns of contemporary philosophic thought as a whole." This American "philosophy of action" reached maturity in pragmatism, but it has its origins in Emerson's alternative to the epistemological options of the seventeenth and eighteenth centuries.[6]

There are, in Sidorov's view, three basic traits of the "paradigm" of the philosophy of action: First, it is anti-speculative; second, it develops a nonclassical understanding of the "rationality of knowledge"; and third, it is inclined toward an idealist and religious conception of the nature and ends of action. The first two of these traits represent the more significant contributions of this strain of American philosophy, while the third embodies its most serious failure. Rejecting speculative deduction as the primary form of rationality is one way, as Dewey will argue, of avoiding the dogmatism so common in the history of philosophy by replacing speculation with an instrumentalist, active understanding of ideas, theories, and the cognitive process. By contrast with the speculative tradition, both rationalist and empiricist, the view that action is a "necessary, decisive factor of knowledge," that ideas are plans of action, is a new and valuable conception of knowledge. It is, Sidorov argues, more flexible than traditional conceptions of knowledge "in that it includes such elements of the cognitive situation as will and conviction, belief and habits, intuition and valuation" (Sidorov 1989, 140). The persistently idealist interpretation of action, however, renders American philosophy of action incapable of adequately grasping the real nature of knowledge and action. Sidorov argued that the Marxist tradition is preferable in that it combines the American rejection of the speculative and contemplative approach to knowledge with a materialist, objectivist understanding of nature, society, knowledge, and action.

It may seem odd at first glance to credit Emerson as the intellectual source of an epistemological alternative to speculative philosophy, in light of his conceptions of the oversoul and the spirituality of nature. But the point is less puzzling when we bear in mind that for Emerson spirit does not represent a closed and finished reality from which nature emanates or to which nature must conform. Spirit, on the contrary, suggests the open possibilities of nature and the inherent creativity of human activity; it embodies the aesthetic and ethical principles providing human nature its most important traits and providing action its proper ends. And these principles require creative, active imagination; they demand inquiry to be known. Emerson's conception of reality and its implications for knowledge and action in turn overcome the dualism implicit in both rationalism and empiricism. The notion that action is inherent in the process of knowing spirit and nature and that spirit, nature, and human action are phases of a unified, seamless process are, in Sidorov's view, the two most significant and positive features of Emersonian philosophy.

Rationalism and empiricism, each in its own way, left an impassable gulf between the human being and the rest of reality, between the knower and the known. In Cartesian hands this gulf is expressed in the technical problem of the relation between mental and material substance and in the broader cultural problem of the place of human being in a mechanical world. Modern empiricism tried to situate the knower in nature by identifying sensation as the source of knowledge, but its passive understanding of sensation left it in skepticism. Kant, dissatisfied with the skeptical consequence of empiricism, tried in his own way to resolve the problem, an attempt that produced a different but no less intractable chasm between the world of possible experience and the thing-in-itself. Romanticism, in turn, avoided the Kantian dualism but often not without asserting yet a new one. Sidorov argues that Ripley, for example, was left with a dualism between individual and divine consciousness and between the spiritual and the practical. By reading action as a matter of individual consciousness, Ripley could integrate neither the individual and the divine nor, as a result, human action and knowledge. Emerson's contribution, Sidorov says, was to overcome Ripley's dualism by developing an idealistic monism. Sidorov here attributes to Emerson a pantheistic interpretation of reality, in which "all subjects perceived and thought manifest a spiritual unity, to be found in their necessary interrelations and determined by a single divine power. This interrelation in which man is organically included is the general life of the universe. According to Emerson, man is a part and embodiment of this life" (Sidorov 1989, 21).

Of course, Emerson too faced the question of the relation between spirit and human being, between the divine "supra-consciousness" and individual consciousness. This issue, in Sidorov's analysis, establishes the parameters that locate Emersonian transcendentalism's cultural problematic, its understanding of action in knowledge, and the ultimate failure of that conception of action. Emersonian pantheism is an expression both of the Romantic alternative to mechanism and materialism and of the religious temper of early nineteenth century American culture. To the extent that Spirit provides the meaning and significance of nature and human being, it is the predominant factor that subordinates nature's materiality and concrete human action. With this, however, Emerson combined the other powerful element of American culture and intellectual tradition: individual freedom. To combine what Sidorov calls "religious supra-consciousness" with individual consciousness in a way that preserves the ubiquity of spirit and the value of individual freedom, Emerson developed a conception of the creative activity of reason (Sidorov 1989, 23–24).

For Emerson, contemplation is not an end in itself and by itself does not bring people closer to understanding. For this, action is necessary. Reason can apprehend the infinite truth of spirit but not without action. In *Nature* Emerson notes the beauty of nature and action and then inverts the point to assert the necessity of action, with intellection, for the apprehension of beauty:

> The intellectual and the active powers seem to succeed each other, and the exclusive activity of the one generates the exclusive activity of the other. There is something unfriendly in each to the other, but they are like the alternate periods of feeding and working in animals, each prepares and will be followed by the other. Therefore does beauty, which, in relation to actions, as we have seen, comes unsought, and comes because it is unsought, remain for the apprehension and pursuit of the intellect; and

then again, in its turn, of the active power. Nothing divine dies. All good is eternally reproductive. The beauty of nature re-forms itself in the mind, and not for barren contemplation, but for new creation.[7]

Spirit, and by implication nature, embodies simultaneously truth, goodness, and beauty, and each of these conditions the others. In his essay "The Poet" Emerson expresses the relation of truth, goodness, and beauty to the modes of the individual's relation to spirit:

For the Universe has three children, born at one time, which reappear under different names in every system of thought, whether they be called cause, operation and effect; or, more poetically, Jove, Pluto, Neptune; or, theologically, the Father, the Spirit and the Son; but which we will call here the Knower, the Doer and the Sayer. These stand respectively for the love of truth, for the love of good, and for the love of beauty. These three are equal. Each is that which he is, essentially, so that he cannot be surmounted or analyzed, and each of these three has the power of the others latent in him and his own, patent.[8]

The knower, the doer, and the sayer are discriminable (each has his own power patent in him), but each also incorporates the other two (each has the power of the others latent in him). The apprehension of beauty, which Emerson here attributes to the sayer, the poet, though he elsewhere attributes it to the artist of any kind, necessarily requires as well the knower, or intellection, and the doer, or action, because beauty cannot be divorced from truth and goodness. For the same reason, action, the apprehension and creation of the good, requires intellection and saying (making), and knowing necessarily involves doing and making. Doing and making are inherent moments of the cognitive process because goodness and beauty are inseparable from truth, and the three together express what spirit and nature are.

Action, knowledge, and artistic creation, then, are inseparable at several levels. They are the correlatives in the human process of the essential traits of spirit and nature, and in any specific instance each requires and implies the others. Thus the apprehension of beauty is not contemplative primarily but active; it makes use of imagination and symbol, and in that creative activity it both presupposes and issues in knowledge. The activity of which Emerson speaks, however, is not restricted to the creative powers of consciousness. It applies as well to the more practical activity of human life. In "The transcendentalist" he chides the "many intelligent and religious persons [who] withdraw themselves from the common labors and competitions of the market and the caucus," and he remarks that "no solid fruit has yet appeared to justify their separation. . . . They prolong their privilege of childhood in this wise; of doing nothing, but making immense demands on all the gladiators in the lists of action and fame."[9] Emerson quickly attacks the contemplative inclinations of the reclusive intellectual and the would-be saint on the grounds that knowledge is not inaction but is the power to act for the better:

> What right, cries the good world, has the man of genius to retreat from work, and indulge himself? The popular literary creed seems to be, "I am a sublime genius; I ought not therefore to labor." But genius is the power to labor better and more available . . . the good and wise must learn to act, and carry salvation to the combatants and demagogues in the dusty arena below.[10]

By reconceiving the relation of knowledge and action, Sidorov says, Emerson "is established as one of the leading representatives of the anti-speculative program of the American philosophy of action" (Sidorov 1989, 30). Emerson is correct, Sidorov argues, in unifying knowledge and action, but his idealist, spiritual conception of the nature of that unity is in the end a mystification: "The essence of this mystification, peculiar not only to transcendentalism but to the philosophy of action as a whole, is that within its framework the bases of action are never connected with the condition of material, practical reality and the social, historical content of the past. In its place is invariably to be found some sort of modification of consciousness, as a rule religious" (Sidorov 1989, 32). Sidorov has no doubt that knowledge and action really are two sides of the same coin, and in support he cites the work of the prominent Soviet psychologists A. N. Leontiev and L. S. Vygotsky. He argues, however, that the integration of knowledge and action derives not from any spiritual unity but from the material and social conditions out of which consciousness and cognition emerge.

Thoreau

However much Emerson understood knowledge to require action, he had in mind primarily the activity of consciousness. Thoreau, Pokrovsky argues, was different. While he was excited by contact with Emerson's ideas, he applied them as direct principles of action. He took seriously transcendentalism's conceptions of the spiritual, moral, and aesthetic significance of nature, and of the appropriate relation of human beings to nature, and he was determined to pursue their implications for human life: "Thoreau devoted all his short life to ever deepening searches for the criteria of moral purity, the beauty of human relations, and the harmony of the world of man and the world of nature." One of the results of his search was that "world culture was enriched by a masterpiece of philosophical prose-Thoreau's *Walden, or Life in the Woods*" (Pokrovsky 1986, 18).

Pokrovsky is aware of the many and divergent interpretations and evaluations of Thoreau's life, his thought, and his legacy. These are, he thinks, due in some measure to the subtlety of Thoreau's ideas but also to a number of tensions, in some cases contradictions, in the development of his philosophy. He often attempted to merge what appear to be distinct and perhaps incompatible positions: philosophy as the pursuit of knowledge of the world and as a way of living; nature as spiritual and as material, as significant symbolically and literally; individual development as requiring a retreat from and an immersion in social affairs; the state as inherently harmful and as perfectible; pacifism and violent social struggle. "Some see Thoreau," Pokrovsky says, "as a symbol of what they refer to as the 'nation's conscience.' Others attack him for his individualism, anarchism, and escape from social reality. . . ." Pokrovsky thinks, however, that when the complexities and tensions in Thoreau's life and thought are sorted out, one can conclude "that there is undoubtedly more truth in the views of those who recognize the progressive significance of Thoreau's heritage than in a flat rejection of it" (Pokrovsky 1989a, 14). In the end, Pokrovsky's Thoreau is a "sincere democrat," determined to locate the conditions of individual moral development, to expose and condemn social injustice, and to participate in "a conscious struggle for the revival of democratic elements contained in state institutions" (Pokrovsky 1989a, 172).

Thoreau's contributions as a philosopher have been largely overlooked, perhaps because he was not concerned with the technical questions that have come to define the subject matter of modern philosophy. Pokrovsky argues, however, that this approach to Thoreau presumes far too narrow a conception of the nature of philosophy and the variety of its traditions. There are more than a few principles of classification in the history of philosophy, of which the most "decisive . . . has always been the distinction between two opposing philosophical positions—'the line of Plato and the line of Democritus.' . . . " In addition to the distinction between materialism and idealism there are also "partial principles", one of the more important of which distinguishes "academic" and "nonacademic" philosophic traditions. Academic philosophy is concerned to achieve knowledge of nature, while the nonacademic trend characteristically interprets the subject matter of philosophy as the search for the meaning of life. In the first case "wisdom" means knowledge, "a rational vision of the world"; in the second case it means a way of living. Nonacademic philosophy begins in the West with Socrates, Pokrovsky says, and has continued in various guises throughout the history of philosophy. "In 19th-century America, the 'nonacademic' tradition was most fully expressed in the life and philosophical ideas of Henry Thoreau" (Pokrovsky 1989a, 16–19).

In the first section of *Walden* Thoreau is clear enough about his disdain for academic philosophers and his understanding of wisdom as a way of living:

> There are nowadays professors of philosophy, but not philosophers. Yet it is admirable to profess because it was once admirable to live. To be a philosopher is not merely to have subtle thoughts, nor even to found a school, but so to love wisdom as to live according to its dictates, a life of simplicity, independence, magnanimity, and trust. It is to solve some of the problems of life, not only theoretically, but practically. The success of great scholars and thinkers is commonly a courtier-like success, not kingly, not manly.[11]

The meaning and relation of theory and practice are central to Thoreau's conception of philosophy. He did not advocate, Pokrovsky suggests, that human lives and social relations be restructured according to some theory or other. This was in part because Thoreau was suspicious of theory, suspecting that it is too distant from people's lived concerns. But it was also the result of his conception of practice, which according to Pokrovsky was not social practice but "merely the introduction of theoretically interpreted ethical norms and conceptions into individual life experiences, for wisdom, as Thoreau saw it, was essentially and profoundly intimate and did not presuppose collective participation and search." Even this lends too much weight to the role of theory, as Pokrovsky himself implies when he says that by understanding wisdom as practice Thoreau advocated "an intuitive-emotional rather than a rational assimilation of the world." The basis of Thoreau's philosophy was not theory but "was to be found in ethical rigorism" (Pokrovsky 1989a, 21–22).

Even in the absence of theory, however, Thoreau's emphasis on the intuitive assimilation of nature still lends to his conception of philosophy and the good life a contemplative air. Observation and contemplation are necessary to appropriate nature's principles and truth, though the philosopher cannot be content with mere contemplation because its results must be useful in human relations. "The search for a synthesis of contemplation and the individual's social activity was an important part of the American philosopher's theoretical and practical work," Pokrovsky remarks, and he suggests that Thoreau "refused to admit the absolute incompatibility of these two views of the world" (Pokrovsky 1989a, 23). Wisdom requires apparently contradictory processes—the philosopher must contemplate without interfering, but must also act and not simply observe. Thoreau was aware of the "antinomy," Pokrovsky thinks, and attempted to resolve it in the concept of philosophical activity, wherein wisdom involves not any sort of practical activity but activity "aimed at the spreading of the right attitude to the world" (Pokrovsky 1989a, 25). Such philosophical activity is accomplished by carefully constructing one's own life, a requirement, Pokrovsky suggests, that entails "yet another contradiction: Philosophical activity became encapsulated within a caste, men were divided into teachers and disciples, and the philosophy of wise men was gradually isolated from life. Thoreau's search thus came full circle"

(Pokrovsky 1989a, 25). Pokrovsky echoes Marx's conception of philosophy as the conceptual side of social transformation when he suggests that Thoreau's "theoretical horizon was limited by the framework of contemporary society, which did not allow him to change the standpoint basically, to see philosophy not only as an explanatory academic discipline but also a science transforming the world" (Pokrovsky 1989a, 26).

Pokrovsky finds in *Walden* one of the clearest expressions of Thoreau's attempt to reconcile naturalism with the Emersonian conception of nature as the symbol of spirit. This is undertaken through the characteristic Romantic use of symbol, or what Pokrovsky calls "image-concept." There are many image-concepts at work in *Walden*, including "flow of water, ocean, pine tree, heaven, night, morning, spring, home sounds, clothes, speed, savage, wilderness, solitude, etc.," all of which "are unusual, ideational image-bearing elements of [Thoreau's] worldview, meaningful units carrying the main ideological content of the text" (Pokrovsky 1989a, 86). The most central image-concept is, however, the lake itself. Pokrovsky identifies four meanings of Walden Pond, the first of which is literal, which is to emphasize the significance of the pond in its temporal and spatial character. Second, Walden represents the general, aesthetic attributes of nature abstracted from any particular natural phenomenon. Third, the language Thoreau uses suggests an indirect sense of the pond as the individual soul-the self. Fourth, Thoreau's discussion of the pond indicates its significance as a symbol of the transcendent meanings of philosophical concepts (Pokrovsky 1989a, 86–88). Thoreau's discussions of the pond flow subtly from naturalistic accounts, some of which are among "the finest landscape descriptions in American literature," to statements that become, "step by step, ever more imageful and at the same time generalized and abstract. The overcoming of the empirically given, even in its artistic, figurative form, is accompanied by a sharp growth in the philosophical content of the text" (Pokrovsky 1989a, 83, 86). Ultimately the lake, without losing its empirical significance, "appears as an example of aesthetic perfection, as a symbol of inexhaustible depth, as a personification of constant mutability (the form remaining stable), as eternity, as a source of moral purity and purification, etc." (Pokrovsky 1989a, 90).

That Thoreau's naturalism is in the end objective idealism, and thus not naturalism at all, or at most a stunted naturalism, is evident in his attempts to provide a more precise even if mythological account of nature and spirit. One of the more outstanding features of material nature is its dynamism, and Thoreau saw that the processes of individual consciousness are no less dynamic: "Following his basic principle of congruence between the physical and the metaphysical worlds, between the domains of matter and spirit, the philosopher postulated a law that covered both these spheres of being; he called that law the law of rebirth, or of renewal" (Pokrovsky 1989a, 113). Thoreau saw in both matter and spirit a cyclical rhythm that expresses eternality and immortality. Pokrovsky cites the following passage from the final page of *Walden* to illustrate the point:

> Every one has heard the story which has gone the rounds of New England, of a strong and beautiful bug which came out of the dry leaf of an old table of apple-tree wood, which had stood in a farmer's kitchen for sixty years, first in Connecticut, and afterward in Massachusetts—from an egg deposited in the living tree many years earlier still, as appeared by counting the annual layers beyond it. . . . Who does not feel his faith in a resurrection and immortality strengthened by hearing of this?[12]

According to Pokrovsky's reading, time and space are inessential to Thoreau's principle of resurrection and revival. The dynamism of nature, natural change, is subsumed under an eternal cyclical process. The conceptual problem with this becomes clearer when one poses the question of the "directedness of movement," of progress and development, because an eternal cycle precludes developmental change:

> The fundamental contradiction of attempting to combine transcendentalism with natural science made it impossible for Thoreau to solve the problem of development. On the one hand, observation and study of the world of nature compelled him to accept the idea of progressive evolution of the species. On the other hand, because of his transcendentalist convictions, the philosopher imposed limitations, in advance, on evolution, for lying above the world of living nature was, in any case, a world of transcendent meaning opposed to any movement forward. Thus the Romantic world picture, incorporating turbulent world cataclysms, the growth of organic nature, etc., had an extremely metaphysical frame. (Pokrovsky 1989a, 115)

To read nature through a spiritual lens requires one set of principles, while to take seriously nature's materiality requires another, and in the long run, Pokrovsky argues, the two are incompatible.

Despite the philosophic inadequacy of Thoreau's transcendental naturalism, there are nevertheless fruitful and profound aspects of his conception of nature. The most outstanding of these, in Pokrovsky's view, concern the relation of nature to the human individual and the relation of both to society. We have already seen that Thoreau regarded nature as the condition of human perfectibility in that it is the embodiment of moral and aesthetic principles. This view, Pokrovsky says, involves significant philosophical ideas:

- Nature is not only an external objective reality but also a source of moral-aesthetic experiences.

- Nature requires an attentive and even worshipful attitude; violation of its harmony has a pernicious effect on human morality.
- Nature permits of contemplative assimilation only; man must neither subordinate nor change nature but merely infiltrate its system cautiously, becoming a silent and thoughtful observer of its harmonious structure. (Pokrovsky 1989a, 146)

The only proper relation of human being to nature, the only relation that does not distort either one and that enables the individual to absorb nature's lessons, is a harmonious interaction between them. Harmony is an aesthetic category, and it is the harmony, the beauty, of nature itself and human being itself that enables the harmony and beauty of their relation. There is a "correspondence," as Thoreau and other Romantics called it, between human being and nature. In this correspondence the human individual participates with the absolute in the experience of the symbolic meaning of nature, and nature is the vehicle of the relation between the individual and the absolute. Of particular importance in Pokrovsky's analysis is that in the triadic relation joining the individual, nature, and the absolute, society has no place. Society in fact is likely to be a threat to the natural harmony.

There are two crucial conceptions in this approach to the relation shared among nature, the individual, and society. One is that society has a pernicious effect on individuals and their relation to nature, and the other is that natural harmony is therapeutic with respect to society. Thoreau himself is clear enough in expressing the deleterious effect of social affairs on the harmony of his relation to nature. In his disgust with the compliance by the state government of Massachusetts with the Fugitive Slave Law, and with the citizenry for not caring, he puts the point forcefully:

> I walk toward one of our ponds; but what signifies the beauty of nature when men are base? We walk to lakes to see our serenity reflected in them; when we are not serene we go not to them. Who can be serene in a country where both the rulers and the ruled are without principle? The remembrance of my country spoils my walk. My thoughts are murder to the State, and involuntarily go plotting against her.[13]

At the same time, as the Walden experiment indicates, it is only by establishing a harmonious relation with nature that individuals are able to correct social evils. This is, Pokrovsky suggests, a "roundabout" approach to the solution of social problems in that it requires as its first stage an abandonment of society. In fact, he says, it is contradictory: society distorts the relation with nature so thoroughly that for Thoreau the very *thought* of his country spoils his walk; yet a harmony with nature must be sustained in order for social relations to be corrected.

Contradictory or not, built into the heart of Thoreau's transcendental naturalism is an interest in social affairs and a concern for social justice. Pokrovsky says that "Thoreau's sociopolitical philosophy rested on three pillars: humanist democratism, transcendental idealism, and consistent individualism," all of which are apparent in his criticisms of contemporary American society, in his conception of what an improved society would be, and in the stages of his understanding of how social progress can be achieved (Pokrovsky 1989a, 181–182). The substance of Thoreau's criticism of his own society is most clear, Pokrovsky feels, in his approach to property, to the division of labor, and in his assessment of business and a commercial culture. Each of these categories is a cornerstone of economic liberalism in general and of the Federalist program that had come to dominate North American society by the early decades of the nineteenth century. Adam Smith had argued that property, the division of labor, and the free market would give rise to a flowering of the individual, of society, and to the "progress of opulence." Thoreau could not have disagreed more. On moral grounds, Thoreau advocated a restriction on the accumulation of property, which Pokrovsky takes "to be one of the links that connected the worldviews of the Enlightenment and Romanticism" (Pokrovsky 1989a, 161).

The Enlightenment worldview Pokrovsky has in mind is the radical, already somewhat Romantic strain of a Jefferson and a Rousseau. And like his two great forebears, Thoreau was disturbed not only by the consequences of the pursuit of property but also by the impact of the division of labor. Pokrovsky notes that Rousseau, and even more so Friedrich Schiller, "had protested against the development of man into a one-sided creature, the child of a false civilization" that they took to be a consequence of the division of labor. Thoreau, too, was convinced that the division of labor was not conducive to personal growth, that it stunted individual development. This is one of the reasons self-development requires removing oneself, at least spiritually, from the mainstream of social life. The fact that so much of his society was inhospitable to the nobler aspects of human nature, that the human being is so fundamentally distorted by society, led Thoreau to talk of the "quiet desperation" of the lives of his contemporaries. Pokrovsky regards the concepts of desperation and despair as central to Thoreau's social thought, and following the American author Robert Dickens he reads them as Thoreau's expressions of alienation. Dickens had identified three forms of alienation in Thoreau's works: of the individual as producer, of the individual as consumer, and in the very processes of industrialization and capitalism. Pokrovsky adds three more: "alienation of man and society from nature, alienation of man from state institutions, and finally, alienation of man from his own essence" (Pokrovsky 1989a, 174).[14]

To mount this kind of criticism of the pursuit of private property and the division of labor is to attack the structural pillars of capitalism and the culture of business. Thoreau leaves no doubt about his disdain for business. Speaking in "Life Without Principle" of the California gold rush, Thoreau intends his comments to apply to the exercise and power of private capital in general:

> That so many are ready to live by luck, and so get the means of commanding the labor of others less lucky, without contributing any value to society! And that is called enterprise! I know of no more startling development of the immorality of trade, and all the common modes of getting a living. The philosophy and poetry and religion of such a mankind are not worth the dust of a puffball. The hog that gets his living by rooting, stirring up the soil so, would be ashamed of such company.[15]

And as if to summarize the point: "I think that there is nothing, not even crime, more opposed to poetry, to philosophy, ay, to life itself, than this incessant business."[16] Business, as Pokrovsky describes Thoreau's view, perverts society's spirit and degrades its morals, and with respect to capitalism in general, "its existence was unjustified, as it did not accord with the higher laws of the spirit" (Pokrovsky 1989a, 180). Thus, Pokrovsky says, "The Romantic protest against the leveling of individuality in society acquired a special significance in Thoreau's worldview, becoming in fact a protest against free enterprise" (Pokrovsky 1989a, 170).

With a criticism of existing social conditions as thoroughgoing as this, the question arises over the appropriate response. Unlike Marx, Thoreau did not see the source of a future alternative to bourgeois society in the working class. He was sympathetic to the conditions and aspirations of working people, but, in Pokrovsky's words, he thought them "too oppressed, downtrodden, and culturally backward . . . to be able to fight evil consciously" (Pokrovsky 1989a, 179). Pokrovsky notes that in his 1833 essay "Society," Thoreau wrote contemptuously of "the mass" and "the mob," giving the impression of a Hamiltonian antidemocratism. Pokrovsky argues, however, that these remarks were made on the occasion of a visit to a cattle show and that they refer not to working people generally but to the landowners and traders who attended such an event. "One goes to a cattle-show expecting to find many men and women assembled," Thoreau says, "and beholds only working oxen and meat cattle," thus expressing the same hostility to the petty bourgeoisie he would later repeat in "Life Without Principle." There he argues that one cannot look to the bourgeoisie, large or small, for a social alternative because they are the problem, and the wage laborer, as a result of his situation, "has not leisure for a true integrity day by day. . . . He has no time to be anything but a machine."

A positive social alternative is available not through the activity of any social forces, but through the individual. As for Thoreau himself, Pokrovsky notes three events that demarcate the stages of his own individual social struggle: the Walden experiment, his arrest for refusing to pay taxes as a protest against the invasion of Mexico, and his solidarity with John Brown. The common perception of Thoreau as an escapist and a pacifist stems from an emphasis on the first two events, but that perception, Pokrovsky suggests, is inconsistent with the third. It is also, as we have already seen, based on a misinterpretation of at least the first. Again, Thoreau's life in the woods was "antisocial only in outward form." As Pokrovsky puts it, "In leaving for the woods, the philosopher in no way negated by that fact man's social experiences and social nature. He wanted but one thing—a radical refashioning of man's consciousness, a cleansing of it from perverted forms of social ideology" (Pokrovsky 1989a, 185). Walden, then, was a form of social action, an overtly transcendentalist form in that its social import was a function of the moral purification of individual consciousness.

Karimsky too, following Pokrovsky, holds that "the Walden experience had a clearly expressed social meaning as part of a wider program." It represents the "internal (moral)" side of Thoreau's social activism in that it seeks "the preliminary moral self-purification of the individual" (Karimsky 1986, 293). The "external (political)" side received its first clear development in Thoreau's defense of nonviolent resistance. The principles that underlay the Walden experiment may have been well grounded in transcendentalist theory, but Pokrovsky suggests that "in trying to break the chain of reproduction at the point of individual consciousness, Thoreau used a patently weak weapon—propaganda of his personal philosophical conditions not based on any mass socioeconomic reforms" (Pokrovsky 1989a, 185–186). Thoreau may have been aware of the problem, and in any case the emergence of a specific social and political injustice, the Mexican War, called for a more active form of protest.

In the context of his argument in "Civil Disobedience" for nonviolent resistance to governmental authority, Thoreau offers a sketch of a political theory. The first paragraph of the essay expresses a hostility to government that has led to the prevalent perception of Thoreau as an anarchist. When he says that the motto "That government is best which governs least" leads naturally to the principle "That government is best which governs not at all," there is little doubt that Thoreau would prefer a situation in which individual moral development is so far advanced that government has no defensible function. That theoretical anarchism is further buttressed by Thoreau's conviction that even though people may not be prepared for no government, that is, even though some government may be necessary temporarily, it is nevertheless more likely that government will act unjustly than for the good: "The objections which have been brought against a standing army, and they are many and weighty, and deserve to prevail, may also at last be brought against a standing government. . . . The government itself, which is only the mode which the people have chosen to execute their will, is equally liable to be abused and perverted before the people can act through it."[17] Pokrovsky, however, emphasizes that the fact that "Civil Disobedience" also contains a political approach quite different from this denial to the state of any positive value, so that Thoreau's political theory, like so much of the rest of his philosophy, is characterized by a tension between opposing positions. Despite his general indictment of the legitimacy of government, Thoreau goes on to distance himself from "those who call themselves no-government men" by asking for "not at once no government, but *at once* a better government. Let every man make known what kind of government would command his respect," he goes on to say, "and that will be one step toward obtaining it." Even for Thoreau the anarchist there appears to be *some* form of government worthy of both respect and the effort required to bring it about.

At the same time, then, Thoreau regards government, like society generally, as an impediment to the more fundamental value of moral development and the individual's relation to nature and spirit—"remembrance of my country spoils my walk"—and as an embodiment of possible social relations well worth struggling for. This, Pokrovsky argues, is the tension between Thoreau the anarchist and Thoreau the democrat, a tension he thinks was never resolved:

> Thus we observe, on the one hand, a nihilism in relation to the state, and on the other, a desire to improve the existing forms of government. In other words, the main methodological contradiction of Thoreau's political critique was that he tried to combine two hardly compatible viewpoints. As a consistent transcendentalist, he could not recognize the existing state norms as legal, for true communities of men only arose, according to Thoreau, on the basis of transcendent spiritual links. As a sincere democrat, though, Thoreau believed that political realities called for a conscious struggle for the revival of democratic elements contained in state institutions rather than for an uncontrolled assault on them. (Pokrovsky 1989a, 172)

The genuinely democratic side of Thoreau, Pokrovsky argues, moved him to respond as he did to political injustice. He argues further that with respect to the form of response, the perception of Thoreau as a pacifist is as one-sided and inaccurate as the perception of him as an anarchist. The nonviolence espoused in "Civil Disobedience" was for Thoreau a natural outgrowth of the Walden experience. It contained the emphasis on individual moral development that was the heart of the Walden period, and it represented an activism that overcame the inefficacy of individual retreat. But Thoreau's development did not stop there. When John Brown and his small group attacked the federal arsenal at Harpers Ferry, Thoreau passionately defended both the goal of the attack and its means. He recognized in Brown's armed insurrection, Pokrovsky says, a triple virtue: "he roused the people from lethargy, demonstrated contempt for the government, and set a personal example of high heroism in doing all this" (Pokrovsky 1989a, 193–194). It appears that in Thoreau's view, when social evil reaches the degree of slavery, transcendentalist principles themselves imply the legitimacy, even necessity, of extraordinary action. This is the reason for his description of Brown as "A man of rare common-sense and directness of speech, as of action; a transcendentalist above all, a man of ideas and principles. . . ."[18] With respect to violent means of social struggle, Thoreau remarks, "I do not wish to kill nor to be killed, but I can foresee circumstances in which both these things would be by me unavoidable." And of Brown's insurrection in particular he says, "I think that for once the Sharpe's rifles and the revolvers were employed in a righteous cause. . . . The question is not about the weapon, but the spirit in which you use it."[19] *This* Thoreau was clearly not the consummate pacifist.

Thoreau's willingness to endorse violent social struggle was not, Pokrovsky argues, a deviation from his earlier views but a consistent development of a single democratic thread:

> The last stage in the evolution of Thoreau's worldview shows that, despite the transcendentalist basis of his views, his democratic convictions were extraordinarily strong. . . . Thoreau's adherence to nonviolence at the early stages of his evolution was explained by the absence of real social forces capable of changing the social system, probably more than by any other causes. But when those forces moved into the forefront, the philosopher decided to join them (Pokrovsky 1989a, 195–196).

On the basis of this kind of interpretation of the course of Thoreau's ideas and action, Pokrovsky sees him not so much as an individualist and recluse but primarily as a singular representative of the radical democratic strain in American thought and culture: "Despite the complexity and contradictions of Thoreau's sociophilosophic worldview, the democratic tendency in it always proved to be dominant and could never be repressed" (Pokrovsky 1989a, 196). This democratism, Pokrovsky argues, coupled with the Romantic conception of nature and the relation of nature and society, is precisely the basis of Thoreau's historical influence on Tolstoy, Gandhi, King, and the American counter-culture, as well as the basis of his continuing role as a theoretical source of contemporary ecologism and left-wing radicalism.

* * *

Pokrovsky's assessment of American transcendentalism differs in one significant respect from that of his Soviet colleagues. Most of them fully recognized transcendentalism's unique place in the development of

American thought and culture and its influence on subsequent technical philosophical and social processes. In general, however, they were inclined to see its philosophical idealism and utopianism as the sources of its ultimate failure. Transcendentalist social ideals, so Karimsky says, have never been realized in practice, and one suspects he would add that they never will. Sidorov echoes this point when he suggests that the goals of the American Romantics were unrealizable and that the philosophic result of the failure of transcendentalism was the simultaneous development of two lines of thought, each extending in its own way the Emersonian philosophy of action—Royce's absolute idealism and the pragmatism of Peirce, James, and Dewey.

Pokrovsky, by contrast, seems to find in transcendentalism more vital philosophic possibilities. We have seen that he regards the conception of nature as the source of ethical principles to be of particular moment, but he appears also to see a more general value in the transcendentalist social vision. He ends his essay "America Lost and Found" with the following passage:

> But when Thoreau, finding no way to break the narrow lethargy of his fellow citizens, climbed the steeple of the town hall and sounded the alarm bell, summoning all to rise in defense of the righteous cause of the emancipation of the slaves, the emancipation of man, we understand now that the troubled sounds of the alarm did not die away in the silence of a pacified Concord. In different places in America and at different times one hears again its uneasy, beckoning ring. It reaches us in the pages of the works of Emerson and Thoreau. Let us attend to it. (Pokrovsky 1986, 20)

Part II

American Philosophy in the Golden Age

Preamble

Despite the growing interest in early American philosophy, the vast majority of Soviet studies of the history of American thought deals with developments in the late nineteenth century and the first half of the twentieth century, American philosophy's so-called classical period or Golden Age. Most of these works have appeared since the end of the Second World War, though there are a few earlier examples. In what appears to be the first post-revolutionary discussion of American philosophy, P. P. Blonsky's *Contemporary Philosophy*, the two volumes of which appeared in 1918 and 1922 respectively, there are accounts of Royce's absolute idealism, pragmatism, and American neorealism. An article on James by V. F. Asmus was published in 1927, and a 1930 book titled *Contemporary Bourgeois Philosophy* includes an article by M. Shirvindt on American Neorealism. Conspicuously absent from the bibliographies of Soviet studies of twentieth century American philosophy are references to works that might have appeared as a result of Dewey's visit to the Soviet Union in the 1920s. In fact, very little discussion appears of any influence Dewey might have had on Soviet thinking during those years. One exception is a remark made by A. V. Gureeva in a study of Dewey's aesthetics, in which she notes that his pedagogical ideas "received some attention in our country." She cites in particular the foreword to a Russian language volume of Dewey's titled *Introduction to the Philosophy of Education*, written by the prominent educational theorist S. T. Shatsky, in which "pragmatist ideas in the area of education, in particular the idea of 'industrial schools,' received a positive evaluation" (Gureeva 1983, 6).[1]

It is worth noting, primarily for its contrast with what was to come, that Blonsky's 1918 and 1922 discussions of then contemporary American philosophy includes little in the way of critical commentary. Blonsky was interested more in simply describing contemporary trends, though he does so because he thinks that American philosophy is becoming increasingly important. "Until very recently," Blonsky says, "American philosophy had an insignificant role. In its past only two names stand out—Jonathan Edwards and Ralph Emerson," though he adds that there were others who are worthy of mention, including Samuel Johnson, Franklin, and Paine, and the transcendentalists Channing, Parker, and Thoreau (Blonsky 1922, 42). By the early twentieth century, however, certain American trends were to be included among the more important in contemporary Western philosophy. Blonsky suggests that the three most significant general philosophic alternatives of his day were various versions of scientific materialism, including dialectical materialism, absolute idealism in its German, British, and American varieties, and the philosophies of action, most notably pragmatism, realism, and the work of Bergson.

The two decades, roughly, following the end of the Second World War saw a virtual explosion of books, articles, and dissertations on recent American philosophy. Most of them deal with pragmatism, though quite a few in addition address American realism, personalism, and Royce's absolute idealism. If there is any, even a vague, sense on Americans' part of a general character of Soviet commentary on American philosophy, it is likely to have derived from works written during this period. Americans are inclined to the view that Soviet philosophical studies were exclusively ideological and, to the extent that philosophy is made to serve ideological ends, unsavory. That conception, if it is taken to apply generally to Soviet philosophical scholarship, is not a characterization but a caricature. And ironically enough it is in large measure the same conception that Soviet works of this period have of American philosophy, also a caricature. Soviet commentaries and analyses written in the late 1940s, the 1950s, and the early 1960s tend to stand out for their extraordinary hostility to recent American philosophy, regarding it as philosophically unsound and as a conceptual tool of indefensible American social, political, and military ends. It should be noted, however, that by the late 1960s Soviet studies of twentieth century American philosophy had become much less ideologically polemical, and that remains true of the vast majority of works written in the 1970s and 1980s. They tend to be no less critical of American thought, but the criticism is made on more technically philosophical grounds. Virtually all of the Soviet studies of classical American philosophy written since the mid-1940s in the end find it wanting for one reason or another.

This tends to apply as well to post-Soviet works. Yuri Melvil, for example, who was perhaps the leading Soviet specialist on American pragmatism and twentieth century American philosophy in general, continued to write until his death in 1993. In his last papers on William James, which we will discuss in the next chapter, Melvil is much more gentle than he had been earlier, and there is no trace of the political criticism so common in earlier analyses of pragmatism. Melvil remains critical, however, in that he continues to find in James an unacceptable degree of subjective idealism. And perhaps more importantly, Melvil continues to object to the pragmatists' theory of truth by arguing that it ignores the relation of knowledge to the objective traits of the world (Melvil 1992a; 1992b). This is in fact the most fundamental technical objection to much of

American philosophy to be found in Soviet and Russian analyses. Melvil makes it again in a review of the 1985 book *New Essays in American Metaphysics* (Melvil 1989).

The ideological component of some Soviet criticism stems in part from the view that American philosophy is related in some way to American society in general and to capitalism in particular. Soviets, like some others, argued that uniquely American philosophic ideas, pragmatism in particular, are philosophic expressions of an "American form of life." In his otherwise descriptive account Blonsky suggests that "pragmatism and realism represent an interesting and typical embodiment of the spirit of 'Americanism'" (Blonsky 1922, 51). More recently, A. S. Bogomolov, noting that pragmatism "was the philosophical 'commodity' with which the United States first entered the international market place of ideas," finds it to be the fulfillment of what McCosh had earlier called for—not another system of the Universe, but something that embodies the typically Yankee "powers of keen practical observation and ingenuity" (Bogomolov 1974, 36).[2] Melvil, probably the most interesting of Soviet specialists on pragmatism because his work was the most extensive and because it spans the years from the mid-1950s to the early 1990s, also finds in pragmatism something distinctly American. In one of his first books, *American Pragmatism*, published in 1957, Melvil, in the context of a discussion of James's equation of truth with utility, argued that though pragmatism did not invent the rejection of objective truth, the specific form in which it casts this rejection relates it to the conditions of American life. Success, he said, is the fundamental principle of pragmatism, and "success determines ends, criteria, and the essence of any activity and any idea." This is fundamentally connected to American life, Melvil argued, since the mainspring of the "American way of life" is the pursuit of private profit, "success" expressed in dollars. American society, according to this view, is one in which all aspects of life are understood in relation to success defined financially, and thus a philosophy that has as its fundamental principle the achievement of individual success is more suited to American society than most others would be (Melvil 1957a, 42–43).

A reading of American society as determining its values and social relations through their "cash value" is to understand it in terms of the means and ends of capitalism, so that to see pragmatism as an expression of those means is also to see it as intimately connected to the ends. Bogomolov made the point explicitly when he said that "pragmatism became as influential as it did because it reflects *subjectively* the very reduction of truth to utility that is found in the *objective* reduction by capitalist society of all social relations to a commodity or cash value" (Bogomolov 1974, 37). Under the extremely tense conditions of the Cold War, especially through the 1950s, the association of pragmatism with capitalism meant that it was also an expression of the interests of the American capitalist class in both its internal exploitation of American labor and its international imperialist designs. Thus at the time Melvil, for example, would write that pragmatism "is the philosophy with which bourgeois ideologies attempt to poison the consciousness of the working class, deprive it of a revolutionary theory, and instill in it the spirit of compromise and class collaboration. . . . In reality pragmatism in both theoretical and political respects is one of the most reactionary philosophical positions in the epoch of imperialism" (Melvil 1957b, 38).

This assessment of recent American philosophy and pragmatism in particular was a complex phenomenon that characterized a specific period of Soviet commentary. In chapter 4 we will look more closely at its claims, its causes, and the arguments that were offered in its defense. It is crucial to realize, however, that beginning roughly in the late 1960s the tenor of Soviet analysis tended to change, primarily in that the earlier ideological concern either disappeared altogether or received much less emphasis. There were, of course, exceptions to this claim. As recently as 1983, for example, one could still hear echoes of Melvil's earlier view: Pragmatism "is a variety of subjective idealism in philosophy and aesthetics, and is one of the most reactionary philosophic trends in the epoch of imperialism" (Gureeva 1983, 5–6). But by the late 1960s this sort of claim had become the rare exception rather than the rule. Melvil himself, from his extensive study of Peirce in 1968 to his last comments on pragmatism and James, abandoned this approach. And other Soviet commentators were also much more circumspect in their treatment of the relation of American philosophy to American society and to capitalism. A good illustration is Karimsky's approach to American naturalism. Though he thinks that there are general characteristics of naturalism that give it a distinctly bourgeois flavor, Karimsky makes a point of saying that "it is not appropriate to regard all bourgeois philosophy as an apologetic for imperialism simply because it is bourgeois" (Karimsky 1972, 37).

With the virtual disappearance of an overt ideological emphasis, more technical philosophic concerns become dominant in Soviet discussions of American philosophy, though in fact they had been there all along. The fundamental philosophic criticism that emerged in Soviet analyses was that all the prominent strains of twentieth century America philosophy, with the possible exception of some forms of naturalism, consist of one or another version of philosophic idealism, including the work of Santayana and others who described themselves as materialists.

The tenor and rationale of this assessment is evident in N. S. Yulina's account of the background of the metaphysical dimension of classical American thought. Yulina argues that twentieth century American metaphysics has tended to take one or another form of empiricism, positivism, or anti-intellectualism, the roots of which she finds in two traits of the American intellectual legacy: the general cultural tendency to value practice over theory, and the process by which American philosophy overcame European absolute idealism and its own transcendentalism. Twentieth century American metaphysics developed out of nineteenth century adaptations of European philosophy, the first great example of which was the transcendentalist transformation of German speculative idealism on the basis of the traditional American emphasis on practice. By the late nineteenth century, American philosophy came to be dominated by the problem of the relation between science and religion, and the major philosophic systems of the period, Yulina suggests, combined a Hegelian historicism, evolutionism, and a religious understanding of human being. The influence of Darwinism and American practicalism engendered a philosophic response in the attempt to strengthen speculative philosophy, one illustration of which was the founding of the *Journal of Speculative Philosophy*. Despite its differences from the general American temper, the adaptation of Hegelianism "was a progressive step for philosophy in the United States during this period" (Yulina 1978a, 38). Its significance is most evident in Royce, who in his appropriation of Hegelianism also crystallized a feature of American philosophy that was to remain prominent long after the overt Hegelianism was discarded. On its Hegelian side, "metaphysics in the United States at the time was monistic and absolutist, its problematics were cosmological, ethical and social, its methods were rationalist and speculative" (Yulina 1978a, 38). The Americanization of Hegelianism, however, was influenced, Yulina says, by the fact that though social and political thought at the time was well developed, social science was not, which meant that metaphysicians could readily paint a picture of "being" as an absolute unity: "A faith in divine providence, in progress, and a social optimism inclined American philosophers to portray being as an absolute harmony, in which the many came together as one" (Yulina 1978a, 39). It was this "faith," which Yulina regards as a cultural and philosophic expression of a religious faith, that influenced subsequent American thought. Pragmatism, Neorealism and Naturalism appeared as responses to absolute idealism, though usually not as a rejection of its "religious" component.

The "new philosophy" represented by these schools of thought had its critical and constructive sides. Critically, it rejected the "monarchical" in philosophy and in so doing abandoned the traditional philosophic dichotomies of substance and accident, mind and matter, and many others. On its constructive side it called for a reconstruction in philosophy, for pluralism, for a "freedom of inquiry" and an "equality of principles." But this "revolution in philosophy" was an illusion, Yulina argues, since the attempt to make philosophy more concrete itself contained an illusion: concrete analysis always rests on specific theoretical premises, she suggests, and thus on some general metaphysical position. Consequently, the "new philosophy" could not reject metaphysics altogether but only replace an old one with a new one. And since their "new philosophy" never freed itself from the older attachment to religion, either in the explicit forms found in Peirce, James, or Whitehead or in the general presumption of the ultimate possibility of a harmonic reconciliation of differences so prominent in Dewey, the parameters of a new metaphysics were fairly limiting. When pushed to their logical limits, Yulina argues, pragmatism, neorealism, positivism, and the other prominent forms of twentieth century American thought turn out to be either subjective idealism or a Platonist variant of objective idealism (Yulina 1978a, 47–48, 283).

As we have already seen, as recently as 1989 Melvil was making similar judgments about more contemporary American metaphysics. Though no longer explicitly concerned with religious questions as earlier American metaphysicians had been, contemporary metaphysical writers have been taking for granted the critique of the modernist epistemology of Wittgenstein, Feyerabend, Kuhn Rorty, Quine, and others. "The essential premise of many of the trends of contemporary Western philosophy," Melvil says," is the thesis that in knowledge and action we deal not with the world itself, or the 'world-in-itself,' but with the world for us, or, in other words, with the world having significance or meaning for mankind. . . [The] new metaphysics . . . effects the replacement of the objective world as the subject of study by a conception of the world, or its perception, or a picture of the world in human consciousness (Melvil 1989, 142). Although there is something of a point here, Melvil thinks, this subjectivist move away from an interest in the world's objective traits continues the same shortcoming that has been at the heart of the bulk of American philosophy throughout the nineteenth and twentieth centuries. It is appropriate, he says, to say that the world is dependent on human conceptions of it and on human action only in an ecological sense. The relations of people to their environment are so essential that what people do can determine the nature of that environment. But this is the extent to which one can reasonably speak of such dependence. American metaphysicians, however, go further: "The fundamental mistake of the interpretation consists in contrasting science as a cultural phenomenon with the capacity of science to explain the role and significance of human culture itself, and the special place occupied by science as the form of the reception and existence of objective theoretical knowledge of the world and of man" (Melvil 1989, 147).

From a Soviet and to some degree post-Soviet point of view, to say that American philosophy is in the end idealist is to identify a defect. Soviet philosophers had traditionally been advocates of dialectical materialism, and many of their philosophic criticisms of American thought are the result of American divergence from dialectical materialist theses. An appreciation of Soviet criticism requires that we bear in mind the constellation of ideas that constitutes the dialectical materialist outlook with respect to nature, knowledge, and human being: nature is objective, which is to say that some or all of natural phenomena have some or all of their traits independently of our thoughts about them, and nature consists of events, processes, and developments that are characterized by lawful regularities; the objective and lawful traits of nature are knowable; knowledge is a reflection in consciousness of objective reality; the process of inquiry, and thus the inquirer, is invariably conditioned and perspectival—it is conditioned by, among other things, class interests, our purposes and intentions, values, the dominant ideology of the culture, our knowledge to date, and so on; human interaction with the rest of nature, including cognition, is creative and active; human beings are fully natural, and human life, unlike most other natural phenomena, is characterized by social interactions that are themselves objective and lawful, that is, defined by laws.

For a host of reasons, some of them more justifiable than others, dialectical materialism has virtually never been taken seriously in the West, including by the majority of Western Marxists, and by the end of the Soviet period a growing number of Marxist philosophers were reevaluating its central concepts. One reason for this has been a Soviet philosophic tendency, though there have been exceptions, to insist on the truth of dialectical materialism rather than to reflect critically on its principles or to use them to advance philosophic inquiry.[3] As a consequence, ideas that may themselves be exceedingly problematic are nevertheless routinely employed as the measure against which to assess other philosophic positions. An example is the claim that knowledge is a reflection of reality, a proposition that plays a prominent role in Soviet criticisms of pragmatism. They have rejected pragmatist theories of knowledge and truth because they have abandoned this aspect of knowledge. Such a rejection, however, rests on the adequacy of a "reflection" theory of knowledge, a theory that is dubious at best. The metaphorical notion of knowledge as "reflection" requires the corresponding metaphor of the knower as "reflector," the mind as the mirror of nature. The problem with this is that even if some sense can be given to the metaphor, there is every reason to think that the mirror by its nature can never be very well polished. Whatever else can be said for or against them, philosophers and philosophic trends for over a century have been demonstrating this in a myriad of ways—from Kierkegaard and Nietzsche to Wittgenstein and Kuhn, from pragmatism to deconstructionism and anti-foundationalism. All of them indicate the necessarily perspectival and conditioned character of inquiry and knowledge, which in turn renders the metaphor of "reflection" virtually senseless.

Interestingly enough, however, the dialectical materialist tradition also embraces the claim that the cognitive process and its products are invariably conditioned and perspectival, a claim made by Marx, Engels, and Lenin. It would appear, then, that dialectical materialism is internally inconsistent. Soviet philosophers tried to resolve this problem by arguing that the conditionality of inquiry does not mean that knowledge is not reflection, but simply that it is never absolute. Knowledge is partial, relative to the conditions and perspectives of the inquirer. However, even if it is true that knowledge is necessarily partial and relative, this neither requires nor rescues the "reflection" theory, though it would require the claims that nature has objectively determinate traits and that the conditionality of inquiry does not preclude knowledge of them.

A philosophically intriguing point emerges here, and I emphasize it for a specific reason. The habit of ignoring dialectical materialism may too quickly incline us to dismiss analyses and arguments made on its basis, in the manner of many Soviet criticisms of classical American philosophy. Of course the criticisms must be evaluated, but it would be a mistake simply to *assume* their inadequacy, in part because the kernel of the dialectical materialist position is not absurd, as philosophers in the West have tended to think and as many in Eastern Europe and the Soviet Union became increasingly prone to suggest. If we jettison the reflection theory, at least in its more traditional form, the following four propositions remain as describing a general approach to nature and knowledge: (1) natural phenomena have objectively determinate traits; (2) the traits of natural phenomena are knowable; (3) the process of inquiry is necessarily conditioned and perspectival; and (4) human interaction with nature, cognitive or otherwise, is active and creative.

This particular set of propositions becomes interesting when considered in the context of the current issue of postmodernism. Postmodernism in all of its versions convincingly argues for the third and fourth propositions, on the basis of which it rejects the first and second. Modernism, on the other hand, assumed the first and the second, and implicitly rejected the third and fourth in its search for the foundations of knowledge and its location of the foundations in rational or empirical reflection. The possibility remains, however, that both sides have overstated the case. The modernist tradition has not, and I think cannot, answer the many arguments in support of the third and fourth propositions and thus has no grounds to posit a foundation of knowledge where and in the ways it traditionally has. But postmodernism tends to make a comparable mistake by rejecting the first and second propositions on the basis of the third and fourth. The postmodernist argument at bottom is that since objective knowledge of nature is impossible, because the cognitive process is conditional and creative, knowledge of the objective traits of nature is impossible; or to push it further, there is no point even to attribute objectively determinate traits to nature, so that, as I heard an advocate of this position claim at a conference not long ago, "The world is whatever we describe it as." This, however, is a non sequitur. From the claim that objective knowledge (reflection) is impossible, it does not follow that knowledge of the objectively determinate traits of nature is impossible, let alone that there are no such traits.

The inadequacy of both sides of the modernist-postmodernist debate suggests the possibility that the answer is, so to speak, to have it both ways, that is, that all four propositions are true. Such a claim would require an extended demonstration, which is beyond the scope of our present concern, though steps in that direction have been taken.[4] In any case, this issue indicates that the kernel of ideas that has traditionally been at the heart of dialectical materialism may not be so inadequate after all, other problems notwithstanding. If so, it may prove to be an interesting perspective for a critical assessment of American philosophy. This may be particularly true for pragmatism, given the extent to which pragmatism has been appropriated in postmodernist arguments.

Soviet philosophers were interested in all facets of twentieth century American philosophy. We will restrict our attention, however, to those figures and movements in classical American philosophy that have proven to be the most influential and enduring: pragmatism, Royce, Whitehead, Santayana, and naturalism.

4

PRAGMATISM

Peirce, James, Dewey, and Recent Pragmatism

THE philosophically significant feature of pragmatism is its recasting of metaphysical and epistemological issues and, as a result, its range of approaches to intellectual concerns from social and political theory to ethics, aesthetics, and pedagogy, on the basis of human action. In this respect it stands in a long line of influential American ideas that have emphasized action, from Jonathan Edwards through the American expression of Scottish "common sense" philosophy in McCosh (Melvil 1968, 480). In fact, one study suggests, pragmatism is the culmination of this line of thought in its American version:

> Pragmatism, then, is the final stage in the evolution of the idea of a philosophy of action. In comparison with the poetic basis of the transcendentalists' free thought and the metaphysical constructs of Royce's principle of moral loyalty, the pragmatists' was undoubtedly a step forward, in that by their thesis of practical faith they attempted to impart to the methodology of the philosophy of action a sobriety with respect to its worldview and its determination of final ends. (Sidorov 1989, 136)

If pragmatism is related to earlier American philosophy, it is no less related to other philosophic developments that arose at the same time, and it is a product in part of processes at work in American society and culture and the West generally in the late nineteenth century. Melvil notes that the theme of human action had begun to generate philosophic interest as early as classical German philosophy and that it had received a materialist treatment in Marx. By the late nineteenth century neo-Kantians are interested, and under the influence of Darwinism attention was paid to human action and adaptation to environing conditions. In the hands of such figures as Nietzsche and Bergson, knowledge became related to the interests of the knower. This new conception of knowledge and truth as related to the interests of the subject "received its full development and completion in pragmatism" (Melvil 1974, 73–77). That the concept of action became a prominent theme across so many otherwise different conceptual outlooks suggests to Melvil a relation between philosophy and broader social processes in Europe and America. The turn to action in the late nineteenth century is not surprising, he argues, considering that the development of industry and transportation and changes in the political, demographic, and cultural character of life had, in the course of two or three generations, thoroughly transformed people's lives. Philosophy could not overlook this and could not help but approach action "not only as a fundamental factor of human existence in the world, but also as a factor having an impact on the world itself" (Melvil 1974, 77).

The obvious efficacy of human action in material and social life may help to account for the widespread philosophic interest in it, but alone it does very little to explain why pragmatism became as influential as it did. For that one must turn to the character of American life, to its cultural traditions, and to the stage of the development of capitalism in America at the turn of the century. "If there is anywhere," Melvil says, "that the themes of action and success could have taken hold of a philosopher's thinking, this would have to have been in America—a country where enterprise, action, and success are valued above all other goods, and where abstract speculations generate little interest. . . . [A]bout the relation of pragmatism to the American form of life there can be little doubt" (Melvil 1974, 78).

Pragmatism and Bourgeois Interests

Virtually all Soviet era discussions of pragmatism addressed its relation to an American form or way of life and, by extension, to the interests of a ruling bourgeois class, though the treatment is not uniform from one period of Soviet commentary to another, nor among the many specialists at any given time. As we have already seen, Melvil in an earlier work reads the pragmatist conception of truth as "success" or "what works" as a reflection of the role of success as a fundamental value in American culture. Melvil's view was not that no relation exists between truth and usefulness, since truth—by which he means the correspondence between the content of an idea, proposition, or theory and its object—really is useful. The curious thing about pragmatism is not that it relates truth to use but that it equates them. Even eighteenth century bourgeois revolutionaries such as Holbach and Diderot had warned against this mistake because they recognized that what was valuable for some, for example religion, was harmful to others. If the problem with identifying truth and success or usefulness was clear enough to earlier bourgeois thinkers, the fact that it was so readily accepted by pragmatists suggests a relation to something distinct about America (Melvil 1957a, 41–42). More recently Sidorov made a similar point: "The methodological reference point of the philosophy of pragmatism was the illusion of the absolute importance for people of practical success, an illusion that is being continuously reinforced . . . by the ideological stereotype of the 'American Dream'" (Sidorov 1989, 93). We should note, too, that Melvil was advancing the same criticism of the pragmatist conception of truth in his last writings on James in 1992. There—although we will see later in the section on James that Melvil was more generous in spirit than he was in his earlier writings—he still regarded the theory of truth as mistaken in its identification of truth with usefulness. James's mistake, he says in the later work, was that he conflates two importantly different things: that which justifies our regarding a concept to be true, that is, its usefulness in practice, with the content of a true idea (Melvil 1992, 13). In his last work, then, Melvil continues the technical criticism, but gone is the older inclination to relate its shortcomings to aspects of American culture.

Even earlier, however, Soviet philosophers did not regard American society, or any society, as homogenous in its values and interests so long as it embodies class divisions in its relations of production, so that the differences in classes and corresponding class interests must be taken into account in the relation of pragmatism to American life. Thus the question of a connection between pragmatism and specifically bourgeois concerns and interests comes up. In one sense, a claim that pragmatism expresses bourgeois interests is a specific instance of the general historical materialist thesis that the prevalent and dominant ideas of any society are the ideas of its ruling class. But Soviet philosophers were inclined to be much more specific about the connection. Certain central epistemological and ontological ideas of pragmatism, they argued, either embody bourgeois values and principles or have implications that support ruling-class social and political designs. By treating ideas exclusively as instruments, which is to say, by denying to ideas and knowledge any "objective content," and in rejecting a correspondence theory of truth, pragmatism is pushed to an ontological conception in which the objects and processes of the world are defined in terms of their roles in our actions and purposes. Peirce's operationalism construes the whole meaning of an idea of an object in terms of the object's effects to a large extent on us; James defines material and ideal objects as cut from a neutral pure experience, depending on the activity, interests, and purposes of the individual; and Dewey describes objects as acquiring their traits by virtue of a situation, that is, in relation to the individual in the situation.

This general pragmatist conception of the world and of knowledge is related to bourgeois values and interests in several ways, as a result primarily of its denial of objectivity to the world and its emphasis on the individual. In one of his early works Melvil said that one of the distinctive characteristics of the bourgeois world view is its subjectivism, by which he means that its most fundamental questions concern the self. Questions such as Who am I, What kind of thing am I, and Where do I fit into the world are for bourgeois thought more central than questions about the nature of the world of which I am a part. Pragmatism embodies just this individualism, Melvil suggested, in its willingness to understand the world in terms of its relation to the individual (Melvil 1957b, 76–77). Furthermore, and perhaps more seriously, the denial of the objectivity of the world not only embodies bourgeois values but serves bourgeois interests. Sidorov, for example, says that pragmatism in the end defends an epistemological, methodological, and axiological pluralism, "the actual content of which serves not a striving for knowledge of the truth, but rather simply a realization in its many forms of class interest" (Sidorov 1989, 137–138). Over thirty years earlier Melvil was more specific about this. If knowledge is devoid of objective content and if the objects and processes of the world acquire their traits wholly in relation to their effects *on* people, or in relation to the purposes and interests *of* people, then the world must be conceived as essentially plastic, amenable to human effort. Melvil would argue that the world is indeed plastic in that human activity affects it and brings about new traits of objects and processes, but for pragmatism "the world is *absolutely* plastic and compliant to our will. . . . [F]or pragmatists to speak of the world as existing independently of human activity would be as absurd as Berkeley speaking of things that no one perceives" (Melvil 1957b, 79). A view of the world as capable of being bent to one's will, he argues, serves bourgeois interests very well, since it means that the ruling class need not be concerned with such matters as objective social laws and conditions but can simply do as it pleases. Pragmatist ontology and epistemology embody a degree of volunteerism, a faith in the ability to make the world over to suit one's interests, which is in turn conducive to the activity of a class the primary interest of which is to dominate others, to subordinate the world to itself. A similar point was made in a more recent study of Dewey: "If the truth of our knowledge is established by its situational use, then truth is nothing but a moment in a continuous process of the reconstruction and enrichment of experience. In relation to science, this gives rise to an extreme agnosticism, while in relation to politics it gives rise to adventurism and unscrupulousness" (Filatova 1985, 10).

Pragmatism and Imperialism

Pragmatism, then, was understood to embody bourgeois values and to accord with bourgeois interests. If pragmatism is especially suited to bourgeois interests, and if bourgeois interests involve imperialist designs, then pragmatism is a philosophy of imperialism, or so it was common to argue, particularly in works from the 1940s and 1950s. Melvil took this view in his book on American pragmatism, itself based on lecturers delivered at Moscow State University in the mid-1950s. Pragmatism, he said, had become "almost the official philosophy of the American imperialist bourgeoisie," and he thought Dewey the most dangerous of the pragmatists: "John Dewey is one of the most negative figures of the ideological reaction of the epoch of imperialism. For more than sixty years he poisoned the consciousness of the American people with his reactionary ideas. . . . Dewey's instrumentalism expresses the union of idealistic philosophy with the reactionary policies of the imperialist bourgeoisie, transforming philosophy into an ideological instrument of monopoly capital" (Melvil 1957a, 5, 64).

Several reasons explain the frequency of this sort of polemical attack on pragmatism. Joining with the claim that pragmatism expresses bourgeois values and interests are also two historical factors, one having to do with the conditions in which pragmatism developed and another with conditions in which the Soviet evaluation was made. Melvil notes that the late nineteenth century was a period that saw the Paris Commune, the First International, the heightening of social antagonisms, the growth of proletarian class consciousness and the worker's movement, and the spread of Marxism, all of which disturbed the ruling class's confidence in the smooth evolution and progress of bourgeois society. This is also the period of the transition from "free" competitive capitalism to imperialism (Melvil 1957a, 6–7). It was the latter development that more than anything conditioned the popularity of pragmatism, which arose, Melvil says elsewhere, not so much from a unique "American form of life" but from the nature of imperialism as a decaying and moribund capitalism (Melvil 1957b, 39). With the successful prosecution of its "splendid little war," the United states had driven Spain out of the Caribbean and the Philippines and had assumed Rudyard Kipling's "White Man's Burden." Following the victory over Spain in "history's first imperialist war," Melvil says, the American monopolistic bourgeoisie needed "a typically American philosophy that could serve as the theoretical underpinning and justification of its form of life, its form of thought, and its policy." Pragmatism, with its view of the world as ready and needing to be made over in the active pursuit of one's interests, was suited to the purpose (Melvil 1968, 339).

It is certainly true that at the turn of the century the United States' ruling circles embarked on the process of empire building, and it is also true that pragmatism gained its popularity at the same time. Whether the two developments were as closely linked as Melvil and his colleagues suggested in their earlier writings is much less obvious, as they themselves might also say today. In any case, the virulence and polemics of the attacks on pragmatism as an imperialist philosophy had as much if not more to do with the international climate of the post–Second World War period than with any relation between pragmatism and imperialism at the turn of the century. Three factors contributed to the Soviet approach. The first was the Cold War and the corresponding tension in Soviet-American relations. Soviet intellectuals in the 1950s, like their American counterparts, saw themselves as enmeshed in a life and death struggle. To the extent that pragmatism could be identified as a distinctly American intellectual movement, the dispute with it was not simply a scholarly disagreement among academics but an ideological component of a struggle of world historic proportions. Second, the Soviet evaluation of pragmatism in this period reflected the struggle being waged between pragmatists and American Marxists, who were under a vicious attack from Senator McCarthy, the House Un-American Activities Committee, and at every level of American society and culture. Some pragmatists played a less than salutary role in this wave of anti-Communism. The case of Barrows Dunham offers one example. In the early 1950s Dunham, then Chair of the Philosophy Department at Temple University, became a victim of the anti-Communist witchhunt and was subsequently dismissed from his position. A few years earlier his first book, *Man Against Myth,* was being prepared for publication. Dunham and the publisher had procured from Dewey a short comment praising the book, and Dewey's remark was to appear on the jacket. After some prompting by Albert Barnes, Dewey changed his mind and in an attempt to disassociate himself from Dunham tried to have the comment removed from the book. At the same time the prominent and influential student of Dewey, Sidney Hook, was advocating in print the dismissal of Communists from teaching positions.[1] For American Marxists under these conditions, pragmatism was not as much a philosophic alternative as it was an enemy that represented the ruling circles bent on destroying them. They responded with analyses of pragmatism that related it to bourgeois and imperialist interests. Soviet academics came to the aid of their American comrades and drew many of their criticisms from the writings of American Marxists.[2]

Finally, the criticisms of pragmatism during this period display a remarkable confidence on the part of Soviet academics that they were in possession of *the* solution to philosophic, economic, social, and political problems. They displayed little, if any, hesitation or doubt with respect to their own philosophic position, a feature of Soviet philosophy which, combined with the larger political struggle, tended to replace inquiry with dogmatic insistence. Over the years this confidence did not wane, though as international tensions relaxed it led less often to the harsh ideological attacks that characterized the earlier work. And it is worth noting that developments in the Soviet Union since 1985 have undermined the traditional Soviet certainty. Not only have overtly anti-Marxist thinkers such as Alexander Tsipko emerged, as have social democrats like Kagarlitsky, but even those who continue to think along more traditional Marxist-Leninist lines had a sense of the dangers inherent in their own ideas. Sidorov, for example, earlier noted with approval Dewey's concern that the rationalist, speculative tradition in philosophy has had harmful consequences for our understanding of social relations in that it rests on a priori conceptions of nature, society, and human nature, adding that just this problem appeared in socialist society and government. Now, Sidorov says, "The Soviet people have to pay a dear price for the mistakes and crimes of the past, committed by those who, with their so-called Marxist-Leninist style of party, soviet, and popular rule, usurped dictatorial power" (Sidorov 1989, 126–127).

Pragmatism and Idealism

Notwithstanding the overt ideological character of the Soviet critique of pragmatism during the 1950s, commentaries from the late 1940s to the end of the Soviet period and beyond share a core of distinctly philosophic valuations, most of them negative. On the positive side, Melvil suggests that pragmatism's most significant contribution is that it introduced into the theory of knowledge the view that the knowing subject is also a subject with interests, and that these two features of human beings cannot be divorced from one another (Melvil 1974, 78). And Sidorov finds the earliest pragmatist association of action and knowledge noteworthy. Pragmatism represents "a genuinely new and decisive step forward in the development of the methodology of knowledge in bourgeois philosophy. Peirce's ideas are the basis for working out a nonclassical, nonspeculative, *active* form of rational knowledge" (Sidorov 1989, 105). But whatever the valuable possibilities might have been, pragmatism failed to develop them in acceptable directions.

Pragmatism's fundamental flaw, in the Soviet critique, is that in the end it has no way to account for the objectively determined traits of the world and for our knowledge of them, a problem rooted in the treatment of ideas solely as instruments. If an idea, and therefore knowledge, is not in some way "about" the world, then we are pushed either to a Kantian chasm between the world of experience and the world in itself, or to the view that the world *is* what we make it in experience. Pragmatists rejected the Kantian position as another of the many artificial dichotomies generated by traditional philosophy, they were not content with the subjectivist and idealist bent of the alternative, and they were aware of the inadequacies of traditional forms of philosophic materialism. The pragmatist response was to attempt to construct a "third line" between materialism and idealism and to overcome the traditional dualism of spirit and matter, subject and object, that had led to skepticism. The Soviet criticism, at bottom, is that this attempt fails and that the best pragmatism can be is a novel form of subjective idealism.

Dewey was familiar with the charge of subjectivism, and he explicitly denied it, and James too acknowledged an independent determinate reality.[3] The question remains, however, whether their philosophic analyses are equal to the task of reconciling pragmatist conceptions of knowledge and truth with a recognition of an objective world. Soviets tended to argue that it does not accomplish this and that both James and Dewey, as Melvil puts it, essentially hold that reality is whatever we determine it to be, though they attempt to avoid that result. Dewey's approach, in Melvil's view more sophisticated than James's, turns on articulating a "third line," an alternative to materialism and idealism, but his attempt to supersede traditional dualism ends up confusing matter and consciousness, conflating material and ideal phenomena. He argues, for example, that the distinction between matter and spirit is a historical and social construct. Melvil agrees with this point but suggests that from it Dewey draws the wholly false conclusion that concepts therefore have no cognitive meaning, which is to say, he rejects the objective existence of matter and its relation to ("reflection in") consciousness: "The sophism of Dewey's reasoning is that he illegitimately identifies the question of the historical origin of the distinction between mental and physical labor with the question of the difference between matter and consciousness and their relation to one another, that is, with the basic question of philosophy" (Melvil 1957b, 55). In other words Dewey in the end identifies matter with consciousness, so that his "third line" becomes a form of idealism.

Pragmatism's ontological idealism is related directly to its epistemology, specifically to the treatment of ideas and knowledge as tools. As ideas become instruments or weapons, they lose objective content, which Melvil has argued is a perversion of the meaning of scientific theories, laws, and concepts (Melvil 1957b, 98–99). According to his view, pragmatism is replete with words and concepts for which the meaning either radically changes, or worse, equivocates. Concepts such as truth, experience, logic, science, knowledge, thought, thing, law, and reality all lose the meaning they ordinarily have. For Melvil, it sounds as if a pragmatist is using ordinary words in ordinary ways but actually means something entirely different by them, so that it is often impossible to divine the meaning. "A particular virtuosity in the use of words with which no determinate meaning can be associated was achieved by John Dewey. But the source of this 'art' is in Peirce" (Melvil 1968, 43). In Peirce's hands, for example, a "natural law" may mean the existing and persistent relations among things, it may mean God's ideas (5.107), and it may mean the "habits of things."[4] Similarly, Peirce will say that reality is that which exists independently of what anyone thinks it is, that it is objective, but then he will say that reality is simply what opinion in the long run takes it to be, which means that it is dependent on human consciousness (Melvil 1968, 44). Equivocation like this makes it nearly impossible to read a consistent position in pragmatism, so that while it embodies a subjective idealism it seems also to be a form of skepticism. The central idea of pragmatism, Melvil has said, is the epistemologically agnostic view that our knowledge cannot penetrate to the essential nature of the reality of which we are a part: "In this respect pragmatism, including the pragmatism of Peirce, was a continuation of the agnostic course in modern idealist philosophy from Berkeley and Hume through Kant" (Melvil 1968, 252).

The most detrimental consequences of pragmatism's reconstruction of the meaning of words and concepts, however, is its understanding of the relation of knowledge and action, of theory and practice. The fundamental problem is that pragmatism makes it impossible to have an adequate understanding of the way theory and knowledge are related to practice and action, because by collapsing the former into the latter, theory and knowledge are essentially eliminated. According to pragmatism, the purpose of thought is to guide human behavior, to direct its activity in changing conditions. But the classical pragmatists persistently avoided the question over whether thought provides true knowledge of reality. Such is the deeply contradictory position of pragmatism, contradictory because while correctly emphasizing the active character of thought and its significance for practical activity, pragmatism in fact rejects the necessary condition under which thought is able to guide action successfully: the relatively accurate reflection of objective reality, the objective situation in which people must act (Melvil 1968, 254).

In an earlier essay Melvil argued that the pragmatist distortion of knowledge reaches its apogee in its theory of truth. If we do not acknowledge that our ideas and concepts have objective content, and thus if we reject the view that truth is the correspondence of our ideas and conceptions with objective reality, then the only remaining possibility is a subjectivist and relativist conception of truth. As in its approach to knowledge, there is something to be said for pragmatism's understanding of truth: "Despite its antiscientific character, the pragmatist theory of truth is not absolutely groundless. Pragmatists in this case exaggerated and absolutized one of the actual traits of scientific knowledge—its connection with practical, expedient human activity, in short, the usefulness of truth" (Melvil 1957b, 105). But the relativism of the identification of truth with use is clear when we remember the always-remaining question of to whom should a given idea be useful. That certain religious myths were useful to the Church in its struggle against a Copernicus or a Galileo, Melvil suggests, is clearly not a condition of the truth of those myths; yet in the pragmatist's definition of truth as usefulness it is. The only way the pragmatist approach would make sense would be if, as James held, the world is inherently plural, a view Melvil thought absurd: "This is an irrational conception of the world, rejecting the unity and lawful character of reality. A 'pluralistic universe' is a chaotic stream of fortuitous events or situations, devoid of internal necessary relations and not subject to any objective laws" (Melvil 1957b, 101).

Based on this reading, pragmatism, despite its several virtues, is in most respects fundamentally flawed. While there are, as we will see, significant differences among the pragmatists, both their successes and failures, in the Soviet view, have their roots in Peirce.

Peirce

The centerpiece of Soviet studies of Peirce is Melvil's 1968 book *Charles Peirce and Pragmatism*, originally written as his doctoral dissertation in 1963. It was the first, and remains the only, extended Russian language account and analysis of the whole of Peirce's philosophic output. Before this Peirce was discussed primarily as the founder of pragmatism, and usually in the context of a broader account of pragmatism in general. Since 1968 all discussions of Peirce reckon in one way or another with Melvil's book. The earlier considerations, many of them by Melvil himself, share the hostility Melvil directed against pragmatism as a whole. In a discussion of Peirce's evaluation of the possible methods of "fixing belief," for example, Melvil referred to Pierce as "hypocritically" endorsing the method of science over the alternatives, suggesting an intentional duplicity on Peirce's part (Melvil 1957a, 18). Beginning with the 1968 book, however, accounts of Peirce's thought became, while still largely critical, far more appreciative.

Peirce tends to be regarded as the most significant American philosopher of the late nineteenth and early twentieth centuries: "Of all the thinkers who perceptively sensed the spirit of their times and attempted to provide a new orientation to philosophy and new forms of philosophic thinking, the first place belongs to the founder of pragmatism, Charles Peirce" (Yulina 1978a, 48). In his logical studies, Melvil feels, Pierce was incomparably greater in comparison with the "irrationalism" of James and in his scientific erudition and competence stood far above Dewey. On the whole, "Peirce is a genuinely outstanding moment in bourgeois philosophy" (Melvil 1968, 15). One of the indications of the extent of Peirce's insight is the degree to which he anticipated so many of the directions in which twentieth century philosophy would develop. Yulina sees two distinct strains of thought in Peirce that lie at the base of the two primary directions of twentieth century American philosophy, a positivist-analytic tendency and a speculative-religious strain (Yulina 1978a, 52). Melvil had made the broader point that Peirce prefigures both American and European ideas. One version of his theory of meaning suggests Bridgeman's operationalism, and through that the Vienna Circle; his metaphysics and evolutionary ideas anticipate Bergson, emergent evolutionism, and even Whitehead; there is something of Husserl in his phenomenology; and Peirce had a direct influence on logic and semiotics (Melvil 1968, 484–485).

Bogomolov echoes the point that seeds of twentieth century logical positivism and semantics, phenomenology and neorealistic cosmology, pragmatism and religious metaphysics can all be found somewhere in Peirce's works (Bogomolov 1974, 38).

Peirce's Contradictions

The sheer diversity of Peirce's ideas indicates the richness of his work, but it also points to its contradictoriness, a characteristic the Soviet commentators made the most general and persistent rubric for their analyses. Peirce, Melvil says, is "one of the most contradictory of philosophical writers," an assessment shared by Bogomolov and Yulina. Melvil notes that many American students of Peirce are well aware of this and have attributed it to the continuous development of Peirce's ideas, but he suggests that there are also fundamental contradictions within any given period of his thought.[5] Furthermore, though many commentators have noted Peirce's various sides, the "bifurcation" between his empiricism and nonempiricist metaphysics or between a naturalism and a transcendentalism, they generally "make no attempt to discover the deeper sources of this bifurcation." The critical point, Melvil suggests, is Peirce's relation to "the fundamental question of philosophy" in its late nineteenth century form—the relation between religion and science: "The conflict between science and religion is the focus and the source of the contradictions, and the key to Peirce's entire philosophy" (Melvil 1968, 33).[6] Bogomolov, citing Melvil, restates this view, and Yulina too agrees, though she puts the point in terms of a contradiction between science and metaphysics. In his articulation of the three fundamental categories of being, in his phaneroscopy, Peirce approaches a theistic treatment of the fundamental problem of philosophy. The categories are highly speculative in the older metaphysical spirit, which, Yulina thinks, contradicts his interest in science (Yulina 1978a, 50).

In Bogomolov's view the difficulties in Peirce can be traced to two basic contradictions that "eat away" at his ideas from within: (1) on the one hand, he adheres to positivist tendencies as they had developed from Hume and Berkeley through Mill, while, on the other hand, he also adopts the classical German tradition's speculative objective idealism in the "climate of opinion" created by transcendentalism and also reflected in Royce; and (2) in his theory of knowledge two conflicting views of logic collide—psychologism and formalism (Bogomolov 1974, 39). Melvil, however, develops his understanding of the contradictions in Peirce more directly in relation to religion and science. In the late nineteenth century developments in the natural sciences and philosophic materialism were threatening the grounds of religious faith. On the one hand, Pierce, by virtue of his sustained interest in science and the fruits of his own research, was committed to a scientific world view. But at the same time he was also convinced that reality reflects a divine creative power (6.505), that knowledge is "knowledge of divine truth" (1.239), and, Melvil suggests, "he went even further than James" in his view that social life and ethics require not only belief in God but a universal church (6.443) (Melvil 1968, 34–35). Pierce, then, needed to reconcile science and religion, and he attempted to do so through a philosophic idealism. Thus "as a scholar Peirce could not and did not want to break with science, with its methods and logical apparatus . . . but at the same time he always took care that no damage was done to religion and its theoretical basis in philosophic idealism" (Melvil 1968, 40).

This would be problematic enough, but Melvil goes on to argue that both sides of this contradiction, philosophic idealism and science, are themselves developed by Peirce in contradictory ways. His theory of knowledge and his understanding of the method of inquiry is a subjective idealism, while his metaphysics, his "Theistic evolutionism," is objective idealism, a newer version of Emerson's transcendentalism and an alternative to the evolutionary views of Darwin and Spencer (Melvil 1968, 46). We will return to the details of Melvil's argument that Peirce's pragmatism is subjective idealism, but at this point it is worth noting some disagreement over the evolution of the tension in Peirce between subjective and objective idealism. Yulina makes much of the contradictions between Peirce's pragmatism and his metaphysics, while Melvil argues that it is more appropriate to see them as two aspects of a single overarching project.

Peirce's thought is characterized more than anything, Yulina feels, by contradictions between his metaphysics and other aspects of his philosophy:

> Peirce supports the transformation of philosophy into a science (or the logic of science), and simultaneously as part of his philosophy he constructs a mythological cosmology; he rejects as senseless the old ontological metaphysics with its speculative conception of reality, and at the same time builds a thoroughly speculative metaphysics; he fights for the introduction into philosophy of the methods of observation and confirmation, and simultaneously creates a conceptual construct which in principle cannot be the object of observation; his was the first expression of the pragmatist maxim, determining the meaning of any concept or judgment in light of its practical or experimental effects, and at the same time he also constructs the theories of phaneroscopy, synechism, etc., which in principle cannot be confirmed by the method; finally, he rejects the possibility of an intellectual demonstration of the existence of God, yet he insists on an instinctive realization of divine reality. (Yulina 1978a, 51)

Melvil agrees that in creating the metaphysical system, Peirce at one level contradicted his own epistemological views but at another level, he thinks, the two converge. It is clear to Melvil that "the goal of Peirce's metaphysics is to set off the scientific and materialist picture of the world against its idealist alternative in order to establish that conception of the universe that would at the same time fully accord with a religious worldview yet retain the appearance of being scientific" (Melvil 1968, 438). Such a metaphysics, however, is ultimately united with Peirce's own epistemology through the anthropomorphism that permeates both. Peirce reads human traits into animals, specifically that animals have ideas (6.418) and into the universe by attributing to nature mind and spirit (1.316). This anthropomorphism "is above all the doctrine of pragmatism, determining the meaning of all, or at least intellectual, concepts in terms of human action, habits, sensation, and feeling." There is, then, no contradiction between Peirce's pragmatism and his metaphysics because "both were for him only different sides of an anthropomorphic interpretation of reality" (Melvil 1968, 446–448).

Much more problematic, in Melvil's view, are the contradictions in Peirce's treatment of science. The nature of scientific inquiry as Peirce develops it has both an objective and a subjective side. In some respects he opposed the positivist conception of science, including, Melvil notes, James's view expressed in the *Principles of Psychology* that science should describe phenomena. For Peirce science is the search for causes and thus involves generalization, a process which he argued requires freedom of inquiry, a non-dogmatic search for truth. He thought that a true picture of the world is possible, that truth is accessible. This is the objective side of Peirce's conception, and in so far as he understood science as the antidogmatic search for objective truth, Pierce is "fuller and more profound than many bourgeois theoreticians of science of his time" (Melvil 1968, 59). There is, however, another, subjective side in that Peirce also regarded science to be the activity of scholars, a form of life:

> This signifies a radical shift in the *meaning* of the concept of science in an anthropomorphic spirit; it signifies a consideration of science not from the point of view of its objective content but as a purely subjective psychological orientation. Peirce shifts the center of gravity in the definition of science from the objective subject matter of science and the process of its knowledge to the subjective motives of the scientist's activity. (Melvil 1968, 57–58)

This goes well beyond antidogmatism to relativism: "An emphasis on the antidogmatic spirit of scientific knowledge was transformed into a disparagement of the cognitive possibilities of science" (Melvil 1968, 59).

For Melvil, then, Peirce held contradictory conceptions of science, inquiry and knowledge, one of which is valuable and the other flawed, and this is the reason Melvil says that "despite significant achievements in logic and semiotics . . . Peirce nevertheless frequently betrayed both science and the scientific methods" (Melvil 1968, 37). The objective, significant aspects of Peirce's thought are related to his activity as a scientist and logician, and the mistakes of his subjectivism, which receive their clearest expression in his pragmatism, are linked to his general commitment to philosophic idealism and religion. Peirce tried, but failed, to have it both ways: "In this, in my view, lies the fundamental contradiction permeating all of Peirce's studies, in this is his tragedy as a scholar, in this is the underlying reason for the fragmentation, incompleteness, and internal discontinuity of his work" (Melvil 1968, 41).

1868: The Critique of Modernism

Peirce's "fundamental contradiction," indeed many of the central ideas to be developed later in his life, appears as early as the 1868 essays in which he engages in a critical study of Descartes and rationalism, concerned primarily with the issue of immediate knowledge. Descartes had argued that immediate, intuitively certain knowledge is necessary as the foundation of deductive inquiries if they are to achieve certainty and to be reliable. Since experience is unreliable, the foundation of knowledge must lie in indubitable rational intuition, specifically immediate knowledge of the self. Peirce attributes four basic traits to Cartesianism: philosophy must begin with universal doubt; the criteria of certainty are to be found in individual consciousness; inference is the fundamental form of reasoning; and explanation requires an appeal to God. One of Peirce's criticisms is that Cartesianism grounds certainty in individual consciousness, which is misleading, Melvil says, since Descartes held that the principles of reason are universal. The more important objection, however, is Peirce's claim that Cartesian doubt is impossible since the inquirer is never free of all assumptions, and inquiry is never without context and purpose. This, Melvil notes, is the fundamental break from modern philosophy. But Peirce's rejection of Cartesian doubt results in a divorce of inquiry from its object and an inadequate conception of reality.

Peirce, Melvil argues, leaves out of his account the distinctive traits of modern science that also characterize Cartesianism, such as Descartes's mechanistic physics and a conception of the natural processes of the cosmos. Perhaps, he suggests, Peirce was focusing on Descartes's method, but still he misses some of what contributed to Cartesian optimism about the unlimited possibilities of reason, specifically the ability of science to provide reliable objective knowledge. In criticizing Cartesian doubt, Melvil argues, Peirce also rejects two theses which, taken together, constitute the virtue of modernism—that the world exists objectively (nature, Spinoza held, is *causa sui*) and that the task of science is to reveal its traits.

In his criticism of intuitive knowledge Peirce argues that knowledge of internal conditions is not independent but is derived through hypothetical reasoning from our knowledge of external facts, that we do not have the ability to intuit, rather that all knowledge is logically derived from prior knowledge and that we cannot think without signs. That we cannot think without signs is, in Melvil's view, the central theme of Peirce's theory of knowledge, since it is his way to show that immediate intuitive knowledge is impossible. Peirce argues that no thought counts as knowledge if it is related only to itself and that the content and meaning of a thought can only be revealed or interpreted by another thought. The problem with this, Melvil holds, is that all thought, and therefore all knowledge, becomes a function of other thoughts: "the process of the interpretation of signs, as Peirce expresses it, . . a purely logical process that never comes into contact with experience, which has no entrée to objective reality" (Melvil 1968, 92).

Peirce's alternative to rationalism is no less a criticism of empiricism and of Kant. Just as there is no immediate rational intuition, neither is there immediate sensible intuition. Sensory impressions, perceptions, are never independent of other impressions, and unlike the empiricist sensationalism of Berkeley and Hume, sensation is not an internal condition of consciousness. Melvil argues that Peirce was right to recognize the complexity of sensation, so that his view in fact improves on the sensationalist approach. Its weakness, however, is the same as in the criticism of Cartesianism. In rejecting the simplistic sensationalism of empiricism, that is, in rejecting the immediacy of sensory impressions, Peirce ultimately divorces impressions from their objects. His mistake, Melvil argues, is to think that because impressions are not intuited as the sensationalists thought, intuitive knowledge cannot be mediated in some other way: "The rejection of the intuitive character of sensation for Peirce is equivalent to a rejection of the conditionality of sensation by its object external to consciousness; in other words it is a rejection of the materialist understanding of the relation of sensation to its object" (Melvil 1968, 97).

Peirce has a similar problem in his account of scientific explanation. Melvil suggests that while Peirce describes it as bringing a particular fact under a general law, since a general law is an idea, and thus a sign, scientific explanation too never leaves the realm of ideas. This is a particularly important point, Melvil feels, since because of this we find the emphasis in Peirce on explanation as the *process* of explanation, on knowledge as the *process* of knowledge or of logical inference or of the interpretation of signs: "Such a view of cognitive activity preserves only the movement toward knowledge, the search for knowledge, or as Peirce and Dewey will later say, the *process of inquiry*, never issuing in any stable results" (Melvil 1968, 105). Here is one of the points where Peirce the scientist collides with Peirce the idealist and postmodernist. He himself describes science as explaining what happens in the external world, which would appear to mean that knowledge is a reflection of the external, objective world. "But

Peirce cannot accept this ordinary thesis, and one which is consistent with his *scientific* interests, for that would mean to accept the materialist point of view, placing Peirce in an irreconcilable antagonism with his own religious idealism" (Melvil 1968, 106). The upshot of severing knowledge from reality is the view that "reality is not the starting point of the process of knowledge but can only be its end," a conception meaning "that our knowledge is reduced to an irrational faith and hope" (Melvil 1968, 106–107).

Melvil's criticism is that Peirce misconstrues the implications of his own otherwise valuable critique of modernism. Peirce is right, he says, in his disagreement with Descartes in so far as he argues that the historical process of knowledge does not begin with an absolute epistemological starting point but always develops from other knowledge, and he is right to criticize the *cogito*, the Cartesian view that we have clear and intuitive knowledge of the self. But he is wrong to reject "a first premise of knowledge in general." There *is* a first premise, Melvil thinks, though unlike for the rationalist and empiricists it is not epistemological but ontological—"the recognition of the existence of the objective world, of nature" (Melvil 1968, 110). Even here, however, Peirce is torn between opposing conceptions. He seems not to reject the existence of an objective, external world, since in arguing against the *cogito* he says that the self can only be known on the basis of knowledge of "external facts." But at the same time he does deny "the possibility of the object immediately determining knowledge of it," a view meaning, as we have seen Melvil argue, that knowledge is divorced from reality and that reality becomes the result of the process of inquiry. Even this view was not consistently maintained, Melvil says, since in the 1873 *Logic* Peirce says that some ideas seem to derive from sensation and not from preceding ideas (7.328). It was nevertheless the conception of knowledge developed in the 1868 essays that Peirce would sustain in his later work. "Without the theory of knowledge from 1868 there would have been no pragmatism," and the 1868 articles also contain the seeds of the later theory of signs (Melvil 1968, 112). Both pragmatism and semiotics, however, also required Peirce's development of the Categories.

The Categories

After an initial formulation of a "table of categories" in a Kantian spirit, Peirce revised the categories to describe three traits or modes of being: firstness, or quality, secondness, or fact, and thirdness, generality and law. The categories are derived from a logical analysis of thought and from experience generally, or what Peirce called phenomenology, or phaneroscopy. Phenomenology, as Melvil describes it, is simply a description of what in any sense appears to the mind, wholly indifferent to the relation between phenomena and reality, truth and falsity, good and evil, and the traits of all human experience, as phenomenology reveals them, are the ground and justification of the categories. They are justified in experience in the sense that if adequate, the categories will be exemplified in specific experience, and if not so exemplified they require revision. There is a value to such a method, Melvil thinks, in that unlike the positivists, Peirce locates verification in the success of the application of the categories in specific conditions and sciences. But as with other of his conceptions, Peirce could not go far enough. In one sense, the method is

> an appeal to the results of all human knowledge, verified and confirmed by sociohistorical practice. But Peirce, as an idealist, stopped short at the first part of this thesis, for the idea of the cognitive significance of social practice, of the highest and final criteria of our knowledge, was to him alien and incomprehensible. He could only go as far as the vague conception of "all experience, natural or poetical" of the experience of our lives in general, i.e., as far as "common sense." (Melvil 1968, 123)

In Melvil's view, the category of firstness, or quality, is the least interesting and significant of the three. It indicates the qualities of sensation, feelings, as they are in themselves, independent of any embodiment. As qualities not necessarily realized, firstness is possibility, "abstract potentiality," and as such is atemporal. This is, Melvil suggests, a kind of Platonism, except that for Peirce qualities are not actualities but possibilities. Firstness suggests for Peirce the reality of chance and indeterminacy, which is the source of multiplicity in the world and which Peirce identifies with freedom. In this respect, firstness captures something akin to James's pluralistic universe, and as pure quality and possibility it anticipates Santayana's realm of essence and Whitehead's eternal objects.

Secondness, by contrast, indicates specific individual fact, by which it is clear, Melvil says, that Peirce means individual objective existences. Such individual existences, Peirce says, are "here and now," spatial and temporal; they are material existences and independent of consciousness. This recognition of objective material existences contradicts, Melvil argues, both the theory of knowledge of the 1868 essays and the general subjective idealism of pragmatism. Peirce denies any contradiction between secondness and a psychological substrate of phenomena (1.436), but Melvil contends that despite this denial, Peirce's treatment of existences is an argument against subjective idealism, though not against idealism generally.

Thirdness, Melvil notes, involves the triadic sign relation so central to Peirce's whole philosophy. It encompasses mediation, regularity, universality, continuity, and natural law. The emphasis on universality indicates Peirce's debt to scholastic realism, but Melvil is particularly interested in Peirce's treatment of law as an exemplification of thirdness.

Peirce's recognition of the objective character of laws, he says, is undoubtedly a positive aspect of his realism, preferable, for example, to a Machian nominalism in which a law of nature is purely subjective. But again Melvil finds more than a few problems in Peirce's approach, one of which is that "his law of nature is divorced from those natural phenomena of which it is a law, and appears as a general principle external to them" (Melvil 1968, 161). There are points, he says, at which Peirce comes close to a correct understanding of laws, for example that a scientific law is a symbolic formula expressing a law of nature, an existing material relation and activity (5.96). But this is a view Peirce could not sustain, inconsistent as it clearly is with his general philosophic idealism. It is more common, Melvil says, for Peirce to approach a law of nature from an empiricist perspective, in which a law simply expresses external repetition and the force or power of a law is explained idealistically.

The Theory of Signs

Easily Peirce's most significant philosophic contribution, in Melvil's view, was the theory of signs. Melvil identifies several sources of Peirce's semiotics. His studies of logic, mathematics, and the role of mathematical symbols are influential. Philosophically Peirce was motivated by several sources: Kant, for whom our sensible intuitions are evoked by things-in-themselves but are not reflections of them; Thomas Reid and the Scottish common sense school; and Emerson, for whom language is a sign of natural phenomena and nature a symbol of spirit.

The triadic relation is central to Peirce's theory of signs. There are, of course, three components of a sign relation—sign, object, and interpretant. In addition, three trichotomies embody the categories and constitute the typology of signs: firstness, or quality of a sign, which includes the qualisign, sinsign, and legisign; secondness, which is a sign's relation to its object, in which a sign is an icon, index, or symbol; and thirdness, or a sign's relation to its interpretant as term, proposition, or argument. Of the many types of signs and their possible relations to objects and interpretants, Melvil is most interested in the icon because, he says, though Peirce did not realize its significance, his understanding of an icon expresses a materialist conception of the reflection of an object in a sign.

As in Peirce's critique of Descartes and in his categories, virtues develop in Peirce's theory of signs, though they are ultimately constrained by inconsistencies and by his inability to see them through. Referring to Marxist work in semiotics, Melvil remarks that while there have been some advances in the field during the past few decades, Peirce's work remains fundamental, and many of his ideas and analyses are retained in contemporary studies:

The most fundamental epistemological result that Peirce achieved through his analysis of the nature of the sign relation and his typology of signs consists in his recognition that:

(1) a sign is determined by some external object, to the objective existence of which one kind of sign, the index, points;

(2) between an object and another kind of sign, the icon, there is a relation of resemblance or similarity. In other words, an icon reproduces or reflects its object;

(3) an icon, being an "immediate image" of an object, is a unique kind of sign, which through exact representation enables the discovery of new truths in relation to its object. Therefore the icon is at the foundation of all scientific reasoning, and also the process of communication. (Melvil 1968, 207)

Melvil, then, locates in some features of the sign relation the germ of a materialist epistemology: "This result of Peirce's research was in fact a rejection of the principles of his subjective idealist theory of knowledge from the 1868 essays, and opened a way to further fruitful analyses of the epistemological function of the sign as a means of the reflection of reality" (Melvil 1968, 207). But as in his understanding of science and his conception of natural law, Peirce's antimaterialist and phenomenalist presuppositions prevented him from pursuing it. His fundamental mistake, in Melvil's view, is the insistence that a sign requires an interpretant, which means that a sign is always determined by another sign in a never ending series. This in turn suggests a rupture between the cognitive process and the object of cognition in that the significant features of cognition are internal to the process, and the relation between a sign and its object becomes less relevant.

The difficulty is crystallized in Peirce's approach to the question of meaning. Melvil remarks that the problem of meaning is an exceedingly difficult one, so that "it would hardly be justified to take Peirce to task for not providing a scientific definition of the concept of meaning" (Melvil 1968, 232). It is nevertheless necessary to point out that Peirce offers a variety of different, sometimes conflicting, descriptions of meaning. It is variously identified with a sign itself, with an "immediate object," with an interpretant, with the triadic sign relation, and also with the sign process, the never ending process of interpretation. The importance of this issue, Melvil argues, is that the concept of meaning is the bridge between Peirce's semiotics and his pragmatism. To bring them together, it was necessary for Peirce to define meaning such that it expresses the principle of pragmatism in terms of the theory of signs.

Peirce's pragmatism

The subjectivist and idealist side of Peirce is clearly expressed, according to Melvil, in his pragmatism. The initial expression of distinctly pragmatist conceptions were the essays "The Fixation of Belief" and "How to Make Our Ideas Clear," in which Peirce developed ideas continuous with both his earlier and later work. In some respects the pragmatism of the 1870s is a logical consequence of the 1868 essays, and, Melvil suggests, though Peirce later tried to refine his ideas and though he would object to the directions in which James and Schiller were to take them, he never fully abandoned them.

In Melvil's reading, the crucial trait of Peirce's early pragmatism was his appropriation of Alexander Bain's notion of belief in a way that placed it at the center of a theory of knowledge. In Peirce's hands a readiness to act is transformed from a criterion of belief into its content, that is into the content of that idea or proposition that one believes. Though it is difficult to ascribe precise meanings to Peirce's concepts of belief or faith, Melvil suggests that two aspects of them pervade Peirce's work: (1) belief is associated with a readiness to act, that is, with a type of behavior; and (2) belief is understood as a certain condition of consciousness, in contrast with doubt. In so far as belief is associated with a type of behavior, or habit, Peirce is again expressing his scholastic realism by deriving the concept in part from Duns Scotus's notion of something being in the mind *habitualiter*. Melvil finds the connection between belief and a readiness to act unsuccessful on the face of it, because in a given case two people may be prepared to act the same way but due to entirely different motives, so that there is no justification to identify a single belief with different people's readiness to act a certain way (Melvil 1968, 261–262). The contrast of belief with doubt, though in the end also flawed, is more interesting in that it represents a challenge to traditional treatments of doubt. In Descartes's case, for example, the alternative to doubt is certainty, that is, objectively true knowledge. Peirce replaces knowledge with belief as the contrast to doubt, which, Melvil says, indicates the antimaterialist and fideistic nature of Peirce's views. For Peirce, we seek to overcome doubt by reaching a condition of belief through a process of inquiry. But the term "inquiry," Melvil suggests, usually means a search for knowledge, an experimental or logical process. The intriguing feature of Peirce's approach is that he does not reject the one meaning for the other, but collapses them.

Of course, Peirce understands that simply declaring that thought is the overcoming of doubt by belief is not enough and that such a conception of thought requires an appropriate method of "fixing belief." Melvil and his colleagues were particularly interested in Peirce's treatment of this question, in part because it reveals certain general features of pragmatism, but more importantly because it leads Peirce to an account of the scientific method. Peirce first considers the method of "tenacity," the insistence on one's beliefs. He rejects this method for several reasons: it will likely result in dogmatism; more importantly the method of tenacity is inevitably unsuccessful because it is inconsistent with social experience. This is an important move, Melvil feels, in that it introduces a social factor, the community, into epistemology. Nevertheless, he says, the principles of pragmatism provide no good reason to reject the method of tenacity in favor of another method:

> But if the sole purpose of thought is to produce belief, and on this Peirce insists without reservation, then even religious belief is no worse than any other: the blind faith of a religious fanatic cannot in principle be distinguished from the proven and confirmed experience of the scholar. The possibility of justifying religion from the pragmatist theory of doubt-belief was used by William James as the basis of his conception of the "will to believe." (Melvil 1968, 274)

If the problem with the method of tenacity is that it is inconsistent with social experience, then perhaps a kind of social tenacity, a method of authority, would suffice. Of course Peirce rejects a method of authority because it is an intellectual slavery; as with the method of tenacity it cannot work because some people will see beyond the bounds of their own social experience and realize that others, in different circumstances, believe otherwise. It is not enough, Peirce says in "The Fixation of Belief," simply to "produce an impulse to believe," but one must "also decide what proposition it is which is to be believed." This is an interesting objection, Melvil thinks, but it makes sense only by assuming that objective criteria exist for evaluating different beliefs, grounds for regarding one belief as more true than another. But for the pragmatist's "theory of doubt-belief," he adds, there are no criteria. Thus as for tenacity, Peirce cannot on his own principles have much objection to a method of authority.

For his own part, though, Peirce does reject a method of authority and wonders whether purely rational inquiry, an a priori method, may be sufficient to fix belief. While an a priori method is more respectable, Peirce says, than tenacity or authority precisely because it is rational, it suffers primarily from the fact that it does not take experience seriously. This criticism, Melvil suggests, introduces a new point, one which is not only not specified by the "theory of doubt-belief," but which is in principle excluded by it—the agreement of belief with observed fact, with experience. Without this neither Peirce's description of the a priori method nor its criticism make any sense, yet pragmatism has no consistent place for it: "Here the contradiction of the theory of doubt—belief reaches its culmination" (Melvil 1968, 282).

To resolve doubt, Peirce says, requires a method "by which our beliefs may be caused by nothing human, but by some external permanency—by something upon which our thinking has no effect" (5.384). Furthermore, Melvil adds, it must lead to the same opinion for all who use it, and this is the method of science. The Peirce here speaking is Peirce the practicing scientist, who knows perfectly well that scientific inquiry can result in knowledge of objectively determinate reality. But there certainly appears to be a contradiction here, since to say of the method of inquiry that it must rely on "nothing human" is quite different from the view that the function of inquiry is simply to produce belief. One might try to reconcile the contradiction, Melvil points out, by interpreting Peirce as holding that while people seek to achieve stable belief, a belief can be stable only when it corresponds with the facts, that is, when it is true. But this interpretation, Melvil quickly adds, cannot be right, since it would attribute to Peirce a scientific materialist position: "There would be nothing of pragmatism in this view. And more than that, the theory of doubt-belief would lose all sense." If the method of inquiry must be tied to objectively determinate reality, then belief has no epistemological role in the theory. The only sense it *could* have, Melvil suggests, is psychological, that is, as a description of the psychological states of a person in the course of cognitive activity:

> The term *belief* itself would become unnecessary, in so far as the issue would only be the truth or falsity of beliefs, in which case the concept 'belief' would add nothing to the concepts 'opinion' and 'proposal,' and would be a superfluous and useless term. A subjective psychological readiness to act on the basis of a given proposal would have no relation to an analysis of its truth. . . . (Melvil 1968, 284)

The only way out of the contradiction is to read Peirce's initial description of the method of science in a way that would have him abandon his pragmatism. But Peirce was not interested in repudiating his conception of inquiry as proceeding from doubt to belief. "On the contrary, he is trying to interpret the genuine method of science in terms of this theory in order to 'rectify' the materialist directions in which it had been leading. At the same time he had to describe the method such that it at least resembled the real method of science, so that it somehow retained its previous traits" (Melvil 1968, 284). This is not to say, he adds, that Peirce was trying to disguise his subjective idealist and antiscientific view with scientific phraseology. "But he wanted to reconcile science and religion, and for that he tried to interpret scientific concepts and the method of science so that not a trace of materialism would remain" (Melvil 1968, 285).

The question remains, however, what Peirce could mean by "some external permanency," by "something upon which our thinking has no effect?" In his description of the scientific method, Melvil says, Peirce accepts the notion of objectivity, that is, a reality existing independently of what we think of it, but Peirce also says that this is a hypothesis, one that science cannot confirm (5.384). Peirce the scientist and scholar cannot doubt that the objective world really exists, but Peirce the idealist cannot acknowledge the materialism implicit in this. "He does not say . . . that the external world *exists* independently of human beings and their thought; Peirce says only that he *cannot doubt* the existence of this world." Peirce suggests that when people use the method that is grounded on a recognition of real things they will have successful results. Does this mean, Melvil asks, that things really exist, that science can achieve true knowledge of the world? He answers that it does not: "All of this signifies only that the scientific method is more successful than other methods in establishing opinion, i.e., belief. The success of the scientific method, in Peirce's view, indicates only the advisability of accepting the method and the inexpediency of doubting it—nothing more" (Melvil 1968, 287).

Peirce's treatment of the methods of fixing belief, then, is problematic at every turn. Pragmatism offers no grounds for rejecting the first two methods, and Peirce's rejection of the third and endorsement of the method of science flatly contradict his pragmatism and antimaterialism. Melvil in fact suggests that on the whole Peirce's thought is so mired in contradictions that one can find all four methods at work:

> As a political conservative he recommends the intellectual enslavement of the masses through the method of authority; as a speculative metaphysician he is wholly at the mercy of the a priori method; as a scholar concerned with the development of science, but also making a place for religion, he adheres to what he calls the method of science; and as a thinker obstinately clinging to the innumerable contradictions and absurdities of his views, he clearly follows the method of tenacity. (Melvil 1968, 288)

Meaning and Truth

Peirce's revision of the Cartesian treatment of doubt and inquiry, and his description and endorsement of the method of science lead naturally to a consideration of the problem of meaning. In "How to Make Our Ideas Clear" he develops a pragmatist theory of meaning, what James called Peirce's Principle, and responds to Descartes's subjectivist understanding of clarity and distinctness. Given his phenomenalism, Peirce is not able to associate meaning with objects in the world, so meaning must be related to the subject, though not in Descartes' mentalistic fashion. His "discovery" is to posit the full meaning of a concept in the practical effects its object might conceivably have. Melvil notes that attempts have been made to minimize Peirce's Principle as a foundation of his pragmatism. He refers specifically to Justus Buchler's attempt to "defend Peirce from Peirce," where Buchler says of Peirce's Principle, "As a statement made in 1878 it is justly famous; but it is a mistake to base a discussion of Peirce's pragmatism on it. Considered relatively to the whole of Peirce's writings it is one of a class of statements that are unprecise."[7] Melvil agrees with Buchler that Peirce's statement is imprecise, but he also thinks that there is no way to avoid the position that this principle "is the source and ground of the entire pragmatist trend in philosophy, and without it there would be no pragmatism" (Melvil 1968, 291).

Melvil suggests two meanings Peirce gives to the expression "practical consequences." The first, consistent with the view that the function of thought is to produce a habit of action, is that the meaning of an idea is the habits it produces (5.400). This, Melvil argues, is an untenable position. Previously habits were the content of belief, but "now it turns out that not only beliefs but also things call forth or include in themselves a habit." If practical consequences, habits, are the meaning of a concept, then we can only know these consequences and never the object that engenders them. An object, he continues, must be different from its consequences, and thus the meaning of the two must be distinguished. But Peirce conflates them, so that in Melvil's words, "the name of an object will merely be the name of some collection of habits." This he thinks is absurd, since it leads either to the view that there are consequences engendered by nothing other than themselves, or to the view that meaning and knowledge have no relation to objects in the world (Melvil 1968, 292). The second meaning of "practical consequences" is that the meaning of a thing is its conceived sensible effects (5.401), a view open to the same objection as the first, since that which has effects cannot be identical to the effects it has.

There is another equally unacceptable implication of the principle. In Peirce's view, an object has, for example, the qualities of hardness and softness "only when we undertake some action. They exist, consequently, as an aspect of our experience, our perception, and nothing more." This is, Melvil adds, a typically subjective idealist position (Melvil 1968, 295). Melvil says that in some cases, with respect to some concepts, the pragmatist maxim is not entirely mistaken, since there are indeed concepts the content of which is revealed in people's actions. Truthfulness or courageousness, for example, are concepts that concern the traits of a human character displayed in actions, though even here we can speak of a truthful or courageous person even when that person is not performing the corresponding actions. He also points to cases in which we know of something only in its manifestations or actions. Peirce's mistake was to apply to every concept an understanding of meaning that is appropriate only to exceptional cases (Melvil 1968, 298–299).

The concept of meaning is related to the concept of truth. There is, Melvil suggests, a more or less commonsensical conception of truth, in that to think or speak about the world at all we need a concept that concerns whether or not we are thinking or speaking correctly. Without such a concept, neither logic nor a theory of knowledge nor science nor practical activity are possible at all. This is a correspondence theory of truth, one that Peirce himself implicitly uses in a number of places. In "The Fixation of Belief," for example, he says that people think in order to reach stable beliefs, whether they are true or false, and that the virtue of the scientific method lies in providing a way for people to accord their opinions with the facts. However, when Peirce deals directly with the epistemological problem of truth, the situation changes and the pragmatist theory of truth has nothing in common with a correspondence theory.

Melvil identifies two conceptions of truth in Peirce. The overt, superficial conception is that if the function of inquiry is to fix belief, then truth is that which enables this end; a true belief is that which can bring about successful activity and lead to the desired end (5.375 N.2; 1.344). There is, however, another "more intricate and contradictory" conception related to Peirce's conception of reality and with which he tries to overcome the subjectivism of the first, "vulgar" view. There are two versions of this more sophisticated conception of truth, one, Melvil says, more primitive and the other more precise. The more primitive version is the view that truth is a state of belief unassailable by doubt, which is to say, that truth is that which we believe (5.416). Peirce attempts to refine this, though, in a way that brings it closer to the conception of truth accepted in science. For a belief to be genuinely stable and free of the possibility of doubt, it must be necessary and universal, so that truth is that which will necessarily be reached by all scholars who study or will study a given question. Melvil suggests that had Peirce been a dialectician and a materialist he would have realized that truth is a process, so that at any given time we achieve *relative* truth in our ideas and propositions. The relative truth of our ideas, furthermore, does not preclude a simultaneous *objective* truth that expresses reality independently of what is known and thought of it. But this is not a position Peirce was able to hold, so he was moved to say that truth is the final opinion to which the application of the scientific method would lead all inquiries, and the object represented in this opinion is reality (5.407). The problem here, in Melvil's view, is that truth loses its "objectivity," without which there is no truth, and that Peirce's definition is not that at all: "The fundamental flaw of Peirce's reasoning is that he passes for a definition of truth something that does not define it. Peirce describes the process as a result of which inquirers are led to the truth and then presents this as a description of truth itself" (Melvil 1968, 309).

A conception of truth, then, is connected directly with a conception of reality, which in Peirce's hands involves the entire community of inquirers. Reality is the object of the opinion that is fated to be agreed to by all who inquire. Peirce is right, Melvil feels, that there is a social character to human thought, that logical thought, or the method of science, has been worked out over centuries and millennia by the entire "community" of people:

All of this is true, but it is far from sufficient. Logical thought is formed not simply as collective, social thought, but as thought that reflects the objective connections, relations, and lawfulness of things and is revealed in the various forms of social practice. This is how scientific thought is distinguished from collective belief, from a form of thought propounded, we might say, by the church; it has an objective content, and its logical form reflects the objective lawfulness of the objective world. (Melvil 1968, 316–317)

Peirce is right when he says that to be logical a person must not be egoistic, but "in order to be logical one must also be objective; one must subordinate one's own thought to the logic of things, and not attempt to violate it in the name of one's own subjective ends." It is precisely this, Melvil says, that pragmatism does not recognize. Peirce himself, he suggests, goes both ways in that he recognizes the role of objective reality but his pragmatism does not allow him to embrace it consistently: "Peirce is of two minds on this point, as on many others, and it proves to be an irresolvable conflict" (Melvil 1968, 317).

The whole problem of pragmatism devolves, in the end, to the question of reality. As we have seen in his defense of the scientific method, Peirce at one level defines reality as that which has its nature absolutely, independently of what anyone thinks of it. The pragmatist principle, though, requires that the meaning of "reality" is in conceived effects, and the sole significant effect of "real things" is that they produce belief. A *true* belief, however, is a function of the scientific method, as Peirce understands it; therefore, that opinion is true which is universally acknowledged by inquirers, and, Peirce says, the object of this opinion or belief is reality. This has two possible meanings. It can mean that reality, being independent of what anyone thinks about it, can be fully revealed only in the course of ongoing research, as a result of which it becomes the object of final belief. Although this interpretation is possible, it is inconsistent, Melvil feels, with Peirce's views. It is an expression of a materialist position against which Peirce struggled and to which his idea that the role of inquiry is to produce belief is an alternative. Peirce must mean something else, and in the end he conflates the real with thought about the real. If, as he puts it, reality consists in the ultimate agreement of the community of inquirers, then the nature of the real turns out to be dependent on how it is conceived (Melvil 1968, 321–322).

Peirce himself, Melvil notes, wonders whether there might be a contradiction here (5.408). He attempts to resolve it by distinguishing between dependence on what any particular individual thinks and dependence on what the community of inquirers thinks in the end. Reality is dependent in the latter sense, dependent that is on "thought in general," Peirce says, and since the process of inquiry is indefinitely extended, reality itself can only be determined in the indefinite future. That he holds this view, however, does not prevent Peirce from asserting the alternative. Melvil cites, for example, a passage from the "Doctrine of Chance" in which Peirce says, "Truth consists in the existence of a real fact corresponding to the true proposition" (2.652). In obvious intellectual frustration, Melvil remarks, "This situation is most typical of pragmatism, due to its ambiguity. One can interpret it any way one pleases" (Melvil 1968, 323). If the existence of a given fact gives a proposition its truth, he asks, then in what way can an existing fact be dependent on a proposition: "This question can be put in a more general form: how can it be that reality both produces belief, which Peirce holds is reality's unique effect, and itself be dependent on belief about it?" Peirce had posed this question as a paradox (7.340), but in fact "its actual resolution from the pragmatist position consists in a rejection of the independence of reality and in the identification of the object of belief with the belief itself" (Melvil 1968, 324).

Pragmaticism

For some years after "The Fixation of Belief" and "How to make Our Ideas Clear," Peirce concerned himself with other issues, but as pragmatism began to gain attention, primarily due to William James, Peirce again turned his attention to it. In one way it is surprising that he returned to pragmatism, since it is inconsistent with the conception he had been developing of pure science. In 1896, for example, Peirce suggested that science and faith are incompatible, that what we call belief has no place in science (1.635). Even in the 1903 *Lectures on Pragmatism,* Melvil notes, Peirce says that actually belief is out of place in pure theoretical science, and in general he was trying to distinguish between a theoretical belief appropriate to science and a practical belief that is the basis of action (5.60). Despite such inconsistencies, Melvil suggests that Peirce continued to pursue pragmatist ideas because they allowed for a non-materialist treatment of science. The years around the turn of the century were also the period in which Peirce developed his speculative metaphysics, and the suggestion is that the new treatment of pragmatism was related to that project. One commentator suggests that while the pragmatism of the 1870s was a subjective idealism and more psychologistic, Peirce's later pragmatism, in its relation to logic and valuation, had more the spirit of his theistic evolutionism and was thus a shift to objective idealism (Ustyantzev 1974, 73–74). In any case, in his later approach to "pragmaticism" Peirce was concerned among other things to distance himself from its more popular versions. Melvil suggests that unlike James, Schiller, Dewey, and others, Peirce thought that "the truth of pragmatism was not at all obvious, that this doctrine was open to all sorts of doubts, and that the correctness of the pragmatist maxim required demonstration" (Melvil 1968, 342). He insisted to James that his own pragmatism had to do with logic and the analysis of concepts, and he also distanced himself from the instrumentalist logic of Dewey and the Chicago School (8.189). However, Melvil says, in his simultaneous concern with logic, science, and pragmatism, Peirce tried to do the impossible, to be both a pragmatist and a scholar. In so far as he was a pragmatist, his disagreements with James, Schiller, and Dewey were not really disagreements of fundamental principle, but in so far as he was a scholar, they were (Melvil 1968, 346).

In the later years Peirce's Principle is expressed in several new variants, and the general trait of them all is the attempt to give the principle a more realist and intellectualist character. There is a behaviorist version, in which the difference between two concepts is understood as the difference between the ways each might change our practical behavior (5.196). This, Melvil thinks, is not yet much of an improvement over the earlier pragmatism. Far more interesting, he thinks, are the intellectualist and experimental versions of the principle. In the former, Peirce shifts the emphasis from a specific concrete action to the type of behavior connected with a given concept or generated by it. Here action and behavior are determined by our ideas, and the meaning of a concept is not our actions as much as another, general idea or concept that embodies a type of action (5.427). Such an approach is interestingly ambiguous, Melvil thinks. On the one hand, to explain the meaning of a concept in terms of a concept is more in the spirit of Peirce's semiotics than the pragmatism of "How to Make Our Ideas Clear," and it is also in this respect more characteristic of his objective idealist metaphysics. This is far from the earlier view, in fact "this is one of those instances where Peirce actually arrives at a rejection of pragmatism" (Melvil 1968, 350).

The most significant of the new variants of the pragmatist principle is its experimental version, where "practical effects" are not concrete actions or types of behavior, but experimental results (5.412). Actually, Melvil suggests, this allows the possibility of both the intellectualist and behaviorist interpretations of the pragmatist maxim, in that the sum of experimental phenomena implicit in a proposition forms the entirety of its meaning for human behavior. In this version of the principle Peirce describes reality in terms of what would be the effects of certain operations or actions. On the face of it this appears to build objectivity into the conception of reality, but in fact, Melvil suggests, it is little different from Berkeley's view that to say something is real is to say that one would perceive it under certain circumstances (Melvil 1968, 353). It is characteristic of Soviet discussions of Peirce to see in him a decidedly Berkeleyan strain. Speaking of the theory of meaning in general, for example, Bogomolov says that for Peirce knowledge of the practical effects of an object *is* knowledge of the object, a distinctly Berkeleyan move in that it replaced "*esse est percipi*" with "practical effects." "Peirce merely overcomes to a certain degree the *contemplativeness* of Berkeley's subjective idealism" (Bogomolov 1974, 50). This is echoed by Sidorov when he says that "Peirce posits a modified version of Berkeleyanism" (Sidorov 1989, 98).

However, Melvil asks, if we overlook the subjective idealism, is there not some way to find a rational kernel in the experimentalist version of Peirce's principle? "Could we not then say that the concept of a thing is revealed precisely in its effects, that in speaking of a thing (or characteristic), we have in mind its possible ('conceived') reactions, interconnections or relations, in short, its practical effects?" (Melvil 1968, 354). Noting the similarity of this version of the principle to Bridgeman's operationalism, Melvil finds it unacceptable for several reasons. First, it never achieves what it sets out to do, to disclose the meaning of a concept, because it replaces 'meaning' with 'denotation.' It describes not what a word or concept means, but what it denotes, that is, the perceived impressions that we might receive from this or that operation. Second, it absolutizes one of the possibilities of scientific practice and thus abandons the fundamental assumption of all of genuine science, that is, that science studies the objective world. Third, in his examples, such as his discussion of the meaning of "lithium," Peirce can develop his pragmatist conception of meaning only by having recourse to the normal, non-pragmatist, meaning of other words and concepts (Melvil 1968, 356). In the end, even this version of the principle collapses the perceived effects of anything with that which is causing the effects, which means that it is impossible to have knowledge of an object. This is inadequate because "in knowing, a person knows not his own action and perception (or better, not only these), but through them he knows the objective world and the things, phenomena, and processes that constitute it" (Melvil 1968, 360).

There are other problems as well. One of them is the essentially contradictory character of the principle: if the existence of a fact consists in the existence of its effects, then the existence of these effects, which are themselves facts, consists in *their* effects, ad infinitum, thus, not only can we not know objects or characteristics themselves, we cannot even know their effects. And finally, there is a degree of inconsistency in Peirce's application of the principle. If the meaning of a concept is its practical effects, then what do we make of those ideas or propositions that have no effects either in the sense of perceptions or on our behavior? They would be, presumably, meaningless, so that "Peirce's Principle" becomes the criterion of intelligibility. This reveals a strong positivist tendency in pragmatism, which, like positivism, often saw itself as an alternative to metaphysics. In Peirce's case, his rejection of "metaphysics" was an attempt to eliminate the "metaphysics" and "ontology" of materialism, that is, "to destroy the concept of objective reality in its materialist sense" (Melvil 1968, 366). The inconsistency is that "he never thought to turn the pragmatist maxim against idealistic and theistic metaphysics."

In his later pragmatism Peirce reconsiders the nature and role of belief. Melvil reads two approaches to belief at this stage, a more rational one deriving from Peirce's scientific and logical research, and a less rational one based in the end on his religious views. The more rational conception appears in Peirce's account of belief as the leading or guiding principles of thought (3.160). The "irrational" strain is his description of belief not in terms of conceptual or intellectual principles but as non-conscious or preconscious stimuli or motives, as instinct (5.498). This is Peirce's "critical common-sensism," the idea that the basis of all general views and beliefs of people is some belief, propositions or judgments that are never doubted, and thus never demonstrated. Peirce understands this "critical commonsense" as deriving from general human experience, but there is, Melvil thinks, a misplaced emphasis here:

> In reality it is not some abstract and indetermined experience that imposes certain beliefs on people, but their productive, practical activity leading to the transformation of nature and the achievement of intended results, rendered meaningful over the course of many centuries, which has led to the discovery of general connections with the world around us, to the observation of stable relations, and to the acceptance of several highly general ideas. (Melvil 1968, 384)

There is also a shift here from the earlier conception of belief, one which both ties Peirce to and distinguishes him from subsequent pragmatists. In "The Fixation of Belief" and "How to Make Our Ideas Clear" Peirce had posited belief as a product of doubt, but in critical common-sensism belief is prior to doubt. Doubt is generated by experience of some kind, specifically experience in which an individual stands at a "fork in the road." In one way this is a description of the "problematic situation" on which Dewey built his instrumentalist logic, though the two are not identical:

> But between the views of Peirce and Dewey there is an important difference. . . . For Dewey doubt arises as a result of a condition of action. Peirce allows for such a possibility, but he is not limited to it, and he holds that doubt may arise from wonder, i.e., it may have a more intellectual origin. Dewey speaks of the "indeterminate situation" in a literal sense, Peirce more figuratively. (Melvil 1968, 388–389)

Despite such differences, Peirce's basic ideas remain essentially pragmatist, and like his earlier pragmatism require a consideration of truth and reality. Melvil identifies four distinct conceptions of truth, the first of which is truth as the satisfactory. Though Peirce was often critical of the identification of truth with success or usefulness, he could never fully abandon this view, Melvil thinks, because to do so would have meant to abandon pragmatism (6.485). A second conception is truth as the indubitable (5.419). Here, Melvil says, Peirce collapses two distinct questions—"What is truth?" and "Under what conditions do we *hold* something to be true?" The pragmatist theory of truth is in the end built on a confusion of these two questions, though Melvil notes that in his objection to truth as the satisfactory Peirce seems to treat truth as one thing and what we believe to be true as something else entirely. The approach most suitable to Peirce, in Melvil's view, is the conception of Truth as the ultimate result of research (2.29). In this way he comes as close as he can to combining the necessary assumptions of science with the distinctive characteristics of pragmatism. As a scholar and scientist Peirce had to hold that truth is objective, but as a pragmatist he could only say that the objectivity of truth consists in the fact that in the end honest and genuine researchers will accept it (Melvil 1968, 395). The conception of truth as the result of research is consistent with the pragmatist maxim that the meaning of a concept lies in the future, it sees truth in terms of doubt and belief, and as formulated in terms of pragmatist principles it seems to allow him in some way to express the objective character of truth. There remains a fourth conception, which is truth as agreement with ideal limits (5.565). Here Peirce tries to connect truth most directly with scientific theory, and in so doing he rejects a pluralist conception of truth so characteristic of other pragmatist versions. In this respect he moves as far as he ever does from pragmatism. Despite Peirce's attempt to formulate an adequate conception of truth, or perhaps because of the attempt, there remains in his later pragmatism the tension between reality as independent of what anyone thinks of it and reality as a function of thought in general, and it remains the case that Peirce the scientist contradicts Peirce the pragmatist (Melvil 1968, 401).

While he acknowledges Peirce's influence on the development of subsequent philosophy in the United States, Melvil asks the question what role in the end pragmatism plays in Peirce's overall philosophy? There is no question, he answers, that many of the fundamental traits of James's and Dewey's pragmatism derive from Peirce and that many of his ideas that are not strictly pragmatist may be given a pragmatist interpretation. Much of his philosophy of science, for example, is strictly speaking not pragmatist, though it nevertheless has that flavor in part due to the centrality of action. On the whole, however, Melvil feels that pragmatism is not the heart of Peirce's philosophy but is itself an expression of a more general philosophic idealism:

> Therefore to the question whether Peirce was a pragmatist, we might answer that pragmatism was a doctrine elaborated by Peirce and applied by him in different periods of his activity, but pragmatism was not the basis of his entire philosophy, nor its most important content, in that his pragmatism itself grew out of the more central

principles of his idealism. Pragmatism was just one of the branches of his idealist philosophy, though one which became detached from the rest and grew into the most influential trend in American philosophic idealism. (Melvil 1968, 479–480)

Its growth and influence was due largely to William James.

James

James, like Peirce, had his intellectual roots in the sciences, in his case medicine and psychology. Also like Peirce James's philosophical work was motivated and characterized more than anything else by an attempt to defend, through a justification of religious belief, the spiritual side of human life threatened by the picture of the world and human being that seemed to be emerging from the sciences. And again like Peirce he found the most potent conceptual tools in the principles of pragmatism. But while in Peirce's case all this produced a sustained and unresolved contradiction between scientific rationality and religious commitment, in James science is ultimately submerged in a philosophic world view that is inherently irrational, or at best arational. This was the general Soviet perspective on James beginning with the 1927 article by V. F. Asmus on James's criticism of and alternative to rationalism. James opposed one of the cornerstones of traditional philosophy—that reason and logic are in themselves valuable cognitive tools. He emphasized instead individual psychological traits, interests and practical activity as crucial epistemological factors. In James not only science but rationality itself is lost in a fairly thoroughgoing anti-intellectualism (Asmus 1927, 1984).

James appropriated the principles of Peirce's 1870s pragmatist essays and developed them in ways that enabled pragmatism to take root in American philosophic culture. One of the reasons his work was so influential, some Soviet commentators have argued, is that his ideas, and even more so his unique expression of them, resonated especially well with the broader American ideology. He argued, for example, for the intellectual legitimacy under certain circumstances of believing what one wills to believe, for a view of the world that confers on us an intellectual "right" to think as we wish: "By so doing, James, like no one before or since, elevated to the rank of philosophic truths the ordinary ideas of the ordinary consciousness of the American bourgeoisie. Precisely this is the reason for his immense popularity in America" (Bogomolov 1974, 80–81). In the 1950s Melvil had made similar points, though in what was at that time a characteristically polemical form. James's conception of a pluralistic universe, he said, can be linked to capitalist society as it appears through the prism of bourgeois consciousness: its splintered interests, its anarchy and crises, its supposedly chance productive events, and its failure to recognize the laws of social development. And in a pluralistic universe God can no longer be a universal source of being, so in James's hands God becomes American, commercial, and essentially utilitarian, "fully adapted to the requirements of the American businessman" (Melvil 1957a, 54, 57).

In later works, as we have seen in his treatment of other aspects of pragmatism, Melvil's discussion of James does not have the hostility of the earlier studies, though he continues to see a connection, perhaps an unconscious one, of James's philosophic ideas with social interests and concerns: "It is possible that James did not recognize the social roots of his own religious aspirations, that the need for an external moral order is for him inseparably linked with the need to preserve the prevailing social-moral order which, in his view, is impossible without the existence of the hope inspired by the religious belief of a majority of people" (Melvil 1983, 50). And in later Soviet era studies, Melvil's and others', the emphasis shifts to a consideration and criticism of the technical details of James's metaphysics and theory of knowledge. Bogomolov emphasizes as a source of his philosophic ideas not bourgeois society so much as his own earlier psychological work. James's pragmatism is anticipated in his psychology most clearly by his rejection of psychological atomism and his conception of consciousness as a stream, one that does not "reflect" reality but out of which we individually "select" our world of experience (Bogomolov 1974, 64–68). Melvil adds that as a result of his psychological orientation James was interested above all in the "spiritual" life of the individual, and he dealt with philosophic problems not in terms of their objective content but in their impact on the subject (Melvil 1974, 89–90).

James's entire philosophic project, Sidorov says, has a religious flavor: "James's desire to strengthen the significance of religious belief and to ground in knowledge its methodological advantages in comparison with science, harkens back to the sources of the idealist tradition in American philosophy," specifically Jonathan Edwards's "religious sense" and Emerson's "intuitive reason" (Sidorov 1989, 112). The many aspects of James's philosophy, both its ontological and epistemological sides, are of a piece; they constitute an articulation and defense of philosophic idealism. Though James regarded pragmatism and radical empiricism as logically distinct conceptions, Melvil has said, they are in fact different aspects of a subjective idealism (Melvil 1957a, 34). More precisely, the latter is logically prior to the former. "In fact, his 'radical empiricism' makes up the general philosophic presupposition of his pragmatist doctrine," Melvil says, and Sidorov argues that with his rejection of experience as simply what is given in sense, and with the alternative view that experience consists of relations, James's radical empiricism is "decisive" for his distinctive philosophy of action (Melvil 1974, 89; Sidorov 1989, 108).

Though he objected to traditional metaphysics, James could not avoid developing a metaphysics of his own, in part because it contributed to his general philosophic concern to sustain a world view amenable to religion, and in part because his pragmatism required it. James's basic objection to earlier metaphysics, Yulina notes, was its adherence to monism and substantialism, and its use of an excessively remote, disembodied speculative method. Substance had become an "absolute," which led to a monistic scheme in which the world was either reduced to it or deduced from it. James rejected both rationalist absolute idealism and more empiricist metaphysics with a critique that had both a theoretical and an ideological character. He struggled against American and English representatives of Hegelianism, primarily Royce, Bradley, and Bosenquet, because their views seemed to him to contradict science and common sense, as well as the principles of democracy and liberalism. Hegelianism collapsed the multiplicity of the world into an unchanging unity, leaving no room for faith, freedom, and moral and emotional activity. At the same time James also opposed the American followers of Spencer, whose philosophic views were inclined to agnosticism, atheism, and amoralism. Spencerism, he thought, ignored the Subject; it had no room for the emotional grounding of human being (Yulina 1978a, 55–56).

James's "third line" between Hegelianism and Spencerism was radical empiricism, an ontological pluralism and neutralism. Yulina describes his empiricism as resting on a recognition of irreducibility as the "eternal element" of experience, and she notes that the ontological foundation of his pluralism was a theory of external relations. Traditional monism rests on a theory of internal relations, which in James's mind leads to determinism. But, James thought, the relations among phenomena are not internally structured. Their relations are functional, not essential. The virtue of such a view, for James, is that it allows for the reality of chance, for the unforeseen, for novelty, for freedom and for the existence of incompatible qualities. While Yulina emphasizes James's pluralism, Bogomolov focuses on the empiricist side of his metaphysics and its corresponding neutralism. James transformed empiricism from a theory of knowledge, in the tradition of Hume, to an ontology, and in the process ruled out any reality independent of experience. He was led to radical empiricism, Bogomolov says, from his conception of reality as two sides of the stream of consciousness.

For Bogomolov James's neutralism is clearly an inadequate ontology, and Yulina is no less critical of his pluralism. James had ambitious ideas about his philosophy, she says, but in the end his radicalism proved to be severely limited: "Frankly believing in the possibility of destroying with one blow the entire structure of scholasticism, metaphysics, and theology, he unwittingly, with the help of 'radical empiricism,' dragged back into philosophy the very thing against which he had earlier struggled" (Yulina 1978a, 57). The problem lies in the combination of pluralism and the pragmatic method. By identifying truth with utility, James identified judgments of fact with judgments of value, which, Yulina argues, inevitably leads to relativism, a theory of "double truths" and the equation of truth with error. To put the point a different way, in a pluralistic universe the pragmatic method can lead to the equal acceptability of incompatible positions because a given view may be useful in some respects while, at the same time, its contrary may be useful in others. James found himself in just this position. Yulina suggests that although he rejected metaphysics and philosophic idealism for specific reasons, in other respects he found a utility for metaphysics, religion, and idealism (Yulina 1978a, 57–58).

One of the distinctive features of James's metaphysics, and by extension his epistemology, is his conception of experience. It is in fact the central concept of radical empiricism, Melvil says, comparable in some ways to the role Spinoza ascribes to substance (Melvil 1974, 90). In his early work Melvil was concerned to illustrate what he took to be the inherently irrational character of James's treatment of experience and its ontological implications: "In the teachings of pragmatism, empiricism goes farther down the path of subjectivism than the empiricism of Berkeley and Mach and is transformed into irrationalism" (Melvil 1957a, 46). Melvil does not object to a conception of experience that would avoid the sensationalism of traditional empiricism, but James's alternative is no improvement. He broadens the meaning of "experience" beyond what is given in sensation but in a way that does not permit certain crucial distinctions. To be sure, Melvil says, things like hallucinations are experiences and thus are of scientific interest for psychology and psychiatry. But philosophically it is significant whether objective reality is given in experience or whether the individual is locked in the circle of the subjective phenomena of consciousness. Melvil interpreted James, and other pragmatists, as in the end taking the latter approach. James regards individual experience to be a construct out of undifferentiated "pure experience," which is already inconsistent with an objectively existing reality. In James's view individual experience is constructed more than anything else on the basis of the individual's purposes, so that "the volitional nature of the human individual is for pragmatism the foundation of all reality" (Melvil 1957a, 48). In this consists James's subjectivism, and it is a view of experience open to the charge of solipsism. James responded by saying that experience is not subjective but is rather a relation to a subject, which Melvil felt indicated his desire to retain a subjective idealism but to escape from the charge of solipsism. Experience, James said, is not a state or condition of consciousness, but consciousness is a state or condition of experience, which is to say that the same experience can be object *or* subject. This conception of experience, James held, is not a rejection of the external world, the world of "common sense," though it does involve the view that the external world is not independent of human being. This is, Melvil argued, a rejection, though somewhat obscured, of objective reality and, so, is little more than an updated version of Berkeley and Mach (Melvil 1957a, 50–52).

Nearly twenty years later Melvil again emphasized the subjectivism he found in James: Whatever there is, is encompassed in experience, a view on the basis of which James constructs a conception of the world and interpretations of traditional philosophic problems. Much of what experience consists is a function of the individual will. Will, however, is related to purposes, and the establishment of ends and the means for achieving them is a function of thought: "Thus, though we are given the material of experience as the stream of sensations, we construct for ourselves all of concrete, determinate reality" (Melvil 1974, 92). Experience, unlike in traditional empiricism, is active and creative, a view especially significant to Melvil because, as he notes, Marx too regarded human activity as affecting reality. The crucial difference is that Marx combined human creativity with objectivity: "But Marx nevertheless characterized the process of labor as an *objective* phenomenon, as the interaction of two material objects or powers. James sees in human activity only a *subjective process of the attainment of ends*" (Melvil 1974, 92; Melvil's emphasis). James does not so much deny an objective world as he articulates a view that does not include it. For James, in Melvil's view, that a world *exists* along with specific sensations and perceptions is not our doing; however, its content, that is, *what* the world is, depends on us (Melvil 1974, 93). And since for James the construction of experience is a result of individual will and purposes, the product is necessarily and inherently a pluralistic universe.

James's pluralism follows from his view of experience and radical empiricism, and it is the alternative to the metaphysical systems and closed, finished universe of absolute idealism. The world, James thought, is not a monolithic entity, not a single whole that follows any discernible, unified laws. Ontologically, since objects are not given in experience but individually constructed, they are not related to one another by objective law. Epistemologically, because no unity or necessity exists in the world, events can be explained in any number of ways, all legitimate to the extent that they meet individuals' purposes. In his early work Melvil criticizes this conception, as Yulina would later do, on the grounds that it results in, in fact encourages, contradictions. A dissatisfaction with contradictions may seem puzzling coming from a Marxist, but there is a crucial distinction to be made in this regard. According to a dialectical view, idealist or materialist, an account of the world may be offered in which the *world* consists of contradictory traits, themselves objectively determined and accessible to inquiry. James's pluralism, by contrast, issues in contradictory *accounts* of the world, which is an entirely different matter. A dialectical account, and there are many possible versions, may not necessarily be right, but it is at least rational in that it permits inquiry, knowledge, and error. But by allowing the equal legitimacy of contradictory views, James essentially eliminates the possibility of inquiry. Inquiry and knowledge become senseless because they presuppose criteria on the basis of which one can adjudicate among inconsistent or contradictory positions, to distinguish between truth and error. If contradictory positions are permissible, the distinction between truth and falsity collapses. By excluding the possibility and sense of inquiry, knowledge, and error, James's pluralism and the radical empiricism from which it follows are irrational and thus "acutely hostile to science and a scientific understanding of the world" (Melvil 1957a, 54).

It is not surprising, then, that one would find contradictions in James's own philosophic views. Melvil mentions a few: James claimed not to reject the existence of the external world, but he nevertheless turns the things of the world into objects of belief; James held that a neutral, pure experience is ontologically primary, yet he reads experience through the flow of human feeling, which renders the individual subject primary; and while he describes truth in terms of usefulness and practical verification, James at the same time allows for truth that has had no practical verification and no recognized use (Melvil 1957a, 52).

This line of criticism, which runs through all the Soviet discussions of James, of course rests on the very conception of knowledge and truth that James directly criticized and that he took his own pragmatism to supersede. His dissatisfaction with absolute idealism, and with materialism, was epistemological as well as ontological. One explanation for neither tradition achieving adequate conclusions—idealism with its closed universe and materialist science with its increasingly emotionless and spiritless world—is that neither was working with an appropriate "form of rationality"; neither took account of the degree to which inquiry and knowledge incorporate human purpose. James's approach, as Melvil describes it, is that "we incline toward one or another system of views not because we regard it to be true; on the contrary, we consent to regard it as true because it corresponds most to our frame of mind, to our emotional state and, if you like, to our interests" (Melvil 1983, 48). Sidorov approaches James's "pragmatic rationality" primarily in its opposition to "logical rationality," the rationality of Hegel, Bradley, and Royce. The "conceptual" logic of the idealists artificially breaks the "flow" of lived experience, while a pragmatic rationality acknowledges the role of the intellect as a weapon for an "effective orientation" in concrete circumstances (Sidorov 1989, 109–110). In reacting against the "intellectualism" of Absolute Idealism, as Bogomolov puts it, James developed a unique pragmatic logic, one which differs in important ways from Peirce's. Peirce's logic is *not* the logic of pragmatism, in Bogomolov's view, because his logic was basically formalist, while a pragmatic logic is basically psychological. It was Schiller and Dewey who were the pragmatist logicians par excellence, but the "irrationalism" they were to develop already appears in James (Bogomolov 1974, 81).

The Soviets have found James's "psychologistic" epistemology unacceptable largely because of its individualism. Melvil criticized James for emphasizing the biological and psychological aspects of human being while ignoring human social constitution (Melvil 1957a, 35). For Sidorov this is perhaps the central flaw of James's philosophy of action. James's mistake was to read human action itself in individual and subjective terms. James is entirely justified, Sidorov argues, in indicating a connection between activity and change, but in doing so he "psychologizes" the content of activity, in that activity is not understood so much as interaction with the world but more with the process of the emotional experience of the actor. Such a conception cannot account for the social nature of consciousness and practical human activity: James's "approach to practice is, again, superficial. He notices, of course, that practice, or in his understanding, activity, has an essential influence on knowledge; however he does not realize that material, practical activity constitutes the law of knowledge" (Sidorov 1989, 115). Roughly the same point can be made in terms of a contrast between the theoretical and practical aspects of knowledge. For James, of course, the significance of knowledge is not its objectivity but that it serves as an orientation in experience, a tool for action. That concepts have a practical side, Sidorov says, is no doubt true, but James errs when he identifies with one another the several aspects of activity: the psychological, logical, cognitive, and practical. They are related but not reducible to one another, and James essentially collapses their differences:

> Therefore, as genuine knowledge he recognizes not the objective, which would be free of the specific traits of individual interest, but rather the subjective, for James elevates the usefulness of knowledge to a criterion of truth, coordinated with practical though merely individual interests. . . . The methodological circle into which James's pragmatism plunges practically oriented knowledge is created precisely because the achievement of truth in his view is connected with ends that are subjectively restricted in their cognitive and practical content. (Sidorov 1989, 119–120)

James's conception of the relation of knowledge and activity is inextricably linked to the centerpiece of his epistemology, the theory of truth. Pragmatism, James says, is primarily a method for reconciling conflicting opinions. This is a clear application of Peirce's Principle, though in James's hands it is transformed from a theory of meaning into a theory of truth. If the very meaning of an idea consists in its practical effects, then an idea's truth as well can lie only in its consequences for us. In his principle of meaning Peirce had already divorced concepts and ideas from any reality independent of those on whom they have practical effects, and in James truth follows suit. Truth can no more be objective than can meaning. This is the point at which all Soviet criticisms of James's conception of truth converge.

Sidorov may put the objection most succinctly when he criticizes James for not distinguishing between objective and absolute truth. James's attraction to Peirce's Principle was due in part to its value for his arguments against absolute idealism. The idealist tradition seeks to articulate a finished, closed system of reality, an absolute truth. It was the absolute character of the idealists' philosophic products that James abhorred, and Sidorov suggests that he also distrusted science for its similar attempt to establish absolute truth. The pragmatist maxim is useful for James precisely because it has no room for absolute truth. Its fundamental problem, however, is that it has no room for objective truth either. James was right to criticize absolute truth, but mistaken in applying the same criticism to objective truth (Sidorov 1989, 116). There is no good reason to accept absolute truth, a truth eternal, unconditioned and unrelated, Sidorov might say, but there is every good reason to accept objective truth, a truth independent of human activity.

We can identify several versions or aspects of James's conception of truth. Melvil has considered James's theory with respect to the relation of truth to usefulness, verification, and knowledge. The truth of an idea resides in its consequences, the most important of which is the utility of the idea for the individual who holds it. For James, to say that an idea is true because it is useful is equivalent to saying that it is useful because it is true. By so abandoning a correspondence theory of truth, Melvil says, the very concept of truth loses its epistemological significance and becomes a category of valuation (Melvil 1974, 94–95). Furthermore, the relation between the truth of an idea and its verification is inverted. If an idea becomes or is made true as it proves its usefulness, then the truth of an idea is not verified by its consequences but rather consists of the process of verification. This, however, cannot be right since "the pragmatists' assertion that truth is constituted by and arises in the process of its verification is refuted at every step by the facts of ordinary life" (Melvil 1957a, 39). We all believe many things without their having for most of us any practical significance, for example that London is on the Thames. Indeed, we may hold any number of ideas to be true without having any sense of their utility. When the Curies discovered radioactivity, Melvil notes, the claims of its existence were accepted as true without people knowing any use of it for them. Pragmatists are not unaware of this sort of point, he notes, and there was an attempt to respond by arguing that potential or initial verification, that is, utility of some kind for somebody, is sufficient to constitute truth for others. But this, Melvil suggests, contradicts the pragmatist position that truth *is* usefulness. In a later discussion he notes both the virtues and flaws of James's idea:

> James's theory of truth makes use of the undeniable fact that true knowledge is useful and that the pragmatic verification of an idea or theory, in one or another form, in the end remains the only reliable criterion of truth. But the fallaciousness of the pragmatist theory of truth consists first in the logically flawed view that if truth is useful then usefulness makes up the entire content of truth, and second in that pragmatism without warrant divorces knowledge from successful activity. (Melvil 1983, 52)

James had tried to handle such criticisms, and as a result he offers several different versions of his conception of truth, not all of which are consistent with one another. Bogomolov identified five aspects of James's theory of truth: (1) truth is created in the process of the verification of ideas; (2) truth is what works, having practical consequences that answer to our expectations; (3) truth is usefulness; (4) truth can be based on faith, the "credit system" of truth; and (5) truth must be consistent with preceding truths and with new facts (Bogomolov 1974, 70).

The first thesis, that truth is made, means that prior to its verification an idea is neither true nor false but simply an idea. This, in Bogomolov's view, is James's first mistake, since it is a conception grounded in "the solipsism of the present moment," ignoring preceding objective conditions and the role they play in the generation and verification of ideas. We acquire truth, Bogomolov argues, using specific means of knowledge, for example sense organs, abstract thought, concepts, judgments, and deduction, and all this comes about on the basis of material, practical human activity and is mediated by it. An idea (concept, judgment, or theory) becomes true or false in the process of its formation depending on whether we correctly or incorrectly use our cognitive abilities and methods. "Verification comes about already in the process of knowledge, and the verification of which James speaks as the process of 'making true' merely completes our cognitive procedure, finally establishing the truth or falsity of the result" (Bogomolov 1974, 70–71).

The second aspect of the theory is that truth is grounded in practical consequences and is what works. But despite what he says, James is really not very interested in human activity and its *objective* results, but simply in the "effects of an idea" on individuals. Furthermore, "by transforming each separate 'practical' act into the evidence of the truthfulness of an idea, the pragmatist eliminates the cognitive significance of practice in general" (Bogomolov 1974, 72).

Regarding the third thesis, that truth is usefulness, Bogomolov echoes Melvil's criticism of identifying the two. He also notes that "not all truth is directly useful for all people" and that in any case one needs to say not only that usefulness is some evidence of truth, but also that truth in the end is useful. The "credit system," basing truth on faith, is, for Bogomolov, James at his worst, since this devalues even the pragmatist theory of truth itself.

Finally, the fifth thesis, in part a statement of a coherence theory of truth, is James's caution against subjectivism. Though he is right to be concerned about this, Bogomolov argues that James has no real way to avoid subjectivism, given the rest of his philosophy. While James says that ideas must be consistent with reality and with our stock of truths, in the end he believes that both an "idea" and "reality" are "two sides of a single stream of consciousness" (Bogomolov 1974, 74). If reality is "selected" by individual volition, then a true idea can only be that which meets individual purposes. There is a vicious circle here from which James cannot escape.

On the whole, Soviet commentators found the inadequacies in James to outweigh by far his philosophic contributions. The virtues of his pragmatism consist in the critique of absolute idealism and, in Sidorov's view, in his conception of action, including cognitive activity, as creative: James "is right in seeing the philosophical meaning of action in the generation of new forms of being, in creativity" (Sidorov 1989, 122). But James's understanding of the creative aspect of human action is marred by a failure to appreciate the relation of human creativity to the objective conditions in which it occurs: "Pragmatism's essential depreciation of the social nature of the epistemological determinations of the objectivity of knowledge and the consequent replacement of the material and practical by the sensually given do not sustain the possibility of an adequate interpretation of the nature of experience and its expression in the forms of knowledge" (Sidorov 1989, 120). And Melvil offers a summary of his objections:

> The philosophy of William James captivated the minds of American bourgeois intellectuals at the beginning of the present century, but its dark sides are too significant: an extreme subjectivism in its views of reality and truth, an overt individualism and antidemocratic ethical, social, and political concepts, an undisguised irrationalism and a militantly antiscientific "radical empiricism," going as far as a justification of spiritualism. (Melvil 1983, 55)

Since as it turned out, Melvil's final public consideration of American philosophy were two papers he presented in Moscow on James, and since these two papers were written and presented in 1992, soon after the collapse of the Soviet Union, it is worth a look at them explicitly. In these two papers Melvil considers some of the same issues that he had addressed in his earlier discussions of James, specifically James's concept of pure experience, his theory of truth, and his idea of a pluralistic universe. What makes these papers interesting is that their tone differs so much from that of the earlier works. For example, Melvil is still interested in the relation between James and American culture generally. In the early works, however, James is described as representing the more crass and commercial traits of American life, looking as he did for the "cash value" of ideas and simply for what "works." In those of his writings, as we have seen, Melvil regarded James as a spokesperson for a philosophy and an ideology that fed neatly into the expansionist and imperialist interests of American capital.

In the 1992 papers, however, James is much more sympathetically treated. Melvil describes him, as a matter of fact, as "genuinely concerned with the presence of immorality and evil in the world, with the existence of wealth and poverty, of oppressors and oppressed. . . . James was a committed opponent of war. . . . He thought that the militarist sense was deeply implanted in people's psyche, but he believed that it is possible to turn them toward another, more peaceful path, to provide them with more peaceful, constructive work." (Melvil 1992b, 3). Not only did Melvil come to see James as a social progressive, but he also altered his view of the sort of Americanism expressed in James. James is no longer the embodiment of base American commercialism, but, on the contrary, he expresses an American sense of the possibilities of the future: "James's universe is an open universe, always in the making. This idea of James is consonant with a typically American conception of the world and of America itself as a country open to all perspectives" (Melvil 1992b, 15). He goes on, in fact, taking his cue from John McDermott, that James embodies a view we find also in Walt Whitman, to the effect that America is not finished and never will be.

Though the greater degree of sympathy is clear, Melvil remained critical of James's central ideas, repeating some criticisms he had made earlier. James's approach to experience and his theory of truth are what concerned Melvil the most. He says, for example, that the concept of experience is so central for James that one can say that it has a "magical character" for him, in the sense that he uses it to explain virtually anything he wants (Melvil 1992a, 7). While James's view had the virtue of overcoming the traditional empiricist break between the subject and object, James went to the other extreme and essentially eliminated the distinction, dissolving both subject and object into "pure experience" (Melvil 1992b, 8–9). The critical philosophic failure, as we have seen throughout, was James's refusal to distinguish between the world with its objectively determined traits and the experiencing, knowing subject standing in relation to those traits. When he fails to distinguish subject and object, or when he does not distinguish between talking about the world and talking about a conception of the world, James may simply be failing to speak precisely enough. In his interest in appealing to a broader audience, Melvil thinks, James often made use of ordinary language when what was required was a language with greater technical precision. He too often collapsed philosophical and ordinary language, and that was the source of his inaccuracy (Melvil 1992b, 10).

The same tendency to overlook crucial distinctions between subject and object are at the heart of the mistake in James's theory of truth, though again Melvil wants to be far more gentle in his criticisms than he had been years earlier. "In this country," he says, referring of course to the Soviet Union, "and not only here, the pragmatist theory of truth has undergone especially bitter attacks" (Melvil 1992a, 11). But these attacks, Melvil goes on to say, including his own, were unwarranted because James's theory of truth was not nearly as primitive as many of his critics thought, and in any case one has to be far more patient and generous with a thinker who is trying to break new ground in such thorny areas as the nature of truth. Despite the weaknesses of James's theory, he ultimately says, we have to bear in mind that after Peirce he was the first philosopher to work out a conception of truth on new theoretical bases. Like any new idea, James's work was prone to exaggeration. This was partly exacerbated by the fact that James was often writing for public lectures and a wide audience, but that does not alter the fact that he was struggling in novel ways with massively difficult ideas, and one should expect some degree of inadequacy under such conditions (Melvil 1992a, 16). None of this however, changes the fact that by too closely identifying truth with usefulness, James's theory fails to do justice either to truth or to practical activity, and Melvil makes his case with many of the same arguments he had been using throughout his life.

In the end, though, Melvil wants to emphasize the depth of James's philosophy, in two specific respects. First, James's view that philosophy is to be understood as our respective, individual ways of representing our lives and its meaning is important. Too often we have wanted philosophy to behave like a science, and that is a mistake. Unlike science, any philosophical analysis or position can stimulate ideas and be worthwhile in some respects, and James's approach can help us to see that. Second, James was able to emphasize the many-sided relationship of human being to the universe, thus helping us to avoid a debilitating narrowness of vision. And finally, James's greatest legacy, Melvil thinks, is his influence on the course of philosophy for the past century (Melvil 1992a, 17–19).

While James's contributions have been to some degree reconsidered in recent years, the same cannot yet be said of Dewey's. The more general of the traditional criticisms of James's pragmatism tended to reappear in Soviet discussions of Dewey.

Dewey

In the United States Dewey has been the most influential of the pragmatists, while traditionally in Soviet commentary he was the most deeply criticized. At the ideological level Melvil in the 1950s would describe him as "one of the most negative figures of the ideological reaction of the epoch of imperialism," and later another commentator would say of his instrumentalism that it is more reactionary than the pragmatism of Peirce and James (Melvil 1957a, 61; Gureeva 1983, 119). In technical philosophic respects Dewey has fared little better, since he "is a less original thinker than Peirce, and perhaps even than James" (Melvil 1974, 97). Dewey stood on the shoulders of Peirce and James, appropriating many of their ideas, but he did so with little effect. In some ways he avoided the mistakes of his forebears, especially James: "If James held that things arise as a result of our belief in their existence and are represented as 'objects of belief,' then Dewey 'corrects' James in the spirit of Peirce, arguing that apparent reality arises in the process of cognition and is represented as the object of scientific inquiry, created by this process" (Melvil 1983, 57). Despite such "corrections," though, Dewey did not advance pragmatist theory, in the Soviets' view, as much as confuse it even further. One of the sources of the confusion, according to Melvil, is the vagueness of Dewey's central concepts. For example, like his pragmatist colleagues Dewey opposed materialism, but he would not characterize his own views as idealist, and this reflects a more general trait of his work: "Dewey's evasiveness with respect to the basic question of philosophy is a specific instance of his evasive position in general, of vagueness and unclarity elevated to a principle. . . . If James tried to express pragmatism in the language of the street and marketplace, Dewey used pseudo-scientific language in which every term defies precise definition" (Melvil 1974, 98). This sort of point, coupled with the many inherent philosophic problems inherited from the pragmatism of Peirce and James, suggests the general if not universal tenor of the Soviet assessment of Dewey's instrumentalism and philosophic reconstruction.

Reconstructing Philosophy

Dewey's program rests in part on his own approach to traditional philosophy, a critical assessment not without its merits. Through his criticism of the European philosophic heritage, he developed an alternative understanding of the nature and function of thought and knowledge, even of philosophy itself. The specific impulse for his critique of the philosophic tradition, Sidorov suggests, came from the pervasive dualisms of the speculative tradition, the incessant bifurcations of the world of experience so inconsistent with what Dewey took to be the continuity of natural development. Accompanying philosophy's tendency to drive a wedge between aspects of the world or phases of experience, between mind and matter, nature and human being, knowledge and action, or fact and value, has been its excessive rationalism, always debilitating and in some respects dangerous. We have, Dewey argued, misunderstood the nature of knowledge and inquiry, and as a result we have missed the genuine possibilities of philosophy and have made it increasingly difficult to solve our problems. This points to the need for a reconstruction in philosophy, for a new conception of philosophy and inquiry. The need is nowhere more apparent than in our continuous inability to resolve social problems, a failure resulting not from the intractable nature of the problems but from an inadequate method. Our tendency has been to approach our problems on the basis of a priori conceptions of social relations, themselves a product of a rationalist and speculative method, and the consequence has been not the resolution but the deepening of social difficulties. The methodological alternative is at hand, however, evident in our own experience. For Dewey, Melvil notes, our own epoch reveals a split between two kinds of human activity or experience. One is science and technology, the most salient characteristic of which has been its profound practical success. The other side of our experience is social life, characterized by contradictions, wars, conflicts, and moral decay. Dewey's proposal is to apply the methods of the first to the second, to explore and extend the application of the method of intelligence as expressed in science (Melvil 1974, 99–100).

"The nucleus of Dewey's program for a radical transformation of philosophy and the methodology of knowledge," Sidorov says, "consists in his critique of rationalist principles of knowledge and the formation of a new type of rationality, expressed in the nonspeculative categories of a philosophy of action" (Sidorov 1989, 123). This overtly epistemological concern was tied to Dewey's treatment of traditional metaphysics, an issue in which Yulina is primarily interested. Although Dewey declared himself opposed to the forms philosophy had taken in the modern period, Yulina suggests, he was in fact a captive of an Enlightenment view that associated metaphysics with a conservative academic tradition and with dogmatism of thought. This she feels explains to some extent his rejection of metaphysics and his use of a historical and genetic method to criticize it. Metaphysics, Dewey argued, had traditionally been an abstract expression of the values and ideal needs of a given culture: "Dewey explained the tenacity and activity of philosophy in terms of its unique function of justifying the social, moral, and psychological convictions of its time and of freeing itself from the social and cultural establishment of a preceding epoch" (Yulina 78a, 61). Once we realize that this in fact has been the role of philosophy, we can more easily see the need to abandon any attempt to discover universal or transcendent traits of being, or foundations of knowledge, and turn our attention to an understanding of ends and values in experience. In the process "what philosophy loses from the point of view of science it gains from the point of view of humanistic knowledge" (Yulina 1978a, 62). In this respect, Yulina suggests, Dewey was an early advocate of "scientific" philosophy, though unlike the positivists he understood this to mean not a rejection of philosophy's relation to values and a "world view," but rather a conscious transformation of it. For Dewey, then, philosophy coincides with education and enlightenment in that its proper concern is not with research into this or that field of facts, since that is the business of science. Philosophy's concern is rather with the educative ends, norms, and ideals that influence the course of social, cultural, and intellectual development.

Metaphysics: The "Situation"

The central flaw in Dewey's interpretation of metaphysics appears, Bogomolov argues, in his treatment of traditional logic. Dewey correctly recognizes, he says, the weakness of the "metaphysical," that is, the antidialectical, nature of formal logic, which is that it alienates thought from our *activity*, from inquiry. But Dewey overextends the significance of this point, and he fails to see how logic nevertheless reflects aspects of reality and practical human activity. By interpreting traditional logic primarily as an expression of classical ruling class biases in favor of "pure thought," Dewey loses an objectivist understanding of logic (Bogomolov 1974, 87–88). Furthermore, Dewey makes a mistake in his own conception of logic, in his theory of inquiry. In Dewey's view, logic must be understood naturalistically, which leads to an emphasis on the biological foundations and conditions of knowledge. Dewey then pursues the biological content of cognitive activity: "the unity of the organism, its surroundings, and the relation between them; the dependence of the surroundings of an organism on the organism's own complexity and function (thus the environment of an animal is wider than the environment of a plant); the dependence of behavior on both the organism's complexity and its environment, etc." (Bogomolov 1974, 84–85). Dewey combines this biologistic approach with the prominent nineteenth century view that life is to be seen as a continuous cycle of the violation of balance and its restoration through trial and error. The upsetting of equilibrium creates need, and the movement toward restoration is inquiry. However, "It is immediately evident that this mechanistic conception essentially oversimplifies the matter," Bogomolov thinks. In his naturalistic logic Dewey correctly emphasizes the point that nothing supernatural distinguishes thought, but he mistakenly takes this to mean that there is nothing "above the biological" about it either, that nothing qualitatively distinguishes thought from the organic behavior of animals, except perhaps for language. This is to read inquiry as a complex form of instinct, and in doing so Dewey does not see the crucial difference between instinct and human behavior. Instinct, Bogomolov suggests, has the two elements of organic need and the biologically conditioned means of its satisfaction, but human behavior also involves an additional, qualitatively distinct set of conditions: "Of course organic needs are retained in human society, but the capacity of their satisfaction becomes social. The human capacities for action and social, productive practice are secured not in the organic behavior of animals but in the laws and forms of human thought" (Bogomolov 1974, 85–86). Thus thought is not so much biological as it is social and cultural. Bogomolov notes that Dewey did in some ways recognize the sociocultural aspects of logic by saying that cultural surroundings do call forth certain modifications in biological organisms. Dewey saw the difference between human beings and animals primarily in the use of language, and he saw "culture" as "the conditions and product of language." But Dewey then grounds language and its cultural products in the human biological condition. Dewey fails to see that the key to culture, and to inquiry, is the essentially social activity of production (Bogomolov 1974, 86).

Dewey's biological approach to the human condition is the source of his fundamental conception of the "situation." The relation between individual and surroundings is a situation, an idea from which flows Dewey's entire epistemology, which in turn conditions the way he is able to understand the ontological character of a situation. A situation may be problematic or indeterminate, though it may also, sometimes as a consequence of inquiry, be determinate or settled. In any case, the most significant generic trait of any sort of situation, for Dewey, is that its constituents are organically interrelated, not simply mechanically related.[8] Dewey used the term *interaction,* and later *transaction,* to express the idea that in their relations with one another the constituents of a situation determine their respective traits. This is a generalization of an "ecological" conception implicit in Darwinism, and it serves Dewey as an alternative to the traditional category of substance. A situation can contain no ultimately discrete or essentially unrelated "things." Rather, "events" occur and are characterized by their continuity with one another, a conception with which Dewey anticipates "Whitehead and other 'process philosophers'" (Yulina 1978a, 65). Dewey developed his understanding of experience and inquiry, of knowledge and action, on the basis of the interaction and continuity in a situation. He was loathe to say much more about the generic traits of situations, in part because to do so smacked of the speculative metaphysical enterprise that he so fervently criticized. But for most Soviet commentators at least one crucial issue must be addressed: whether the constituents of a situation have objectively determinate traits. Dewey's reluctance to pursue this question may account for Melvil's remark that "the problematic situation is the central and at the same time the most cloudy concept of Dewey's instrumentalism, in which is embodied his attempt to synthesize several ideas of James's and Peirce's pragmatism" (Melvil 1974, 100). However reluctantly, Dewey did eventually offer a more explicit account of the ontological character of a situation, and in so doing he revealed what Soviets tended to argue is the philosophic inadequacy of the category.

The issue, again, is the conflict between materialism and idealism. Dewey himself had rejected the choice, arguing that neither materialism, in its mechanical and determinist sense, nor idealism, objective or subjective, is philosophically adequate.[9] Many traditional ontological conceptions either presumed or produced sharp and irreconcilable dichotomies between the individual and the world, between matter and mind, or else entirely subsumed one under the other. The interactional character of the constituents of a situation, Dewey thought, neither assumed nor generated unacceptable dualisms, and thus overcame and rendered obsolete the choice between materialism and idealism. But the specific way Dewey understood the interaction between the individual and environing conditions in a situation indicates the failure of his alternative, or more precisely that it is no alternative at all. The problem is that Dewey's conception of a situation does not refer to an objective condition of things but to a "contextual whole" that includes a subject (Bogomolov 1974, 88). The concern is not with contextuality and interaction but with the philosophic inability of Dewey's conception to account for the objectively determinate traits of the constituents of a situation. For all its value in overcoming an earlier mechanical understanding of relation, Dewey so "absolutized" his conception of natural, social, and cognitive interaction or transaction that it eliminates the constituents of the interaction, in the sense that subject and object are so "continuous" that they exist only as aspects or sides of the transaction (Bogmolov 1974, 104). As Melvil puts it, the continuity in a situation between the knower and the known, or between subject and object, is such that the known "exists" only in knowledge, reality arises in the process of knowledge, objects arise in interaction (Melvil 1957b, 61).

In one of his early essays Melvil considers Dewey's example of the consequences of the discovery of America.[10] Dewey here criticizes the conception of discovery as simply an encounter with or finding of a preexistent reality, as a "mere stumbling over a chair in the dark." Rather, discovery, and by implication the process of inquiry that may lead to it, is ontologically, existentially creative; it transforms nature. It can be said that the Norsemen "discovered America" only in the sense that "the newly found and seen object was used to modify old beliefs, to change the sense of the old map of the earth. . . ." This change in the sense of the old map was not simply an alteration of states of consciousness or of people's ideas of the world. On the contrary, "the modification was one in the public meaning of the world in which men publicly act," and "changing the meaning of the world effected an existential change." To change the map is not simply to change "a piece of linen hung on a wall" but to generate meanings and possibilities for the old world that did not exist prior to the discovery, "to produce consequences previously impossible." America became "a potential object of further exploration and discoveries . . . a source of gold; an opportunity for adventure; an outlet for crowded and depressed populations, an abode for exiles and the discounted . . . in short, an agency of new events and fruitions. . . ." The discovery of America created a new relation that changed the traits of Europe and Asia, and Dewey concludes that "In some degree, every genuine discovery creates some such transformation of both meanings and the existences of nature."

Melvil does not object to Dewey's epistemological point that knowledge and inquiry are active and fruitful and that they change the world. His concern is with the corresponding ontological conception that Dewey associates with this. As Dewey puts it immediately prior to his discussion of the discovery of America, "That there is existence antecedent to search and discovery is of course admitted; but it is denied that as such, as other than the conclusion of the historical event of inquiry and its connection with other histories, it is already the object of knowledge." To be an object of knowledge, then, to be an aspect of the world as known, is to be a product of the process of inquiry; the world we know is a world we make in the process of coming to know it.

"Dewey's entire argument is built on the conflation of two meanings of the expression 'to change the world' and on the confusion of two different questions," Melvil says. The first question is whether the discovery of America changed the world in the sense that it changed the structure of the terrestrial sphere, and the second is whether it changed the world in the sense that is had serious historical consequences for the world's people? Obviously it did not create a new continent, though it did "imply a whole series of transformations in economic and political life," and "*in this sense* Columbus's discovery genuinely changed the world" (Melvil 1957b, 65–66; Melvil's emphasis). For Melvil it is essential to grant the previous, objective existence of America in order to understand how its discovery could have the creative consequences it did, but this is a distinction Dewey essentially elides. First, the discovery of America is not in any significant sense an acknowledgment of a preexisting reality as a result of which we alter our understanding of the objective world or "change our map," since "a change in the map involves other and still more important objective changes," Dewey holds. Second, "every genuine discovery creates some such transformation . . . of the existences of nature." And third, Dewey "scoffs at the view according to which an object exists independently of us and that we 'stumble upon' or discover it" (Melvil 1957b, 66). In equivocating between different meanings of "change," Melvil argues, Dewey rejects the objective existence of the world, collapses the existence of a thing with knowledge of it, identifies objective reality with its reflection in consciousness, blends the object with the subject, and in general defends a subjective idealism: "Dewey's idea is very simple: so long as we do not know a particular thing, it does not exist as that thing."

Dewey's ontological conception has both a Berkeleyan and Kantian flavor. In so far as "the object of knowledge" is nothing "other than the conclusion of the historical event of inquiry," Dewey's idea is a close relative of Berkeley's view that "to be is to be perceived." Unlike Berkeley, however, for Dewey an "existence antecedent to search and discovery is of course to be admitted." What, then, is the relation between an "antecedent existence" and the object of knowledge that is the product of inquiry? In the context of a discussion of existence and consciousness later in *Experience and Nature,* Dewey draws a distinction between events and objects. He has been arguing for a conception of consciousness as a "phase of a system of meanings which at a given time is undergoing re-direction, transitive transformation. . . . Consciousness *is* the meaning of events in the course of remaking."[11] Consciousness, and by implication perception and awareness generally, is a matter of meanings, or the meaning of events, and not of events themselves. However, "when it is denied that we are conscious of *events* as such it is not meant that we are not aware of *objects*. Objects are precisely what we are aware of. For objects are events *with* meanings."[12] The distinction between events, or existences, and objects, or events with meaning, is an ontological bifurcation. That it is ontological is clear from the fact that Dewey's entire project is an attempt to read meanings into nature, to avoid conceptions that treat meanings either as supernatural or as wholly individual and subjective. So objects, events with meanings, are fully natural phenomena, but in one crucial way they differ from events, which are also fully natural. Natural existences that are events by definition cannot be known because knowledge is a matter of meanings, and an event "in itself," that is, "nature" as it is independent of our activity, has no meaning. As Dewey puts it, "theories which identify knowledge with acquaintance, recognition, definition and classification give evidence, all the better for being wholly unintended, that we know not just events but events-with-meanings."[13] Precisely here is the Kantianism of Dewey's ontology. The world as known is a world made by us as we imbue events with meaning, while the objective world, Dewey's "antecedent existence," is in principle unknowable. Melvil saw much the same problem in Dewey's view that science constructs the physical world, or that physical science leads to the organization of the physical world (Melvil 1957b, 67).

If this sort of Kantian moment arises in Dewey's ontology, it is in all likelihood an inadvertent backsliding on his part. One of his most persistent concerns was to avoid or, more precisely, to develop an alternative to the very chasm between aspects of nature, or between the individual and the rest of the world, which his distinction between events and objects reintroduces. Dewey's desire was to reconstruct philosophic conceptions of nature and knowledge on the basis of continuity, a "novel twist," Yulina says, since traditional modernist empiricism had been characterized by the drawing of distinctions and differences. Soviet commentators are sympathetic to his intent, in that "in principle Dewey was right to posit the question of the unity of knowledge" in the face of traditional, absolute demarcations between philosophy and science, between judgments of fact and judgments of value (Yulina 1978a, 67–68). The criticism is not that Dewey's purposes were wrong but that he failed to achieve them. The culprit tends to be a pragmatism that understands the determinate traits of objects as functions of objects' relations to subjects. Notwithstanding Dewey's laudable concern with natural continuity, "the too general a formulation of this question, the underestimation of the necessity to specify and qualify the many forms of knowledge, as well as the subjectivist aims of instrumentalist logic, made it impossible for him to substantiate this unity convincingly and with certainty" (Yulina 1978a, 68).

Despite such objections, there is value in Dewey's treatment of ontological continuity in a situation. In what may have been the most sympathetic treatment of Dewey in all of Soviet literature, D. M. Khanin considers the role of continuity in a situation in Dewey's conception of aesthetic experience. Khanin is interested primarily in the interaction of the rational and emotion in aesthetic experience, and he finds Dewey's aesthetic theory to be particularly valuable in the way it treats this question. He notes that Dewey's approach rests in part on a break from traditional psychological categories that had enclosed an individual's emotional traits in an atomized self. Dewey was able to offer a more fluid conception of human nature deriving from an understanding of experience that reflects his interest in the changing and precarious. In addition, Khanin notes the centrality for Dewey's aesthetics of the pragmatist principle that both subject and object arise in a situation, and are determined according to specific ends. One of the distinctive features of Khanin's discussion is that unlike other Soviet commentators he emphasizes the fruitfulness of the very aspects of Dewey's views that others tend to criticize. In the end he is critical, though somewhat perfunctorily, suggesting that "Dewey remains in the very individualist and subjectivist orientation that he so masterfully criticizes" (Khanin 1985, 35). But he nevertheless notes the significance of the integration of subject and object in a situation and, interestingly enough, the role of the objective in Dewey's aesthetics. One of the more important contributions of Dewey's theory, in Khanin's view, is as a basis for a criticism of explicitly individualist conceptions of artistic expression in which art is an activity motivated by isolated subjective concerns of the artist. By contrast, "Dewey holds that aesthetic theory cannot stop short at the constitution of the purely imaginative emotional and personal character of expression, but rather should be turned to inquiry and exposure of the character of reality itself, of the conditions in which the active individual is realized" (Khanin 1985, 26). It is precisely Dewey's conception of a situation that generates what Khanin takes to be the virtue of his aesthetic theory over others, both objectivist and subjectivist. The situation enables Dewey to bring to the fore the interaction of the individual with the surrounding environment so that neither objective conditions nor the role of subjectivity are short-changed (Khanin 1985, 34).[14]

Experience and Inquiry

As Khanin points out, the way Dewey treats the ontological traits of a situation engenders his general conception of experience. The category of experience is so fundamental for Dewey, and so pervasive in its signification, that in some respects it takes the place of the classical categories of being, substance, and reality (Yulina 1978a, 67). Melvil remarks that "The central concept of his philosophy was the concept of 'experience,' in which the Jamesian concept of the stream of consciousness is combined with the idea of the active interaction of the individual with the environment, the organism with its surroundings" (Melvil 1986, 111). The relation to James is real but partial. For one thing, "If for James the model of experience was religious and moral, for Dewey it was more moral and political," and furthermore "Though in essence Dewey's and James's understanding of experience is the same, there is a difference in that Dewey gives experience a more dynamic character, including in it the entire sphere of active human life, taken, however, exclusively from its subjective side" (Melvil 1974, 99). Experience is public for Dewey, but the public is determined in relation to a subject.

Melvil, Yulina, and Bogomolov all find Dewey's conception of experience to be "vague," in part due to its somewhat obscured subjectivism, but also because in Dewey's hands the concept has so many differing aspects. For example, both Bogomolov and Melvil object to the view of practice implicit in Dewey's concept of experience, and both illustrate their objection by contrasting Dewey's view with a Marxist understanding of practice. Melvil had been interested in Dewey's treatment of practice from his earliest book to a later article, in part because, as he notes, many people have seen a parallel between Dewey and Marx on this point. The grounds for suggesting a similarity are that in reconstructing the concept of experience Dewey rejects the "given" and an approach to human being as passive, that is, merely reflecting the world in consciousness. In Dewey's hands people are active agents in the construction and reconstruction of their world. This all sounds a good deal like Marx and would be were it not for the fact that unlike Marx Dewey's understanding of practice is essentially idealist. Marxism, Melvil says, regards practice as the human being's active influence on objective reality, as the creative activity of people leading to the transformation of material reality, nature, and society. Such transformation, however, is accomplished in the context of the objective laws of that reality, traits of our world that are not themselves the product of inquiry. Dewey in his approach to human practical activity makes use of the fact that conscious transformation of material reality is a result of people's physical and intellectual capacities and abilities, but unlike Marx Dewey "absolutizes" this aspect of practice. Dewey emphasizes the role of human will, but he does not fully bear in mind that activity is directed at a material object, that it is subordinate to objective laws (Melvil 1957a, 68–69). Bogomolov makes essentially the same point when he describes experience as the interaction of people with the objective world. There are, he says, two kinds of such interaction. One is the practical, material transformation of the world, and the other is the cognitive, ideal reflection of the world in human consciousness. In the practical interaction with the objective world, people change it, while in the cognitive interaction we do not. And any systematic efficacy of creative practical activity rests to a significant degree on an acknowledgment of the objective traits of the world in which we act as well as our knowledge of them (Bogomolov 1974, 97). One of the ways the crucial differences between Dewey and Marx are obscured, Melvil argues, is by attributing to them both not "practice" but "praxis," a term that "has acquired a distinctly subjective-idealist meaning, replacing the concept of objective reality" (Melvil 1986, 114).[15]

While the relational character of individual and surroundings defines a situation, and the interaction of individuals with their surroundings is experience, knowledge is the action of individuals on their surroundings to resolve problems. In Sidorov's description of Dewey's "reconstruction of philosophical rationality," knowledge, with respect both to its logical content and historical expression, is based on neither speculation nor imminent laws of pure reason, but on the practical necessity to support and enhance progress, individual and social. Knowledge, then, is to be understood as the expression in ideal forms of practical needs that arise and are fulfilled in the course of concrete practice and lived experience.

If thought is active, practical and instrumental, then the question arises as to the form it should take to be an effective instrument. Dewey's answer, of course, is that thought, inquiry, must be experimental if it is to be a useful tool in the resolution of problems. "In this, perhaps, is his important positive idea: it is necessary to act not on the basis of authority, a priori ideas, chance, etc., but by searching for better methods and variants of ideas, by testing and verifying them to select the most effective" (Melvil 1974, 102). Melvil and others describe Dewey's schema for experimental inquiry, from the perception of a problem through the construction of hypothetical means for its resolution to the testing and verification of the hypotheses in practice. Despite the virtues of the experimentalism of the theory of inquiry, there are nevertheless several serious problems with Dewey's conception. One of them has to do with the role of theory:

Dewey's suggested schema gives no notion of what is involved in the real process of scientific knowledge, even though Dewey considers the experimental method of modern science. It is true that modern knowledge of nature is based on experimentation, but it is experimentation which is penetrated by theory, and which is established and modified on the basis of theoretical estimations and generalizations, and takes into account the preceding development of scientific theory. (Melvil 1983, 57–58)

With respect to the issue of objective reality, there are several versions of the criticism of Instrumentalism, all of which have in some way to do with Dewey's conception of the relation between knowledge and action. In his early book on pragmatism Melvil located the problem in Dewey's treatment of thought as adaptation, in which "Dewey completely misinterprets the nature and essence of the thinking process. Thought, for Dewey, does not reflect objective reality. It is merely a means of adapting to one's environment." It is a principle of science as old as Bacon, Melvil argues, that to influence and change nature one must know its objective laws. Knowledge of the objective laws of nature is a necessary condition of the success of human practice. But for Dewey the purpose of thought is not knowledge in this sense, but activity. Thus Dewey's mistake is that by regarding thought as a function of the biological adaptation to the environment he dismisses the view that thought is in some way a reflection of objective reality.

Bogomolov describes the mistake in Dewey's epistemology somewhat differently, though the upshot is the same. The problem on Bogomolov's view is not so much that Dewey replaces knowledge with activity, but that he collapses the two and thus fails to make certain crucial distinctions. Dewey held, he says, that knowledge brings about an existential transformation and reconstruction of the material with which it deals, which is to treat the consciousness of an ideal "plan" of action as the action itself. Dewey is resting here on two genuine aspects of knowledge, that consciousness and knowledge have their expression in behavior, and that there is a relation between knowledge and practical activity. But by not distinguishing between consciousness and knowledge, on the one hand, and behavior and activity, on the other, in other words, by collapsing knowledge and action, Dewey makes the "known" world something that knowledge itself can change. Bogomolov suggests that there are two possible ways to construe Dewey's view here, neither of them satisfactory. Either the real world is "woven" out of human activity, or all of human activity, including knowledge, is an undifferentiated, purely objective process, a practical alteration of coarse existences:

In the first case one loses the objective world and can speak of a real organism and its behavior in a real external environment only in a figurative, "Pickwickian sense." In the second case one loses the distinctive characteristics of consciousness and knowledge as "fitting" a "coarse reality," without which human activity is ultimately transformed into "blind striving," into the method of trial and error, defying as a result of the uniqueness of a situation even elementary regulation. Dewey constantly vacillates between these two alternatives. (Bogomolov 1974, 101–102)

The problem of the relation of knowledge to objective reality also appears in the context of the instrumentalist conception of truth. Melvil notes that Dewey, much like James, talks of assertions being warranted by their success in resolving problems, but he adds that this way of talking "already lacks any hint of the relation of assertions to objective reality or to an objective state of affairs" (Melvil 1983, 59). Elsewhere it is suggested that if truth is a matter of the successful resolution of a particular problematic situation, then "truth is nothing other than a moment in the continuous process of the reconstruction and enrichment of experience," having nothing to do with objective conditions (Filatova 1985, 10). And Sidorov suggests that despite Dewey's protestations, instrumentalism's reputation for collapsing the truth of knowledge into its usefulness is not merely the fault of its detractors. An inadequate conception of truth results because in his treatment of the nature and purposes of knowledge Dewey does not grant that knowledge has an objective side, that its function is to convey accurately the nature of things. This is crucial not only for a philosophy of knowledge but also for an understanding of philosophic knowledge itself, since "philosophy should be a study of the objective, not permitting however the vulgar concept of objectivity characteristic of the superficial conceptions of speculative ontology" (Sidorov 1989, 134–135)

If Dewey was an unwitting victim of subjectivism in his ontology, he attempted at least to guard against it in his epistemology. The conception of inquiry as motivated by a problematic situation, and of knowledge as that which resolves the problem, seems to be consistent with the pragmatist, especially Jamesian, equation of truth with usefulness. As Sidorov puts it, Dewey sees the basic condition of knowledge or certainty produced by inquiry, which again is the satisfactory resolution of a problem, in terms of an emotional valuation of the sufficiency or effectiveness of a resolution. He adds, however, that Dewey strongly objected to the criticism that his views rest on individual and personal success. To that end he insisted on distinguishing between illegitimate ends, such as personal ambition, and genuine ends that are directed toward the development of human culture, so that truth cannot simply be equated with usefulness of just any kind (Sidorov 1989, 133–134). Dewey argued that the failure to make this distinction was the fundamental flaw of utilitarianism. In order to avoid the equation of "truth" or "good" with individual usefulness, Dewey carefully defines the nature of a problematic situation and the differences between legitimate and illegitimate ends in the resolution.[16] As Melvil notes, for Dewey a problematic situation is not simply a matter of the individual in the situation experiencing doubt, but of the situation itself being doubtful. The problem is not "in" the individual but "in" the complex of relations among the individual and environing conditions that constitutes the situation. Consequently, simply satisfying the individual is not enough to resolve a problem; resolution requires finding satisfactoriness with respect to the problem. To make this point clearer, Dewey drew a distinction between the satisfying, that which for whatever reason and in whatever way satisfies the individual, and the satisfactory, that which in fact resolves the problem. Comparable distinctions can be made with respect to a range of terms of valuation, for example between the desired and the desirable, the pleasant and the pleasurable. In this way the resolution of a problem, that is, knowledge, truth, and the good, is determined not simply by individual choice but by the traits of the situation of which the individual is a constituent. Thus Dewey attempts to avoid an overt epistemological subjectivism (Melvil 1974, 102–103).

Sidorov and Melvil both find Dewey's attempt to solve the problem of subjectivism to be laudable, but they also both argue that it is unsuccessful, and for the same reason. It is not enough that Dewey's proposed solution satisfied *him*, since a genuine resolution of the problem of subjectivism must be adequate from the point of view of the problem. It is not, they argue, and the culprit again is Dewey's ontology. The distinction between legitimate and illegitimate ends, and between the satisfying and the satisfactory, is a valuable one. But it avoids subjectivism only if legitimate ends and the genuinely satisfactory are *objectively* determined, that is, if they arise from objectively determinate traits of the situation, and only if it is possible for objectively determinate traits to be known (Melvil 1974, 103). Both conditions are, however, impossible given Dewey's ontology. If, as Dewey argues, the objects of knowledge are the products of inquiry, then the constituents of a situation lose their objectivity, or at least whatever objectively determinate traits a situation has and are in principle unknowable. Dewey removes the resolution of a problem, knowledge, from purely individual valuation, only to place it in a situation that is itself a product of the individual's process of inquiry. The absence of objectivity, ontological and consequently epistemological, is the fatal philosophic flaw of Dewey's instrumentalism (Sidorov 1989, 134).

Had Dewey been able to reconcile the active nature of inquiry and experience with the objectivity of the conditions in which individuals are located, he would have been much closer to the truth. Even so, however, his epistemology would suffer from a failure to understand or incorporate the social conditionality of inquiry and knowledge. Soviet philosophers traditionally endorsed the view that among the many factors that condition human activity, including cognitive activity, a crucial place is held by a society's mode of production, more specifically by the form of social relations that prevails in a given society. In some respects Dewey shared this view, as when, for example, he argued that the contemplative, excessively intellectualist conception of philosophy stemming from the Greeks was a reflection of the Greek aristocracy's reliance on slave labor, its distinction between physical and mental activity, and its deprecation of the former.[17] But despite Dewey's understanding at one level of the social nature of knowledge and inquiry, he fails at another level to account for the social conditionality of the process of inquiry. One of the indications of this is that Dewey's description of the stages in the process of inquiry includes no necessary or inherent place for the influence of social factors on cognition.

The Soviet presumption here is that at every level knowledge and inquiry are conditioned by a range of social factors, from the dominant forms of social relations to widely accepted ideological perspectives. Inquiry as Dewey understands it is grounded in a sense that there is something wrong and in the recognition of the problematic nature of a situation. But Dewey fails to build into this the extent to which even at this initial level social factors are at work. Whether we regard a given situation to be problematic at all can depend on characteristics of the social order. The same is true for the hypotheses we might entertain as possible ways to proceed, as well as for what we will regard as a sufficient solution. In medieval Europe, for example, the practice of charging interest came to be regarded by many as a problem. The perception of *this* situation as problematic was conditioned by ideological commitments, largely religious and ethical, which prevailed because they were consistent with and supported other aspects of medieval economic and social life. Under different social conditions the charging of interest is not felt to be a situation that poses a problem. Furthermore, the medieval European solution of the problem was also socially conditioned. The function of providing interest-bearing loans was relegated to those outside the dominant Christian communities. This practice deepened social divisions and racism in medieval Europe, but the prevailing social relations and ideology allowed it to count as a solution. Dewey has a sense of this when he considers specific problems, as for example when he argues that the influence of eighteenth century values prevents us from responding successfully to contemporary problems. But the powerful role of social factors seems to disappear from his more generic account of the process of inquiry.[18] In Melvil's view Dewey's conception of the process of inquiry presupposes that the process is unrelated to broader social phenomena: "By conflating the various 'interacting components' of social life, such as art and politics, education and commerce, production and ethics, he rejects not only the determinate significance of these factors, but also the lawful character of social development in general" (Melvil 1983, 59).

History and Social Development

A failure to understand the nature of human sociality is problematic in several respects. In addition simply to painting an inaccurate picture of human nature, it makes it virtually impossible to appreciate the fact that human life at its social level, as well as the physical, chemical, and biological, has a lawful character. That history and social development are characterized to some degree by objective laws is of course a view that Dewey rejected; in fact it was one of his central objections to Marxism.[19] To treat history and society as lawfully determined seemed to Dewey to leave no room, or at least insufficient room, for the efficacy of human action. From the traditional Soviet point of view, by contrast, a refusal to recognize the lawfulness of social processes makes it impossible to have a general theory of society, which in turn means that there can be no general scientific understanding of social development. The value of science is not in descriptions of isolated phenomena but in its accounts of general lawful relations, without which inquiry and knowledge can have no systematic efficacy. This places Dewey's social philosophy in double jeopardy. The first danger is that his conception of social development is not general, theoretical, and scientific, but piecemeal and pluralist. The resolution of problems is situation specific, so that there can be no meaningful conception of social progress: "For Dewey, the development of society is determined not by objective necessity, but rather, as for James, by the will and desires of people" (Melvil 1957a, 105). Thus for Dewey, as for many of his forebears in the American philosophic tradition, the problem of social development is primarily a moral problem. But even here there can be no general moral norms because moral problems are themselves "moral situations," and their resolution is situation specific (Bogomolov 1974, 113).

Dewey's denial of objective lawfulness in history and society thus generates the theoretical shortcoming of "pluralism." Its second jeopardizing problem is more practical. If Instrumentalism on its own epistemological principle can have no theory of lawful social development, then neither can it offer a general program of social change. This point is at the heart of Soviet criticism of Dewey's social philosophy. Soviet writers acknowledge Dewey's many criticisms of capitalism and his own willingness to be described as a socialist. But whatever his views on these matters may have been, they argue, the fact remains that an epistemology in which knowledge and the resolution of problems is "situation specific" is not consistent with a conception or program of thoroughgoing, fundamental change. An instrumentalist conception of change, then, approaches problems as they come up, with no theoretical basis or guidance for understanding the relations among various social problems and for transforming their most fundamental roots. Instrumentalist social philosophy is inherently reformist, which in the context of American capitalist society means that while it will seek to resolve this or that problem as it arises, it will avoid challenging the material sources of those problems. Or even when it does challenge them, as Dewey did in his criticisms of private property, it can be expected neither to sustain the critique nor to offer well-grounded alternatives. This is the reason Soviets tended to read Dewey's social philosophy as a reformist attempt to save bourgeois society rather than, as others have read it, as a radical critique of capitalism[20] (Melvil 1957b, 130–131).

Melvil offered this interpretation in his earliest study of pragmatism. To Dewey's credit, he "acknowledged the existence of various contradictions and the collision of opposing forces in society. He denied only those contradictions which, as ascertained by Marxism, determine the development of society. Dewey could not remain completely silent about the basic contradictions of the capitalist mode of production, about the contradiction between the forces and the relations of production." In the same vein Melvil adds that Dewey "reproached capitalists for the mercenary pursuit of their own ends and for their neglect of the interests of society" but that he "remained silent only about exploitation, which is the basis of all social conflicts." But despite his recognition of contradictions is capitalist society, Melvil argues that Dewey misunderstood them in that he did not see the extent to which they derive from the inherent and necessarily conflicting interests of those differently related to property in the capitalist mode of production. Dewey instead saw the more serious problems of capitalist society as a consequence of a contradiction between science and technology, on the one hand, and moral ideals, on the other, so that for Dewey the basic problem of philosophy is to address the relation between our conception and knowledge of nature and our conception of values. Thus, Dewey appears to be socially and politically progressive in his criticisms of many of the traits of capitalist society. But, for Melvil, the fact remains that in his failure to appreciate the nature and consequences of the conflict between capital and labor Dewey overlooks the basic components of social and historical development. The result is that this program for social change, for the resolution of capitalist society's problems, calls not for a victory of labor over the power of private capital but for a reconciliation of the two social forces, and this, wittingly or not, is to lead the American people down the garden path of class collaboration (Melvil 1957a, 100–104).

Human Nature and Values

The view that Dewey's social and political thought is inadequate, largely due to its pragmatist philosophic underpinnings, informs Soviet discussions of the details of his social philosophy, from his treatment of human nature and ethics to his conceptions of democracy and education. With respect to human nature, Khanin attributes to Dewey an important conceptual break from the traditional view of the atomized individual by developing a view of human nature as much more fluid (Khanin 1985, 17). Bogomolov, however, is much less enthusiastic. He notes that in general the concept of human nature has been central to political thought throughout the history of philosophy in that apologists for an existing social order have tended to appeal to the immutable nature of human being, while those opposed to the prevailing order have often taken it to task for an incorrect understanding of human nature. Marxism, he argues, does not rely in this way on human nature, having "shown that the essence of human being, human 'nature,' is an historically formed aggregate of social relations" (Bogomolov 1974, 105–106). By contrast Instrumentalism, notwithstanding its claims to novelty, turns to the "old fiction" of human nature in its conception of social possibilities and ideals. It is not so much that Dewey provides a finished definition of human nature, but more that he offers, most clearly in *Human Nature and Conduct*, relatively stable psychological and biological human traits. In one way Dewey is right, Bogomolov argues, in his repudiation of the idea of an immutable human nature as a fiction created to serve existing social relations. But in his alternative Dewey does not go as far as he should, in that he does not see the predominantly social determination of the human character. Rather than seeing human beings as changing in fundamental ways by virtue of the social relations in which they reside, Dewey holds that there is a biologically determined human character that takes different forms in differing social conditions. Bogomolov attributes to Dewey a "centrist" position with respect to human nature. Dewey rejects what he calls the view of the "quasi-revolutionary," according to which human nature is completely pliant, as well as the view of the conservative, for whom human nature remains identical regardless of social change (Bogomolov 1974, 106–107).

Dewey's de-emphasis of the sociality of human nature leaves him, Bogomolov argues, with the philosophic problem of the relation of the individual and society. This problem has historically been particularly acute because traditional bourgeois thought treats the human character as a cause of social structures and relations, but usually fails to realize the degree to which the causal relation also works the other way. Dewey falls into the same trap, Bogomolov thinks, which can be seen from the fact that for him the most important means for achieving reform and social transformation is education, that is, the transformation of the individual. Dewey is undoubtedly correct in thinking that if a sufficient number of individuals are influenced in the right ways toward the right ends social consequences will develop. But there remains something quixotic about Dewey's faith in the socially transformative power of education if, as Bogomolov and Marxists generally hold, individual character is in large measure a product of the prevailing social system. Dewey's own interest in social change, on this view, is undermined by an overly individualist conception of human nature.

In one of the rare discussions of Mead in Soviet philosophic literature, Bogomolov compares Dewey's treatment of human nature with Mead's social psychology. Although Dewey was influenced by Mead's "social behaviorism," in Bogomolov's view Mead's approach is in some respects more fruitful than Dewey's. With his conception of the "social act" Mead can appreciate "the dialectics of the individual and the social" in ways Dewey does not. Through the differentiation in the self of the two aspects "I" and "me," "Mead's conception offered much greater range for an analysis of the social nature of the individual than Dewey's naturalistic conception, which relied too much on a 'human nature.'" However, despite this advantage, and despite Mead's valuable influence on American social psychology, Mead did not any more than Dewey see "the real possibility and actual threat of the alienation of the individual in capitalist society" as clearly as, for example, the existentialists saw it (Bogomolov 1974, 111).

In these remarks on Mead, Bogomolov is echoing the spirit of a paper that had appeared in *Voprosy Filosofii* five years earlier. In that piece, I. S. Kon and D. N. Shalin argued too that Mead's analysis of the social nature of the self was a major step forward from the subjectivist and associationist approaches of the modern period. James, they note, had the idea too, but he never developed it as fully as did Mead. Mead's achievement, and the respect in which he was able to go beyond James, was in his view that in all its aspects, that is, the genetic, physical, and mental or spiritual, the individual self develops from the social (Kon and Shalin 1969, 91). However, like other discussions from this period of American figures, Mead does not compare well with Marx. Mead, they argue, was interested in the interrelations of individuals in separate social groups and situations, while Marx was concerned with the objective system of social relations, in the context of which is the only way to understand the actual nature of social interrelations. Mead does say, they point out, that to understand the self one has to look not only at the relations among individuals, but to the relation between an individual and the society as a whole. "However, there is no way to unpack this idea, to make it concrete, within the terms of Mead's social theory: for that, one would turn to a generally developed theory of social structure, to trace the interactions of social norms, groups, institutions, etc." (Kon and Shalin 1969, 95).

To return to Dewey. If an inadequate theoretical individualism is the result of Dewey's "naturalistic" (read "biologistic") conception of the situation, his instrumentalist treatment of the activity of individuals in situations cannot overcome a relativism in ethics, or so Melvil has argued. Ethics, or the nature and role of values, has a central place in Dewey's thought, so central, in Melvil's view, that a flawed conception of values casts a pall over his entire philosophy. The questions of value and valuation are not isolated issues for Dewey, not merely additions to a list of "philosophic problems." On the contrary, Dewey takes great pains to argue that values and valuation are at the heart of the epistemological process, inseparable from inquiry and from the means by which inquiry is effected and knowledge achieved. Cognitive activity is engendered by a problematic situation, and the purpose of inquiry is to resolve the problem, which in turn implies that inquiry invariably has specific purposes, that it is necessarily directed toward ends. The ends inherent in inquiry, Dewey's "ends-in-view," are the values the nature and origins of which constitute the enterprise of ethics. Dewey objected to the traditional conception according to which values are absolute, eternal principles awaiting discovery and articulation. They are, instead, phenomena that arise, like all other phenomena, in the changing, precarious course of natural processes. To that extent Soviet philosophers had no quarrel with Dewey, since they too reject a conception of ethical values as absolute and eternal. But here the agreement ends, because in a Marxist view values arise primarily in relation to social and historical processes, whereas for Dewey their source is individual situations, and here lies Dewey's ethical relativism. The uniqueness of situations, as we have seen Melvil and others argue, essentially eliminates the possibility of general theory with respect both to natural science and historical development. In the same way, if situations are unique, and if unique situations are the source of values, then generality is no more possible with respect to ethics than to science and history. As Melvil puts it, though Dewey tries to avoid dogmatic, eternal, and ahistorical moral principles, he posits instead a view in which each moral situation is unique and can be resolved only on the basis of what is taken to be the good in that case. This means that "Dewey in fact rejects any moral norms and principles at all" (Melvil 1957b, 119). Dewey may wish to assert general norms, but any such assertion is undermined by his own ontology and epistemology.

There are other problems as well. Not only are values relative to unique situations, but they are also relative to subjects. Dewey, in other words, in overcoming the absolute character of values also denies them objectivity. The point is not that Dewey endorsed subjectivist ethics. He did not, any more than he endorsed subjectivism with respect to knowledge of any other kind. In fact the means he used to try to avoid a subjectivist epistemology are also employed against a charge of subjectivism in ethics. Just as knowledge, truth, or the resolution of a problem is not simply what is subjectively satisfying to the individual but what is satisfactory with respect to the problem, so too the values that serve as ends-in-view are appropriate not because they are individually appealing but because they direct a course of action that resolves the problem. This move, however, does not save the objectivity of the constituents of a situation, as several commentators argue, and neither does it save the objectivity of values. As the objects constitutive of a situation have their traits only in relation to an individual subject, a situation has significance only given a subject's interest in it. The problematic character of a situation, its resolution, and the values toward which action is directed are at least indirectly subjectively determined (Melvil 1983, 60).[21]

Democracy and the Public

That Dewey's approach to the resolution of social and political problems does not in the end go beyond the bounds of bourgeois theory is the central theme of I. P. Filatova's 1985 dissertation on Dewey's social and political philosophy. The foundation of Dewey's view of the state, she argues, is his concept of the "public," people living in a condition of association with one another. In an extension of the pluralist side of the founders' constitutionalism, Dewey held that the distinctive trait of government is to organize and control the indirect effects of associated living, to balance differing groups in society so that none of them dominate the others (Filatova 1985, 14–15). The crucial political question for Dewey becomes the question of means, the methods the public might employ to reconcile diverse interests and resolve social problems. The choice of method is basically between force and "intelligence." Concerned with the irrationality and detrimental consequences of the use of force, and extending his more general experimentalism, Dewey urges the method of intelligence in social and political affairs. For Dewey this meant an open-minded experimental approach to problems, as opposed to a tenacious and dogmatic insistence on one's preconceived ideas and categories. That the method of intelligence as Dewey understood it would bring to bear in politics a degree of rationality often precluded by violence may well be true, but its efficacy would require that irreconcilable differences do not lie at the root of social problems. If there are irreconcilable differences among social groups constituting the public, then the method of intelligence either misunderstands or ignores them. Dewey urges the method of intelligence as a way to overcome force, but among other things this amounts in particular to an attempt to sidestep the class struggle, and it is this that reveals Dewey's essential bourgeois liberalism (Filatova 1985, 15).

Dewey certainly did not ignore class differences and conflicts, but neither did he see them as necessarily central among the causes of social problems. He tended to argue, rather, that social difficulties grew from the conflict of old and new ideas, or between old ideas and new conditions. This would have to be true if the method of intelligence is to be a successful political tool, but it reflects the severe limitations of Dewey's analysis:

> The fact is that the thesis of a conflict between "old and new ideas" as the cause of social contradictions is the pet argument of revisionism and anti-Communism, for it calls not for a revolutionary replacement of the old by the new, but for a restructuring of the old through a union with the new, advocating a harmony of the old and

the new on the basis of the accomplishment of slow, gradual changes and the maintenance of the prevailing status quo. (Filatova 1985, 16)

Dewey, given this reading, was concerned not to envision something genuinely new and forward looking, let alone revolutionary, in social and political life, but to preserve the basic character of American society by "updating" its principles. The appropriate response to the society's social problems, then, was to restructure or, better, reconstruct its initial and still central concepts. For social and political matters generally, the fundamental ideas of freedom, the individual, and intelligence required redefinition and transportation from their eighteenth and nineteenth century contexts to twentieth century conditions. This process entailed also a rethinking of economic concepts and relations. Dewey criticized many of the prevailing principles of capitalist economic practice and aspirations as having arisen and having had their value under conditions of a competitive market system of production and distribution that by the twentieth century no longer existed. Some have read Dewey's criticisms of laissez faire capitalism as evidence of his opposition to capitalism in general and as an expression of a form of socialism or anarchism. The predominant Soviet reading, however, was that in rejecting laissez faire economic and political practices Dewey was attempting to reconstruct traditional principles to accord with modern conditions of corporate, state monopoly capitalism. As Filatova sees it, while Dewey understood the basic importance of economics in social and political life, his own conception of appropriate economic relations was akin to Keynesianism, for which in fact he provides a philosophic foundation (Filatova 1985, 12).

Dewey's rethinking of social concepts included the principle of democracy, his own conception of which was central to his political thought and, Filatova says, is important for its influence on American political thinkers of both the right and the left. In Dewey's hands the concept of democracy is transformed from a formal political category, the significance of which rested largely on individual decision making and political responsibility, to a principle of much broader social significance. Democracy became not so much a method for filling governmental offices and for crafting governmental policy but a kind of human association, a form of life. Furthermore, democracy as Dewey understood it did not presuppose generally isolated individuals but, on the contrary, was a way of living and of carrying on social affairs defined by a commitment to ever-broader community and communication. This approach to democracy has its roots in a more or less Jeffersonian political tradition, but it was nevertheless a considerable change from the prevalent American conception of democratic political organization. To that extent Dewey's treatment of democracy was of a piece with this general reconstruction of social categories and principles, but it no more challenged the underlying character of bourgeois society than did the reconstructed concepts of freedom and individualism. Dewey's is essentially a bourgeois conception of democracy in that it is both idealist and utopian. Dewey's idealism, as Melvil has put it, is clear in that for Dewey the nature and possibility of democracy do not derive from concrete social conditions but are determined by the method of intelligence, by how we think, by "freedom of thought" (Melvil 1957b, 132). Its utopianism has the same source: "consistent with his view that class relations do not determine the essence of political phenomena, Dewey tries to avoid the view of democracy as a historically determined form of government generated on the basis of the relations of property and instead paints a utopian picture of 'pure,' classless democracy" (Filatova 1985, 17).

Melvil and others argued in the 1950s that Dewey's social and political philosophy, in fact his Instrumentalism and pragmatism generally, in various ways reflected the interests of the ruling class of American society. Though in a milder tone and a different literary style, largely the same interpretation was defended some thirty years later. Several of the characteristic traits of Dewey's social and political philosophy, Filatova argues, serve as justifications of the policies of contemporary American imperialist bourgeoisie. First, his attempt to apply pragmatism to the conditions of state monopoly capitalism, she suggests, involved just the sort of mixture of anti-intellectualism and scientism that came to dominate the thought of the American ruling class and exerted an influence in all the non-philosophic spheres of American thought. Second, Dewey's general Darwinism emphasized the adaptation to existing conditions, so that when there are problems they are due to the failure of individuals to adapt to new conditions. Problems are to be solved, then, not by a fundamental challenge to the conditions but by the gradual transformation of individuals and social institutions without affecting the "foundations of the system." Third, Dewey's "new" liberalism is perfectly consistent with conditions under state monopoly capitalism. The emphasis on achieving "success" in pragmatism generally is transformed into the ideas of profit and social success. This is precisely the concept, in Filatova's view, that constitutes the basis of the revisionism and reformism in the contemporary American labor movement. And finally, Dewey's conception of the uniqueness of America's contributions to the development of world civilization are transformed in practice into American domination over the world (Filatova 1985, 20–21).

Recent Pragmatism

"By the time of his death in 1952," Melvil notes in a later article, "John Dewey had become the most respected philosopher in America. But at the same time the influence of pragmatism as an independent philosophic movement had begun to decline," to be replaced for a time by "analytic philosophy" (Melvil 1986, 115). Pragmatism was kept alive during this period by "commentaries" and "historical" analyses of the views of Peirce, James, Dewey, and Mead. Bogomolov puts the point somewhat differently. Dewey, he said, had exhausted the intellectual potential of pragmatism, and those who followed tended to combine it with other philosophic tendencies. In Bogomolov's view the two most interesting figures in this respect were Sidney Hook and C. I. Lewis. Hook had attempted to combine pragmatism with Marxism, and Lewis to bring to bear on pragmatism analytic categories and methods (Bogomolov 1974, 260).[22] As we will see in the next chapter, Yulina and to a degree Karimsky are prepared to read Hook as a naturalist, but Bogomolov explicitly rejects this. Hook had tried to develop an ontology to suit Dewey's concept of an "instrument," and in so doing produced a clearly pragmatist position: "Hook establishes a one-sided relation of instrument to thought—an instrument is determined by thought, by intentions. Genuine naturalism, not to mention materialism, rather tries to derive an instrument from nature on the principle of imitation." Instruments, including thought, are inseparable from their reality, yet Hook distinguishes between nature and instruments so sharply that any pretension to naturalism has no grounds (Bogomolov 1974, 262). Hook's treatment of the relation between ideas and reality is also fully pragmatist, breaking with any sort of correspondence theory more decisively than Dewey or even James had. He rejected the notion that an idea can correspond to an object on the grounds that ideas and objects are very different categories and thus cannot correspond in any meaningful way; he also found senseless the effort to regard an idea as resembling an object, because to perceive such a resemblance we must already have a direct representation of the object. Such objections, however, fail to take account of the process of practical verification as securing a relation between idea and object. And when Hook holds that a judgment is a rational plan of action transforming the existing condition of things, "He simply chooses not to attend to the fact that a rational plan of action must and does issue from an understanding of the existing condition of things, i.e., from the *reflection* in consciousness of existing conditions" (Bogomolov 1974, 263).

On the basic philosophic questions, then, Hook is fairly clearly a pragmatist, and his reading of Marx is "through the prism of instrumentalism." This makes it virtually impossible for him to have an adequate understanding of Marxism, Bogomolov says, so there is little surprise in the many objections he has to dialectical and historical materialism. Nor is there any surprise in the fact that eventually Hook abandoned even his own earlier "pseudo-Marxism" in favor of a militant anti-Communism and anti-Sovietism. This point, however, "leads us far from the sphere of philosophy" (Bogomolov 1974, 268).

C. I. Lewis's philosophic program, however, was far more promising. His concern focused on how to relate a logical calculus with facts, and his resolution of the problem was to unite a neopositivist conception of logic as an analytic discipline with a pragmatist criterion of the choice of a logical system applied to experience. Lewis's most valuable general contribution to pragmatism was that he took seriously both the subjective and objective aspects of knowledge. His most basic shortcoming is that he is not able successfully to bring them together. Lewis's theory of knowledge vacillates between two extremes: "Knowledge always exceeds the bounds of the given, of direct experience, he says, thus overcoming the subjective idealist limits of pragmatism. But knowledge cannot be a reflection of an object independent of our consciousness of the world. Rather, the world reflects our common categories" (Bogomolov 1974, 270). Lewis emphasizes the relativity of knowledge, though not necessarily the world, as a result of the role of logical categories. From this he infers that ideas and concepts cannot be reflections of objective reality. This in Bogomolov's view is his mistake. The relativity of knowledge does not preclude reflection, and the resemblance of our ideas to objective reality can be confirmed in practical experience. Without such resemblance there is no way to connect knowledge and its objects. As Bogomolov puts it, for all his contributions, Lewis cannot escape the Kantian contradiction between the subjectivity and the objectivity of the objects of knowledge (Bogomolov 1974, 276).

Lewis's general program was carried on by Willard Van Orman Quine and Nelson Goodman, each in his own way. In the end, however, the marriage of analytic, "neopositivist" methods and categories with pragmatism invariably fails because the logical formalism of neopositivism and the psychologism of pragmatism are necessarily opposed to one another: "The 'reunification' of pragmatism and analytic philosophy returns the neopragmatist hybrid to the internally contradictory combination of psychologism and formalism that permeated Charles Peirce's philosophy and that was one of the reasons for its demise" (Bogomolov 1974, 293).

Writing in the early 1970s, Bogomolov of course could not have anticipated the directions pragmatism yet could take. In 1992 a short article by V. N. Shtinov appeared in *Filosofskie Nauki*, titled "The Philosophy of Richard Bernstein as an Alternative to Analytic Philosophy" (in Russian). In it Shtinov remarks that the 1980s saw the weakening of the influence of analytic philosophy in the United States. While the most prominent critique of that tradition has been Richard Rorty, Shtinov is interested in pointing to the degree to which Bernstein had earlier drawn from Dewey and the pragmatists in general his alternative approaches to science, scientific research, and to other philosophic and methodological concerns. Bernstein, Shtinov argues, helped both to undercut the hegemony of analytic methods and assumptions in American philosophy and to reassert the pragmatist tradition as a viable and living alternative (Shtinov 1992). Melvil, however, had already taken note of the reemergence of pragmatism a few years earlier, in particular the pragmatism of Richard Rorty. In the

1970s works began to appear that tried to introduce "some new ideas" into traditional pragmatism, in particular Richard Bernstein's *Praxis and Action* and Nicholas Rescher's *Methodological pragmatism*. However, "The pragmatist views worked out in recent years by Richard Rorty are of significant interest" (Melvil 1986, 116).[23]

Melvil notes Rorty's arguments against knowledge as the reflection of reality and philosophy as a "mirror of nature." At the same time he points out that Rorty's position is not simply a restatement of traditional pragmatism since he does not endorse, for example, any of the various pragmatist epistemological theories nor a conception of truth as usefulness. Rorty's pragmatism revolves around an understanding of knowledge and philosophy as matters of "conversation" and prevalent social practice. Of course, Melvil says, Rorty is right that knowledge is socially conditioned, and he is also right to recognize and explore the "unity of cultural life and human activity," but on the basis of these otherwise valuable insights he develops a conception of philosophy, and by implication of inquiry and knowledge generally, that is "highly vague and careless" (Melvil 1983, 213–214).

There are, Melvil argues, two kinds of problems that undermine Rorty's ideas, one of them more theoretical and the other more social. The absence in Rorty of a dialectical approach, he says, becomes apparent in his refusal to make certain distinctions among the many aspects of cultural life. To be sure they are all socially conditioned—art, science, philosophy, literature, and the rest—but they do not all serve the same function or function in the same way. According to Melvil's reading Rorty tends simply to treat them all as aspects, more or less equivalent in their various roles, of the ongoing human conversation. This implies that, for Rorty, any one form of cultural activity, for example science, can be significantly different from the others—perhaps scientific inquiry can in a unique way produce accurate knowledge of reality—only if that form differs from all others in all or most fundamental respects. Since it does not—science no less than the others is a socially conditioned process or cultural activity—Rorty seems to think that we are compelled to reject any essential epistemological differences among them. This is an inference that strikes Melvil as neither necessary nor adequate (Melvil 1983, 213).

The social difficulty in Rorty is what Melvil identifies as a rather deep-seated conservatism. This is not so much a judgment about political ideas as it is of a more general cultural conformism, an attachment to prevailing official practice, standards, and norms (Melvil 1983, 223). This Melvil suggests helps to explain why Rorty would refuse to make any evaluative judgments in his account of the conflict between Galileo and Cardinal Bellarmini; and it helps bring into focus the fact that Rorty treats the aggregate opinions of a prevailing society as the final criterion and authority for any theoretical, conceptual, or generally cultural questions. In the same vein Melvil is struck by Rorty's refusal to address certain questions about the prevalent aggregate of opinions: why does a society at a given time accept one set or system of beliefs over another, and why does one set of beliefs, norms, and standards of thought change into another? Melvil would argue that to understand human activity and cultural life, these and similar questions must be asked and that the key to their answers is to be found in objectively determinate social and historical processes. For Rorty, by contrast, even to ask the questions is simply to make another move in the conversation, and, in any case, no answer that genuinely points beyond the conversation itself is possible. This "evasiveness" is one of the fundamental weaknesses of Rorty's ideas, and Melvil notes that it is another respect in which Rorty differs from the pragmatist tradition. Even Bernstein, he says, points out the importance of these questions, as had Dewey himself (Melvil 1983, 218).

In some respects, then, Rorty breaks from the pragmatist tradition and offers his own unique ideas. In general, though, he shares a good deal with the tradition. He agrees with Peirce that there is no foundation of knowledge and no foundation of philosophy. Of his view that philosophy is simply another cultural activity, Melvil remarks that "even if philosophy is understood as one voice in the human conversation, it does not follow that that voice may speak in any way it pleases" (Melvil 1983, 214–215). But Rorty, he says, holds James's view on this point: that there *is* a world is a given, but *what* it is is determined by us through our concerns, interests, ideas, wills, and discourse. In the end, Melvil suggests, Rorty offers little or nothing that in one way or another is not already in his "philosophic heroes": the active role of the subject in knowledge; that no single theory no matter how complex and abstract can describe the phenomena of the world as they absolutely are; that all theory is approximate; that all theory constructs idealized objects and often appeals to metaphor; that all theory is formulated in relation to conceptual schemes. With all of this Melvil has no quarrel. Rorty's mistake, one that repeats and in some ways exacerbates what is perhaps the fundamental philosophic flaw of pragmatism, is to think that this suggests that we do not know or cannot attempt to know what the world in reality is like (Melvil 1983, 214–217). Melvil argued for some forty years that this position is part and parcel of pragmatism and that it is absurd. When he makes the following comment about Rorty, one can imagine that he has all the pragmatists with the possible exception of Peirce in mind: "Only a philosopher in the quiet of his study can speak ironically about the 'contact' or 'contiguity' of science or theory with reality" (Melvil 1983, 218).

5

IDEALISM, REALISM, AND NATURALISM

THE philosophic milieu out of which pragmatism grew was permeated by the influence of German idealism. It would make itself felt in Peirce, especially in his metaphysics; it was the frame of mind in which Dewey would complete his graduate studies at Johns Hopkins; and it was for James the chief contender, the "closed," "block" universe that so stifled him emotionally and goaded him philosophically. German idealism had emigrated to America in the early nineteenth century and had been given an American cast by the transcendentalists, Emerson in particular. During the course of the century new immigrants, most notably through the St. Louis school, kept its influence fresh. It was the Hegelian William Torey Harris who founded *The Journal of Speculative Philosophy*, the first professional and technical philosophic journal in the country. And still in the final third of the century, when young American scholars and intellectuals went to Europe to study, the speculative spirit of Hegelianism and neo-Kantianism prevailed.

In the late nineteenth century absolute idealism was the primary alternative to pragmatism in American philosophy. As a school of philosophic thought, however, it was quickly to dissipate on both sides of the Atlantic, and by the early twentieth century in America the argument against pragmatism was for the most part taken up by realism. Until the 1950s, at which point the methods and problematics of "analytic" philosophy became dominant, American philosophy in the twentieth century was characterized in Soviet readings by pragmatism and one or another form of realism-neorealism, critical realism and naturalism. There were of course other philosophic ideas and trends in American philosophy in the twentieth century, such as Thomism, existentialism and phenomenology, but with few exceptions they had not been developed in distinctly American forms. In addition to pragmatism and realism, however, several less influential schools of thought evinced a more American flavor and drew the interest of Soviet scholars. Among them are personalism and, as we have seen, some of the post-Deweyan forms of pragmatism.

Soviet scholarship since its inception analyzed modern American philosophy under these general rubrics. In the earliest Soviet study, for example, P. P. Blonsky identified the main movements in American philosophy other than pragmatism with Royce, whose views he described as a synthesis of absolute and personalist idealisms, and with R. B. Perry's neorealism (Blonsky 1918, 42, 45). Though the inclination to categorize American philosophic development in terms of a set of schools of thought continues in contemporary scholarship, Soviet specialists realized that the relations among them all are complex and shifting, and that in many respects these otherwise distinct philosophic conceptions overlap. While it is true to say, for example, that absolute idealism and pragmatism are very different philosophic positions, it is equally true to say that absolute idealism in Royce's hands acquires a decidedly pragmatist flavor. In fact, one of the central theses of Sidorov's book is that Royce was enough of a "pragmatist" to have been one of the primary contributors to a unique American "philosophy of action" (Sidorov 1989, Chap. II). Similarly, though neorealism arose in part as a response to pragmatism, the neorealists like the pragmatists saw themselves as overcoming the traditional dichotomy of idealism and materialism, as offering a "third line" in philosophy (Yulina 1974, 40). Furthermore, despite their opposition to the ontological implications of pragmatist and instrumentalist epistemology, the neorealists in the end borrowed heavily from James's "neutral monism" and his pluralism in the development of their own ontological views (Bogomolov 1974, 152–153). And like pragmatism, neorealism turns out to be a philosophy of experience in the sense that it reads experience into nature by understanding nature through the categories of experience (Yulina 1978a, 282).

The relation of critical realism to the other prominent schools of thought is no less complex. Even though in its early formulations critical realism sought an alternative to the neorealists' epistemological presentism and its corresponding ontology—in the persons of Santayana and Whitehead, their most outstanding representatives—the two traditions converge in Platonism (Yulina 1978a, 84). Critical realism also dovetails in several ways with pragmatism. In the concept of animal faith, Santayana's approach to knowledge is as biologically grounded as Dewey's interactions. Soviet commentators saw in Santayana the culmination of one line of development of critical realism. The other line eventually issued in naturalism, the pivotal figure for which was Roy Wood Sellars, and naturalism too converged with pragmatism in Dewey.

The complex overlapping of ideas and approaches in modern American philosophy is due in part to the fact that all of its trends and tendencies are rooted in the same or similar philosophic, cultural, social, and ideological sources, though responses to them sometimes differed. In general, American philosophy in the late nineteenth and early twentieth centuries was conditioned by the accomplishments of science, by the relation of science and religion, by developments in mathematics and logic, and by the rapidly changing character of American economic, social, and political life. In his 1974 dissertation on Royce, Sidorov refers to W. T. Harris's remarks in the first issue of the *Journal of Speculative Philosophy* concerning the tasks of speculative philosophy. In Sidorov's description they were (1) to reform the philosophy of religion, since traditional dogmas had lost their significance; (2) to enable social philosophy to correspond to the new level of national consciousness; and (3) to reconsider the scientific method in order to eliminate its narrow empiricism. The social and religious tasks, Sidorov argues, were related in that the necessity to establish "the spiritual unity of the American nation" required replacing traditional Calvinist principles with an individualism that would at the same time subsume individuals in the whole: "From this point of view a social philosophy was required that could ground the necessity of both individual freedom and its limits in the form of full loyalty to the capitalist state." This program, he continues, generated a "golden age" of American objective idealism, the leading figure of which was Royce, who in turn influenced not only his immediate followers but also such diverse figures as "the pragmatist William James, the critical realist George Santayana, and the existentialist Gabriel Marcel" (Sidorov 1974, 3–5).

The reconstruction and support of religion to help it prevail in the contemporary world was also a central concern of personalism. From its nineteenth century expressions in Borden Parker Bowne and George H. Howison to its prominent twentieth century versions in Mary Calkins, William Ernest Hocking, R. T. Flewelling, and Edgar S. Brightman, personalism was motivated, among other things, by a perceived conflict between religious and spiritual values, on the one hand, and what it took to be the materialism of science, on the other. The personalists had to deal with the issue of science, and they were inclined to do so. The task was to show that science was not fully able to explain nature and human activity. For example, Hocking, Flewelling, and others, Bogomolov notes, held that spiritual sources were necessary to account for the arising of novelty in nature. In Bogomolov's view, the personalist commitment to religion, and its consequent depreciation of science, generated a wholly indefensible world view: "Attempting to reconcile science and religion (at the expense of science, of course!), personalism in fact produced a naive, anthropomorphic conception of the world." In an age when we know as much as we do about scientific dialectics, "Personalism's concept of a cosmic 'Person' is an oversimplification, making of philosophy a religious fantasy" (Bogomolov 1974, 129).

Absolute idealism and personalism were not alone among American philosophic trends in their commitment to religion. Whitehead, for example, stands out as one for whom religious issues were a central philosophic concern. But unlike Royce and the personalists, the significance of religion did not require submerging nature and the sciences in a spiritual realm. In that respect Whitehead shares the approach of many twentieth century realists that science and the scientific method must be appropriated by any adequate philosophic perspective. This was particularly true of neorealism. In the works of Ralph Barton Perry, Edwin B. Holt, William P. Montague, Edward G. Spaulding, Walter T. Marvin, and Walter B. Pitkin, neorealism arose as an attempt to reorient philosophy to contemporary science, to place philosophy on a scientific footing.[1] This involved a critique of pragmatist epistemology and its voluntarism, and it placed neorealism in a broader movement that included neopositivism. In its interest in the positive results of science and scientific methods, however, neorealism shared with pragmatism a hostility toward speculative philosophy and metaphysical generalization, and the neorealists were to a degree inclined to reject specifically philosophic knowledge. The accomplishments of science indicate the value of scientific methods, and if philosophy is to be equally fruitful it has to break with its own past, with traditions that rest on entirely different methods. To the neorealists this meant that philosophy and philosophic inquiry had to be severed from the history of philosophy, and it meant also that descriptions of reality, "metaphysics", had to be emancipated from epistemology because the unacceptable subjectivism of modern philosophy was the result of taking the knower and the process of knowing as the point of departure. In Yulina's description, the neorealists emphasized the methodological traits of science, especially analysis over synthesis, induction over deduction, and observation over speculation, as the appropriate philosophic methods, all of which constituted an "essential break with the traditions of American philosophy and speculative philosophy in general" (Yulina 1978a, 74).

Yulina argues that in its generally defensible concern to take science seriously, the neorealist approach suffered from inadequate conceptions of both philosophy and science. Neorealism faltered in several respects, specifically in its disassociation of philosophy from the history of philosophy, its devaluation of epistemology, and in the implications of its vacillation on the question of the nature and possibility of metaphysics. With respect to the first issue, philosophy requires that its own history be both appropriated and built upon:

> There was a grain of truth in their idea of reconsidering the legacy of past philosophy. However, their proposed thesis of "the separation of philosophical research from the study of the history of philosophy" was at its roots incorrect. It is evident that philosophic reasoning that does not address itself to problems given in the history of philosophy and does not go beyond solutions offered by preceding generations of thinkers will be either a special scientific reasoning or reasoning from the

point of view of common sense, but it will in no way be philosophic reasoning. (Yulina 1978a, 74)

Similarly, in their call to emancipate metaphysics from epistemology, the neorealists were engaging in justifiable polemics with the subjectivist tendencies of Kantianism, Humean empiricism, Machism, and so forth, but their alternative was no more adequate because philosophic reasoning cannot be removed entirely from an understanding of the means of acquiring knowledge, that is, from epistemology. Finally neorealism's interest in science and its suspicions about speculative philosophy left it with a problematic conception of metaphysics.

In one sense, Yulina argues, the neorealists tended toward "scientism," toward an approach that deals only with those issues amenable to the methods of science—empirical observation, induction, analysis, and verification. Scientism, while a protest against traditional forms of philosophy, is in the end a "fetishization of science and a devaluation of the distinct traits of philosophic activity" (Yulina 1978a, 78). It is an approach which, if its implications were followed through, would have led the neorealists to neopositivism, a complete break with metaphysics. But the neorealists were not prepared for such a radical break with the philosophic tradition, and their scientism led not to positivism but to "a reorientation of philosophy from speculative and rationalist methods to empirical methods, from substantialism to phenomenalism." While maintaining its commitment to science, neorealism appealed to a Jamesian neutralism and functionalism and in the end produced novel appropriations of the philosophic tradition: "In a word, the attempts to force philosophy into the mold of the scientific method, contrary to the scientistic designs of the neorealists, led them to a revival of traditional schemes of metaphysics, in part to the metaphysics of Platonism" (Yulina 1978a, 84). In its American version, the neorealists in the name of science left room for the grand speculative system of Whitehead.

Critical realism too had an ambiguous relation to science. As the name suggests, it is a close relative of neorealism, opposed to the speculative absolutism of objective idealism and to the subjectivism and instrumental treatment of knowledge in pragmatism. And like neorealism it recognized the independent existence of an objectively determinate world. In the 1920 anthology *Essays in Critical Realism*, however, the authors distance themselves from neorealism, primarily its theory of presentism or immanence.[2] In perception, they argued, the object is not in any significant sense "present" to or "immanent" in the knower. It is, rather, "represented" in perception and consciousness. The "given" is not an independent object immediately present in consciousness, but something else—essence. The way essence was understood distinguished different critical realist theories of knowledge and approaches to science. Bogomolov makes the distinction between essence as an epistemological and as an ontological category. Those who regarded essence epistemologically included James B. Pratt, Arthur. O. Lovejoy, and Roy W. Sellars. The group that gave essence ontological significance included Charles A. Strong, Durant Drake, Arthur K. Rogers, and, most prominently, George Santayana.

The conception of essence as an ontological category, the view of some critical realists, leads to a symbolic view of science, and the approach to essence taken by other critical realists results in a different understanding of science, of inquiry in general, and of their relation to nature. This other line of thought, exemplified most clearly by Sellars, developed critical realism into naturalism. In his 1972 study of American naturalism, Karimsky argues that its origins in the 1920s were conditioned not so much by the successes of natural science but by the "deep crises" of philosophic idealism's inability to handle or "digest" the accomplishments of the sciences (Karimsky 1972, 12). By collapsing nature into experience, pragmatism loses the independent existence of the subject matter of science, while the critical realism of Santayana dissociates scientific knowledge from its object. Naturalism sought to be a realist alternative to the former and to incorporate science and its methods more adequately than the latter. Another of the distinctive features of modern American naturalism was that while aspiring to a more careful and fruitful understanding of science it also sought "to restore as methodologically and epistemologically legitimate ontological problematics to the level of philosophic theory" (Karimsky 1972, 10). Other late nineteenth and early twentieth century philosophic trends, when facing the question of the relation of science to philosophy, tended either to eliminate the significance of one or the other or to subjugate one to the other. Naturalism by contrast tried to understand the relation while retaining the cultural and cognitive significance of both. As we will see, Soviet commentators tend to be more sympathetic to twentieth century naturalism than to any other trend in mainstream American philosophy, and this is one of the reasons. At the same time, a tension between science and philosophy, that is, metaphysics, has pushed the development of naturalism in various directions. Differences are determined in part by whether emphasis is placed on the methods of science or on metaphysical generalization; thus, Nagel differs from Randall or Buchler. Philosophic disagreement within modern naturalism can also result from what Yulina has called "images of science." If the nature of science and its methods are construed based on the "image" or model of physics, the philosophic result will differ from an understanding of science based on a biological model (Yulina 1990). The relation between naturalism and science is, according to Soviet readings, exceedingly complex, but it is clear enough that a concern with science lies at its roots, as it has for nearly all the influential developments of twentieth century American philosophy.

American philosophy with some few exceptions has developed in active opposition to a philosophic materialism that Soviet philosophers had traditionally regarded as the only general world view implicit in and consistent with contemporary science. Opposition to materialism has taken one of two forms. One of them is to reject materialism in favor of an explicit idealism, as in Royce and personalism. The other, found in Dewey and James, is, first, to reject the dichotomy between materialism and idealism by criticizing traditional versions of both and then to offer a view thought to be neither one nor the other. Yulina and Bogomolov attribute this approach also to neorealism and then argue—as they, Melvil, and others had with respect to pragmatism—that it is not a genuine alternative at all, but at best a novel form of idealism. Realism arose, Yulina notes, as a response to nineteenth century absolute idealism and also to the solipsistic implications of sensationalist epistemology and subjective idealism generally. At the same time it was also a rejection of traditional mechanistic materialism and, thus, able to conceive itself as free of the inadequacies of both materialism and idealism (Yulina 1974, 39–40). She had suggested in an earlier article devoted primarily to Santayana that the realists avoided *objective* idealism by acknowledging both the existence of objects of knowledge as independent of human beings and the objectivity of knowledge; they avoided *subjective* realism by attempting to build their theory on "the elements of experience." This attempt was unsuccessful, she thinks, and the entire history of American realism indicates that on the whole it remained within the confines of philosophic idealism (Yulina 1963, 294–295). Bogomolov agrees, and he proposes that realists are able to see themselves as offering something genuinely new only because their proposals were a unique sort of synthesis of objective and subjective idealism (Bogomolov 1963, 252).

The relation of critical realism to materialism is more ambiguous still. The critical realists were not as averse as most of their contemporaries to philosophic materialism, though in the 1920s few described themselves in that way. One exception was Santayana, who would say of himself that "in natural philosophy I am a decided materialist—apparently the only one living."[3] Yulina suggests that what inclined some critical realists to consider themselves materialists is that they endorsed the objective existence of the material world and its independence from essences. Also, she notes, critical realists did not in principle reject the view that consciousness depended on material human existence. This, however, is not enough, since while the critical realists recognize "the genetic connection of consciousness with the physical world, they are not in a position to explain convincingly the epistemological dependence of the ideal on the material, the fact that the content of perceptions, representations, and concepts always derives from material reality and is a reflection of it" (Yulina 1974, 62). It is insufficient simply to acknowledge the existence of the material world. Even

Plato had done so, though in his case the distinction between the ideal and material was as much or more a moral valuation as an ontological point, and Santayana is careful to distinguish his view from Plato's in this respect. Nonetheless, an adequate materialism requires a recognition of both the existence of the material world and a certain conception of the relation between the material and the ideal. Remember, Yulina advises us, that "a consistent materialism is based on the practical and theoretical interrelation of human beings with their surrounding reality; consciousness always presupposes the existence of the external world and an active relation to it." She notes that critical realism had a different approach: "For the central epistemological relation it takes not the human being as a subject cognizing the objective world, nor the real practical interrelation of the subject with the world, but consciousness, or more precisely *self-consciousness*." If Santayana's realm of essence belies his claim to materialism, so too does his realm of spirit. The corresponding epistemological view is that "the relation between subject and object is a transcendent interrelation of two forms of being, that the object of perception and the content of perception are two absolutely different things having between them nothing in common." And in Santayana's case an independent realm of truth further clinches the case against his "materialism": "In a word, there is an absolute truth about the world, but it apparently is inaccessible, in that knowledge always remains relative and subjective" (Yulina 1974, 64–65).

If critical realism in Santayana's variety claims but does not achieve materialism, it comes much closer in the strain that runs through Sellars to mid-century naturalism. Though Sellars explicitly prefers the term *naturalism* to the term *materialism*, Bogomolov says that in his specific criticisms of materialism, Sellars has in mind either nineteenth century natural scientific materialism or mechanical, metaphysical materialism in general. And Sellars's criticisms in many respects would win agreement among dialectical materialists. In his positive views Sellars avoids many of the pitfalls of other realists, particularly with respect to the relation between the subject and object of knowledge. Neither is reduced to the other, yet they remain related. Later in his life Sellars also approached materialism in his articulation of something like a reflection theory of knowledge and in the specific way he treated practice as a criterion of our belief that we have achieved knowledge of the surrounding world. While Bogomolov also locates a number of problems and insufficiently developed conceptions in Sellars, he nevertheless thinks that his work was "an important step forward in the development of American philosophy. In it is found an embodiment of the irresistible materialist tendency in the history of philosophy" (Bogomolov 1974, 217).

A materialist strain runs through other versions of American naturalism as well. There are those, Karimsky notes, who have been rather clearly materialists, among whom in addition to Sellars he includes Corliss Lamont, Marvin Farber, and Abraham Edel. Even those who would have rejected the label tended to fluctuate between idealism and materialism—Ernest Nagel, Yervant Krikorian, Sterling Power Lamprecht, John Herman Randall Jr., and Harold Larrabee (Karimsky 1972, 11). The details of their views will be considered below, but it is important to realize that the materialist strain in American naturalism is one of the central reasons for its generally favorable evaluation by Soviet commentators, and they are explicit about this point. Karimsky has said that he is sympathetic to naturalism because "in a number of respects naturalism is congenial to philosophic materialism . . ." (Karimsky 1990, 1).

With common roots in cultural, scientific, and philosophic sources, twentieth century American philosophy developed in several directions. Besides pragmatism and personalism, the latter of which appears to be interesting to Soviet philosophers not for any philosophic value but as an expression of American cultural traits, the high points have been reached in Royce, Whitehead, Santayana, and in naturalism.

Royce

Josiah Royce, in Bogomolov's estimation, was a pivotal figure in American intellectual history. In his objective idealism he was genuinely the last of the nineteenth century American philosophers, while his "personalism," "pragmatism," and reliance on mathematics for his metaphysics made him the first American philosopher of the twentieth century (Bogomolov 1974, 35). Despite such a unique place in American thought, however, the philosophic influences on Royce were from the beginning primarily German—Kant, Fichte, Schopenhauer, and Hegel. The impact of Hegel was particularly interesting, since for all his interest in logic, Royce was influenced not by the technical Hegel of the *Logic* but by the *Phenomenology*. For Royce the crucial Hegelian concept was the paradox of consciousness—to know oneself one has to see oneself through an other, a conception that leads him to the absolute (Bogomolov 1974, 24–25).

For Bogomolov and Sidorov, the two Soviet philosophers who commented most extensively on Royce, the most significant of his ontological concerns is his treatment of the relation of the one and the many. In Royce's hands this involved the relation of individuals with one another and, more generally and importantly, the relation of individuals to the absolute. Throughout his life Royce continually addressed the latter question, and he offered various conceptions of the nature of the absolute and of the way the many are harmonized in relation to it. While the absolute was always identified with divine experience, Royce variously conceived it as the Logos, the Individual of Individuals, and finally as the Spirit of the

Beloved Community (Sidorov 1974, 7). Similarly, Royce described differently at different stages of his thought the harmony of the many that the absolute makes possible. In *The World and the Individual* the principle by which the many are united is metaphysical duty, in *The Philosophy of loyalty* it is loyalty to loyalty, and in *The Problem of Christianity* it is the ongoing process of interpretation (Sidorov 1989, 91).

Royce's philosophy is dominated by his understanding of the absolute, but for him the absolute was not a philosophic point of departure or a given. It was invariably a conclusion to be drawn, a deduction, and his specific conceptions of it were derived above all from epistemological considerations. Sidorov in his dissertation on Royce and Bogomolov in his account are both interested primarily in a description and criticism of Royce's metaphysics. In his more recent book, however, Sidorov focuses not so much on Royce's metaphysics as on a distinctive thread that runs through his epistemology. The most significant trait of Royce's approach to the nature of knowledge is its voluntarism. It is this that places Royce in the American tradition of a philosophy of action, and that allows his philosophy to be described as an absolute pragmatism. It may be tempting to assume that a voluntarist, active conception of knowledge is a result of Royce's interaction with James, and their ongoing debate no doubt had some effect. But it would be more appropriate to see in Royce's epistemology a reflection of the same Kantian roots that were a source, each in its own way, of Emersonian transcendentalism and of pragmatism.[4] Royce's view is not an offshoot of pragmatism; rather, Royce and the pragmatists, and Emerson as well, are distinct branches of the same conceptual tree. Despite the centrality of action in their conceptions of knowledge, however, there are fundamental differences between Royce and pragmatism:

> The essential trait of Royce's philosophic program was his methodological opposition to pragmatism: if the pragmatists were inclined to be satisfied with a phenomenalist treatment of experience and saw the criteria of truth in the efficacy of an idea, then Royce, while holding that an idea is a plan of action, attempted to discern the general conditions of the intelligibility of experience and the criteria of truth in relation to the absolute. (Sidorov 1989, 56)

In pragmatism an active, voluntarist epistemology produced a subjective idealism, while in Royce it is expressly and persistently merged with an objective idealist metaphysics. In that respect Royce is closer to Emerson than to James or Dewey, though in contrast with the aesthetic idealism of transcendentalism. Royce's is an ethical idealism, concerned above all with the problem of moral and social harmony (Sidorov 1989, 90). Royce's unique blend of ideas and methodological procedures gives his entire philosophy an overtly ethical and religious cast.

The centrality of epistemology in Royce's work is evident in his earliest deduction of the absolute, the well-known argument from error. Royce developed this argument in *The Religious Aspect of Philosophy*, published in 1885, and it contains elements that were to reappear in later work. The argument begins with a concern with skepticism and relativism, that either truth is unattainable or that there is no truth independent of a perceiver or someone offering a judgment. Royce makes short work of the "relativity of truth" by asking us to consider the proposition that error exists. If the proposition is false then error exists, and if it is true then error exists. When we ask, however, how error is possible, or what are its logical conditions, an answer is less clear. A mistaken judgment, Royce says, is defined as one that does not agree with its object, in which subject and predicate are combined in a way that does not correspond with the object. On the face of it this does not seem to present a difficulty, but the situation becomes problematic when we consider the nature of the supposed agreement or correspondence between a judgment and its object. A particular judgment is not about just any object at all, or any one of a set of similar objects, but rather it has a particular object. A judgment "picks out as its own" a particular object, and it does so by intending the object. A judgment is about an object, has an object, only when the individual making the judgment intends just that object. But to intend a particular object, the individual must to some degree know the object, and here is the dilemma. To judge, one must intend an object; to intend, one must know the object; thus, a false judgment can only be about an object which one knows. Error is only possible about that which is known.

One may be tempted to resolve the dilemma by distinguishing between an object as intended by a judgment and the same object as it is independent of the judgment. But a judgment has as its object an intended object, so that the question still arises, how can one be in error about an object as one conceives it? It appears that one cannot be mistaken about an object as conceived, because however it is conceived, so it is. Error, then, must somehow be in the relation between the object as intended or conceived and the object as independent. But a judgment requires intention, so an object unintended bears no relation to a judgment. The only way this dilemma can be resolved, Royce argued, is through the presence of a third term in the relation. The agreement or disagreement of the intended object of a judgment with the independent object requires that both be present to, or observable by, a third, more inclusive consciousness that is able to compare them and to know whether the judgment is true or in error. With this idea in mind, consider the case of a judgment that concerns the future. Here the possibility of a judgment, true or false, seems even more remote because we assume that the future does not exist, which is to say, no object exists for such a judgment to intend. Yet we do make judgments, including false judgments, concerning the future, and they are possible only on the supposition that the judgment and its object, the future, are present to a consciousness that relates them. In the end this implies a single, all-inclusive absolute thought in which all reality, all past, present, and future, is realized as intended object. The existence of error implies, then, the reality of absolute consciousness.[5]

Neither Sidorov nor Bogomolov develops an extended criticism of Royce's argument, presumably because its shortcomings are obvious enough. No account of human activity, including knowledge, is adequate if it does not take into account human practice. Judgments arise in lived circumstances, and their truth or falsity is determined in the efficacy of practical activity, not by a dialectical articulation of ideal, logical conditions. Royce's general mistake, in the argument from error and elsewhere, is that he "ignores socially determined material and practical activity as the determining basis of the process of knowledge. Therefore his deduction has not only an a priori character but is also distinguished by an extreme subjectivism in that it absolutizes the role of the subjective factor in knowledge" (Sidorov 1974, 8). Despite such shortcomings, however, Royce's argument from error is intriguing because of what it reveals about the character of his thought. We find in it that "paradox of consciousness" that Bogomolov identifies as the Hegelian concept most crucial for Royce—that knowledge of any sort, including self-knowledge or self-consciousness, requires an other, ultimately an absolute other. Royce's argument also suggests the fundamental role in his thought of triadic relations, to be developed years later, under Peirce's influence, through the concept of interpretation.

Royce did not rest content with the argument from error nor with the conception of the absolute developed in *The Religious Aspect of Philosophy*. The next significant refinements came in 1892 in *The Spirit of Modern Philosophy* and in what Sidorov describes as the more clearly argued essay "The Implications of Self-Consciousness." In the latter Royce offers a sharp critique of Cartesianism, as Pierce had done in his 1868 essays, arguing that one cannot draw any epistemological implications from individual self-consciousness. The reason, unlike for Peirce, is that a given fact is subject to study not through such psychological categories as clarity and vagueness but through the philosophic categories of truth and falsity. And the latter, continuing the line of thought of the argument from error, imply a higher, absolute reality and truth. Thus philosophy, and knowledge generally, do not concern an "objective world" independent of consciousness as much as they concern the absolute, the unity of experience and rational necessity, freedom and law, the infinite and the finite, the irrational and the rational. To this end philosophy requires corresponding concepts. Royce finds them in the distinction between the "world of description" and the "world of appreciation," categories he considers in

The Spirit of Modern Philosophy and in 1899 in *The World and the Individual.*

The world of description is the world of observation and empirical experience; it is the world studied and described by the sciences. Our descriptions of that world, and whatever we regard as aspects of it, are the result of social interaction. We take as aspects of the world of description that which we find in our experience to be shared with others. Thus the world of description requires the reality of other individual conscious beings like ourselves. However, the nature of other individuals, their "inner reality," their consciousness, is not revealed to us in empirical observation. Their inner nature is a necessary condition of the world of description, but it is not part of that world. The inner reality of consciousness is the world of appreciation, which in Royce's view is "superior to" or "higher than" the world of description in several respects. First, that world is a condition of the world of description. Second, the methods of knowledge appropriate to the world of description, that is the sciences, are themselves not able to achieve genuine knowledge of that inner world without being augmented by methods appropriate to the world of appreciation. The reason for this, again following the line of thought of the argument from error, is that scientific judgments are necessarily intentional and thus require the "selection" of their objects by consciousness. In that such selection or intention is an activity, knowledge is inherently purposive and moral, and the purposes and ends of consciousness, on which the world of description depends, are not available to descriptive knowledge. And finally, the world of appreciation, because it is the world of inner individual consciousness, is at the same time the realm of the absolute.

By the time Royce delivered his Presidential Address to the American Philosophical Association in 1903, "The Eternal and the Practical," he had been for some twenty years refining his understanding of the active and volitional nature of thought and knowledge. Sidorov discusses his article "The Two-Fold Nature of Knowledge: Imitative and Reflective," written in 1883 but published only in 1966, in which Royce tried to distance himself from the view then widely held by idealists that knowledge is a purely mental, speculative process (Sidorov 1989, 69). The most significant theoretical development of Royce's volitional, voluntarist conception of knowledge came in the concepts of internal and external meaning. In *The World and the Individual* Royce used these concepts to reformulate the intentional nature of judgments from *The Religious Aspect of Philosophy*. All ideas have both an internal and external meaning. The internal meaning of an idea, reflecting the earlier concept of an idea's intention, embodies the individual's purpose. It is the selection by consciousness of some object for a reason. This is the respect in which an idea is a plan of action, that is, a plan to fulfill its purpose. The external meaning of an idea is the object it selects, the referent of the idea. Here Royce must face the same questions he did earlier—how should we understand the relation of an idea and its object and in what consists the truth or falsity of an idea? Now, however, the terms of the questions must be somewhat different since now, as Sidorov puts it, "the essence of an idea consists not in its relation to reality, but in the interrelation among the modifications of its own internal and external meaning" (Sidorov 1989, 71). Royce describes the relation between the internal and external meaning of an idea in terms of the individual's purposes. An idea either fulfills its purpose or it does not, and in that lies its relative truth or falsity. In this respect, as Sidorov points out, Royce shares James's view that the truth of ideas is related to purposes. But what are the conditions, Royce asks, that enable an object to fulfill an individual's purpose? His answer is that this is possible only because an object or an external meaning is itself an embodiment of the purpose partially expressed by the internal meaning of an idea. An idea would be wholly true when its object is a "fully determinate" fulfillment of purposes. Objects, which are the external meaning of finite ideas, are the internal meaning, the purposes, of the absolute. Reality in general, in other words, is pragmatically conceived. It is the expression of absolute Will, a realm of ends.[6]

In *The World and the Individual* Royce combined a pragmatic treatment of meaning, will, and knowledge with a mathematical account of the absolute as a self-representational system. While there remained unresolved problems and contradictions, Bogomolov notes what he takes to be the achievements of Royce's ideas, specifically his mathematical concepts. Royce was able to articulate the interrelation of individual phenomena, thus avoiding atomistic individualism. At the same time he overcame one of the difficulties of F. H. Bradley's idealism by being able to show the relation between individuals and the absolute, the one and the many, the individual and the world (Bogomolov 1974, 28–29). For Sidorov, however, the most outstanding feature of *The World and the Individual* is its voluntarism, embodied most directly in the concept of internal meaning. By virtue of internal meaning ideas are purposeful, and Royce extends this point to argue that in their volitional nature ideas "share" in absolute thought.

Royce's unique conception implied at the ontological level, that reality embodies the purpose and meaning of absolute experience, that reality is a realm of ends, and that the absolute and the world, the one and the many, have an inherently moral character. Epistemologically, Royce's voluntarism is the feature of his work through which he stands with Emerson and the pragmatists as a source of a distinctively American philosophy of action. Though he finds Royce's contribution valuable, Sidorov nevertheless notes what he takes to be among the mistakes of Royce's epistemology. First, Sidorov had raised against the argument from error the objection that it overlooks the social factor in knowledge. Royce's general mistake, again, is that he "ignores socially determined material and practical activity as the determining basis of the process of knowledge." One might wish to respond to Sidorov that Royce does not at all ignore the social. His account of the world of description presupposes social interaction, and the entire philosophic conception of his later life is expressed in terms of community and the social interrelation of its members. Sidorov will respond to these points by suggesting the difference between what he means by *society* and Royce's use of the term. To be sure, as Sidorov notes, in Royce's view human beings are constituent elements of a wider end, a "social order," and he does indeed try to develop a social conception of knowledge that rests to a great degree on Peirce's concept of interpretation. But Royce's "society" is only spiritual, and while the issue of interpretation is an important one, it will not do, in Sidorov's critique, to treat it, as Royce does, as a kind of spiritual activity. Royce's mistake is in his idealism, Sidorov argues, since the spiritual realm is not a source of social relations but finds its explanation in material, practical human relations and activity (Sidorov 1989, 79–81). Second, Royce's entire conception of knowledge and reality deprives knowledge of its profound value—rationally conceived scientific knowledge. One of the problems is that the distinction between the worlds of description and appreciation sharply limits the applicability of science. By describing science as appropriate to the world of description and by placing consciousness in the world of appreciation, Royce essentially removes human beings as possible objects of scientific inquiry (Sidorov 1974, 14). More generally, while he charges science with inadequacy, Royce proposes to orient knowledge not on a consciousness of aims and actions but on a mystical access to the absolute (Sidorov 1989, 77–78).

Again, one might be inclined to reject this last criticism on the grounds that Royce himself was highly critical of mysticism, largely because it underestimates the significance of the many, of the world of description. Sidorov is aware of this and even suggests that Royce had foreseen the danger that his views would be interpreted in irrational and obscurantist ways. Royce in turn tried to forestall too mystical a reading by applying his general philosophic ideas to specifically human problems (Sidorov 1989, 78). His understanding of the ontological issue of the one and the many and his active and voluntarist epistemology are both further developed in the context of social and ethical questions. Of particular importance for Royce was the nature of human being. He treats the individual person as an "ethical individual," an individual embodiment of absolute meaning, whose activity is organized around "life tasks." The specific way Royce relates the human individual and the absolute had, in Sidorov's view, both virtues and shortcomings. On the one had, as we have seen, by relating human ideals to the divine, Royce avoids in his voluntarism the overly subjectivist and relativist treatment of ideal ends characteristic of pragmatism (Sidorov 1989, 78). What is more, in doing so he explicitly tried to avoid the common pitfall of absolute idealism of subsuming and dissolving the many into the one. On the other hand, this in some ways insightful approach left him with insoluble problems and contradictions. For Royce, Sidorov feels, people's interests and requirements have no practical grounds in that the meaning and content of human activity is determined by absolute ends. There is an "excessive idealism" and "ahistoricism" in his conception of the person and consequently in his social theory (Sidorov 1974, 17).

The idealism of Royce's ontology, epistemology, and social theory is of course unacceptable to a dialectical and historical materialist. His epistemological optimism, as Sidorov puts it, which rests on his view of the absolute and absolute reason, is unfounded. Nonetheless, in important ways Royce's aspirations are noteworthy: "The humanistic motive of the American philosopher's attempt to express and defend the vital importance for human beings of higher ends of activity and knowledge of course deserves respect . . " (Sidorov 1989, 92).

Whitehead

In defense of his absolute idealism Royce was engaged for most of his career in polemics with the pragmatism of James and Dewey. In the early twentieth century, however, a group of American philosophers who advocated a "new realism" sought an alternative to both Royce and the pragmatists. One of the fundamental concerns of the neorealists was to reorient philosophy to the perspectives and methods of the natural sciences. However the movement as a whole was ambivalent about the relation of philosophy and science, in some cases looking to turn philosophy into a science, in others to achieve solutions to philosophic questions that would accord with the practice and results of contemporary science and at the same time "preserve all the variety of life and experience" (Yulina 1978a, 78). Bogomolov identifies a related division in American neorealism, an epistemological trend concerned to construct a realist theory of knowledge, and a cosmological trend that attempted on the basis of evolutionism to build an all-embracing philosophic system (Bogomolov 1963, 256). As a distinct movement neorealism dissolved in the 1920s, though its philosophic concerns did not disappear. Of its two dominant trends, the cosmological turned out to be more stable and influential than the epistemological, reaching its zenith in the process philosophy of Whitehead (Bogomolov 1974, 162).

"In his speculative cosmology Whitehead tried to resolve the most significant problems of contemporary science," Bogomolov remarks. He was in a unique position to undertake such a task, and given his background it would seem that he had every possibility to succeed: he was a specialist in mathematics, mathematical physics, and logic, and he had a broad understanding of the history of science and philosophy. "Nevertheless, his attempt ended in failure" (Bogomolov 1963, 261). The dominant theme of Yulina's discussion of Whitehead and Bogomolov's more extensive analyses attempts to explain why and how he went wrong. Both locate the most fundamental flaws of Whitehead's philosophy in its idealism and theism, of which there are more than a few illustrations. In his earliest American book *Science and the Modern World* Whitehead argues that the theories of contemporary, early twentieth century science and their fundamental categories require philosophic attention. Newtonian science had been based on the concept of material particles with simple location in space. The new science, beginning with Maxwell, required an entirely new world view, and the conceptual structure Whitehead developed to serve that function he called a philosophy of organism. One of the central characteristics of Whitehead's conception of organism is that spatial objects and intervals of time all "appropriate" (prehend) one another, that each is a "prehending unity" and to that extent constitute one another. This "deeply dialectical" insight concerning the interaction of natural objects and events, however, is developed into an idealist construction. In Bogomolov's view Whitehead should have pursued a dialectical conception of matter but that with the concept of organism he moved in a different direction:

> At this point we already encounter an idealist tendency: where mechanism attempted to reduce organic nature to an aggregate of mechanistic processes, "organism" tries to reduce the inorganic to the organic and find in it a form of "life." But Whitehead does not stop there. The organism in turn is treated as a process of organic synthesis, in the course of which arises something new, something not reducible to its source. Whitehead finds the analogy to this process in the act of experience, and his attempt to replace the "materialist abstraction" of the immediate given of experience results in the view that reality is an aggregate of "actual occasions" as "acts of experience." (Bogomolov 1974, 165)

Finally, for Sidorov, Whitehead's admirable philosophic project fails, perhaps primarily, because of its theism. For all his interest in formal mathematics and the sciences, Whitehead remained convinced that those disciplines contributed to a picture of reality devoid of ends, value, and meaning, and he thought that religion more than anything was the arena that could accommodate them. Thus one of his most basic concerns was to combine science and philosophy with religion, "a combination of ordinary science with a flight of religious and metaphysical fantasy" (Bogomolov 1974, 163). For Bogomolov, whatever cultural, anthropological and historical significance religion and theological categories may have, they never have genuine philosophically explanatory power. To appeal to religion and theology as an inherent feature of a philosophic system is to admit failure. Thus the evidence of Whitehead's failure "is more than anything the appeal to the idea of God—the genuine *testimonium paupertatis* of a philosophic system aspiring to a scientific solution to a question" (Bogomolov 1963, 261). The question of *how* Whitehead went wrong remains, and an answer requires turning to the development and details of his thought.

Nature and Its Events

Bogomolov identifies four stages in Whitehead's philosophic development: (1) the period of logical and mathematical studies, (2) a positivist period, (3) the period of concern with the "philosophy of science," and (4) the period of his speculative cosmology and metaphysics. This periodic division must of course be applied fairly loosely. Bogomolov notes, for example, that despite the fact that the first period was dominated by formal mathematical concerns culminating in his and Russell's *Principia Mathematica*, Whitehead had already during these years turned to conceptual questions raised by developments in the sciences. In his 1906 article "Mathematical Concepts of the Material World," Whitehead addressed mathematically relevant distinctions between a classical model—where the world is an aggregate of spatial points, moments in time, and material particles—and a model based on the theory of relativity, where the properties of space and time are indissolubly connected with the properties of matter and arise from them. While the primary result of the first period of Whitehead's thought was the view developed in the *Principia* that logic is the foundation of mathematics, in the second period he held that logic was also the basis of science, which led him to a positivist view of both science and philosophy.

Whitehead's most distinctive and enduring philosophic contributions, however, began to emerge with the publication in 1920 of *The Concept of Nature*. In this period of his thought, in Bogomolov's interpretation, Whitehead moved away from the more or less subjective idealism of positivism to an objectively idealist neorealism. Unlike Mach and others, who reduced reality to "neutral elements" and in the end to sensation, Whitehead held that the "ultimate facts of experience," and thus the basic elements of nature, are events. At this point Whitehead is raising the problems and introducing the concepts that would extend to his speculative cosmology (Bogomolov 1963, 264–265).

Whitehead approaches the conception of nature in neorealist fashion, as independent of thought, and through a criticism of traditional conceptions. In the past philosophers in their understanding of nature have taken "things" to be the real constitutive parts of the natural world, when in fact things are abstractions. The result has been a series of bifurcations in nature—between what is given in perception (the world as experienced) and what is given to science (atoms, electrons etc.); between primary objective qualities and secondary subjective qualities; between nature comprehended in perception and nature as the cause of perception. Whitehead objects to these and related dichotomies, and he argues that nature must somehow be conceived as a seamless fabric inclusive of individual experience. In that spirit Whitehead held another wholly neorealist position, that as fully characteristic of nature experience is independent of the individual and of knowledge. This conception enabled him to be rid of the subjectivism in the distinction between nature consisting of atoms and molecules and nature consisting of sensibly perceived elements.

Whitehead, Bogomolov argues, was right about much of this: that there is just one nature revealed to both reason and sensation; that natural science reveals the interrelations of real processes, though it abstracts from some aspects of reality; and that one must locate the connection of sensible qualities with physical quantities without deriving them from an interrelation of the physical world and consciousness (Bogomolov 1963, 267). But Whitehead begins to go astray at this point, and the problem is comparable to the implications of the neorealist epistemological theory of immanence. Whitehead asks the question, What objectively exists in nature, independent of perception, when, for example, we have the perception of red? Bogomolov suspects here an attempt to avoid a traditional bifurcation between nature and nature perceived by eliding the distinction between the process of the acquisition of knowledge and the object of knowledge.

That Whitehead wants to avoid the distinction between the process and object of knowledge is further suggested by his remarks about the "why" and the "what" of knowledge. We cannot, Whitehead says, explain the "why" of knowledge (which Bogomolov interprets as the "how"), but only the "what." "Knowledge is a fact of nature, Whitehead thinks, and like all facts it is subject to description but not explanation. But this is not true: we may speak exclusively of the content of knowledge and the interrelations of its internal elements only to the extent that we do not face the task of demonstrating the truth of our knowledge, or to the point where we confront the fact of the error of our knowledge". The process of the acquisition of knowledge, Bogomolov holds, conditions the object insofar as it is known, so that in our philosophy and our science we need always to distinguish carefully, to the extent that we are able, those traits that the object of knowledge has as a result of coming to be known and those traits that it has independently of knowledge. If we are not careful about this distinction, there is the danger that we will attribute distributively to all natural phenomena traits that are peculiar to or the result of a knowing, experiencing subject or the processes of knowledge and experience themselves. In other words, the danger arises of reading nature in general as a human world writ large. The neorealist theory of immanence falls prey to this danger, as does Whitehead when he reads experience into nature. For Bogomolov, the fact that we can be mistaken indicates the need to make the distinction Whitehead apparently wants to avoid. The question of truth and the fact of error requires a consideration of the relation between the objective world and the world as we think we know it: "In that case it is necessary to distinguish between the external world perceived by us with the aid of sense organs, and the 'world' of our knowledge which is a reflection of the first, and in relation to which the first is the source, the prototype" (Bogomolov 1963, 268). Whitehead might have avoided Bogomolov's point because it may well have seemed to him to be an example of the very thing he was reacting against:

> Whitehead would likely call this view a "bifurcation." But in fact there is no bifurcation here at all. . . . Originating in material, productive activity, knowledge reveals the laws of reality and becomes a guiding principle for action. But it does not create a special "world"; it is an activity, a function, a property of highly organized matter, and it can be contrasted with the other properties of the material world only conditionally and relatively. . . . (Bogomolov 1963, 268–269)

Whatever problems of this sort Whitehead may or may not have had, his attempt to avoid the many dichotomies of traditional philosophic ideas produced a new approach to nature. His rejection of a mechanistic conception of nature led Whitehead to the view that nature is a process composed of events, that this process of nature gradually gives rise to novelty, and that the events that constitute nature are fleeting and transient. This new conception raises an immediate question, however. If nature is a continuous process constituted entirely by transient events perpetually originating and perishing, how then is scientific knowledge, that is knowledge of stability, regularity, and law, possible? Whitehead's answer introduces what Bogomolov refers to as a new bifurcation between events and objects. Events are quantitative and changing within nature, objects their qualitative stability; events are concrete, objects abstract; events are particular, objects universal; events are transient, objects eternal; events are in space and time, whereas objects are not; events are continuous, objects discrete. This, however, raises yet another question: How are such contradictory existences combined in nature? From this point forward, the attempt to answer this question drives Whitehead's thought.

Whitehead regarded the method of extensive abstraction, technically a way of deriving geometrical elements from experience, as an implication of the theory of relativity, that such simple entities as a point are essentially complexes of relations or possible relations among things. But the specific way Whitehead understood "thing" and "object" at this point proved to be inconsistent with the method: "Whitehead understood by 'things' events with their spatio-temporal properties, and by geometrical elements he understood constancies, objects. And this metaphysical point of departure inevitably led to the failure of the method itself" (Bogomolov 1963, 271). Whitehead's familiar illustration of the method is a series of squares with a common center and progressively diminishing sides, and a series of rectangles with progressively diminishing heights. The series of squares will end up in a point and the series of rectangles in a line, thus the point and the line are limits toward which the series tend.[7] This approach, however, could not satisfy Whitehead because with it a geometrical element is regarded as a process, as a never ending approximation to its initial element, and this is inconsistent with Whitehead's understanding of geometrical elements as "simple entities" or "scientific objects," strictly determined and unchanging concepts. He tried first to refine the method, and eventually he abandoned it: "This metaphysical, anti-dialectical interpretation of 'object' obliged Whitehead to reconceive the method of 'extensive abstraction' such that it would lead to an acknowledgment of immutable 'objects,' but in fact it led him to a rejection of the method itself in favor of the postulation of the existence of such objects." To put the point a different way, Whitehead's problem was that "the application of the method of 'extensive abstraction' having as its aim to show the essence of the interrelation of 'events' and 'objects' already presupposes the 'theory of objects.'" Bogomolov adds that "apparently this was clear even to Whitehead himself, since in further consideration of the 'theory of extensive abstraction' the 'theory of objects' figures as a speculative presupposition" (Bogomolov 1963, 272–273). Whitehead realized, in other words, that his understanding of "object" and "event" were even more fundamental concepts than a method as general as extensive abstraction. This realization led him both to his assertion of the necessity of carefully articulated speculative categories and to the details of his philosophy of process. Whitehead came to think, Bogomolov suggests, that the resolution of the problem of the relation between events and objects could be achieved only on the basis of an explicitly developed objective idealism and ultimately a direct appeal to a divine being.

Speculative Metaphysics

Whitehead's ontology and cosmology are an expression of his conception of metaphysical generalization. His own experience in the sciences and mathematics convinced him that it is not possible simply to observe facts, since facts will invariably be approached and understood from the perspective of some set of general ideas. It is also impossible to engage solely in analytic reasoning, since that no less than empirical observation presupposes more general concepts. To avoid fundamental concepts that are either arbitrarily or dogmatically held, science, mathematics, and philosophy require a direct consideration of conceptual generalizations. The process of metaphysical generalization is meant to produce a system of general ideas which, as Bogomolov puts it, has both a rational and an empirical side. Rationally, the system of ideas must be coherent and logically necessary, while empirically it must be applicable and adequate to experience. Traditionally philosophy has tended to emphasize either the rational or the empirical aspects of inquiry to the detriment of the other. Whitehead, by contrast, wanted to construct a universal philosophic system that would retain all the multiplicity of the world and of knowledge (Yulina 1978a, 87). Yulina wonders, however, whether metaphysical generalization as Whitehead understood it is sufficient to the task. For one thing, he seems to go two different ways with respect to the power of reason. He rejects the possibility of strict rational thought on the grounds that analytic consciousness cannot capture the totality and creativity of experience, in that emotion, valuation, aesthetic feeling, and the goal-directed nature of experience permeate thought. At the same time, though, he regards rational thought capable of achieving a metaphysical "ultimate." Furthermore, Yulina questions whether a single system of concepts can be adequately empirical and rational to do the job: "Whitehead felt he could combine the incompatible—i.e., create a system of ideas that reflects the unique composition of experience and at the same time is sufficiently formal to apply to all possible experience" (Yulina 1978a, 100).

Despite the claim that metaphysical generalization is crucial for inquiry of less general sorts, "Whitehead sees the important practical value of philosophy not in this but above all in its relation to religion" (Bogomolov 1963, 274). Yulina does not make this sort of claim, though she does note that Whitehead's is a metaphysical scheme that has its point of departure in experience and its terminus in God. In her estimation, however, this points not so much to religion as a motivating factor but rather to the question of the adequacy of metaphysics and the relation of metaphysics to science. Pre-Kantian philosophy, Yulina notes, offered many examples of metaphysical systems that moved conceptually from experience to God, and Kant was more than justified in raising the questions he did about them: what is the relation of metaphysics to science, and what are the criteria of adequacy of a metaphysical system? (Yulina 1978a, 92).

Both of these questions were very much in the philosophic air in the early twentieth century, having been taken up by the logical positivists in their reworking of the nature of philosophy and its relation to science. Whitehead of course rejected the positivists' contrast of metaphysics to science. Metaphysics cannot be judged by the same criteria as science, because since its adequacy is in its applicability, the criteria appropriate to metaphysics are internal logical consistency, integrity, the necessity of its principles, and so forth. In any case, metaphysics is necessary, again, because scientific procedures and results always flow from a system of ideas, and it is the role of metaphysics to establish and justify such a system. Whitehead's primary objection to the positivist conception of science, however, is that its method does not allow for recognition of a crucial aspect of nature, that is, the natural status of ends and creativity. Religion can and does meet this concern to some extent, but in Whitehead's view metaphysics merges the rigor of science with the imagination of religion, and only a metaphysical synthesis can overcome both the limits of science and the dogmatism of religion (Yulina 1978a, 94).

Yulina is particularly interested in a comparison of Whitehead and the positivists on the question of the relation among metaphysics, science, and religion. Like neopositivism, she says, Whitehead's conception of philosophy is another of the many "revolutions" characteristic of bourgeois philosophy in the first half of the twentieth century:

> Whitehead's philosophy was formulated in the same social and ideological context as the philosophy of neopositivism. Like the neopositivists, Whitehead carried on a "settling of accounts with the classics" and was inclined to devalue the classical heritage. In his own philosophic research he was, like the neopositivists, oriented toward science, drawing from it the fundamental ideas of his philosophic constructions. Finding himself at the point of the breakdown of the theoretical, methodological, and conceptual apparatus of science, he was captivated by the idea of taking a fresh look at philosophy and the construction of a new theoretical and conceptual apparatus for it. Like the neopositivists, he was concerned with the range and limits of the applicability of scientific methods and with the possibility of utilizing the methods and calculus of mathematical logic for the expression of the multiplicity of experience and being. (Yulina 1978a, 95–96)

Whitehead described his ontological and cosmological system as a philosophy of organism. For Yulina, his view of the universe as organism was intended to serve two functions: (1) to deal with internal philosophic issues, specifically to overcome such traditional philosophic antinomies and dichotomies as those between the material and the ideal, the theoretical and the empirical, value and fact, and scientific and ethical-humanistic knowledge; (2) to deal with the external problem of bringing the philosophic theory of being into conformity with contemporary natural scientific conceptions of the world and to offer a philosophic interpretation of these conceptions (Yulina 1978a, 104–105). At the heart of Whitehead's approach to these tasks is an attack on substantialism. He rejected all forms of substantialism, including physical objects, absolute spirit, "neutral thing," and "thing in itself," but his primary target was mechanistic materialism.

Whitehead's central objection to traditional mechanistic materialism was that on its terms matter is static and inanimate, and the corporeal is without feeling, value, and ends. These kinds of objections to mechanistic materialism have been made for thousands of years, and in the early twentieth century they were advanced in one or another version by philosophers from various camps. Whitehead was not alone in his philosophic concerns, though he did not fit neatly into any of the prevailing alternatives. While he flirted, Yulina suggests, with the physical idealists' inclination to reduce matter to energy, mathematical symbol, or sensation, in the end he defended a view different from those of the physical idealists, symbolists, instrumentalists, and pragmatists (Yulina 1978a, 105).

Along with an attack on substantialism, Yulina says, one of the keys to Whitehead's concept of organism is that it was an attempt to combine physics and biology. He of course took seriously an evolutionary, developmental biological paradigm, but unlike many of his contemporaries for whom Darwinism was crucial, Dewey comes to mind, Whitehead was as much concerned to take account of Einsteinian relativity. He accepted relativity in the concrete sciences, but again unlike many of his contemporaries, he rejected the attempt to generalize relativity (or relativism). into a world view, specifically a relativist view of the absence of a firm foundation of knowledge and the impossibility of objective criteria of valuation: "His entire philosophy is an attempt to demonstrate the opposite—the presence of an absolute foundation, a firm ontological structure, and the ability of the intellect to comprehend that structure" (Yulina 1978a, 106).

In the philosophy of organism Whitehead generalizes his earlier concepts. In particular, the categories of event and the several kinds of objects of his "philosophy of science" are replaced by the categories of actual entity (actual occasion) and eternal object. Actual entities, the "final real things," are defined as "drops of experience," so that the world is an aggregate of experiential processes. Actual entities, or actual occasions, express the dynamic side of process. Its static, qualitative side is conveyed in the category of eternal object, or pure potentiality. The connection between static eternal objects and dynamic actual entities is through the "ingression" of eternal objects in actual entities. The concept of ingression, Bogomolov suggests, weaves together two strains of thought, one from mathematics analogous to variables entering into propositional functions, and the other that Whitehead calls the "ontological principle," according to which actual entities are the ultimate reasons or causes (Bogomolov 1974, 168).

The question of the relation of the dynamic and the static, the changing and the eternal, is for both Bogomolov and Yulina the key to Whitehead's entire philosophy. The attempt to solve the problem generates the rest of his specific categories, and the way Whitehead is finally compelled to solve the problem reveals the most fundamental shortcoming of his metaphysics. Whitehead confronts the problem of stability and change through the concept of process. To regard nature as process had several virtues from Whitehead's point of view. It accommodates advances in the sciences and mathematics in that contemporary scientific and mathematical theories deal with the nature of *development.* These theories, however, to a significant degree deprecate what for Whitehead is philosophy's point of departure and its central concern—its connection with religion, and religion is in the end more significant than science since it seeks to ascertain the connection of rational thought with the ends and emotions of subjects. To regard nature as process, then, accommodates the accomplishments of science and mathematics, and to regard it as an experiential process supplies what they are missing (Bogomolov 1974, 169–170).

The concept of process offers a revitalized picture of nature, but the specific character of the creative process, of development, remains to be described. In the course of the account of development arise two noteworthy manifestations of the problem of the relation between the dynamic and the stable: the distinction between actual entities and eternal objects and the distinction between the continuous and the discrete. Process, the "creative advance into novelty," is essentially the perpetual becoming and perishing of actual entities. This is the dynamic, the unstable, the ever-changing character of reality. Whitehead's view is complicated, however, by the presence of eternal objects, the fixed, stable, unchanging potentialities that neither become nor perish. Since eternal objects are the qualitative traits of actual entities, the generation of novelty in some way involves the relation in development of the qualitative and quantitative aspects of reality.

Philosophy in the nineteenth century, Bogomolov remarks, was dominated by a mechanical conception of development, where novelty is a combination of previously existing unchanging elements. Bogomolov's own dialectical materialist understanding of qualitative novelty is that it is the result of quantitative change. Unlike either of these, theories of "creative evolution" "onesidedly understand development as purely qualitative change, ignoring quantitative changes as the cause of qualitative. . . ." Such approaches invariably treat creativity as an ideal force, and Whitehead's is no exception (Bogomolov 1963, 280). Whitehead's problem, in Bogolomov's view, is that to a degree he wants a dialectical understanding of development, but he does not have the appropriate categories necessary to understand it. He realizes that novelty is both quantitative and qualitative. It is quantitative in that it is new actual entities that arise, and it is qualitative in that the process involves the ingression of eternal objects. But given the sharp distinction between actual entities and eternal objects, "The real process of development, in which qualitative and quantitative sides are located in a continuous unity, turns out to be irreparably divided" (Bogomolov 1974, 171).

In the *Adventures of Ideas* Whitehead grants that his conception has "an air of paradox" about it. The paradox, as Bogomolov describes it, is that the novel arises not from nothing but from the past, but it is a past in which the novel does not exist. In other words, there is no ex nihilo creator, yet the perpetual becoming of novel actual entities seems to suggest creation of some kind.[8] "Whitehead has no way out of this contradiction," Bogomolov says, "other than to postulate a mysterious, intuitively grasped 'metaphysical principle.'" But this is not much of a resolution: "If all processes are realizations of certain possibilities, located in a realm of 'eternal objects' and 'entering (ingressing)' in the world of 'events,' where here is the novelty? As possibility, perpetual novelty in fact does not arise but merely acquires a new status—from possible it becomes actual; there can be nothing genuinely new" (Bogomolov 1963, 280).

Whitehead also faces another kind of difficulty, Bogomolov suggests, in that the ontological principle requires that all elements of the world process be some kind of actual entity. But in this case what happens to eternal objects, which though not actual are yet elements of the world? Whitehead deals with this, he says, through the concept of God—eternal objects are God's primordial nature, while the world of actual entities is God's consequent nature. Here in fact, Bogomolov and Yulina both argue, is Whitehead's resolution of the entire problem of the relation between the stable and the dynamic, between eternal objects and actual entities. "This dual nature of God reveals the mystery of Whitehead's speculative construct: everything possible and actual is divine experience" (Bogomolov 1974, 172). Or as Bogomolov put it earlier:

> The contradiction of events and objects is transferred now to "God's nature." With this we now discover the "secret" of Whitehead's speculative philosophy: all existence is transmuted into God's "experience"—logical categories are the unity of eternal objects in God's "primordial nature," and physical experience is the "ingression" of eternal objects in the world of space and time and the formation of "actual entities." (Bogomolov 1963, 280)

The other aspect of the concept of process that mirrors the problem of the dynamic and the stable is the relation between the continuous and the discrete. Whitehead agreed with Zeno that continuity leads to contradictions, so he proposed an "epochal," atomistic theory of reality, which he took to accord with conceptions in quantum mechanics. Whitehead's atomism of actual entities was, Yulina notes, a "social" atomism, in which nothing exists in isolation and complete independence, including God. It is the social nature of this atomism that generates his specific problem: "The 'atomic' understanding of reality and the process of its development poses for Whitehead the problem of the unity of the discrete with the continuity of change" (Bogomolov 1963, 283). One of the ways Whitehead distinguishes the two is to recognize continuity in the relation between an actual entity and other actual entities available for objectification in the process of its becoming, while the actual entity is atomistic in relation to others arising contemporaneously with it, since they are not available to it for objectification. Bogomolov, however, says that Whitehead's resolution to the question is to distinguish two kinds of change. One is an actual entity's process of becoming, the other the transition or transformation of an actual entity into another, into something else. Change, Whitehead held, is always of the first sort, never the second. Actual entities arise and perish, but they do not themselves become something other than what they are. "This however is a false, one-sided solution," portraying, in Bogomolov's estimation, a stunted conception of development. Of course, he says, if a thing is changed or transformed into another, then it has vanished or ceased to exist as that thing. But such elimination is at the same time a result of something new, a "qualitative leap" with regard to the thing undergoing transformation (Bogomolov 1963, 283). Again, for Bogomolov, Whitehead is unable to appreciate the relation between quantity and quality, and is pushed to a wholly quantitative conception of change in which transformation has no part and is, indeed, impossible.

Whitehead himself, Bogomolov notes, likened his view to Hegel's, with the difference that in place of Hegel's hierarchy of the categories of thought, the philosophy of organism involves a hierarchy of the categories of feeling.[9] In this respect, however, "Whitehead's philosophic conception is essentially impoverished by contrast with the Hegelian view" (Bogomolov 1974, 171). For Bogomolov, Whitehead is right in his view that the conception of reality as an ongoing concrescence is much like Hegel's idea of development as the ascent from the abstract to the concrete. But Bogolomov sees a central difference: for Hegel this is a logical process, while for Whitehead it is analogous to a psychological process, in that concrescence functions through feelings. It is precisely the psychological analogy that Bogomolov opposes, because "sense knowledge is only one of the particular cases in the dialectic of development, and it cannot be attributed to the whole of reality" (Bogomolov 1963, 285). Whitehead attributed sense knowledge to all of reality, in part, because he took the concept of organism to be central to all of contemporary science: "But Whitehead's own understanding of 'organisms' is far from the way the sciences understand them: identifying them with actual entities and events, he sees the organic like the psychological, like the process of 'experience,' and so 'overcomes' mechanism by means of idealism, transferring his understanding of the processes of knowledge to the whole of the real world" (Bogomolov 1963, 286).

Whitehead's view of reality as developing through prehension and concrescence, combined with his unique conception of change, also means for him that nothing is preserved in the creative advance. An actual entity achieves its "satisfaction" and then perishes. However, actual entities perish only "subjectively," since they have "objective immortality" as data for other prehensions, and ultimately in God's nature. What, Bogomolov asks, could this mean? The answer points to the ethical and religious dimensions of Whitehead's thought: "In order to understand the essence of the concept of 'objective immortality,' it is necessary to turn to Whitehead's 'moral' valuation of 'process' as a whole" (Bogomolov 1963, 287). In *Process and Reality* Whitehead describes the perpetual perishing of actual entities as "the ultimate evil in the temporal world."[10] But to whom, Bogomolov wonders, does such perishing present a problem, to whom is the present such a virtue that its disappearance is the "ultimate evil?" More inclined than Yulina to identify social and ideological sources of Whitehead's thought, Bogomolov finds them here. The perpetual perishing of the present is the ultimate evil "only to that class to which this development denies a future, to the class dying and heading for ruin" (Bogomolov 1963, 287).

Such ideological matters aside, Whitehead's handling of the general nature of development illustrates both important insights and crucial shortcomings. Whitehead had a dialectical understanding of the process of development, at least insofar as he understood that in some way development has both quantitative and qualitative aspects. But the creative character of development can be understood on the basis of the dialectical transition from quantitative changes into qualitative, while Whitehead tries to understand the relation by analogy with the cognitive process. "Naturally, from this point of view the qualitative aspect of development turns out to be alienated from the quantitative and embodied in 'eternal objects'" (Bogomolov 1974, 172). Yulina, too, underscores the problems created for Whitehead by the absence of a method that would have been appropriate for his own ideas:

> Whitehead approached the resolution of the problems of describing multiplicity, creativity, development, experience, etc., and the embodiment in them of general metaphysical traits, armed with the old, traditional method of formal logic. Having rejected the mechanistic representation of reality, Whitehead did not find the adequate epistemological means for the expression of the uniqueness, mutability, and qualitative determination of experience, and as a result he was compelled to introduce an irrational ontological and epistemological principle—God. (Yulina 1978a, 103)

These and similar points can be generalized in an evaluation of Whitehead's thought as a whole. Despite the methodological problems,

Whitehead "better than many contemporary thinkers in bourgeois society understood the contradictions of this world. Existence and change, immutability and transience, universality and particularity, quality and quantity, abstract and concrete—these are the opposing categories in which the philosopher's thought moves." As a result, in his work "dialectics more and more decisively made its way through, and exerted an influence on bourgeois philosophy" (Bogomolov 1963, 291).

In the Soviets' final analysis, however, Whitehead's contributions do not outweigh his flaws, at times because he pushes even his insights too far or in the wrong directions. When he posits organism as the central concept of his theory of being, for example, he is doing more than simply replacing models from physics with a biological concept, since he likens "organism" not to biological organisms generally but to psychological processes (Bogomolov 1962, 303–305; Yulina 1978a, 112). The resulting panpsychism is then reinforced on epistemological grounds: "Whitehead justifiably criticized Hume for his rejection of the immediate perception of causal connections, seeing in this the source of Hume's subjectivism. However, recognizing that people can perceive them, he turns objective causality into a kind of immediate knowledge and thus attempts to replace real relations with epistemological ones" (Bogomolov 1963, 281). Yulina makes the additional objection that Whitehead's method is essentially reductionist in an attempt to reduce the multiplicity of the world to its "building blocks" and "first forms." A resulting problem is that this makes it all the more difficult to explain qualitative multiplicity adequately. This proved to be a serious stumbling block for Whitehead, and to deal with it he was forced to pile categories upon categories, ultimately violating Ockham's Razor (Yulina 1978a, 112–113). And finally, if Yulina suggests that Whitehead had too many categories, for Bogomolov they are simply the wrong ones. Whitehead identifies the formative elements of reality as creativity, a realm of ideal entities, actual occasions and God. In so doing he commits "the very 'fallacy of misplaced concreteness' which he opposed" (Bogomolov 1963, 292–293).

Santayana

A direct interest in Santayana's philosophy on the part of Soviet scholars began in the late 1950s with a study by V. D. Endovitzky of his philosophy of culture. In the ensuing years he and others continued to address Santayana's aesthetic theory, while in 1963 Yulina published an extended article devoted primarily to Santayana's metaphysics and epistemology. These works have been the background of Soviet studies of Santayana, including more recent dissertations dealing with his epistemology and with his aesthetics (Endovitzky 1958; Endovitzky and Korovin 1984;

Yulina 1963; Degesis 1983; Kandareli 1983). Santayana seems also to have attracted some interest among Russian philosophers in the immediate post-Soviet period. As with the very recent discussions of other American philosophers, the accounts of Santayana tend to be more sympathetic than they had been before. In a talk given at a conference on Santayana in Seville, Spain, for example, Tigran Yepoyan makes the commonplace point that Santayana felt more at home in the world of spirit and imagination than in the world of matter and science, but then he adds, "So do I" (Yepoyan 1993, 23). This is a remark one would not have seen during the Soviet period. In a similar spirit, V. K. Shokin wrote sympathetically in 1992 of Santayana and his appropriation of aspects of Indian philosophy. Santayana, he says, was "one of the most sensitive Western interpreters of the Eastern worldview, above all the heritage of Indian thought" (Shokin 1992, 118). He goes on to say, by way of introduction to a Russian translation of an excerpt from Santayana's *Soliloquies in England and Later Soliloquies*, that Santayana was "one of the most fruitful thinkers of our century" (Shokin 1992, 120).

Remarks like that were not characteristic of earlier considerations of Santayana. The most common approach to Santayana among Soviets had been to place his thought within the context of the critical realist movement, specifically its objective idealist strain. Yulina describes Santayana's as the most striking speculative interpretation of the principles of realism, though she also notes at least one respect in which he differed: "At a time when the majority of neorealists and critical realists aspired to the construction of a scientific philosophy, or at least a philosophy that accorded with contemporary science, Santayana sharply opposed taking science as the ideal for philosophic knowledge" (Yulina 1963, 301, 308). This way of reading Santayana in relation to his contemporaries raised the question of his relation to naturalism. It is common among American commentators to regard Santayana as one of the early representatives of twentieth century American naturalism, and he described himself as a materialist. Soviet scholarship, however, tended fairly sharply to distinguish between naturalism and critical realism and its objective idealist forms. Yulina follows this distinction in her 1963 article, where, while she notes that Santayana thought himself a naturalist and materialist, she claims for reasons to be made clear below that "in reality Santayana was never either a naturalist or a materialist" (Yulina 1963, 326). Karimsky has suggested much the same thing. In his history of American naturalism he argues that the term has had such a variety of meanings and has been used so loosely that there is a good deal of room for carelessness in understanding what it involves and whom it includes. This had led to attempts by instrumentalists, theologians, and overt objective idealists to portray themselves in naturalist garb, and he mentions Santayana as one of many "pseudo-naturalists" (Karimsky

1972, 18–19). Despite all this, in her book on metaphysics in twentieth century American philosophy Yulina herself includes Santayana in "the first generation of naturalists" insofar as he was opposed to supernaturalism and mysticism (Yulina 1978a, 119–120).

The question of typology is relatively insignificant in relation to a description and evaluation of philosophic views, and whether a naturalist or not, Santayana's is at bottom a moral philosophy. "In Santayana's view naturalism is not a metaphysical theory but a moral position in relation to the world," Yulina remarks (Yulina 1978a, 129). In her earlier study she makes the same point in greater detail. Santayana's thought, she says, is essentially a "philosophy of life": "With the ideas of Emerson, Thoreau, and other American philosophers of culture as points of departure, Santayana attempts within the limits of an idealist world view to understand the dual consequences of civilization for morals, philosophy, and religion, and the contradictory processes in the development of material and spiritual culture." His most basic questions, even when doing metaphysics and epistemology, are these: "How are happiness and freedom possible? What should be the relation to a world where an increase in wealth does not afford people the possibility to find truly human existence, where practice dominates the individual's spiritual life, destroying those subjective aspirations that do not conform to its inherent course of development?" (Yulina 1963, 302–303).

With questions like these at the heart of his concerns, Santayana rejected philosophy's traditional role of acquiring knowledge of the nature of things and of system building. He regarded his own philosophy, by contrast, as "common sense," as the critical and skeptical position of contemporary human being. For Santayana, as Yulina puts it, "philosophy should concentrate its attention on 'personal experience' and the moral aspects of being." Moral philosophy is at the core of Santayana's thought, not in the sense of constructing ethical theories but in the sense of "the art of achieving freedom and happiness" and "the ability to achieve harmony with oneself and one's surroundings." In rejecting philosophy's pursuit of knowledge Santayana also rejected all other forms of that pursuit in its traditional sense, from science to religion; he "takes all human explanations of the world for illusions," and he accords fantasy and imagination a higher role than science and rational knowledge in general (Yulina 1963, 303–304).

Despite his misgivings and even sarcasm about philosophic truth claims, Santayana's thought merges with the philosophic tradition in the ontological and epistemological studies of *Skepticism and Animal Faith* and *The Realms of Being*. He did not, however, regard these inquiries to be inconsistent with his general vision of what philosophy should and should not be. For one thing, Santayana writes in the preface to *Skepticism and*

Animal Faith, "My system, accordingly, is *no system of the universe.* The Realms of Being of which I speak are not parts of a cosmos, nor one great cosmos together: they are only kinds or categories of things which I find conspicuously different and worth distinguishing."[11] Perhaps Santayana shared Whitehead's view that any discipline or inquiry necessarily involves general ideas that are themselves in need of explicit articulation and defense. If so, then his general ontological and epistemological concepts are part and parcel of the overriding moral concern. This, in any case, is how Yulina reads it: "The ideas of *The Realms of Being* are called upon to serve as the theoretical foundation for the determination of the role of spirit and the practical dimension of human life and correspondingly for the determination of a moral position with respect to the social reality of the twentieth century" (Yulina 1963, 308).

Santayana draws his realms of being from "moral experience" and from "common sense." These are vague concepts, but their vagueness has advantages for him. It allows him to avoid being restricted to narrow empirical problematics, and the "moral" treatment of experience frees him from any necessary ties to the sciences and their methods. More importantly still, Santayana's point of departure allows him to take seriously the fact that an individual's perception of and activity in the world is invariably perspectival, conditioned by a wide range of biological, social, and personal factors.

Yulina and Bogomolov both regard Santayana's sensitivity to the conditionality of human life as perhaps the most valuable of his philosophic insights. The "positive movement" in Santayana's general conceptions, Bogomolov says, is the idea that the reality of the objects of knowledge is not simply a postulate based on "common sense" or general human agreement, but is a necessary aspect of the biological nature of human beings. His biological argument shows the inherent relation of human life with real physical objects (Bogomolov 1974, 189–190). That there is an independent material world, that there is a past and will be a future, and other such fundamental ideas, are not inferred from anything "given" in experience or rationally deduced from necessary premises. They are rather an "animal faith," engendered by the "shocks" that the organism undergoes in its ongoing relation with the rest of the world. Similarly, in a way superior to an empiricism based on the "given," Santayana recognized not only the biological but also the social conditionality of the theoretical position of any individual thinker (Yulina 1963, 309–310). Unfortunately, however, Santayana distorts these otherwise valuable insights. His acknowledgment of biological conditionality is essentially a materialist point, but the ontological categories and the conception of knowledge he derives from it transforms it into something irrational (Bogomolov 1974, 190). With respect to social factors, instead of analyzing the nature of this sort of conditionality and working with historical and social practice in order to distinguish the subjective, relative aspects in knowledge from its objective side that can reflect reality in its true light, "Santayana proposes the eternal inadequacy of human perception of reality" (Yulina 1963, 310).

A result of this is an overblown subjectivism in the conception of knowledge. For his part, Bogomolov is concerned with what he calls the epistemological "irrationalism" inferred from what Santayana called the "irrational impulses" that engender rational thought. In *The Life of Reason* Santayana treats the development of human reason in a way comparable to Hegel's *Phenomenology of Spirit*, though without presenting the history of ideas as a process of cosmic evolution. Santayana's point of departure is that insofar as the human individual is a rational *animal*, the entire "life of reason" is controlled by the individual's animal, biological life, from which he infers that ideas are not rational reflections of anything, but have a purely symbolic significance. Furthermore, the life of reason is an ongoing accommodation or adaptation of internal relations to external, which is to say, of poetic constructs to facts and possibilities. Reason, then, is a play of the imagination, science as much as art, at bottom because the progressive organization of irrational impulses creates rational thought. For Bogomolov it is significant that Santayana regards these biological "impulses" to be "irrational," rather than perhaps simply "arational": "The irrationality of these impulses consists in the fact that they arise as primordial and initial factors, thrust on human beings by the outside world and unrelated to their aims, hopes and anticipations." Because of this, Bogomolov suggests, Santayana's ideas often come close to the irrationalism of existentialism. The "irrationalism" of the epistemology Santayana develops is evident especially in his concept of "normal madness," and in his view of science as a species of poetry.[12] In the end his "biologism" forced him into skeptical doubt about the capacity of knowledge to reflect the external and independent world (Bogomolov 1974, 191–192).

The Realms of Being

Comparable problems, Yulina argues, are evident in Santayana's corresponding ontology. In the technical philosophic works that followed *The Life of Reason,* Santayana distinguishes on the basis of his "biologism" the realms of being: essence, matter, spirit, and truth. Like critical realism generally, Yulina suggests, Santayana sharply contrasts the material with the ideal, and in his hands the process of the human interaction with the world "begins to be broken up into several self-sustaining elements, independent of one another and without connections among them: cognitive content, the psychical act, and the material object" (Yulina 1963, 310). At the outset, and in this respect unlike those critical realists more confined to the empirical tradition, Santayana saw these elements of the process of knowledge in terms of a wider social and cultural life. The ideal, for example, expressed not the contents of individual consciousness but a "realm of essence." Similarly, the process of thinking itself expressed a "realm of spirit," the ideal reproduction of all existence a "realm of truth," and the object of knowledge a "realm of matter." Along the way, however, what are initially "moral" categories are transformed into ontological distinctions, and a point of departure that had something materialist about it is replaced by an ontological pluralism. Such a pluralism, which for Yulina is a term of criticism, consists not in acknowledging the existence of different sorts of things, but in erecting them into distinct "realms" that in the end have little if any relation. A preferable alternative, which Yulina attributes to dialectical materialism, would be to avoid, as Santayana does, reducing the various elements of reality to one another, while at the same time exploring their essential relations and interdependence, which he does not do: "Santayana, proceeding from the fact that matter is the single substance engendering everything, including the brain with its capacity for thought, acknowledges the genetic dependence of consciousness on matter. But he rejects the second side, the epistemological correlation of the ideal contents of consciousness with matter. The result is pluralism" (Yulina 1963, 312–313). Santayana's ontological pluralism in the end contributes to the same epistemological positions that bothered Bogomolov in *The Life of Reason*. Ideas are cut off from the material reality that engenders them, truth claims can have no independent criteria of evaluation, and distinct ideas are wholly incommensurable. This is a thoroughgoing relativism, or, to use Bogomolov's term, irrationalism.

While Santayana's general ontological view is a crucial ingredient of his philosophic position, the most significant and problematic of his categories, and the one that most interests Yulina and Bogomolov, is essence. The concept of essence and the role it plays in his system was not of course original with Santayana, although he gave it his own unique coloration. There is a Platonic element in it, and to that extent Santayana shares a tendency not uncommon among his contemporaries, Whitehead and Husserl in particular (Yulina 1963, 316). The most direct source of the concept, however, was the critical realist Charles A. Strong, who argued that the "immediately given" is not an object as the neorealists argued, nor is it a content of consciousness, as the more sensationalistic empiricists would have it, but "essence." Objects are not directly accessible to us, yet they are in some way "expressed" through their essence, and we know them only to the degree we perceive their essence.[13] In this conception essence is something general, a kind of universal, and it is primarily this feature of the critical realist concept of essence that Santayana inherits and develops (Bogomolov 1974, 184).

An essence, as Yulina describes it, is anything that has been thought or can be a content of consciousness, including even unthinkable and ideal qualities (Yulina 1963, 313). Essences, Santayana argues, are available to "intuition," and in that respect they emerge as contemplative knowledge, as "intellectual experience" in which essence is the rational structure of the world (Bogomolov 1974, 194). As a result, essences are not material, but logical and aesthetic objects and ultimately express ethical and religious values. Essences are neither spatial nor temporal, and they prevail in their own unique "realm." In Santayana's language, the material world—the world of space, time, and motion—is the "existing" world. Since essences have none of these traits, since they are not aspects of the existing world, they have being but do not exist. The import of this peculiar sounding claim is that it is a way for Santayana to distinguish his conception of essence from other related interpretations of universals, Plato's ideal forms in particular. Plato's Forms are causally related to the material world, and they are "above" the material, changing world in a hierarchy of being. Santayana's essences involve no such hierarchy and no causal relation to the material world because they bear no relation to it at all. We intuit essences, but it is we who associate them with the existing world.

These points suggest Santayana's approach to the concept of essence in *Skepticism and Animal Faith*, while in *The Realms of Being* the concept develops further. Yulina suggests that Santayana ran into some of the same problems as did Plato and the scholastic realists. If essences are wholly self-identical, and if they share no traits with the material world, then it would seem that they can be related neither to one another nor in any way at all, even through intuition and imagination, to the existing world. As a result Santayana has to introduce the concept of pure being, and by contrast that of nonbeing. It is in their "possession" of pure being that all essences are essences and that they are related to one another, all "comparable modes on one plane of reality," as Santayana puts it. Essences, then, are defined by participation in pure being and by their contrast with the material world. The material world, as the contrast to pure being, is nonbeing. In the end, in Yulina's reading, the being of essences is enabled by the nonbeing of everything else, above all the nonbeing of matter. Ultimately, Santayana subsumes all essences under one essence, pure being, "and this single essence fulfills in his system the function which in ordinary theological views God fulfills" (Yulina 1963, 317–318).

In developing his conception of the realm of essences, Yulina says, Santayana begins with the correct and philosophically important realization that the ideal, the contents of consciousness, are not unique or peculiar to or the private possession of individuals. However, he distorts the implications of this otherwise significant point:

> The basic moment that Santayana idealistically perverts is the uniqueness of spiritual culture, the specific role that ideal products of spiritual production fulfill in social life. Essences, if we discard their mystical aspects, are in fact elements of spir-

> itual culture: aesthetic and moral values, concepts, theories, contents of art, literature, religion, etc. And the isolation of the ideal in a self-sustaining sphere of being is not so much a revival of Platonism . . . as a manifestation of the tendency, widespread in contemporary bourgeois philosophy, to ontologize the products of spiritual activity. . . . (Yulina 1963, 318–319)

The problem is not in the distinction between the material and the ideal, but in "the *absolute opposition of the material and the ideal* . . . One may say that the ideal exists, that it is real, but this in no way means that it possesses its own unique being independent of the spatio-temporal material world" (Yulina 1974, 61–62). That Santayana and so many others are misled in this way is due in part to "an idealistic view of human nature and a failure to understand the social essence of consciousness," to a misreading of the real role of ideal forms, specifically that they are ideological expressions of social processes (Yulina 1974, 62; 1963, 319).

Yulina suspects that the metaphysical speculation of Santayana, and of Whitehead and others, about the nature of the ideal and of "higher being" have not so much epistemological as social and essentially religious motives: "The opposition of a 'realm of essence' to existence is necessary to him as a foundation of the superiority of spiritual life, or more precisely, life in the sphere of the fictions of bourgeois consciousness, over practical cognitive activity." In the end, Santayana's conception of ideal essences is a theoretical basis for his conception of religion that would have as its object pure being, "Thus in both theoretical and moral respects Santayana's theory of essences is a contemporary variant of the old theological theme of an eternal divine being that is revealed to an individual in immediate contact, in intuition and revelation" (Yulina 1963, 324–325).

Interestingly enough, Yulina sees the same religious motivation behind Santayana's category of matter and his conception of the realm of matter: "Like all religious philosophy, contrasting the divine with the diabolic, the spiritual with the corporeal, Santayana's 'intellectual religion' logically requires an acknowledgment of body. This role is fulfilled in his philosophy by the category of matter." Another consideration buttresses this point, one that ties together the religious and social motives and concerns. "Social reality, or bourgeois practice, invades" the life of the spirit—art, literature, religion, poetry—and "imposes its laws and norms. But it comes as an irrational force . . . violating the 'harmony of the spirit' and destroying beauty. Therefore the moral meaning of Santayana's theory of matter is to determine that relation to practical reality in which a harmonic life would be possible" (Yulina 1963, 325).

While the category of matter may be necessary for Santayana's more fundamental purposes, his own understanding of essences makes it exceptionally difficult, probably impossible, to say or know much about matter.

If the human individual constructs the world out of essences, and if essences are a realm or mode of being wholly independent of matter, then there are no conceptual grounds to assert even the existence of a material world, let alone its traits. Santayana understood this, Yulina points out, which is why he held that the reality of the external world is undemonstrable. Any conception of the existence and nature of the material world can be based only on animal faith (Yulina 1963, 326). The distinction between the intuition and contemplation in which essences are available, and the practical interests and activities, the animal faith, from which belief in the reality of the external world arises, is crucial for Santayana. Ontologically it is responsible for the vagueness of his view of matter, but more generally it feeds his moral, religious, and aesthetic concerns.

Essences, or qualities, are revealed through intuition and contemplation free of practical interests, while matter by contrast lays claim to reality only by virtue of practical interests, activity, and animal faith. One of the implications of this is that the philosophic conception of matter is devoid of any qualitative determinations: "All the qualitative determinations of matter are derived from the 'realm of essence.' Consequently, matter is practically transformed into 'nonbeing,' into Plato's *me on*" (Bogomolov 1974, 196–197). In one sense the vagueness and indeterminateness of Santayana's view may not be entirely inappropriate to a general, purely philosophic conception of matter. Bogomolov suggests that, after all, materialism derives the conceptual material for its generalizations not from philosophic speculation but from the sciences. But Santayana, again due to his understanding of essences, has made even this next stage in the study of the material world impossible. If science is symbolic and poetic, then even with it we cannot achieve truth about the nature of the material world; Santayana has cut himself off from science (Bogomolov 1974, 197–198). The consequence is a view of matter as an "irrational force," a "hazy principle of existence" (Yulina 1963, 327).

As dissatisfied as Yulina is with Santayana's concept of matter, she thinks that together with his view of essence it suits his purposes very well. His conception of matter contributes to a resolution of the problem of the ideal and the material, specifically the greater value and significance of "being" relative to "nonbeing," of essence to matter. The ontological valuation in turn "serves as a theoretical foundation for a solution to the question of the relation between the material and spiritual sides of human life and correspondingly as an answer to the question how happiness and freedom are achieved." Santayana's position coincides with the classical Greek distinction between the eternal and the mutable, the rational and the practical. And like the Greeks, Santayana finds the source of happiness and freedom in the contemplation and imaginative manipulation of the ideal: "Life in the sphere of art, literature, poetry, and religion, that is, in the sphere of the fictions of bourgeois consciousness, appears as the true life, and it is contrasted with bourgeois practice, which is 'lower' and 'animal'" (Yulina 1963, 331). Also like the Greeks, the superiority of the ideal to the material, the life of the mind to the life of practice, is tied for Santayana to a social elitism: "The opposition of essence to existence and the ideal to the material takes the form for him of an opposition of the activity of the 'spiritual life' to the masses, to the activity of practical labor" (Yulina 1963, 332).

Despite sharing with the Greeks a sense of the higher value of the spiritual life over the practical, and of essence over matter, Santayana departs from the Greek view of knowledge. While he agrees that the spiritual life has access to the ideal, spirit does not achieve knowledge, even lower order knowledge, of the material. Plato and Aristotle, each in his own way, had argued for a causal relation between the ideal and the material, so that access to the ideal was necessarily knowledge, even if only in the form of "opinion," as for Plato, of the material. Without such a connection, contemplation of ideal essences has little to do with matter. If there is an ontological link for Santayana between essence and matter, it is not in any direct relation between them but appears in the category of spirit. In his understanding of spirit, Bogomolov notes, Santayana is an epiphenomenalist. Spirit arises from nature, from matter, but in itself is not material. It expresses itself in feeling, intellect, and imagination; it is the "shadow" of matter but has no influence on it. Spirit has its source in matter, while its activity concerns essence, and in that respect Santayana's epiphenomenalism "is transformed into a purely idealist understanding of human knowledge as the 'free expression' of the contemplative life of the spirit" (Bogomolov 1974, 199).

The opposition between the material and the ideal, regardless of spirit's epiphenomenal character, means that knowledge cannot be reflection, and Santayana explicitly rejected a mirror metaphor of mind: "Consciousness, Santayana holds, is not in a condition to go beyond itself and cross a bridge to the world of things. Knowledge of the world will invariably be subjective interpretation, symbolic, and the truth of an interpretation can never be demonstrated" (Yulina 1963, 333).[14] The fact that for whatever is objectively true of the world our cognitive relation to it can at best be agnostic did not strike Santayana as a problem. This is because knowledge of the objective world did not concern him: "His entire interest is concentrated not on the objective but on the subjective elements of our knowledge." His interest is in the dramatic, the imaginative, the fanciful, and the poetic play of spirit.

Knowledge and Symbol

Santayana's epistemology begins with what Yulina describes as a "behaviorist" conception, where the individual experiences shocks from the external world and reacts to the shocks. At the cognitive level, at the level of consciousness, the individual's response is mediated by essences. Thus there is no direct contact with material reality, since material reality is perceived only through the prism of essences. The result is a conception of knowledge as symbol rather than reflection. The impossibility of reflection, in Santayana's view, is implied both by the biological location of organisms and by the view that consciousness deals only with essences. In an analysis that for us has a contemporary ring, Santayana held that knowledge cannot be reflection because the process of knowledge is grounded in the organism's natural condition, and the individual cannot achieve a sufficiently divorced or "objective" position from which to "reflect" the traits of his own natural condition. Yulina finds this point somewhat compelling: "With one of the most weighty arguments against the reflective capacity of a concept, Santayana argues that consciousness itself is located in the 'stream of nature.'" The argument is "weighty" because Santayana is right about the natural context of the individual and of cognition. Yulina does not accept his conclusion, however, because in her view the reflective capacity of knowledge functions because the process of cognition is not only biologically grounded but also social and practical.

Mistaken or not, Santayana's view holds that knowledge is invariably symbolic and that our means of representing reality are free constructions of consciousness. The concept of symbol is a cornerstone of Santayana's approach to knowledge. Though he does not analyze the concept, he gives it a much wider range than have others who make use of it. For Santayana, Yulina suggests, the "symbolic" is whatever is related to the subject. It includes the psychological form of perceived knowledge, the abstract contents of thought, and the means of their expression—speech and written language: "Logic, scientific symbols, religious myths, moral norms, fine arts, religious rituals, and human behavior—all appear in the single category of 'symbol.'" That Santayana is prepared to cast all knowledge as symbolic suggests a religious foundation: "Santayana sees symbolism, and ultimately the arbitrary creation of fantasy, not only in perceptions and concepts, but also in all forms of social concepts, in artistic creations, philosophy, science, etc. Symbolism for him develops into mythologism" (Yulina 1963, 335).

Santayana arrives at this view by means of a transference of the specific traits appropriate to one ideological form, religion, to all forms of social consciousness. Seeing religion essentially as the basic form of the explanation of reality, Santayana sees in the fact of religious mythologism and in the changing of religious ideologies evidence in favor of the general view of the mythological and poetic character of the human interpretation of reality (Yulina 1963, 341).

Regarding all knowledge as symbolic raises several questions, one of which has to do with science. One way to pose the question is to ask whether it is possible to speak of science generally as a system of knowledge that differs in any significant way from delirium or hallucination? The question comes up because our experience indicates that the results of scientific inquiry are confirmable, or disconfirmable, in our practical activity. Consequently, another way to pose the question is to ask how our theoretical constructs and practical life coincide so well if knowledge is imaginative, symbolic representation? Yulina remarks that "for an explanation of the fact of the 'miraculous' coincidence of theory and practice, of human ideas and the objective world, Santayana turns to pragmatism" (Yulina 1963, 341). If the speculations of the intellect turn out to be true, it is not due to a reflection of any true moments of reality but because it blindly and instinctively adapts to the surroundings.

Another question suggested by the symbolic conception of knowledge addresses whether the activity of consciousness traps the individual in his own symbolic constructions. Although reason is a game of fantasy and science, a subjective construction, Santayana "does not think that there are no ways out of the prison of subjectivity." The individual moves beyond merely subjective and self-referential consciousness in poetry, religion, and art. These activities differ from science, in Santayana's view, in that they are free of the dogmatism that attends to science as a result of its attempt to achieve nonsymbolic knowledge, its transformation of mythological forms into "cognitive" principles. In poetry, religion, and art "the spirit feels itself free, and this freedom creates greater possibilities for intuition 'to grasp' the truth in all its fullness and concreteness" (Yulina 1963, 344). As with other issues, Yulina says, Santayana here distorts an otherwise valuable point. That art can better reflect some aspects of reality than other activities is in itself not a problem. But Santayana's view is that poetry is "higher" than science not only in its capacity to understand the perceptible multiplicity of phenomena but also in providing knowledge of the essential nature of things. This much bolder position is not peculiar to Santayana, Yulina says, in that we find it also in Schopenhauer, Nietzsche, Bergson, the existentialists, and others, but in none of them is there sufficient evidence for it (Yulina 1963, 345).

In the end, the fact that Santayana values "intellectual experience," the life of the mind, and the symbolic activity of art and religion over more mundane and practical matters reflects a complex relation to the realities of social life. His motive for opposing poetry, art, and religion to science is not as much epistemological as social, and it suggests at one and the same time a profound practical alienation from and an ideological commitment to the dominant traits of his society. It is a way "to escape from bourgeois reality, from the pragmatist practice of bourgeois society and the utilitarian character of scientific thought. . . . At the same time this contrast has as an end to present a mythological world perception as the natural interpretation of reality, in other words, to present the conscious acceptance of bourgeois illusions as the only possible objective position" (Yulina 1963, 345–346).

Naturalism

While there had been some discussions of it earlier, Soviet specialists turned to a serious and detailed consideration of twentieth century American naturalism only in the early 1970s. The first and still the most extensive study was A. M. Karimsky's dissertation, published in 1972 as *The Philosophy of American Naturalism* (in Russian). Since then the various strains of naturalism and their more prominent representatives were discussed by Yulina, Bogomolov, Karimsky, and others in books, articles, and dissertations. In American naturalism Soviet scholars found a tendency "congenial to philosophic materialism," as we have already seen Karimsky note, and one that, of all the forms mainstream American philosophy has taken, comes closest to the dialectical materialism Soviet philosophers traditionally endorsed. Yulina admires it because despite its many varieties and contradictions, naturalism's basic traits—nature as the central philosophic category, an orientation toward science, the struggle against overt forms of supernaturalism—place it on the left wing of American bourgeois philosophy in the struggle against overt idealism, theism, and scientism: "Proceeding from the basic assumption of the significance of nature, naturalists attempt to solve the problem of the unity of nature and human being, of human being and history, and to provide an objective philosophic foundation for humanism" (Yulina 1978a, 159). Bogomolov has been no less complimentary, admiring naturalism for the respects in which it approaches Marxism:

> The philosophy of naturalism has an undoubtedly progressive philosophic, social, and political significance in the contemporary ideological struggle. It embodies an ongoing tendency toward materialism, and its representatives often moved beyond the bounds of bourgeois ideology, accepting several important propositions of Marxist philosophy, or arriving at them themselves. The quest of contemporary American naturalism, its basic scientific and humanist position, cannot but elicit a deep sympathy. (Bogomolov 1974, 308)

The Roots of Naturalism

The roots of American naturalism lie in a complex of factors that includes nineteenth century naturalism, a "crisis" of philosophic idealism, turn-of-the-century scientific materialism, and a number of characteristics of American culture. In the eighteenth and nineteenth centuries naturalism was defined by a rejection of the supernatural and was thus associated with materialism, as well as with either open or secret atheism. This was a naturalism, Karimsky says, that was "an extrapolation of concrete scientific knowledge to confer on it a philosophic status" (Karimsky 1990, 5). But this was only one trait or tendency in earlier naturalism, and it had its antipode in "naturphilosophie," which in the absence of concrete information compensated with speculative assumptions and inquiries: "This inevitably resulted in ungrounded ideas and fantastic hypotheses, but at the same time also in profound conjectures and insights, stimulating and anticipating scientific discoveries" (Karimsky 1990, 5–6). Earlier naturalism, then, had two trends, one grounded in natural science and the other in speculative metaphysics, both of which were to merge in twentieth century naturalism.

The sciences at the turn of the century also conditioned naturalism in another way. The results of the natural sciences in these years produced what Karimsky calls a "spontaneous" or "scientific" materialism, to be distinguished from a dialectical materialism, and naturalism was in some ways related to it. This materialism was "spontaneous" in that developments in the sciences, especially in physics by the early twentieth century, made it clear that materialism, that is, the recognition of the objective character of reality, was the only philosophic perspective consistent with the scientific method and the necessary assumptions of scientific research. This spontaneous, scientific materialism was decidedly non-positivistic in that it took seriously the philosophic issues that arise from the practice of science. Nonetheless, Karimsky says, it tended to avoid a direct and explicit development of his own philosophic inclinations. It was in large measure empirical, he adds, "and often concrete scientific solutions substituted for the philosophic aspects of an issue (especially in the understanding of matter, consciousness, space, and time, causality etc.)." Scientific materialism, furthermore, often spontaneously advanced dialectical and historical materialist theses, though it never pursued them systematically. Naturalism is in many respects similar to this "timid" materialism, particularly in its reliance on the sciences and in some of the philosophic positions it inferred from science (Karimsky 1972, 22–30). Yulina makes a similar point in different terms. One of the defining characteristics of American naturalism, she says, is that it attempted to occupy an intermediate position between "extreme forms of philosophy"—speculative idealism, on the one hand, and radical variants of scientism, on the other. Despite attempts to avoid scientism, however, aspects and trends in it, nevertheless, have inclined toward the same "fetishization" of science and in that respect resemble the "spontaneous materialism" that Karimsky describes (Yulina 1978a, 117–126).

While Yulina and Karimsky have similar views of the roots of modern American naturalism in the natural sciences, they appear to disagree somewhat about the relation of naturalism to American culture. Citing Harold Larrabee's essay "Naturalism in America," Yulina contends that naturalism, in its secularism and more or less "positive" concerns, embodies the characteristically American traits of "practical materialism" and utilitarianism; and in its flirtations with instrumentalism, functionalism, and operationalism it often reflects the anti-intellectualist tradition in American thought (Yulina 1978a, 123–124). Yulina was not the first Soviet to make this claim. Karimsky had referred to a 1964 book titled *Contemporary Philosophy and Sociology in the Countries of Western Europe and America*, in which it is suggested that "The greatest role in the formation of the ideas of naturalism was played by the 'practical materialism of American life,' the spirit of 'sober efficiency' that penetrated the whole of American culture." In Karimsky's opinion this suggests a philosophic or ideological expression of the more negative traits of American culture, which he thinks is true of pragmatism but not of naturalism: "Naturalism by no means expresses the 'practical materialism of American Life', and it did not encroach upon the laurels of pragmatism, which at the time was at the height of its popularity and was brilliantly fulfilling its own social function" (Karimsky 1972, 12). On the contrary, naturalism, due primarily to its humanism, represents the most admirable features of the American tradition: "Naturalists make much of, and see themselves as the successors to, the humanistic, materialistic, and democratic traditions in philosophy and social thought in the United States." In this sense modern American naturalism is heir to the deism of Jefferson, Adams, Franklin, and Paine, the materialism of Priestly, Cooper, and Buchanan, and in some respects even the humanist, democratic idealism of transcendentalism (Karimsky 1972, 35–36).

Karimsky raises the question why naturalism flourished as it has in the United States in the twentieth century, and his answer suggests that naturalism is related not only to long-standing American intellectual traditions but also to more contemporary features of American culture. By the 1930s and 1940s the United States had become a leading center of bourgeois philosophic thought, both indigenous (pragmatism, realism, and personalism). and imported (positivism). At the same time the United States was rapidly becoming the scientific center of the Western world. The latter development especially contributed to the crisis of philosophic idealism and to the alternative of naturalism. In addition, Karimsky adds, it is intriguing that some naturalists, for example Larrabee, saw in naturalism an alternative to dialectical materialism. Among other factors, the "anti-Communist psychosis" of the United States disinclined otherwise like-minded intellectuals from embracing Marxism or dialectical materialism directly, so they developed a closely related alternative in naturalism. Among the traits of modern American society, indeed the whole of the capitalist world, are the intense contradictions within the ruling class and the consolidation of democratic forces. Naturalism, Karimsky argues, expresses the ideological side of the latter process in attempting to provide a general theoretical foundation of democratic social ideals. This, he says, together with naturalism's materialist tendencies, is the general trait that determines the character of modern naturalistic philosophy (Karimsky 1972, 163–166).

While naturalism is related to American culture in these and perhaps other ways, in its relation to science there is nothing peculiarly American about it. The development of naturalism was influenced by scientific progress, but Karimsky suggests two additional aspects of science that have contributed to naturalism's distinctive character. The results of the sciences have been noteworthy both theoretically and practically, but the practice of science has generated two serious problems. One is that the world described by the sciences seems to be divorced from central characteristics of human life, and in light of this it became one of the concerns in naturalism to attempt to overcome any apparent division between scientific knowledge and ethical and other values. The second problem created by the sciences concerns the application of its results. Though few doubt, Karismky says, that only the development of science will resolve general human problems and create the conditions for human happiness, science, in fact, also creates the possibility of the abuse of its achievements, most seriously in weapons of mass destruction. An awareness of and concern over the abuse of science has led many scientists and scholars to take seriously the struggle for peace and the movement for democracy. This same awareness and concern has contributed to the humanism and democratism of American naturalism (Karimsky 1972, 160–161).

The problem of the relation between the world of scientific description and the world of human values, and its place in naturalism, requires more extensive discussion. For both Karimsky and Yulina, the world of human values is the province of philosophic inquiry and the material world the province of science, so that the question of their relation is also the question of the relation between science and philosophy. Furthermore, Karimsky has said that another of the distinctive traits of modern American naturalism is that it has sought to restore "metaphysical" and ontological problematics to the center of philosophic theory, in which case the problem of the relation of science and philosophy becomes the problem of the relation of science and metaphysics (Karimsky 1972, 10). Yulina, in turn, defends this rehabilitation of metaphysics and argues that in fact one cannot understand naturalism without an appreciation for the various ways naturalists have handled the relation of metaphysics and science. With respect to the value of metaphysics, Yulina notes that for many twentieth century philosophers the very term "metaphysics" appears anachronistic.

She argues, however, that "the content of the term is fundamental for philosophic knowledge. For example, the problems that naturalists consider under the rubric of metaphysics, such as the nature of the world, human nature, the historical process and the forms of social consciousness, the correlation of the principles of being and knowledge, ontology and humanism, etc., undoubtedly have a theoretical significance of the highest degree for philosophy" (Yulina 1978a, 118). While Yulina agrees with the emphasis on metaphysics that characterizes some strains of naturalism, she is also aware that some representatives of American naturalism opposed the notion of metaphysics. She argues, in fact, that the most useful criterion for distinguishing among the many tendencies in naturalism is their respective "approach to metaphysics" (Yulina 1978a, 118–119).

In general, both "prometaphysical" and "antimetaphysical" trends have gathered under the rubric of naturalism, and the differences between turn largely on their respective treatments of the relation of philosophy to science (Yulina 1978a, 119). The way a philosopher or group of philosophers is oriented toward science, either explicitly or implicitly, determines approaches to metaphysics in general and to specific sets of problems, methodology, and a general style of thought (Yulina 1990, 1–2). Naturalists early in the century emphasized the continuity of the physical, biological, and spiritual, and their central concern was consciousness. Later, naturalists concentrated more on the continuity of the natural and the social, and, correspondingly, at the center of their interests were questions of the nature of values, ends, ideals, the social nature of human being, and the character of social and historical processes. In their treatment of these problems naturalists tended to advocate emergent, "ascending" principles of creative evolution, and they were inclined to view nature as the source of qualitatively ascending levels of life, chance, and novelty. But this still left crucial problems, in particular determining the criteria for distinguishing between reality and fiction, the material and the ideal, truth and falsehood, facts and values. While answers to these questions often produced diametrically opposed positions, naturalists were nevertheless generally committed to the methods of science, conceived broadly enough to include the social sciences. Some naturalists followed the approach to the scientific method of Morris Cohen and Ernest Nagel, which in their 1934 book *An Introduction to Logic and Scientific Method* they identified with a broadly conceived notion of rational thought that included hypotheses, the value suppositions of inquiry, metaphysical views, and a wide understanding of verification. Even this broad a conception of science and its method, however, leaves open the question of the role of philosophy and whether philosophy has its own subject matter: "If science successfully proves itself with respect to the knowledge of nature, is a philosophical knowledge of being necessary? In other words, should philosophy be metaphysical or antimetaphysical?"

(Yulina 1978a, 135). In response to these questions some, like Nagel, held that philosophy should concern itself with the logical and methodological analysis of the sciences. Others of the "antimetaphysical trend," in which Yulina includes Dewey and Hook, concentrated on social and ethical "human" problems. On the other side, those who saw a value or necessity for metaphysics, including John Herman Randall Jr., Sterling Lamprecht, Abraham Edel, Corliss Lamont, and others, advocated a kind of Aristotelian study of being as the central role of philosophy (Yulina 1978a, 136).

Varieties of naturalism

The variety of differing "naturalisms" can make it difficult to discuss and evaluate the movement as a whole. It is many-sided and contradictory, Karimsky says, "But it is integral in the sense that it includes all philosophic areas from ontology and epistemology to axiology and ethics," and its general traits can be described:

> in its world view, a realization of the active, practical interaction of human beings and the world, of subject and object; in social philosophy, chiefly a secular-humanist orientation and a normative historical optimism; in the moral and anthropological sphere, individualism and egoism (in the positive sense), an informal code of working ethics and criteria of practical effectiveness; in methodology and epistemology, a scientific orientation and commitment to rationality, and a suspicious attitude toward speculative thought and irrationalism. (Karimsky 1990, 3)

A more precise account of naturalism as a whole is difficult, however, because there are so many versions and representatives: "the evolutionary naturalism of R. W. Sellars, the critical naturalism of Dewey, the experimental naturalism of Hook, the naturalist humanism of Lamont, and the ordinal naturalism of Buchler" (Karimsky 1990, 4). Bogomolov regards the term "naturalism" to be "vague," describing only a line of thought resting on empiricism and scientific knowledge and in which all radical differences are dissolved, above all the distinction between materialism and idealism (Bogomolov 1974, 294). Whether vague or not, the variety has raised the question in Soviet literature over who is and who is not a naturalist. The tendency in works from the early 1970s was to exclude a number of figures as "pseudo-naturalists." Bogomolov does just that to Dewey, Hook, Santayana, Pratt, and Woodbridge, since they are pragmatists, idealistic critical realists, or theists. Karimsky also dismissed Santayana, Woodbridge, Pratt, and Dewey as pseudo-naturalists, though in his most recent work he appeared to hold a conception of naturalism broad enough to include them (Karimsky 1972, 18–19; 1990, 4).

The figures Bogomolov and Karimsky did not include, with the exception of Hook, are nearly all of what Yulina refers to as the first generation of twentieth century American naturalists. One of the few generally accepted members of the first generation whom Bogomolov and Karimsky regard as a genuine naturalist is Roy Wood Sellars. Though she too recognizes the relevant differences among them, Yulina had from the beginning a more liberal and flexible conception of naturalism. The first generation of naturalists included Dewey, Woodbridge, Santayana, Perry, Sellars, Montague, Cohen, and others. While their ideas differed in many fundamental ways, they nevertheless shared a distinctive set of general views: "an opposition to all forms of idealism (in fact, though, only to overt forms of idealism such as supernaturalism, irrationalism, intuitivism, mysticism, etc.); an attempt to offer a philosophic explanation of reality, i.e., nature; and a demand for the maximum application in philosophy of methods worked out in the sciences" (Yulina 1978a, 119–120). One of the other distinctive characteristics of the members of the first generation was that many of them tended to hold views that are not at all naturalist. Woodbridge, on the one hand, advocated an Aristotelian "first philosophy" with a naturalist conception of being, and he acknowledged the primacy of natural existence in relation to the individual intellect. On the other hand, "Like the neorealists Woodbridge could not sustain his naturalist position in the consideration of the problem of the creative possibilities of consciousness and the status of the ideal content of consciousness . . . [N]ature for him turns out to be necessarily associated with thought," and his naturalism is ultimately an objective idealism.[15] Santayana too, despite his "materialism," in the end "created a metaphysical system that was a modernized variant of Platonism" (Yulina 1978a, 128–130).

The work of Dewey, however, is the most controversial. He had, Yulina says, an especially great influence, and some of his ideas determined many of the characteristic traits of American naturalism. He was critical of dualism, he rejected any impenetrable boundaries among the physical, biological, and spiritual, he endorsed the continuity of nature and experience, and he interpreted matter and consciousness as different characteristics of natural events. Furthermore, many later naturalists followed him in trading traditional speculative methods for the methods of contextualism, functionalism, and instrumentalism. In these respects and given the extent of his influence, Dewey was certainly a naturalist. But still, with his instrumentalism and understanding of experience Dewey produced a subjectivism no less inimical to naturalism than the objective idealism of Woodbridge or Santayana: "Dewey held that to view knowledge outside of the contextual limits of experience and its functional roles renders problems related to it insoluble. This abstractly correct view was accompanied for Dewey by the philosophically false, subjectivist thesis concerning the identity of the object of inquiry with the content of experience, its functions, etc." (Yulina 1978a, 126–127).

Yulina was prepared to read Dewey both ways, but Karimsky was not, in part because his conception of naturalism as a distinct philosophy required that it be distanced from pragmatism. In Karimsky's view, though Dewey regards nature to be all there is, his understanding of it in terms of the "interaction" of a subject with its environment reduces nature in the end to experience. The naturalist counter-argument rests on the opposite presumption that since the world exists without experience it is therefore independent. Dewey's mechanism for breaking down traditional philosophic bifurcations is the inclusion of the objective in the subjective. Naturalism, by contrast, does not "merge" the spiritual with the non-spiritual but takes the essentially materialist approach that what we call consciousness or mind is a complex function of matter (Karimsky 1972, 41–43). The epistemological implication of this further separates Dewey from naturalism. From the naturalist criticism of the pragmatist conception of experience flows the important inference that the instrumental value of knowledge does not exclude its being a reflection of reality, due to the fact that the question of the truth or falsity of theories is not at all deprived of sense, as instrumentalism would have it (Karimsky 1972, 14). In his most recent discussion of this issue Karimsky may be prepared to grant that the history of American naturalism was sufficiently diverse to include Dewey, but he continues to argue that a consistent and worthwhile naturalism must be divorced from instrumentalism: "Pragmatism's war against dualism signified the immanence of the world. It was more than anything a war against ontology in the naturalistic sense, and it undermined the basis of an adequate epistemology, which is impossible without realist assumptions" (Karimsky 1990, 14).

Of all the early twentieth century representatives of American naturalism the most consistent position can be found in Sellars. Soviet specialists have been interested in Sellars first because of all the early naturalists his work is the least tainted by instrumentalism or objective idealism. Furthermore, Sellars lived and worked long enough to be an important figure in later naturalist philosophy. Naturalism experienced a resurgence in the 1940s, its "second generation," and Yulina identifies two strains of thought in it. The first was expressed in the 1944 volume *Naturalism and the Human Spirit* and represented a naturalism that compromised with pragmatism. The second was a strain much closer to materialism, and it found its voice in the 1949 collection titled *Philosophy for the Future*, of which Sellars was one of the editors (Yulina 1978a, 130–131).

As early as his first book *Critical Realism*, published in 1916, Sellars was developing an epistemology that avoided what the Soviets regarded as the more common mistakes others were making. Unlike the neorealists, he argued that the objects of knowledge cannot be identified with thought, so that the known world is independent of the process of knowing it. At the same time, the objects of knowledge cannot simply be identified with sensations or perceptions. Sellars was critical of such a common sense or naive realism, yet his criticism took him not in idealist but in materialist directions. Bogomolov summarizes the advantages of Sellars's realist epistemology:

> The strong side of this conception of knowledge is that despite the subjectivist and agnostic dogmas that prevail in bourgeois philosophy, Sellars maintained the reality of the external world, emphasizing the active, selective relation of the subject to it. And the subject and object of knowledge are relatively correctly interpreted. A material object is a physical thing and independent of knowledge. Their interaction is not passive contemplation, but an active, practical connection. Finally, the cognitive process is understood as a causal relation, the conditionality of the content of consciousness by the external world. (Bogomolov 1974, 207)

Despite the merits of his views, Bogomolov contends that Sellars's epistemology never overcame two crucial problems. He never adequately took account of the social aspects of the process of knowledge, and as a result he misunderstood the necessary conception of practice. Sellars's tendency was to approach epistemology through a consideration of perception, which he distinguished from sensation. His treatment of perception had the virtue of avoiding subjectivism in that he understood it as an active, organic response to the influence of the external world. But still, Bogomolov says, two issues remain: (1) one cannot stop at perception, since the social side of the process of knowledge is involved in conceptual thought and language; and (2) even in his otherwise valuable analysis of perception Sellars does not address the fact that the "living meaning" of perception includes the capacity to determine human conduct. Sellars's approach to perception was largely biological and physiological, and "leaves the social character of human thought in the shadows" (Karimsky 1972, 76). Sellars's failure to appreciate the sociality of knowledge is reflected in the issue of practice. On the one hand, his view of perception as active did lead him to consider the place of practice in the theory of knowledge. He argued that practical success justifies our belief that we have achieved knowledge. This is an approach different from, and preferable to, the pragmatist view. "However, Sellars does not treat the concept of practice from its 'technological' and generally cultural side. From our point of view, this means that the development of productive powers, of human productive practice, serves as the basis of the development of science. It is precisely social, productive practice that confronts people with theoretical problems and compels the development of knowledge" (Bogomolov 1974, 210). There is, in other words, an individualism in Sellars that damages his understanding of both perception and practice.

Sellars stopped short of an adequate materialist epistemology, and the same is true of his general conception of nature. He had argued directly against idealism and defended the essentially materialist conceptions of the objectivity and substantiality of the world. However, he also argued against materialism, specifically the atomism and mechanism of traditional materialism.[16] While Sellars preferred the term *naturalism* for a general characterization of his own views, Bogomolov notes with approval that his objections to both idealism and mechanistic materialism are shared by dialectical materialists. And in many of its details his alternative is also closely related to Bogomolov's own view. One of the features of Sellars's naturalism that Bogomolov finds most important is his use of the concept of substance. Sellars, and naturalists generally, rejects the traditional conception of substance as something that underlies changing qualities. Some have abandoned the concept altogether in favor of a view of nature as constituted by events or processes. Bogomolov, Karimsky, and other Soviet commentators have been suspicious of this move, concerned that the independence, individuality, or "thingness" of material objects will be dissolved into the events or processes. As a result Bogomolov approves of Sellars's use of the concept that substance itself develops; on this basis he constructed his theory of emergent evolution.[17]

Sellars's emergent evolutionism differs from and is an improvement on earlier versions of the view; nevertheless, Bogomolov argues, it does not go far enough. Sellars did not think, for example, that the new qualities that emerge in natural, developmental processes are unforeseeable and unknowable. Such evolutionary process can be understood and explained, he thought, which is to say that it is possible to know how one form of organization moves to another. Bogomolov agrees, though he adds that the transition from one natural condition to another should be understood in terms of the relation between quantitative and qualitative changes. Sellars, however, had rejected this view on the grounds that it was little more than a vestige of speculative Hegelianism.[18] A second aspect of other emergent evolutionary theories with which Sellars broke was a tendency to regard the moving forces of development as ideal. The natural world has its own principles of movement and development and has no need of external, ideal sources. Again, however, Bogomolov thinks that Sellars's point is right but that he missed the fact that "the *contradictions* of the objective world are the source and moving force of development" (Bogomolov 1974, 214). Sellars had no more use for contradictions than he did for the conception of quantitative change leading to qualitative change, and for the same reasons. In Bogomolov's view, and Karimsky agrees, Sellars to his credit was more of a materialist than he knew, while his failure was that he was not enough of a dialectician.

Nature and Knowledge

Naturalism posits as the central philosophic category not matter or spirit but nature, and philosophic inquiry is not primarily the study of the material world or knowledge, but of nature, of which matter and knowledge are aspects (Yulina 1978a, 122). Nature is the broadest possible philosophic category in that it includes whatever there is. The scope of the category of nature creates something of a paradox, Karimsky thinks, in that a concept of nature as "whatever is" is contentless, underscoring only the breadth of the term. This in part accounts for the diversity among specific naturalist accounts of nature and inquiry. While naturalists agree that nature is "whatever there is," there has been disagreement over just what it is that nature includes (Yulina 1978a, 132). Nonetheless, despite the lack of content of the category, it has been and continues to be an important means of exposing and answering idealist concepts of panlogism, panpsychism, theism, and so forth (Karimsky 1972, 39–41).

The generality of the category of nature generates the question of the relation between nature and experience, the answer to which Karimsky calls a "watershed" in the naturalist view. One way to provide content to the concept of nature is to describe it as including "all facts—'natural,' spiritual, social—that is, everything that enters or can enter into the sphere of experience" (Yulina 1978a, 132). To describe nature this way leaves open the question whether nature should be read through experience or whether experience is one of the many aspects of nature. Dewey, as we have seen, tended to take the first approach, while many others have taken the second. While Yulina acknowledges both trends within naturalism, Karimsky has argued that the distinctively naturalist approach is the second. A genuine naturalism insists on the objectivity of natural phenomena, and Karimsky regards this to be among its most valuable philosophic traits. Nature or, better, natural phenomena are objective, which is to say that among their innumerable determinate traits is an indefinite number that either in whole or in part are not products of knowledge, mind, consciousness, or experience and, indeed, may not be related to those qualities at all.

The objectivity of nature in no way precludes a continuity between nature and experience, since experience is a fully natural process with its own determinate traits. For earlier naturalists, Yulina suggests, this point led to a focus on the natural status and character of individual experience and consciousness, while later naturalists tended to concentrate more on the continuity of the "natural" and the social, that is, the status and character of social processes and traits. In general, the continuity among the physical, biological, experiential, and social aspects of nature was understood in terms of emergent, "ascendant" principles of creative evolution, in which nature is characterized by qualitatively ascending levels of life, novelty, and chance (Yulina 1978a, 133). One of the specific forms the naturalist concept of emergent evolution took was the theory of levels. Sellars, Abraham Edel, and others argued, in Karimsky's view, that the active, evolutionary character of matter generates new levels of its complex organization and that different levels function according to different principles. There are several advantages to this conception of natural levels: it overcomes reductionism, it distinguishes naturalist materialism from any mechanical materialism, and more specifically it allows naturalists to avoid the "biologization" of the social level, as for example in Sellars's rejection of social Darwinism (Karimsky 1972, 45–47).

One of the components of a naturalist concept of nature that most concerns Karimsky, and Bogomolov and Yulina as well, is the category of substance. We have already seen Bogomolov speak approvingly of Sellars's use of the concept, and Karimsky, at least in his 1972 book, was of like mind. Naturalists rejected any traditional conception of substance as "primordial matter" or a concrete substratum, but some thought it worthwhile to retain the term. For some of those who did, the concept of substance, as Karimsky describes it, implies nothing more than a certain "togetherness," which in his view makes it possible to speak of the real "substantiality" of nature without excluding a recognition of its qualitative multiplicity and complexity of organization. This, Karimsky argues, is far preferable to the approach of those, like Randall, who identify substance with activity and process, or of those who want to abandon the category altogether. The danger of the latter approaches, he seemed to think, is that the unity, the identity, the "thingness" or "togetherness" of natural entities, especially material objects, is liable to be dissolved in a web of relations and processes. For some naturalists, then, the concept of substance expresses a more or less materialist understanding of nature, while those who either reject it or define it in terms of relations or process are engaged in a compromise with idealism and agnosticism (Karimsky 1972, 44).

It is not clear that Karimsky would have made this claim later in his career. In his last formal discussion of American naturalism, for example, he speaks fairly highly of Buchler's concept of ordinality, and Buchler is certainly one of the naturalists for whom the category of substance has no place. One might argue that if Karimsky's concern is to retain the "togetherness" of natural entities, then the category of substance is not important. The issue is not "substantiality," but individuation and identity. It may be possible to offer an adequate categorial account of identity and stability without substance. Buchler has attempted precisely this as an aspect of his ordinality, and if there is merit to his or similar attempts, then a construal of natural phenomena in terms of the relations among their traits need not imply that identity and stability are dissipated into vague and indeterminate processes.

Like its ontology, naturalist epistemology, in the Soviet view, begins as an improvement over its predecessors and contemporary alternatives, though the directions it has taken leave something to be desired. The decisive step in the development of naturalism out of critical realism, Karimsky has said, was Sellars's realization that realist metaphysics was badly in need of an epistemology that could uncover the natural mechanism of sensible knowledge, and that only by resurrecting truth as the correspondence of knowledge with its object could realism be a defensible world view. In this respect "Sellars's epistemological position was inextricably linked to an ontology that bore a materialist character" (Karimsky 1990, 7–8). Sellars most explicitly represents the materialist strain in naturalist epistemology and to some extent expresses its most general and valuable traits. The world is knowable, primarily through the sciences, and knowledge is itself a natural process. The world as known is independent of knowledge of it, in the sense, for example, that inquiry does not create scientific laws but reveals them. In its conception of truth naturalism emphasizes practice as a confirmation of truth and in this way avoids both a narrow empiricism and the "vulgar instrumentalist" interpretation of practice as the source of truth. And in their conception of the independence of the object of knowledge, naturalists avoid both subjective idealism and agnosticism (Karimsky 1972, 68–69).[19]

While these traits characterize naturalist epistemology generally, they are more thoroughly and consistently developed in Sellars's materialism than in the directions taken by other prominent naturalists. Marvin Farber, for example, was taken by Husserl's phenomenological method, attempting to divorce the method from the rest of Husserl's system and apply it in a more naturalistic spirit. Farber was right, Karimsky and Bogomolov both argue, to reject Husserl's subjectivism and to hold that a theory of reality must not be subordinated to a theory of cognition. But Farber failed to realize that the phenomenological method is itself idealist and thus inconsistent with the materialist naturalism he otherwise endorsed (Karimsky 1972, 81; Bogomolov 1974, 305). In addition to Sellars's materialism and Farber's phenomenology, the naturalist in whose epistemological ideas Soviet commentators have had the most interest is Ernest Nagel.

The central issue of Nagel's epistemology, as Karimsky and Bogomolov read him, is the relation of methodology and inquiry to reality, of logic and the scientific method to being. His conception of knowledge has realist, operationalist, and positivist moments, and the evaluative question concerns the relations among them. In a later paper Karimsky rejects the temptation to read Nagel in too positivistic a vein. His concept of "logic without ontology" is often misunderstood, Karimsky says. Nagel was not opposed to metaphysics, nor did he reject the correlativity of logic and ontology. He rejected rather the view of logical and methodological principles as isomorphous of the laws of being, holding that cognitive practice has its own specific regularities. In this respect Nagel, Farber, and Sellars are of one mind: "Knowledge in all its components is natural, and consequently all cognitive levels are genetically and functionally interrelated, though the mechanism of the relation is far from clear" (Karimsky 1990, 9, 11). In his earlier work, however, Karimsky was less enthusiastic about Nagel's treatment of logic and science, and Bogomolov followed Karimsky's lead. The realist, operationalist, and positivist moments of Nagel's epistemology are, according to this reading, in an unstable marriage, producing conceptual traps from which Nagel cannot escape.

Nagel's epistemology is concerned above all with the general structure and characteristics of the scientific method and its results.[20] Three conceptions of the nature of scientific theories have been widespread: (1) theory is true or false in relation to reality; (2) theory is not true or false but instrumental; and (3) theory is a "description" of facts. The first is a materialist view, the second pragmatist, and the third positivist. Nagel rejected all three in their pure forms, seeing valuable elements in each. He held, for example, that theory describes reality but at the same time cannot be merely description of facts. Scientific theory concerns not only empirical generalization but also reveals necessity in nature. This is the realist and materialist aspect of Nagel's view, and it distances him from a strict Positivism (Karimsky 1972, 83–84). Nagel also argued that scientific theories are concerned to explain natural phenomena, further distinguishing himself from positivism and pragmatism. Nagel's realist and materialist side is evident too in his treatment of such issues as determinism in nature. He rejects mechanistic determinism, yet holds that scientific description and explanation requires determinism in some sense, an approach that is "correct and fruitful" (Bogomolov 1974, 302).

One of the problems Nagel addresses in his analysis of scientific theory and explanation concerns the fact that no single theory or kind of theory appears to cover all phenomena. Bogomolov puts the issue in terms of two problems: (1) whether we can decide what is to be done with phenomena that cannot be subsumed in an existing theoretical system, that is, the problem of changing or enriching theories; and (2) whether we can speak of qualitatively distinct phenomena that require distinct theories not reducible to one another. An adequate treatment of such questions, Bogomolov argues, requires acknowledging qualitatively distinct yet related phenomena correlated with distinct yet related theories. Dialectical materialism, he says, proceeds from the existence in nature of different forms of movement and levels of development, qualitatively unique yet lawfully related to one another. These distinct phenomena and processes are reflected in scientific disciplines, each with its own unique categorial apparatus, methods, and theories that remain, at the same time, essentially connected. A correlation obtains between, on the one hand, objectively existing forms of movement and levels of development and, on the other, their cognitive expression in scientific knowledge.

Bogomolov stresses this issue because he thinks that Nagel's treatment of it indicates the most serious and general flaw of his epistemology. Nagel, he says, treats one side of the issue, in that he recognizes the legitimacy of distinct and irreducible theories, for example mechanistic and organic explanations. His mistake, however, is that he does not make the connection between theory and objectively existing reality (Bogomolov 1974, 302–303). This is Nagel's "logic without ontology," the separation of logical principles from the logic of things. Nagel enters dangerous ground here, Karimsky feels, because he slides into a positivist conception of logic in that scientific principles no longer depend on the object of knowledge, and the significance of logic and mathematics becomes largely operational (Karimsky 1972, 85). The realism of Nagel's earlier conception of logic and the scientific method is diluted by a collapse into positivism and pragmatism: "This materialist, or at least clearly naturalist, position is cheapened in its general significance by the rejection of the objective ('ontological') content of logic and the scientific method" (Bogomolov 1974, 298).

The complex of ontological and epistemological issues that characterize American naturalism—the nature and relation of science and metaphysics, the problem of substance, the pragmatist elements of functionalism, contextualism, and operationalism—converge in a different way in the philosophy of John Herman Randall Jr. Randall was a participant in what Yulina calls the "back to Aristotle" movement that played an important role in the development of twentieth century American philosophy, and it took several specific forms. Following Woodbridge, the Columbia school interpreted Aristotle in the spirit of contextualism, pragmatism, and functionalism, in Chicago in the spirit of neoscholasticism, and by Catholics in the spirit of Thomism. Yulina suspects that much of this reflected a psychological motive to ground one's views in an authoritative tradition. Randall's case, however, demonstrates more than simply the wish to use Aristotle's name for support. Randall's appeal to Aristotle, on the contrary, is a component of the American interest in a "reconstruction in philosophy" and a reinterpretation of the foundations of philosophical knowledge (Yulina 1978a, 146). Specifically, in the tradition of Woodbridge and Dewey, Randall combines a naturalistically rendered Aristotelian metaphysics with a pragmatist theory of experience. The result is a unique, distinctly objectivist conception of philosophy, its subject matter, and its history, one that distinguishes Randall's from overtly idealist, subjectivist, irrationalist, and scientistic philosophic positions, and that contrasts sharply with contemporary phenomenological, personalist, neopositivist, and existentialist points of view.

Randall rejects the Platonist and neo-Platonist attempts to reduce reality to one or another kind of thing, or to a set of distinct kinds of entities. It is not the function of philosophy or metaphysics to provide a "reality list."

On the contrary, he takes seriously the breadth of the naturalist concept of nature, and holds that whatever is encountered is in some way real. The point, as Randall put it, is not to determine what is or is not real, but in what way this or that is real, a formulation that anticipates what Buchler would later call the principle of ontological parity.[21] One of the tasks of metaphysics, then, is to determine through categories of the broadest possible scope the general traits of the plurality and multiplicity of reality. As central as this is, however, it is only one of the tasks of metaphysics. For Randall metaphysics is also concerned, Yulina notes, to unify the multiplicity and contradictions of experience and to correlate this unity with nature. Metaphysics fulfills the analytic and critical function of correlating the cognitive and mythological forms of the interaction of human beings with their world. One of the most important examples of the latter is religion. Like Santayana, Randall felt that religion is, among other things, a poetic expression of human aspirations, and metaphysics or philosophy must be put to the task of explaining the meaning and function of religion in relation to the other factors of social existence (Yulina 1978a, 138–139).

The meaning and function of science also come under the purview of metaphysics, though the relation of metaphysics to science differs from its relation to religion. Metaphysics, in Randall's view, is akin to science in that both are theoretical, cognitive, and demonstrative disciplines, and as such both are cumulative, progressive, and developing spheres of knowledge. Of course metaphysics and science are not identical. Metaphysics is more general, and thus includes the philosophy of science within it, and unlike science, metaphysics does not attempt to explain, to answer the question "why" things are this way rather than another. Metaphysics differs from science, then, in its subject matter, its categorial apparatus, its degree of generality, and in its cultural-humanistic functions. It nevertheless resembles science in its cumulative and progressive character, its ongoing attempt to fill the "gaps" and "omissions" left by its predecessors in the general account of nature (Yulina 1978a, 140–143).[22]

Randall's view that philosophy or metaphysics is cumulative and progressive conditions his valuation of the history of philosophy. He was engaged, as we have said, in the reinterpretation and reconstruction of philosophy, and to that extent was, like many of his colleagues, in "rebellion against the classics." The specific target of his criticism was the "epistemologism" and "reductionism" of philosophy in the modern period. However, unlike so many other critics of modernism, in Randall's day and now, the critique of modernity did not lead him to abandon philosophy or its history. "As a historian of philosophy," Yulina says, "he categorically rejected the view that the theoretical legacy of the past was obsolete with respect to the resolution of contemporary problems." Randall, to his credit, combined a critical eye toward the history of philosophy with an appreciation of its cognitive and cumulative character. This sets him apart from many other twentieth century American philosophers, Dewey in particular: "In this respect he differed from Dewey who, as we recall, saw in the philosophic systems of the past an ideological product, a continuing need of moribund classes to provide an intellectual justification for their conservative social, political, and moral beliefs" (Yulina 1978a, 146–147). For Randall the history of philosophy is at the same time cultural expression and a continuous process of the accumulation of knowledge of nature in all its multiplicity.

Randall's appreciation for the cognitive character of philosophic inquiry led him to insist that fundamental problems of worldview, including the problems of metaphysics, are unavoidable. Yulina finds two aspects of Randall's own metaphysics most significant and revealing, his interpretation of the category of substance and his methodological conceptions. His approach to substance reflects his attempt to rehabilitate the naturalist side of Aristotle, indeed the entire historical tradition of the naturalist-substantialist system of views.[23] As Bogomolov and Karimsky had argued with respect to Sellars, Yulina sees Randall's category of substance as his way of retaining the objectivity of natural phenomena, and it is consequently the more valuable of his metaphysical contributions. "In this," Yulina says, "he is undoubtedly right, in so far as his defense of the Aristotelian line in the history of philosophy is in large measure objectively expressed as a defense of materialism. . . . Randall is absolutely right to proceed from the assumption that the question of the adequacy of a metaphysics rests on the supposition of the objectivity of substance" (Yulina 1978a, 147). Randall's naturalist Aristotelianism, however, is woven together with a pragmatist methodology, which, Yulina argues, is its undoing. His metaphysics employs the methods of functionalism, contextualism ,and operationalism, which were developed primarily in Dewey's instrumentalism, Mead's social pragmatism, and Bridgman's operationalism. On the one hand, Randall's own insistence on the objectivity of substance led him "to soften and neutralize" the subjectivism of pragmatism's biological treatment of "context," its substitution of operations for objects, and its utilitarian treatment of truth (Yulina 1978a, 138). In the end, however, Randall's methods contradict his approach to nature, and the objectivity of substance cannot withstand the relativizing force of pragmatist methods.

Like other naturalists, Randall rejected the notion of substance as substratum, either material or psychological, in his case in favor of an Aristotelian conception of substance as "primary existence," reality in all its variety of manifestations, as nature. He regarded his own view as similar to pragmatism, though without the latter's drawbacks. Dewey's mistake, Randall argues, was in treating the object of knowledge as the result of knowledge, or as the consequence of the activity of cognitive tools. Dewey had been right, however, to emphasize context and interaction in his conception of nature. Randall's category of substance is an attempt to avoid Dewey's subjectivism while retaining his contextuality. Substance is the totality or context of a situation, and the ongoing interactions that characterize situations. More specifically, substance is process. Randall develops the concept by specifying two aspects of the structure of substance. Substance has a formal structure, which is the stable capacity of the elements of a process or situation to be in relation to one another. Substance also has a functional structure, the interaction among constituents of a particular process, context or situation. The formal structure of substance, Randall held, is invariant through differing contexts, while in its functional structure substance is relative to specific events, relations, and activities. Yulina is clearly sympathetic to Randall's project here, in that he wants to maintain both the structural, objective traits of natural phenomena while incorporating their active, changing character in relation to specific situations. She argues, however, that there are two aspects of his approach to substance that defeat him. One is an excessively broad interpretation of functionalism, contextualism and operationalism, and a second is a consequence of his "anti-epistemologism" (Yulina 1978a, 148).

In themselves, Yulina says, functional, contextual, and operational methods are not without value. They can be applied effectively in concrete scientific research and even in the resolution of some philosophic problems. But when they are generalized into metaphysical principles they are unsatisfactory. Understanding processes functionally, as Randall does, ultimately relativizes them. If forms of cultural expression such as myth, science, philosophy, and religion are treated functionally, in terms of their relations to certain ends, little room is left to understand the objective processes that engender and condition them. Furthermore, if knowledge and the various forms of inquiry are treated instrumentally, activities such as science or philosophy lose their cognitive value because they lose their relation to objective reality:

> Consider, for example, the use by naturalists of the method of functionalism. Advanced as a contrast to absolutist and universalist conceptions of the forms of culture, it explains these forms as socially conditioned, dependent on a given concrete context and subordinate to the practical ends and interests of a given group. In this way, the essence of the forms of culture is reduced to the operations or functions that they fulfill. If one or another form of culture or social consciousness "works" in a given concrete area, if it fulfills its task or traditional function, it is taken to be "natural." The operational, functional approach to cultural forms, to forms of knowledge, is accompanied by a relativization, deprivation, or depreciation of their theoretical significance and appropriate epistemological criteria of evaluation. This approach glosses over the theoretical differences between myth and science, between philosophy and religion. We see just this tendency in, for example,

Randall's *The Role of Knowledge in Western Religion.* With the functionalist approach to cultural forms they all turn out to be of equal standing, i.e., socially equivalent. But this is far from true. (Yulina 1978a, 148–149)

If functionalism relativizes such activities as science and philosophy, myth, and religion, when generalized into a description of natural phenomena, substance no longer retains the objectivity that justified the category in the first place. By understanding substance as functionally conditioned process, Randall, intentionally or not, replaces its theoretical and epistemological determination and role with the concrete and historical.

The other serious problem Yulina finds in Randall's metaphysics is a consequence of his rejection of modernist "epistemologism." He wants to avoid the subjective, epistemological point of departure of modernist metaphysics, but in the process he misses an important contribution of the modern period:

In the heat of the polemics against substantialist dualism, epistemological monism, reductionism, "substantivism," etc., Randall missed a very important point, namely, that the modern period, above all Descartes, Locke, and other thinkers, formulated the problem of the subject, which was the foundation for an understanding of the active, creative essence of human being. (Yulina 1978a, 150)

The German idealists had developed this line of thought, and to the extent that they did, Yulina says, they were superior even to the preceding contemplative materialism. Randall's approach is in a sense a throwback, in that the subject is dissolved in situations and processes, in which the active and reflective sides of cognition, and their relation, cannot be accounted for.

Yulina's objection to Randall in the end is that interpreting substance as process dissolves both the object and the subject. The functionalist account of process at one stroke eliminates the objectivity of natural phenomena and the subjective traits of human activity, especially cognition. An adequate ontology and epistemology, Yulina maintains, requires both.

Human Nature and Society

Naturalist discussions of human nature and social philosophy reflected both the advantages and shortcomings of its conceptions of nature and knowledge. The naturalist understanding of human nature posits the human being wholly in the course of natural development. Human being is a product of the evolutionary process of nature, a conception that is both advantageous and, in its naturalist versions, problematic. To see the human as a fully natural being avoids supernaturalism and dualism, and it opposes any conception of human nature or essence as eternal and immutable. In this reading, nature is not an alien or hostile force with respect to human being, nor is the human regarded as the culmination or centerpiece of nature. And naturalism, with the aid of such ideas as Sellars's theory of levels of natural development, can avoid reductionism, in particular biological reductionism. If, for example, the social is a distinct level of the processes of nature not fully describable or explainable in biological or physical terms, there is far less compulsion to read human nature through strictly biological or physical categories. As a result, many naturalists—Karimsky explicitly mentions Sellars, Farber, Lamont and Edel—have been able to see the social character of human nature, in the sense that the self is a product of both natural development and of social and historical relations (Karimsky 1972, 95–97).

This same point, however, indicates the fundamental difficulty in the naturalist treatment of human nature. It is one thing to be able to avoid a biological reductionism by recognizing the social as a distinct level of natural development, but it is quite another to understand the precise relations between social factors and human nature. At this point, Karimsky and other Soviets have argued, the naturalist interpretation of human nature fails. As Karimsky puts it, naturalism is a successor to earlier forms of materialism, and it inherited the historical idealism of its predecessors, specifically the failure to realize the role of material production in history and as a causal factor in the formation of human beings (Karimsky 1972, 64). The same claim is defended in a dissertation by S. A. Nikolsky on the interpretation of human nature in American naturalism. Some naturalists, Nikolsky mentions V. J. McGill in particular, have argued that history can be explained on biological grounds, which is to say that historical principles are not themselves factors in the formation of human beings (Nikolsky 1977, 10–12). And even those who, like Sellars, are more likely to see the social factors in human development, in the end tend to "biologize" both human nature and society. Nikolsky defends the historical materialist thesis that human labor, production, under the lawful conditions of social development, is the key to the process of human development, and he argues that Sellars and others have failed to incorporate this insight into their evolutionary naturalist approach. Although he notes that "Sellars categorically rejects the possibility that the social can be reduced to the biological and also the treatment of human being as a passive product of surrounding conditions," Nikolsky argues that ultimately Sellars reads society as developing primarily by adaptation to its conditions, and to that extent he essentially biologizes social development. This, Nikolsky argues, is characteristic of naturalism, so that despite attempts to understand human beings as active, a biological interpretation of social development leads to a largely passive conception of human beings as developing through adaptation to their environment (Nikolsky 1977, 13–19).

Several undesirable consequences develop from this. One of them is that naturalists tend to miss the actual traits of human sociality. As Bogomolov put it, "Human consciousness has always been a stumbling block for naturalist conceptions, which reduce all phenomena to nature, and as a result of this they cannot see the social nature of consciousness" Krikorian, for example, clearly argued for a view of the psyche as a function of fully material beings, but more or less leaves it there: "This essentially materialist view of the psyche is supplemented by behaviorism, but leaves alone the psyche's social origin and essence" (Bogomolov 1974, 295).[24] Karimsky makes largely the same objection, though in somewhat different terms. The view of human being as a part of nature correctly indicates its biological character, he says, but such an abstraction does not reveal the individual's nature as subject, which arises through the web of social relations:

> Naturalism unjustifiably simplified and distorted the relations between human being and nature, ascribing to them a direct and immediate character. Unlike all other biological forms, the human relation to nature is mediated through labor and the system of social relations. Naturalists have not understood the role of these relations, in the context of which productive activity arises. By dissolving the human being in nature, they lose the real subject of the social sciences—human society and the concrete—historical person. (Karimsky 1972, 66)

And finally, even in those respects in which naturalists argue for the sociality of human nature, since in general they have failed to discern the laws of historical and social development, there is a tendency to regard any and all social factors as equally significant and causally relevant (Karimsky 1972, 98).

The fact that as a rule naturalists have not appreciated the extent to which and the precise ways in which historical and social factors have conditioned human nature affects a good deal of naturalist social theory. One of the more significant areas is ethics. The most extensive and thorough naturalist treatment of ethics, in Karimsky's opinion, is Abraham Edel's. Naturalistic ethical theory proceeds from a rejection of a "non-natural" character of ethical principles. Since ethics arises as an aspect of human culture, it is unacceptable to divorce it from its cultural and social context, and it is equally unacceptable to deal with it other than through the methods of science broadly conceived. Thus ethics cannot be regarded as either intuitive or transcendental.

Edel is aware not only that ethics has a social and cultural context, but he also appreciates the more precise point that ethical norms and principles have a class character. Despite this point, however, Edel tends to ground his ethical theory in a conception of human nature that too heavily emphasizes biological factors. He attempts specifically to derive ethical principles from a biological conception of human needs. Edel's approach, Karimsky argues, reveals a characteristic unstated assumption: Though any ethical norm reveals under concrete historical analysis a specific class or group orientation, normativity in general must be regarded objectively, "scientifically," not from a specific class position. Here naturalism demonstrates its tendency to employ an approach to meta-ethics that is independent of class, and that represents its own position as the point of view of humanity in general (Karimsky 1972, 104). Edel's alternative to a class analysis is to ground ethical principles in a naturalistic conception of human needs, in which biological and social factors are accorded equal weight.[25] This, Karimsky argues, is Edel's fundamental mistake, since he fails to see that "need" is primarily a social category. Needs are not internal "urges" arising from people's common biological conditions but rather involve the conditions necessary for their own satisfactions. Social relations and social practice are the context of human needs, and, consequently, ethical theory must be grounded primarily in the social conditions of human life (Karimsky 1972, 108, 113).

Bogomolov extends Karimsky's criticism. To avoid strained and artificial constructs, he argues, it must be clear that moral principles are engendered not by biological and psychological factors but by social relations, in part by relations of private property. Biological factors are certainly related, but they do not determine the origin and character of ethical principles. This becomes especially clear when naturalists try to ground biologically the value of cooperation and the feeling of sympathy, as if they were independent of social and class differences: "Deriving this 'common human' ethics from the biological characteristics and needs of people does imply individuals' activity and a moral responsibility for their actions. . . . But for all the attractiveness of this point of view, it overlooks the compulsory power of social conditions, moral and otherwise, which in a society characterized by class antagonisms appears as an active, alienating force" (Bogomolov 1974, 296–297). In the end a note of tragedy sounds in the naturalist approach. Nagel expressed it himself when he said that the human individual is in a situation with no guarantee of eternal existence or reward for unwarranted suffering. Human suffering, in Nagel's view, can be alleviated only by the wide application of a method of knowledge that can master the power of nature.[26] For Bogomolov, however, if tragedy imbues the human condition, that is not due to a failure to employ adequate methods of inquiry, but to a failure to appreciate the real character of social processes and relations: "The tragedy of human fate does not lie in the individual's being a powerless atom in an all-inclusive nature. The human individual is rooted in social and class antagonisms, which not only are not alleviated by the rational and practical mastery of the power of nature, but more often than not are aggravated as a result of that 'mastery,'" which so often serves those who rule society (Bogomolov 1974, 297).

Nagel's disinclination to see the significance of social and class relations for ethics and the human situation generally is reinforced in his case by an explicit rejection of the possibility of social and historical laws, "the weakest of his ideas" (Bogomolov 1974, 305). Karimsky in fact argues that the rejection of objective and lawful necessity is one of the fundamental weaknesses in naturalist social and political thought. Notwithstanding Nagel's "tragic" chord, naturalist humanism is in many ways an exceptionally optimistic philosophy, as a rule committed to the possibility of progress and social and individual improvement. For many, however, such optimism seems to require a rejection of necessity in favor of open possibilities for the future. Naturalism, Karimsky notes, rejects the view of human beings as fully determined, in that determinism implies predetermination. While the naturalist alternative does not go as far as the existentialist view of the individual as "free" and "uncaused," many have extended it to a repudiation of any social and historical necessity. Corliss Lamont, for example, in his interpretation and defense of social and individual freedom grounds it in the reality of chance and the rejection of historical necessity.[27] This, in Karimsky's view, is the essential flaw in Lamont's position. Contrary to Lamont's supposition, determinism and chance are in reality correlated, not in the sense that they supplement each other, but in the sense that they assume each other. In all human choices, Karimsky argues, one or another historical tendency, historical necessity, dominates the situation. The individual, in other words, is not free to choose his or her own conditions, but does choose within the range of conditions generated in part by social and historical necessity. Contrary to the naturalist view, effective freedom of choice, and by implication the possibility of progress, requires not a rejection of historical necessity, but a knowledge of the objective laws that condition one's situation (Karimsky 1972, 136).

Naturalists, Karimsky cautions, do not reject necessity altogether, but whatever necessity they may recognize they do not ground in historical law. For example, the desire for a just social order, itself a prominent feature of naturalist humanism, is understood not in terms of the laws of history but rather in terms of the degree to which social ideals are taken up and defended by the population. Edel, for example, grounds whatever social necessity there may be in an *ethical* necessity, lending naturalist social ideals and aspirations a utopian, idealist cast. Furthermore, a serious disadvantage of refusing to acknowledge social and historical law is that it becomes virtually impossible to isolate and understand those factors of the social situation that are more causally relevant to the possibility of social progress. Naturalists may recognize economics as a factor in social life, but they do not realize that it is the basis of other factors. Not every relevant feature of human life is equally significant in determining its course of development, any more than every aspect of inert matter is an equally significant factor in its process. Only by understanding the laws of natural development, in this case social development, are we able to discriminate among its more and less significant components: "The basic theoretical flaw of naturalism's social conception follows from its lack of understanding of the dialectical interrelation of the factors forming the course of social development; the flaw also inheres in naturalism's failure to isolate both the principle and less significant determinants of the historical process" (Karimsky 1972, 142).

The naturalist mistake concerning social freedom, in the Soviet critique, is directly reflected in the approach to political freedom. Even the most progressive naturalists, Karimsky says, understand both political freedom and the path to a more democratic society in essentially idealist ways. Democracy, and socialism for those naturalists who have advocated it, are but ideals, for the most part not understood in relation to the material conditions of social progress. All of this, in Karimsky's view, relates to the naturalist understanding of chance and necessity. If chance, or choice, is not essentially related to necessity, then no need arises to ground one's social ideas in lawful historical processes (Karimsky 1972, 152). For all its commitment to humanism and democracy, naturalism in one way or another short-circuits its social and political thought by sharply contrasting chance and necessity and rejecting the latter: "Lamont's attempt to base human freedom solely on chance, Edel's substitution of the necessity of morals for historical necessity, and Nagel's attempt to interpret social phenomena in terms of statistical probability all reveal the fundamental trait of naturalist sociology: the rejection of historical necessity and general laws of historical development" (Karimsky 1972, 145).

The naturalist approach to social and political freedom follows logically, Karimsky says, from its conception of nature. We will recall that in an attempt to find room in nature for indeterminacy and chance, naturalism has tended to endorse an ontological pluralism. Karimsky objected to this pluralism, not because it acknowledged plurality and multiplicity in nature, nor because it is a rejection of nature as a whole or a single system, but because it is a conception of the plurality of nature that neither recognizes nor understands the lawfulness of the events and processes that constitute nature. Karimsky referred to this as the fundamental flaw of naturalist metaphysics (Karimsky 1972, 55). Analogous to that flaw, in Karimsky's objection, is the mistake in naturalist social and political theory. His concern is not that naturalism acknowledges pluralism in society, nor that it avoids a view of society as a total, or totalitarian, system, but that it will not account for the lawful relations among the multiplicity of social events, factors, and processes. In both its metaphysics and social theory naturalism pulls up short at the same, crucial point. In Karimsky's view this is a failure to pursue a consistent materialism: "Making a considerable effort to overthrow positivism, naturalism succeeded only to the extent that it was guided by philosophic materialism (which is of unquestionable advantage in its understanding of nature and in its general worldview). But by abandoning the materialist position in its understanding of human being, it turned out to be a captive of positivist philosophy" (Karimsky 1972, 145).

* * *

In his last relevant article Karimsky turned briefly to a discussion of contemporary American naturalism, in particular Buchler's ordinal naturalism and the movement to naturalize epistemology. He finds Buchler's ordinality both promising and problematic. Buchler, as other naturalists had, opposes the conception of the world or nature as a "whole," and emphasizes the plurality of orders and complexes having differing relations with one another.[28] "One can agree with this," Karimsky says, "if 'wholeness' is understood in the sense of a supernaturalist holism or a mechanism. The idea of ordinality seems to me to be consonant with the theory of levels and, in my view, has methodological value. The ordinal approach allows a more precise assessment of traits without resorting to reductionism" (Karimsky 1990, 15–16). Buchler may, however, encounter the same problem other naturalists had in his conception of the plurality of nature. As Karimsky puts it, Buchler contradicts himself when he rejects the unity of the world while endorsing its "integrality." Both points can be consistently maintained, Karimsky thinks, but only by retaining a conception of the material world as the basis of the multiplicity of complexes. While Buchler himself does not take this view, his ontology may offer a way to conceive "the relations among forms of the movement of matter, levels, and universal laws" (Karimsky 1990, 16–17).[29]

One of the deficiencies of traditional American naturalism, in Karimsky's view, has been its reluctance to avail itself of developments in logic and the philosophy of language, and in general to adopt and utilize analytic procedures. The contemporary trend in naturalized epistemology, however, is a promising rapprochement between naturalism and analytic philosophy.[30] These two prominent trends in naturalist epistemology and ontology are representative of a general trait of philosophic naturalism. Naturalism has traditionally been oriented toward scientific clarity, while at the same time it has had a metaphysical orientation. As a general point of view, Karimsky suggests, it has performed a kind of regulative function. The relation between scientific knowledge and metaphysics, both of which are necessary, has been a long standing philosophic problem. Kant had tried to develop the relation in his transcendental idealism, "but he did not build a bridge between them." On the whole philosophy ever since has not fared much better:

> The poverty of twentieth century philosophy has been that its approaches to philosophic problems have been too polarized: compare the anti-metaphysical positions of positivism, pragmatism, and scientism with the speculative metaphysics of holism, process philosophy, and theism. Naturalism has happily avoided these extremes, and it may be a contemporary way to construct that bridge. (Karimsky 1990, 21)

CONCLUSION

Since the vast majority of the work that has been surveyed here was written during the Soviet period, it is natural to wonder at this point what the consequences of the dissolution of the Soviet Union and the ousting of the Communist Party from power have been for the study of the history of American philosophy. The answer is that so far, while there has been some impact, the end of the Soviet Union has not been a watershed event as far as the character of Russian thinking about American philosophy is concerned. The fact is, as we have seen, that Russian studies of American philosophy had been undergoing a change since the 1960s in that they had been becoming far less ideologically oriented. This was a development that had been occurring, in other words, during the Soviet period, and is not simply a result of the end of the domination of Marxism. The character of Russian commentaries since 1991 has continued in the same vein, and by now ideological considerations play virtually no role in the most recent literature. Melvil's late discussions of James are a clear illustration.

Along similar lines, even without the overt ideological layer, commentaries on the history of American philosophy during the Soviet period tended to have a "know the enemy" flavor to them. Even at their most even handed and insightful, the point in any number of Soviet studies of American philosophy was often not so much to study a philosopher or philosophical movement for the purpose of learning something but more for the purpose of exposing inadequacies. Something undoubtedly dissatisfying hovers about a body of literature in which the point of departure is that fundamental flaws lie at the root of the subject of study. And yet this is precisely the mistake made in most Western studies of Soviet philosophy during the cold war period. Just as Soviet philosophical "Americanologists" studied Western philosophy in order to know the enemy, Western philosophical Sovietologists, for the most part, did the same. There were exceptions, of course. In my view the one significant Russian specialist in American philosophy whose work never reflected the arrogance of looking only to expose the others' flaws is N. E. Pokrovsky. His studies of Thoreau in particular, but also his analyses of Colonial thought in general, contain an unusually high degree of sensitivity and sympathy with the ideas being discussed. One finds some of this too in the discussions of naturalism, especially in the last works of A. M. Karimsky. When he died Karimsky was working on another book on contemporary American naturalism. It is a pity that that book will never be written. The work of others, too, was especially evenhanded and thoughtful, and, fortunately, some of them are still writing. N. S. Yulina comes to mind as a significant example. Her studies of American metaphysics are carefully considered and insightful. Whatever the variations in the tone of Soviet studies, the character now of Russian commentaries has none of the feel of looking primarily at what is wrong with the enemy. Since we are presumably not enemies, this is as it should be.

While the quality or character of the Russian study of American thought has not altered significantly from the late 1980s to the present, a change in its quantity is measurable. One of the more striking features of the Russian situation in the several years since the end of the Soviet period is that relatively little work is being done on the history of American philosophy. Between 1992 and late 1995, for example, *Voprosy Filosofii* published only an article on Santayana (Shokin 1992), a piece by Yulina on feminism (Yulina 1994), and an article on Rawls (Alekseeva 1994). The emphasis seems to have shifted to the translation of American philosophers into Russian. The same years have seen the publication of excerpts of works by Santayana, John Rawls, John Lachs, and Richard Rorty. In addition, *Voprosy Filosofii* has begun a section it calls "Panorama," under the joint editorship of N. E. Pokrovsky and John Lachs, the latter of Vanderbilt University. The purpose of the Panorama section is to publish Russian translations of articles by American specialists in aspects of the history of American philosophy. The first piece, by James Campbell on "Freedom and Community," appeared in 1992, and since then articles have appeared by Beth J. Singer, Sandra Rosenthal, Mitchel Aboulafia and Susan Haack. While it is good for these philosophers to receive the exposure of publishing in Russia, and while it is good for Russians to have such material available to them, one wonders if translations like these are replacing the study of the history of American thought. It does appear that the Russian philosophical audience may today be more interested in what American philosophers are currently saying than in our past. These two interests are of course not mutually exclusive, and one hopes that for the sake of interested Russian philosophers as well as for the health of the study of the history of American philosophy in general, a balance may be struck.

The future of Russian philosophy and Russian studies of American philosophy is open, as is the future social and political direction of that and the other countries once constituting the USSR. Whether Russian philosophers will retain the lively interest in American philosophy that they have had in the past is itself an open question. An unfortunate possibility presents itself here, that with the changed relation between Russia and the

United States, America in general will be of less interest to Russians than in the past and that, consequently, American philosophy will no longer command the attention it once did. This may already be happening and may help to explain the decrease in published work on American philosophy the past few years. How the future looks in this regard will be shaped in large measure by its own past, and that past is represented by the studies that we have examined here.

NOTES

Introduction

1. Richard T. DeGeorge, Introduction to Dahm, Blakeley and Kline 1988, p. 2, and Lewis S. Feuer 1964.

Preamble to Part I. Early American Philosophy

1. See Flower and Murphy 1977, Vol. I, p. xiii.
2. The philosophic background and commitments of the Founders are discussed in Wills 1979 and 1982, and White 1987.

Chapter 1. The Colonial Period

1. Karimsky's reference is to Schneider 1963, 9.
2. Pokrovsky's reference is to Schneider 1963, 4.

Chapter 2. The American Enlightenment

1. Stephen Toulmin argues for the influence of the social and political upheaval of the early seventeenth century on Descartes's philosophic development in *Cosmopolis, The Hidden Agenda of Modernity.*
2. See, for example, Richard Rorty, *The Consequences of Pragmatism,* and Cornel West, *The American Evasion of Philosophy.*
3. Jefferson's letter to Adams in Peterson 1975, 569–574.
4. Ibid., 540–544.
5. There is a fascinating discussion of religion and the state during the late eighteenth and early nineteenth centuries in John T. Noonan Jr., "'Quota of Imps.'"
6. Fairfield 1961, 17–18.
7. Madison 1976, 196.
8. Peterson 1975, 396–397.
9. Madison 1976, 196.
10. The reference is to Charles Beard's *An Economic Interpretation of the Constitution of the United States.*

11. The argument that follows is developed more fully in J. Ryder, "Private Property and the U.S. Constitution."

12. Fairfield 1961, 18.

13. Madison 1976, 194.

14. Ibid., 194.

15. Fairfield 1961, 23.

16. Ibid., 19.

Chapter 3. Transcendentalism

1. "Self-Reliance," in Emerson 1981, 145.

2. "Civil Disobedience," in Thoreau 1966, 11.

3. Batalov cites Parrington 1954, 2:384, who quotes Emerson from the *Journals*, 10 vols. (Boston, 1909–1914), 4:95.

4. Emerson, *Journals*, 3:369.

5. "Civil Disobedience," in Thoreau 1966, 1.

6. The importance of Emerson for subsequent American philosophy is becoming more apparent. See especially Cornel West, *The American Evasion of Philosophy*, ,and Russell B. Goodman, *American Philosophy and the Romantic Tradition.*

7. *Nature*, in Emerson, 1981, 18.

8. "The Poet," in Emerson, 1981, 243–244.

9. "The Transcendentalist," in Emerson, 1981, 99–101.

10. Ibid., 103.

11. *Walden*, in Bode 1975, 270.

12. Ibid., 571–572.

13. "Slavery in Massachusetts," in Thoreau 1966, 40.

14. Pokrovsky's reference is to Robert Dickens, *Thoreau: The Complete Individualist.*

15. "Life Without Principle," in Bode 1975, 638–639.

16. Ibid., 632.

17. "Civil Disobedience," 1.

18. "A Plea for Captain John Brown," in Thoreau 1966, 45.

19. Ibid., 61.

Preamble to Part II. American Philosophy in the Golden Age

1. This is the Russian translation of Dewey's *Democracy and Education.*

2. Bogomolov's quotation from McCosh is drawn from Schneider 1963, 219.

3. Exceptions to this generalization include Lektorsky 1984,

Dubrovsky 1983, and more than a few others. To give just one example, in an endnote to chapter 5 of his book on Peirce, Melvil considers the difficulties in the concept of "reality." "It should be noted that it is not at all easy to give a full definition of 'reality.' 'Reality' is one of those terms burdened by multiple layers of meaning." Melvil is concerned to avoid too simplistic a conception of reality, such as one which identifies it with matter, or even one which, as he notes is all too common, defines reality simply by contrast with fabrications or fictions. Thus he asks, "for example, whether the heroes of Shakespeare's plays are real?" Some of them are real, he answers, in the sense that they had existed as historical figures—Julius Ceasar, Brutus, Richard III—while others are fabrications. "But as human types, as characters, Shylock and Othello are no less real than Anthony and Cleopatra." They are real in the sense that "we at this point cannot change their character. . . . In this sense the heroes of Shakespeare's plays are as fully real as a Michelangelo sculpture, a Raphael painting, or the music of Beethoven." Melvil goes on to suggest other distinctions, but he makes the point that for materialist philosophy the "real" is to be understood as that, whether fiction or not and whether material or not, which has traits independently of what individuals choose to think of it (Melvil 1968, 331–332 n. 46).

4. One interesting possibility for reconciling aspects of modernist and post-modernist epistemology is with the concept of "foundherentism" in Susan Haack 1982–1983, 1989, and 1995a. Another possibility is represented by Justus Buchler's ordinal metaphysics. See in particular Buchler 1990 and 1976. I have worked through some of the relevant issues, particularly in Ryder 1991b and 1993.

Chapter 4. Pragmatism

1. For an account of Dunham's experiences see Fred Zimring. Sidney Hook's argument first appeared in *The New York Times Magazine*, February 27, 1949, and is reprinted in John C. Wahlke, ed., 1952.

2. The study of Pragmatism by an American Marxist most influential on Soviet scholars was Harry Wells, *Pragmatism: The Philosophy of American Imperialism*.

3. Dewey asserts the existence of an independent reality in *Experience and Nature*: "That there is existence antecedent to search and discovery is of course admitted" (Dewey 1925, 124). James grants the point, among other places, in responses to possible objections to his conception of truth in chapter 15 of *The Meaning of Truth* (James 1970, 287–298).

4. I have in some cases included the references to specific passages in Peirce that are cited in the Soviet originals. In all cases the references are to

the eight-volume *Collected Papers*, and they follow the standard form of citing first the volume number followed by the paragraph number.

5. Throughout his book Melvil makes use of the full range of the studies of Peirce that had appeared by the mid-1960s. On the specific question of the contradictory nature of Peirce's ideas he refers to Wiener 1949, Nagel 1954, Murphy 1961, Goudge 1950, Gallie 1952, Feibleman 1960, Buchler 1939, and Thompson 1953.

6. Melvil had sketched the argument for this interpretation in an English language article two years earlier. See Melvil 1966. See also a response in P. Wiener 1967.

7. Buchler 1939, 94, n. 3.

8. I have elsewhere used the expression "constitutive relations" to describe Dewey's view of the relations among constituents of a situation. See Ryder 1988.

9. Dewey's relation to philosophic materialism is somewhat ambiguous. In "Antinaturalism in Extremis" he rejects both materialism and supernaturalist idealism by rejecting the philosophic significance of the terms *matter* and *spirit* (Dewey 1943, 48). A year later, in 1945, Dewey coauthored an article with Hook and E. Nagel that responds to the "charge" that naturalists are materialists. In this piece, titled "Are Naturalists Materialists?" the authors explicitly reject traditional mechanical and reductive materialism, though in turn they endorse a version of materialism that has a good deal in common with the Marxist tradition. See Dewey et. al. 1945, and also Ryder 1988, 238.

10. Dewey considers this example in *Experience and Nature*, 124–125.

11. Ibid., 233.

12. Ibid., 240.

13. Ibid., 249.

14. It should be mentioned that in 1990 Khanin left the Soviet Union and soon after joined the faculty of Colgate University in Hamilton, New York.

15. For a variety of recent discussions by Americans of the relation between Dewey and Marx, see the essays in Gavin, ed., 1988. In his remark about the transition from "practice" to "praxis" Melvil refers to Bernstein's *Praxis and Action*.

16. Dewey's clearest consideration of this issue is the essay "The Construction of Good" in *The Quest for Certainty*.

17. There are several places in which Dewey develops this view. Among the best are *Reconstruction in Philosophy* and several chapters in *Democracy and Education*.

18. For Dewey's accounts of the power of socially accepted ideological conceptions on our perception of and ways of responding to social problems, see *Liberalism and Social Action* and *Freedom and Culture*.

19. Two valuable recent discussions of Dewey's approach to Marx are William L. McBride, "Science, Psychology, and Human Values in the Context of Dewey's Critique of Marx," and James Campbell, "Dewey's Understanding of Marx and Marxism."

20. A radical, in fact anarchist, reading of Dewey appears in Peter T. Manicas, "John Dewey, Anarchism, and the Political State," his "Philosophy and Politics: An Historical Approach to Marx and Dewey," and in Arthur Lothstein, "From Privacy to Praxis: The Case for John Dewey as a Radical American Philosopher."

21. The reader will note that I have left out of this brief account of Dewey's ethics any mention of Trotsky. There are two reasons for this. First, the debate between Trotsky and Dewey on questions of ethics is already well known, and the relevant literature has long been available in English in Leon Trotsky, *Their Morals and Ours*. Second, by the time Trotsky and Dewey were engaged in their debate Trotsky had already been exiled and intellectually ostracized, so that his views did not represent directions in which mainstream Soviet thinking would travel.

22. Bogomolov's analysis of Hook appeals to *The Metaphysics of Pragmatism*, *The Quest for Being* and his several works on Marx and Marxism. With respect to C. I. Lewis, he works with *Analysis of Knowledge and Valuation*, *Mind and the World Order* and *Our Social Inheritance*.

23. Melvil discusses Rorty's *Philosophy and the Mirror of Nature* and his *Consequences of Pragmatism*.

Chapter 5. Idealism, Realism, and Naturalism

1. These were the authors of "The Program and First Platform of Six Realists," the initial statement of the neorealist school. It originally appears in *The Journal of Philosophy* in 1910. This and several other central works of American realism are reprinted in Herbert Schneider 1964.

2. The authors of *Essays in Critical Realism* were Durant Drake, A. O. Lovejoy, J. B. Pratt, A. K. Rogers, George Santayana, Roy W. Sellars and C. A. Strong.

3. *Scepticism and Animal Faith*, vii.

4. Much the same interpretation of Royce is defended by Bruce Kuklick in his *Josiah Royce, An Intellectual Biography*.

5. Royce's argument from *The Religious Aspect of Philosophy* is reprinted in McDermott 1969, 1:321–353.

6. See McDermott 1969, 1:491–542.

7. Whitehead's method of extensive abstraction has a prominent role in *The Concept of Nature*. However the illustration of its meaning that Bogomolov cites is from the earlier *An Enquiry Concerning the Principles*

of Natural Knowledge. Victor Lowe suggests that the conceptual origins of the method can be found as early as Whitehead's paper "On Mathematical Concepts of the Material World." See Lowe 1941.

8. *Adventures of Ideas*, 236.

9. *Process and Reality*, 166.

10. Ibid., 340.

11. *Scepticism and Animal Faith*, vi. Emphasis in original.

12. Santayana develops the concept of "normal madness" in *Dialogues in Limbo*.

13. Bogomolov's reference is to Strong's contribution to *Essays in Critical Realism*, "On the Nature of the Datum."

14. Santayana's rejection of mind, or rather "discourse," as a mirror, and consequently of knowledge as reflection, is in *Scepticism and Animal Faith*, chapter 18, 179.

15. Yulina is referring here to Woodbridge's *The Realm of Mind*.

16. See especially Sellars's essay "Why Naturalism and not Materialism?"

17. Bogomolov quotes from Sellars's article "Verification of Categories: Existence and Substance."

18. See Sellars's "Reflections on Dialectical Materialism."

19. Karimsky refers here to Lamprecht's *Empiricism and Natural Knowledge*, Lamont's *The Philosophy of Humanism* and Sellars's "Panpsychism or Evolutionary Naturalism."

20. Karimsky and Bogomolov are working primarily with Nagel's "Logic without Ontology," *Sovereign Reason, Logic without Metaphysics* and *The Structure of Science*.

21. See Randall's *Nature and Historical Experience*, 131, and Buchler's *Metaphysics of Natural Complexes*, 30–51.

22. In her account of Randall's conception of metaphysics, Yulina draws from his "Metaphysics: Its Function, Consequence and Criteria," "Metaphysics and Language" and *The Role of Knowledge in Western Religion*.

23. The significant works on the category of substance are "Substance as Process," *Nature and Historical Experience* and *Aristotle*.

24. Bogomolov is referring to Krikorian's "A Naturalistic View of Mind."

25. Karimsky refers to Edel's *Ethical Judgment, Method in Ethical Theory*, and, with M. Edel, *Anthropology and Ethics*.

26. Bogomolov quotes from an article, edited by Sidney Hook, titled "American Philosophy Today," which appeared in Russian in the U.S. Government-sponsored journal *Amerika*. In it several prominent American philosophers offered short statements of their general views.

27. Karimsky cites from Lamont's *Freedom of Choice Affirmed*.

28. See in particular Buchler's "On the Concept of the 'World'" and "Probing the Idea of Nature."

29. One attempt to address this issue is my "Ordinality and Materialism."

30. Karimsky mentioned explicitly Quine, Searle, and the collection *Naturalism and Rationality*, edited by Newton Garver and Peter Hare.

REFERENCES

I. Russian Sources

This list of Russian language works includes more than those explicitly referred to in the text. This portion of the bibliography is a compilation, as complete as I could make it, of Soviet and Russian studies of the history of American philosophy.

Alaev, L. B., M. L. Gasparov, A. B. Kudelin, and E. M. Meletinsky, eds. 1988. *Vostok-Zapad* (East-West). Moskva: Izdatel'stvo "Nauka."

Alekseeva, T. A. 1994. "Dzhon Rouls i ego Teoriya Spravedlivostu" (John Rawls and his Theory of Justice). *Voprosy Filosofii* 10: 38–52.

Antonovich, I. I. 1967. *Amerikanskaya Burzhuaznaya Aksiologiya na Sluzhbe Imperializma* (American Bourgeois Axiology in the Service of Imperialism). Minsk: Nauka i Tekhnika.

Aleksandrov, G. F. 1947. "Filosofskie Oryzhenostzy Amerikanskoi Reaktzii" (The Philosophical Henchmen of American Reaction). *Bol'shevik*, no. 11.

Alekseeva, T. I. 1988. "Sovietskie Istoriki ob Ideologicheskikh Problemakh Amerikanskoi Revolyutzii XVIII Veka" (Soviet Historians on the Ideological Problems of the American Revolution of the XVIIIth Century). Kazan. (Candidate dissertation.)*

Asmus, V. F. 1927. "Alogism Uil'yama Dzhemsa" (The Irrationality of William James). *Pod Znamenem Marksizma*, no. 7/8. Reprinted in Asmus 1984, 262–300.

———. 1984. *Istoriko-Filosofskie Etyudi* (Studies in the History of Philosophy). Moskva: "Mysl.'"

Bandura, O. A. 1974. "Instrumentalizm i Operatzionalizm i Problema Nauchnogo Ponyatiya" (Instrumentalism, Operationalism and the Problem of the Scientific Concept). Kiev. (Candidate dissertation.)

*In the Soviet and Russian academic system the Candidate degree is the functional equivalent of our Ph.D., and it requires a scholarly work similar to our Ph.D. dissertation. A scholar may earn a Doctoral degree, but it is possible only well into his or her career, and it requires another dissertation. As a rule Doctoral dissertations are published in book form, and Candidate dissertations may also be published. All Candidate dissertations, however, are accompanied by a twenty to thirty page abstract, called an "Avtoreferat." References in the text to Candidate dissertations are all to their corresponding Avtoreferati.

Baskin, M. P. 1955. *Filosofiya Amerikanskogo Prosveshcheniya* (The Philosophy of the American Enlightenment). Moskva: Izdatel'stvo Moskovskogo Universiteta.

Baskin, M. P., and M. Sh. Bakhitov, eds. 1957. *Sovremenny Subektivny Idealizm* (Contemporary Subjective Idealism). Moskva: Gosudarstvennoe Izdatel'stvo Politicheskoi Literatury.

Batalov, E. Ya. 1985. *The American Utopia*. Moscow: Progress Publishers.

Batalov, E. Ya., and O. Alyakrinsky. 1983. "V Poiskakh Utrachennoi Utopii: Sotzial'naya Utopiya i Utopicheskoe Soznanie v SShA" (In Search of the Lost Utopia: The Social Utopia and Utopian Consciousness in the U.S.A.). *Novy Mir*, no. 8: 258–262.

Blinov, A. L., and V. V. Petrov. 1988. "Davidson D.: Sovremennaya Analiticheskaya Filosofiya v SShA" (D. Davidson: Contemporary Analytic Philosophy in the U.S.A.). *Voprosy Filosofii*, no. 3: 138–140.

Blonsky, P. P. 1918, 1922. *Sovremennaya Filosofiya* (Contemporary Philosophy). 2 Vols. Moskva: Russky Knizhnik.

Bogomolov, A. S. 1962a. *Filosofiya Anglo-Amerikanskogo Neorealizma* (The Philosophy of Anglo-American Neorealism). Moskva.

———. 1962b. *Ideya Razvitiya v Burzhuaznoi Filosofii XIX i XX vekov* (The Idea of Development in Nineteenth and Twentieth Century Bourgeois Philosophy) Moskva.

———. 1963. "Neorealizm i Spekulyativnaya Filosofiya (A. N. Uaitkhed)" (Neorealism and Speculative Philosophy (A. N. Whitehead). In G. A. Kursanov, 252–293.

———. 1964. *Anglo-Amerikanskaya Filosofiya Epokhi Imperializma* (Anglo-American Philosophy in the Epoch of Imperialism). Moskva.

———. 1974. *Burzhuaznaya Filosofiya SShA XX Veka* (Twentieth Century Bourgeois Philosophy in the U.S.A.). Moskva: Izdatel'stvo "Mysl.'"

———. 1977. *Sovremennaya Burzhuaznaya Filosofiya i Religiya*, (Contemporary Bourgeois Philosophy and Religion). Moskva.

Borob'ev, N. V. 1954. "Kritika Filosofskikh Osnovanny Logicheskikh Teory Amerikanskikh Pragmatistov i Neopozitivistov" (A Critique of the Philosophical Foundations of the Logical Theory of American Pragmatists and Neopositivists). *Vestnik Moskovskogo Universiteta*, no. 4: 35–45.

Brodov, V. V. 1949. "Instrumentalizm Dzhona D'yui na Sluzhbe Amerikanskoi Reaktzii" (John Dewey's Instrumentalism in the Service of American Reaction). Moskva. (Candidate dissertation.)

Brutyan, G. A. 1985. "Filosofiya i Metafilosofiya" (Philosophy and Metaphilosophy). *Voprosy Filosofii*, no. 9: 85–90.

Butenko, A. P. 1989. "Vinoven li Karl Marks v 'Kazarmennom Sotsializme'"? (Is Karl Marx to Blame for "Barracks Socialism"?). *Filosofskie Nauki*, no. 4. English translation in *Soviet Studies in Philosophy* 29, no. 2 (Fall 1990): 32–47.

Bykhovsky, B. E. 1959. "Filosofiya Neopragmatizma" (The Philosophy of Neopragmatism). In *Znanie*.

———. ed. 1968. *Amerikanskie Prosvetiteli*, T.2 (*Figures of the American Enlightenment*, 2 Vols.). Moskva.

Degesis, L. A. 1983. "Gnoseologicheskie Problemy v Filosofii Dzhordzha Santayany" (Epistemological Problems in the Philosophy of George Santayana). Vilnius. (Candidate dissertation.)

Dobren'kov, V. I. 1980. *Sovremenny Protestantsky Modernizm v SShA* (Contemporary Protestant Modernism in the U.S.A.). Moskva.

Dubrovsky, D. I. 1982. "Kontzeptziya 'Emerdzhentistskogo Materializma'" (The Concept of "Emergent Materialism). *Voprosy Filosofii*, no. 2: 133–136.

———. 1983. *Problema Idealnogo* (The Problem of the Ideal). Moskva: Izdat'stvo "Mysl.'" English translation 1989, Moscow: Progress Publishers.

———. 1987. "Ot 'Nauchnogo Materializma' k 'Emerdzhentistskomu Materializmu'" (From "Scientific Materialism" to "Emergent Materialism). *Voprosy Filosofii*, no. 4: 130–141. English translation in *Soviet Studies in Philosophy* 27, no. 1 (1988): 51–76.

Dubrovsky, D. I., and I. S. Narsky. 1983. "Po Povodu Stat'i Dzh. Margolisa 'Trudnosti Teorii Gomunkulusa'" (Concerning J. Margolis' Article "Problems with the Homunculus Theory). *Filosofskie Nauki*, no. 6: 105–108.

Endovitzky, V. D. 1958. *Kritika Filosofii Amerikanskogo Kriticheskogo Realizma: Filosofiya Kul'tury Dzhordzha Santayany* (A Critique of the Philosophy of American Critical Realism: George Santayana's Philosophy of Culture). Moskva.

Endovitzky, V. D., and V. F. Korovin. 1984. "Evolyutziya Predstavlenii Dzh. Santayany o Prekrasnom" ("The Evolution of G. Santayana's Conception of Beauty). *Vestnik Moskovskogo Universiteta*, no. 3: 47–55.

Estetika Amerikanskogo Romantizma. 1977. (The Aesthetics of American Romanticism). Moskva.

Fedorov, V. M. 1977. "Kritika Naturalisticheskogo Pragmatizma Sidneya Khuka" (A Critique of the Naturalistic Pragmatism of Sidney Hook). Moskva. (Candidate dissertation.)

———. 1985. "Naturalistichesky Pragmatizm i Religiya" (Naturalistic Pragmatism and Religion). In *Aktual'nye Problemy Ateizma i Kritiki Religii*, 43–50. Moskva.

Filatova, I. P. 1984. "Instrumentalizm: Kritichesky Analiz Kontzeptzii Demokratii Dzhona D'yui" (Instrumentalism: A Critical Analysis of John Dewey's Conception of Democracy). In *Teoreticheskie Problemy Razvitogo Sotzializma*, sektziya 4, pp. 75–77. Moskva

———. 1985. "Sotzial'no—Politicheskaya Filosofiya Dzhona D'yui" (John Dewey's Social and Political Philosophy). Moskva. (Candidate dissertation.)

Gaidadymov, E. B. 1986. "K Voprosu o Genezise Burzhuaznoi Kontzeptzii 'Prav

Cheloveka' v Sotzial'noi Filosofiya SShA" (On the Question of the Genesis of the Bourgeois Conception of "Human Rights" in the Social Philosophy of the U.S.A.). *Vestnik Belorusskogo Gosudarstvennogo Universiteta*, seriya 3. Minsk.

Geevsky, I. A., A. A. Mishin, V. M. Nikolaichik, V. A. Vlaskhin, S. A. Chervonnaya, E. N. Ershova, and E. V. Zhukova. 1987. *SShA: Konstitutziya i Prava Grazhdan* (U.S.A.—The Constitution and the Rights of Citizens). Moskva: Izdatel'stvo "Mysl.'"

Gogoberishvili, V. G. 1966. *Filosofiya Pragmatizma* (The Philosophy of Pragmatism) (in Georgian). Tbilisi.

Gol'dberg, N. M. 1965. *Svobodomyslie i Ateizm v SShA (XVIII–XIX VV.)* (Freethinking and Atheism in the U.S.A. [17th–18th Centuries]. Moskva.

Grigoryan, A. G. 1967. *Ekzistentzializm v SShA* (Existentialism in the U.S.A.). Moskva.

Grigoryan, B. T. ed. 1986. *Burzhuaznaya Filosofskaya Antropologia XX veka* (20th Century Bourgeois Philosophical Anthropology). Moskva: "Nauka."

Gryaznov, A. F. 1988. "Posleslovie k Stat'e Dzheimsa Maklellana" (Afterword to the Article by James McClellan). *Filosofskie Nauki*, no. 11: 80–83.

Gureeva, A. V. 1972. "Kritichesky Analiz Pragmatistskoi Estetiki D. D'yui" (A Critical Analysis of John Dewey's Pragmatist Aesthetics). Moskva. (Candidate dissertation.)

———. 1983. *Kritichesky Analiz Pragmatistskoi Estetiki D. D'yui* (A Critical Analysis of J. Dewey's Pragmatist Aesthetics). Moskva: Izdatel'stvo Moskovskogo Universiteta.

Kandareli, T. R. 1983. "Kritika Irratzionalisticheskoi Estetiki Dzhordzha Santayany" (A Critique of the Irrationalist Aesthetics of George Santayana). Tbilisi. (Candidate dissertation.)

Karimsky, A. M. 1972. *Filosofiya Amerikanskogo Naturalizma* (The Philosophy of American Naturalism). Moskva: Izdatel'stvo Moskovskogo Universiteta.

———. 1973. "Sotsial'naya Filosofiya Amerikanskogo Puritanizma" (The Social Philosophy of American Puritanism). *Voprosy Nauchnogo Ateizma*, no. 14.

———. 1976a. "Pedagogicheskie Idei Amerikanskoi Revolyutzii" (Pedagogical Ideas of the American Revolution). *Sovetskaya Pedagogika*, no. 7: 109–119.

———. 1976b. "Problema Cheloveka v 'Deklaratzii Nezavisimosti' i Sovremennaya Ideologicheskaya Bor'ba v SShA" (The Problem of Man in the 'Declaration of Independence' and the Contemporary Ideological Struggle in the U.S.A.). *Vestnik Moskovskogo Universiteta*, no. 4: 53–62.

———. 1976c. *Revolyutziya 1776 Goda i Stanovlenie Amerikanskoi Filosofii* (The Revolution of 1776 and the Formation of American Philosophy). Moskva: Izdatel'stvo "Mysl.'"

———. 1978. *Problema Gumanizma v Sovremennoi Amerikanskoi Filosofii* (The Problem of Humanism in Contemporary American Philosophy). Moskva: Izdatel'stvo Moskovskogo Universiteta.

———. 1981. Problema Gumanizma v Sovremennoi Burzhuaznoi Filosofii SShA (The Problem of Humanism in Contemporary Bourgeois Philosophy in the U.S.A.). Moskva. (Doctoral dissertation.)

———. 1986. "Amerikanskaya Romanticheskaya Utopiya" (The American Romantic Utopia). *Problemy Amerikanistiki*, vol. 4. Moskva: Izdatyel'stvo Moskovskogo Universiteta, 276–294.

———. 1988a. "Konstitutziya SShA i Problema Prav Cheloveka" (The U.S. Constitution and the Problem of Human Rights). In A. A. Mishin, and E. F. Yaz'kov, 235–264.

———. 1988b. "Problema Chelovkeka i Obshchestva v Filosofii Amerikanskogo Prosveshcheniya" (The Problem of Man and Society in the Philosophy of the American Enlightenment). In A. A. Mishin, and E. F. Yaz'kov, 26–44.

———. 1990. "Filosofiya Amerikanskogo Naturalizma: Vzglyad Izvne" (The Philosophy of American Naturalism—A View from Abroad). Society for the Advancement of American Philosophy, Annual Conference, State University of New York at Buffalo, March 1990.

———. 1992. "American Naturalism for a Non-American Perspective," *Transactions of the Charles S. Peirce Society* 28, no. 4: 645–665

Kasavin, I. T. 1987. *Teoriya Poznaniya v Plenu Anarkhii* (The Theory of Knowledge as the Captive of Anarchy). Moskva: Izdatel'stvo Politicheskoi Literatury.

Khanin, D. M. 1985. "Sootnoshenie Emotzional'nogo i Ratzional'nogo v Khudozhestvennom Vospriyatii" (The Relation of the Emotional and the Rational in Artistic Perception). In M. G. Ovsyannikov, and D. M. Khanin, 5–37.

Khmel', T. A. 1982. "Metodologicheskaya Nesostoyatel'nost' Sovremennoi Amerikanskoi Burzhuaznoi Pedagogiki" (The Methodological Groundlessness of Contemporary American Bourgeois Pedagogy). *Sbornik Nauch. Trud./Mosk. Ped. In-T Inostr. Yaz.*, no. 184: 3–8.

Klimenkova, T. A. 1988. "Filosofskie Problemy Neofeminizma 70–X Godov" (Philosophical Problems of Neofeminism in the 1970s). *Voprosy Filosofii*, no. 5: 148–157.

Kolesnikov, A. C. 1997. *Filosofia Richarda Rorty i Postmodernizm Konza XX veka* (The Philosophy of Richard Rorty and Postmodernism at the End of the 20th Century). Sankt-Peterburgsky: Gosudarstvennii Universitet.

Kolodii, A. F. 1989. "K Diskussii o Doktrinal'nykh Predposylkakh Deformatsii Sotsializma" (A Contribution to the Discussion of the Doctrinal Preconditions of the Deformation of Socialism). *Filosofskie Nauki*, no. 12: 61–68. English translation in *Soviet Studies in Philosophy* 29, no. 3 (Winter 1990–1991): 69–63.

Kon, I. S. and D. N. Shalin. 1969. "D. G. Mid u Problema Chelovecheskaya Ya" (G. H. Mead and the Problem of the Self). *Voprosy Filosofii*, no. 12: 85–96.

Kopnin, P. V., and V. V. Mshvenieradze. 1966. *Sovremennaya Burzhuaznaya Filosofiya SShA: Kritichesky Ocherk* (Contemporary Bourgeois American Philosophy: A Critical Essay). Kiev.

Kosichev, A. D., V. V. Bogatov, and A. F. Zotov, eds. 1984. *Nekotorye Voprosy Istoriko-Filosofskoi Nauki* (Some Questions in the History of Philosophy). Moskva: Izdatel'stvo Moskovskogo Universiteta.

Koval'chuk, S. N. 1988. "Filosofskaya Problematika v Protestantskom Modernizme SShA" (The Philosophical Problematic in Protestant Modernism in the U.S.A.). Moskva. (Candidate dissertation.)

Kovalev, Yu. V. 1972. *German Melvill i Dvizhenie Amerikanskogo Romantizma* (Herman Melville and the American Romantic Movement). Leningrad.

———. 1982. "Amerikanskii Romantizm: Khronologiya, Tipografiya, Metod" (American Romanticism: Chronology, Typography and Method). In Ya. N. Zasursky, ed., 1982, 27–54.

Krylova, L. V. 1973. "Filosofskaya Sushchnost' Semiotiki, Ch. S. Pirsa" (The Philosophical Essence of C. S. Peirce's Semiotics). Irkutsk. (Candidate dissertation.)

Kursanov, G. A., ed. 1963. *Sovremenny Obektivny Idealizm* (Contemporary Objective Idealism). Moskva: Izdatel'stvo Sotzial'no-Ekonomicheskoi Literatury.

Legostaev, V. M. 1972. "Filosofskaya Interpretatziya Razvitiya Nauki Tomasa Kuna" (Thomas Kuhn's Philosophical Interpretation of the Development of Science). *Voprosy Filosofii*, no. 11.

Lektorsky, V. A. 1971. "Analiticheskaya Filosofiya Segodnya" (Analytic Philosophy Today). *Voprosy Filosofii*, no. 2.

———. 1973. "Filosofiya, Nauka, 'Filosofiya Nauki'" (Philosophy, Science, and the "Philosophy of Science). *Voprosy Filosofii*, no. 4.

———. 1984. *Science. Object. Cognition*, Moscow: Progress Publishers.

Leont'ev, A. N. 1977. *Deyatel'nost'. Soznanie. Lichnost'.* (Activity, Consciousness and Personality). Moskva.

Lominadze, S. G. 1987. "Progressivnye Mysliteli SShA XX v. Protiv Religii" (Progressive 20th Century American Thinkers Contra Religion). *Filosofiya i Mirovozzrenie*, no. 2: 171–175.

Lukanov, D. M. 1968. *Gnoseologiya Amerikanskogo Realizma* (The Epistemology of American Realism). Moskva.

———. 1981. "Problema Neposredstvennogo i Oposredovannogo Poznaniya v Gnoseologii Amerikanskogo 'Realizma'" (The Problem of Immediate and Mediate Knowledge in the Epistemology of American "Realism). In *Aktual. Probl. Kritiki Sovrem. Burzhuaz. Filosofii i Sotziol*, 4:16–32. Leningrad.

———. 1982. "Ekzistentzial'naya Filosofiya v SShA i Dzhordzh Santayana" (Existentialist Philosophy in the U.S.A. and George Santayana). Gorky. (Doctoral dissertation.)

———. 1988. "Traditziya Ekzistentzial'noi Filosofii v SShA" (The Tradition of Existentialist Philosophy in the U.S.A.). In *Spetzifika Filosofskogo Znaniya i Problema Cheloveka v Istorii Filosofii*, 70–77. Moskva.

Mel'vil', Yu. K. 1954. *Amerikansky Personalizm—Filosofiya Imperialisticheskoi Reaktzii* (American Personalism—A Philosophy of Imperialist Reaction). Moskva.

———. 1957a. *Amerikansky Pragmatizm* (American Pragmatism). Moskva: Izdatel'stvo Moskovskogo Universiteta.

———. 1957b. "Pragmatizm—Filosofiya Subektivnogo Idealizma" (Pragmatism—A Philosophy of Subjective Idealism). In M. P. Baskin, and M. Sh. Bakhitov, 38–139.

———. 1966. "The Conflict of Science and Religion on Charles Peirce's Philosophy," *Transactions of the Charles S. Pierce Society*, 2:33–50.

———. 1968. *Charlz Pirs i Pragmatizm* (Charles Peirce and Pragmatism). Moskva: Izdatel'stvo Moskovskogo Universiteta.

———. 1974. "Pragmatizm" (Pragmatism). In L. N. Mitrokhin, T. I. Oizerman, and L. N. Shershenko, 2–106.

———. 1983. *Puti Burzhuaznoi Filosofii XX Veka* (The Course of Bourgeois Philosophy in the 20th Century). Moskva: "Mysl.'"

———. 1986. "Pragmaticheskaya Filosofiya Cheloveka" (The Pragmatist Philosophy of Human Being). In B. T. Grigoryan 1986, 104–119.

———. 1989. "Novie Veyaniya v Metafizike SshA" (New Tendencies in American Metaphysics). *Voprosy Filosofii*, no. 6: 138–147.

———. 1992a. "Filosofia Uil'yama Dzhemsa" (The Philosophy of William James). Unpublished.

———. 1992b. "Filosofia Uil'yama Dzhemsa, 1842–1910" ("The Philosophy of William James, 1842–1910). Unpublished.

Minitaite, G. V. 1977. "Noveishie Tendentzii v Amerikanskoi Moral'noi Filosofii" (Current Tendencies in American Moral Philosophy). Moskva. (Candidate dissertation.)

Mirskaya, L. A. 1982. "Sootnoshenie Individual'nogo i Sotzial'nogo v Amerikanskoi Ekzistentzial'noi Fenomenologii" (The Relation of the Individual and the Social in American Existentialist Phenomenology). *Vestnik Moskovskogo Universiteta*, seriya 7, no. 1: 43–50.

———. 1987. "Amerikanskaya Ekzistentzial'naya Fenomenologiya" (American Existentialist Phenomenology). Kishinev. (Candidate dissertation.)

Mishin, A. A. 1988a. "Konstitutziya SShA—Pervaya Pisanaya Burzhuaznaya Konstitutziya" (The U.S. Constitution—The First Written Bourgeois Constitution). In A. A. Mishin, and E. F. Yaz'kov, 67–85.

———. 1988b. "Thoughts on the U.S. Consitution." State University of New York—Moscow State University Conference on the U.S. Constitution, State University of New York College at Cortland, January 1988.

Mishin, A. A., and E. F. Yaz'kov, eds. 1988. *Konstitutzia SShA: Istoriya i Sovremennost'* (The U.S. Constitution in History and the Present). Moskva: "Yuridicheskaya Literatura."

Mitrokhin, L. N. 1960. *Kritery Istiny v Filosofii Pragmatizma* (The Criteria of Truth in the Philosophy of Pragmatism). Moskva.

Mitrokhin, L. N., T. I. Oizerman, and L. N. Shershenko, eds. 1974. *Burzhuaznaya Filosofiya XX Veka* (20th Century Bourgeois Philosophy). Moskva: Izdatel'stvo Politicheskoi Literatury.

Morozova, T. L. 1982a. "Literatura SShA XIX veka: Osnovnye Tendentzii Razvitiya" (Basic Tendencies in the Development of 19th Century American Literature). In Ya. N. Zasursky, ed., 1982, 10–26.

———. 1982b. "Uchenie Emersona o 'Doverii k Sebe' i Problema Individualizma v Amerikanskoi Obshchestvennoi i Dukhovnoi Zhizni" (Emerson's Doctrine of 'Self Reliance' and the Problem of Individualism in American Social and Spiritual Life). In Zasurky, ed., 1982, 101–159.

———. 1985. "O Natzional'nom Svoeobrazii Amerikanskogo Prosveshcheniya" (On the National Uniqueness of the American Enlightenment). In Ya. N. Zasursky 1985, 160–185.

Mukovozov, Yu. I. 1977. "Kritika Idealisticheskikh Osnov Protestanskoi Teologii Reingol'da Nibura" (A Critique of the Ideological Foundations of the Protestant Theology of Reinhold Niebuhr). Leningrad. (Candidate dissertation.)

Nadtochaev, A. S. 1983. "Kritichesky Analiz Filosofii K. I. L'yuisa" (A Critical Analysis of the Philosophy of C. I. Lewis). Moskva. (Candidate dissertation.)

Nemirovskaya, E. M. 1973. "Semanticheskaya Kontzeptziya Iskusstva: K. Krit. Analizu Semant. Filosofii Iskusstva S. K. Langer" (The Semantic Conception of Art: Toward a Critical Analysis of S. K. Langer's Semantic Philosophy of Art). Moskva. (Candidate dissertation.)

Nesmelova, O. O. 1981. "Vliyanie Ekzistentzializma na Amerikanskuyu Literaturu" (The Influence of Existentialism on American Literature). In *Razvitie Obshchestvennykh Otnosheny Zrelogo Sotzializma,* 60–64. Kazan.

Nikol'sky, S. A. 1977. "Problema Sootnosheniya Sotzial'nogo i Biologicheskogo v Filosofii Amerikanskogo Naturalizma" (The Problem of the Relation of the Social and the Biological in the Philosophy of American Naturalism). Moskva. (Candidate dissertation.)

Nikonov, V. A. 1988. "The Adoption of the U.S. Constitution as Viewed by Soviet Historians," State University of New York—Moscow State University Conference on the U.S. Constitution, State University of New York College at Cortland, January 1988.

Nosov, D. M. 1983. "Problema Samootchuzhdeniya Cheloveka v Ekzistentzializme U. Barreta" (The Problem of the Self-Alienation of Man in the Existentialism of W. Barret). *Istoriya Filosofii: Problemy, Metody i Ideologii,* 116–138. Moskva.

Oizerman, T. I., and P. S. Trofimov. 1951. *Protiv Filosofstvuyushchikh Oruzhenostzev Amerikano-Angliiskogo Imperializma* (Against the Philosophical Henchmen of American and English Imperialism). Moskva: Izdatel'stvo Akademii Nauk SSSR.

Ovsyannikov, M. F., and D. M. Khanin, eds. 1985. *Dialektika Emotzional'nogo i Ratzional'nogo v Khudozhestvennom Tvorchestve i Vospriyatii* (The Dialectic of the Emotional and the Rational in Artistic Creativity and Perception). Moskva: Akademiya Nauk SSSR.

Panova, E. 1980. "Kuain i Problema Ontologicheskoi Relyativnosti" (Quine and the Problem of Ontological Relativity). *Vestnik Moskovskogo Universiteta*, seriya 7, no. 6: 59–70.

Pavlychko, S. D. 1983. "Nekotorye Problemy Filosofskoi Esseistiki R. U. Emersona" (Some Problems in R. W. Emerson's Philosophical Essays). In *Ideino-Khudozhestvennye Iskaniya Zarubezhnykh Pisatelei Noveishego Vremeni*, 192–207. Kiev.

———. 1984. *Filosofskaya Poeziya Amerikanskogo Romantizma* (The Philosophical Poetry of American Romanticism). Kiev.

Pechatnov, V. O. 1984. *Gamil'ton i Dzhefferson* (Hamilton and Jefferson). Moskva.

Pilipovsky, V. Ya. 1986. "Tekhnokraticheskie Tendentzii v Sovremennoi Burzhuaznoi Pedagogike" (Technocratic Tendencies in Contemporary Bourgeoise Pedagogy). *Sovietskaya Pedagogika*, no. 6: 115–120.

Podgorny, Z. R. 1978. "Naturalisticheskaya Kontzeptziya Tzennostei v Amerikanskoi Burzhuaznoi Filosofii XX Veka" (The Naturalistic Conception of Value in 20th Century American Bourgeois Philosophy). Leningrad. (Candidate dissertation.)

Pokrovsky, N. E. 1977. "Filosofskoe Mirovozzrenie Genri Toro" (The Philosophical World View of Henry Thoreau). Moskva. (Candidate dissertation.)

———. 1983a. "Dzhefferson i Federalisty: Protivoborstvo Filosofskikh Vzglyadov" (Jefferson and the Federalists: A Conflict of Philosophical Views). *Problemy Amerikanistiki*, 2:269–289. Moskva: Izdatel'stvo Moskovskogo Universiteta.

———. 1983b. *Genri Toro* (Henry Thoreau). Moskva: Izdatel'stvo "Mysl.'"

———. 1986. "Amerika Poteryannaya i Obretennaya" (America Lost and Found). Introductory essay to N. E. Pokrovsky and N. Sibiryakov, eds., 3–20.

———. 1988. "Through the Beautiful to the Human," Frontiers in American Philosophy Conference, Texas A&M University, 1988. Forthcoming in *Texas A&M Studies in American Philosophy*, College Station: Texas A&M University Press.

———. 1989a. *Henry Thoreau*. English translation of *Genri Toro* by Sergei Syrovatkin. Moscow: Progress Publishers.

———. 1989b. *Rannyaya Amerikanskaya Filosofiya. Puritanizm* (Early American Philosophy. Puritanism). Moskva: Izdatel'stvo "Vysshaya Shkola."

———. 1995. *Ralf Uoldo Emerson. V Poiskax svoei Vcelennoi* (Ralph Waldo Emerson. In Search of His Universe). Concord Mass: Center for American Studies.

Pokrovsky, N. E., and N. Sibiryakov, eds. 1986. *Ralf Emerson, Genri Toro* (Ralph Emerson and Henry Thoreau). Moskva: Izdatel'stvo "Khudozhestvennaya Literatura."

Porus, V. N. 1977. "'Struktura Nauchnykh Revolyutzy' i Dialektika Razvitiya Nauki" (The Structure of Scientific Revolutions and the Dialectic of the Development of Science). *Filosofskie Nauki*, no.2.

Rogulev, Yu. N. 1988. "The 'Nationalization' of Socio-Economic Doctrines in Contemporary Constitutional Law," translated by Leanne G. Wilson, State University of New York—Moscow State University Conference on the U.S. Constitution, State University of New York College at Cortland, January 1988.

Romanova, A. P. 1982. "Kritika Kontzeptzii Religii P. Bergera" (A Critique of P. Berger's Conception of Religion). In *Problemy Nauchnogo Ateizma*, 25–34. Moskva.

———. 1985. "Fenomenologichekoe Napravlenie v Sovremennoi Burzhuaznoi Sotziologii Religii" (The Phenomenological Trend in Contemporary Bourgeois Sociology of Religion). *Voprosy Filosofii*, no. 7: 135–142.

Rutkevich, A. M. 1983. "Ekzistentzial'naya Psikhologiya R. Meya" (The Existentialist Psychology of R. May). *Vestnik Moskovskogo Universiteta*, seriya 7, no. 3: 75–87.

———. 1984. "Ekzistentzial'ny Psikhoanaliz i Religiya: Kritichesky Analiz Logoterapii V. Frankelya" (Existentialist Psychoanalysis and Religion: A Critical Analysis of V. Frankel's Logotherapy). In *Nekotorye Voprosy Istoriko-Filosofskoi Nauki*, 122–132. Moskva.

Sabirov, Kh. F. 1961. "Sotzial'naya Filosofiya Amerikanskikh Prosvetitelei i ego Znachenie v Sovremennoi Ideologicheskoi Bor'be v SShA" (The Social Philosophy of the American Enlightenment and Its Significance in the Contemporary Ideological Struggle in the U.S.A.). Moskva. (Candidate dissertation.)

Sagatovskii, V. N. 1989. "Dialog ili Vzaimnye Obvineniya?" (Dialogue or Mutual Accusation). *Filosofskie Nauki*, no. 12: 57–60. English translation in *Soviet Studies in Philosophy* 29, no. 3 (Winter 1990–1991): 62–68.

Sentebov, L. S. 1956. "Reaktzionnaya Sushchnost' Etiki Amerikanskogo Pragmatizma" (The Reactionary Essence of the Ethics of American Pragmatism). Moskva. (Candidate dissertation.)

Sevost'yanov, G. N., and A. I. Utkin. 1976. *Tomas Dzhefferson* (Thomas Jefferson). Moskva.

Sheguta, M. A. 1983. "Vul'garno-Materialisticheskaya Tendentziya v Kontzeptziyakh Realisticheski-Naturalisticheskoi Orientatzii" (A Vulgar Materialist Tendency in the Conceptions of Realistic Naturalism). In *Voprosy Obshestvennogo Razvitiya v Domarksistskoi i Sovremennoi Burzhuaznoi Filosofiya*, 160–180. Voroshilovgrad.

Shershenko, L. A. 1950. "Bor'ba Progressivnykh i Reaktzionnykh Sil v Sovremennoi Amerikanskoi Filosofii" (The Struggle of Progressive and Reactionary Forces in Contemporary American Philosophy). Moskva. (Candidate dissertation.)

———. 1963. "Amerikansky Personalizm" (American Personalism). In G. A. Kursanov, 350–377.

Shershenko, L. A., and I. S. Vdovina. 1974. "Personalizm" (Personalism). In L. N. Mitrokhin, T. I. Oizerman, and L. N. Shershenko, 259–290.

Shevchenko, V. N. 1989. "Sotsial'naya Filosofia Marksizma: Klassika i Sovremennost" (The Social Philosophy of Marxism: The Founders and the Present Day). *Filosofskie Nauki,* no. 7: 3–16; no. 9: 3–16. English translation in *Soviet Studies in Philosophy* 29, no. 2 (Fall 1990): 49–91.

Shirvindt, M. 1930. "Amerikansky Neorealizm" (American Neorealism). In *Sovremennaya Burzhuaznaya Filosofiya.* Leningrad.

Shklyarik, E. N. 1984. "Problema Obosnovannaya Morali v Filosofii Amerikanskogo Naturalizma" (The Problem of the Basis of Morals in the Philosophy of American Naturalism). Moskva. (Candidate dissertation.)

Shkrobova, E. D. 1984. "Filosofiya Nauki Charlza Pirsa: Kritichesky Analiz" (Charles Peirce's Philosophy of Science: A Critical Analysis). Leningrad. (Candidate dissertation.)

Shlaifer, N. E. 1983. "Problema Cheloveka v Filosofii Amerikanskogo Protestantizma" (The Problem of Man in the Philosophy of American Protestantism). Dnepropetrovsk. (Candidate dissertation.)

Shokin, V. K. 1992. "Dzh. Santayana i Indiiskaya Filosofiya" (G. Santayana and Indian Philosophy). *Voprosy Filosofii,* no. 4: 118–124.

Shorokhov, I. M. 1982. *Personalizm kak Amerikanskaya "Filosofiya XX Veka"* (Personalism as the American "Philosophy of the 20th Century"). Kuibyshev.

Shpotov, B. M. 1982. *Fermerskoe Dvizhenie v SShA* (The Agrarian Movement in the U.S.A.). Moskva: Izdatel'stvo "Nauka."

Shtinov, V. N. 1992. "Filosofiya Richarda Bernstaina kak Al'ternativa Analiticheskoi Filosofii" (The Philosophy of Richard Berstein as an Alternative to analytic Philosophy). *Filosofskie Nauki,* no. 2: 168–173.

Shvartzman, K. A. 1991. "Zapadnaya Etika i Problema Dobrodetelei" (Western Ethics and the Problem of Virtue). *Filosofskie Nauki,* no. 11: 65–79.

Shvyrev, V. S. 1983. "Problema Otnosheniya Nauki i Metafiziki v Sovremennoi Anglo-Amerikanskoi Filosofii Nauki" (The Problem of the Relation of Science and Metaphysics in Contemporary English and American Philosophy of Science) in *Problemy i Protivorechiya Burzhuaznoi Filosofii 60-70-X Godov XX Veka,* 29–59. Moskva.

Sidorov, I. N. 1974. "Absolyutny Idealizm Dzh. Roisa: Kritichesky Analiz" (The Absolute Idealism of Josiah Royce: A Critical Analysis). Leningrad. (Candidate dissertation.)

———. 1989. *Filosofiya Deistviya v SShA: Ot Emersona do D'yui* (The Philosophy of Action in the U.S.A.: From Emerson to Dewey). Leningrad: Izdatel'stvo Leningradskogo Universiteta.

Skrypnik, V. R. 1982. "Transtzendentalizm Ral'fa Uoldo Emersona" (The

Transcendentalism of Ralph Waldo Emerson). Moskva. (Candidate dissertation.)

Sogrin, V. V. 1983. *Osnovateli SShA: Istoricheskie Portrety* (The Founders of the U.S.A.: Historical Portraits). Moskva.

Solov'ev, E. Yu. 1966. *Ekzistentzializm i Nauchnoe Poznanie* (Existentialism and Scientific Knowledge). Moskva.

Sovremennaya Filosofiya i Sotziologiya v Stranakh Zapadnoi Evropy i Ameriki (Contemporary Philosophy and Sociology in the Countries of Western Europe and America). 1964. Moskva: "Nauka."

Stetzenko, E. A. 1985. "Tomas Pein i Problemy Prosveshcheniya" (Thomas Paine and Problems of the Enlightenment). In Ya. N. Zasursky 1985, 232–260.

Subbotina, Z. A. 1984. "Teoreticheskaya Nesostosyatel'nost' 'Novoi' Religii Erikha Fromma" (The Theoretical Groundlessness of Erich Fromm's 'New' Religion). In *Aktual'nye Problemy Nauchno-Ateisticheskogo Vospitaniya Molodezhi*, 47–50. Moskva.

Sukhomlinsky, V. A. 1973. *O Vospitanii* (On Education). Moskva.

Tomashov, V. V. 1987. "Problema Otvetstvennosti v 'Kriticheskom' Ekzistentzializme U. Kaufmanna" (The Problem of Responsibility in W. Kaufmann's 'Critical' Existentialism). In *Teoretiko-Metodologicheskie Problemy Formirovaniya Kommunisticheskogo Mirovozzreniya*, 118–123. Yaroslavl'.

Tregubova, E. A. 1987. "Osobennosti Primeneniya Logiko-Semioticheskikh Metodov v Esteticheskoi Kontzeptzii N. Gudmena" (Peculiarities of the Application of Logical-Semiotic Methods in N. Goodman's Aesthetic Conception). In 118–123.*Filosofsko-Estetichesky Sbornik*, 313–324. Moskva.

Trofimova, Z. P. 1984. *Sovremennaya Ateisticheskaya Mysl' v SShA i Velikobritanii* (Contemporary Atheistic Thought in the U.S.A. and Great Britain). Moskva.

———. 1987. "Problema Gumanizma na Stranitzakh Amerikanskogo Zhurnala 'Religiozny Gumanizm'" (The Problem of Humanism in the Pages of the American Journal *Religious Humanism*). *Voprosy Filosofii*, no. 10: 134–139.

Tsipko, A. 1989. "Istoki Stalinizma" (The Sources of Stalinism), parts 1 and 2. *Naukai Zhizn* (Science and Life), nos. 11–12 (1988). The first essay, from no. 11, 1988, pp. 45–55, has been translated into English—"The Sources of Stalinism," *Soviet Studies in Philosophy* 29, no. 2, (Fall 1990): 6–31.

———. 1991. *Is Stalinism Really Dead?*, New York: HarperCollins.

Tz'rlina, T. V. 1987. "'Tzennostnoe Vospitanie' v Pedagogike SShA: Kritichesky Analiz" ("Values Education" in American Pedagogy: A Critical Analysis). *Sovietskaya Pedagogika*, no. 1: 123–127.

Tzurina, I. V. 1987. "Kritichesky Analiz Ekzistentzializma v SShA" (A Critical Analysis of Existentialism in the U.S.A.). Moskva. (Candidate dissertaton)

Udarand, T. 1987. "Naturalisticheskaya Teoriya Tzennosti R. B. Perri" (R. B. Perry's Naturalistic Theory of Value). In *Velikaya Oktyabr'skaya Sotzialisticheskaya Revolyutziya i Sovremennost'*, 69–71. Tartu.

Ust'yantzev, A. A. 1984a. "Kritika Pragmatistskoi Kontzeptzii Deyatel'nosti" (A Critique of the Pragmatist Conception of Activity). Moskva. (Candidate dissertation.)

———. 1984b. "Kritika 'Pragmatitzisticheskoi' Versii Subekta Deyatel'nogo Otnosheniya" (A Critique of the 'Pragmaticist' Version of the Subject of the Active Relation) in A. D. Kosichev, et al., 69–74.

Veish, Ya. Ya. 1985. "Lingvistiko-Analiticheskaya Religioznaya Apologetika kak Slozhivsheesya Napravlenie v Sovremennoi Filosofii Religii" (The Linguistic, Analytic Religious Apologetic as a Formative Trend in Contemporary Philosophy of Religion). *Voprosy Filosofii*, no. 3: 139–147.

Voronkova, L. P. 1976. "Kritichesky Analiz Teologicheskoi Antropologii R. Nibura" (A Critical Analysis of R. Niebuhr's Theological Anthropology). Moskva. (Candidate dissertation.)

Vygotsky, L. S. 1956. *Izbr. Psikhol. Proizv.* (Selected Psychological Works). Moskva.

Yepoyan, T. 1993. "The Sunstantiation of the Possibility of the Spiritual Life in the *Realm of Spirit*." Unpublished.

Yulina, N. S. 1963. "Filosofiya D. Santayany i Amerikansky 'Realizm'" (The Philosophy of G. Santayana and American "Realism"). In G. A. Kursanov, 294–349.

———. 1974. "Realizm v Amerikanskoi i Evropeiskoi Filosofii XX v." (Realism in 20th Century American and European Philosophy). In L. N. Mitrokhin, T. I. Oizerman, and L. N. Shershenko, 38–71.

———. 1978a. *Problema Metafiziki v Amerikanskoi Filosofii XX Veka* (The Problem of Metaphysics in 20th Century American Philosophy). Moskva: Izdatel'stvo "Nauka."

———. 1978b. "Problema Metafiziki v Burzhuaznoi Filosofii SShA XX Veka" (The Problem of Metaphysics in 20th Century Bourgeois Philosophy in the U.S.A.). Moskva. (Doctoral dissertation.)

———. 1985. "Analiticheskaya Filosofiya v XX Veke" (Analytic Philosophy in the 20th Century). In , *Noveishie Tendentzii v Sovremennoi Analiticheskoi Filosofii*, 5–40. Moskva.

———. 1986a. "Problema Cheloveka v Filosofii Fizikalizma" (The Problem of Human Being in the Philosophy of Physicalism). In B. T. Grigoryan 1986, 133–159.

———. 1986b. *Teologiya i Filosofiya v Religioznoi Mysli SSha XX Veka (Theology and Philosophy in 20th Century Religious Thought in the U.S.A.)*. Moskva: Izdatel'stvo "Nauka."

———. 1988. "Problyemy Zhenshchin: Filosofskie Aspekty" (The Question of Women: Philosophical Aspects). *Voprosy Filosofii*, no. 5: 137–147.

———. 1989. "Zhenshehina i Patriarkhat" (Women and Patriarchy). *Kinostzenarii* 2: 177–180.

———. 1990. "Obrazy Nauki i Naturalizm" (Images of Science and Naturalism). Society for the Advancement of American Philosophy, Annual Conference, State University of New York at Buffalo, March 1990.

———. 1994. "Zhenshchina, Sem'ya i Obshchectva. Diskussii b Feministskoi Mysli SshA" (Woman, Family and Society. Discussions in American Feminist Thought). *Voprosy Filosofii*, no. 9: 132–146.

Zaborova V. V. 1972. "Kritika Kontekstualistskoi Estetiki S. K. Peppera" (A Critique of S.K. Pepper's Contextualist Aesthetics). Sverdlovsk. (Candidate dissertation.)

Zakharova, M. N. 1971. "G. Toro: ot Neprotivleniya k Soprotivleniyu" (H. Thoreau: From Non-Resistance to Opposition). *SShA: Ekonomika, Politika, Ideologiya*, no. 11 .

Zasursky, Ya. N., ed. 1982. *Romanticheskie Traditzii Amerikanskoi Literatury XIX veka i Sovremennost'* (The Romantic Tradition in 19th Century and Contemporary American Literature). Moskva: "Nauka."

———. ed. 1985. *Istoki i Formirovanie Amerikanskoi Natzional'noi Literatury. XVII—XVIII VV.* (The Sources and Formation of American National Literature. XVII–XVIII Centuries). Moskva: Izadatel'stvo "Nauka."

Zykova, E. P. 1988. "Vostok v Tvorchestve Amerikanskikh Transtzendentalistov" (The East in the Works of the American Transcendentalists). In L. B. Alaev, et.al., 86–109.

II. Other Sources

Aboulafia, Mitchell. 1995. "Mid i Mhogogolocie Universal'nosti" (Mead and Many-Voiced Universality). *Voprosy Filosofii*, no. 5: 143–156.

Aptheker, Herbert. 1959. *A History of the American People: The Colonial Era*. New York: International Publishers. Russian translation, *Istoriya Amerikanskogo Naroda. Kolonial'naya Era*. Moskva, 1961.

Barrett, Robert, and Roger Gibson, eds. 1989. *Logic, Words and Objections: Perspectives on the Work of W. V. Quine*. Oxford: Blackwells.

Beard, Charles A. 1935. *An Economic Interpretation of the Constitution of the United States*. New York: Free Press.

Bernstein, Richard. 1971. *Praxis and Action*. Philadelphia: University of Pennsylvania Press.

Bode, Carl, ed. 1975. *The Portable Thoreau*. New York: Penguin.

———. 1981. *The Portable Emerson*. New York: Penguin.

Buchler, Justus. 1939. *Charles Peirce's Empiricism*. New York: Octagon Books.

———. 1976. "Reply to Anton: Against 'Proper' Ontology." *The Southern Journal of Philosophy* 14, no. 1: 85–90. Reprinted in Buchler 1990, 200–206.

———. 1978a. "On the Concept of 'The World.'" *The Review of Metaphysics* 31, no. 4: 555–579. Reprinted in Buchler 1990, 224–259.

———. 1978b. "Probing the Idea of Nature" *Process Studies* 8, no. 3: 157–168. Reprinted in Buchler 1990, 260–281.

———. 1990. *Metaphysics of Natural Complexes.* 2d edition. Edited by Kathleen Wallace, Armen Marsoobian, and Robert S. Corrington. Albany: State University of New York Press.

Campbell, James. 1988. "Dewey's Understanding of Marx and Marxism," in William J. Gavin, ed., 1988, 119–145.

———. 1992. "Svoboda i Soobshchestvo" (Freedom and Community). *Voprosy Filosofii,* no. 12: 112–126.

Cohen, Morris R., and Ernest Nagel. 1934. *An Introduction to Logic and Scientific Method.* New York: Harcourt, Brace.

Dahm, Helmut, Thomas J. Blakeley, and George L. Kline, eds. 1988. *Philosophical Sovietology.* Boston: D. Reidel.

Dewey, John. 1916. *Democracy and Education, The Middle Works* (*MW*), vol. 9. Carbondale: Southern Illinois University Press, 1980.

———. 1920. *Reconstruction in Philosophy, MW,* vol. 12, 1982.

———. 1922. *Human Nature and Conduct, MW,* vol. 14, 1983.

———. 1925. *Experience and Nature, The Later Works* (*LW*), vol. 1, 1981.

———. 1929. *The Quest for Certainty, LW,* vol. 4, 1984.

———. 1935. *Liberalism and Social Action, LW,* vol. 11, 1987.

———. 1938. *Experience and Education, LW,* vol. 13, 1988.

———. 1939. *Freedom and Culture, LW,* vol. 13, 1988, 63–188.

———. 1943. "Anti-Naturalism in Extremis," *LW,* vol. 15, 1989.

Dewey, John, Sidney Hook, and Ernest Nagel. 1945. "Are Naturalists Materialists?" *LW,* vol. 15, 1989.

Dickens, Robert. 1974. *Thoreau: The Complete Individualist.* Buffalo, N.Y.: Prometheus.

Drake, Durant, Arthur O. Lovejoy, J. B. Pratt, A. K. Rogers, George Santayana, Roy W. Sellars, and C. A. Strong. 1920. *Essays in Critical Realism: A Coopertive Study of the Problem of Knowledge.* New York: Macmillan.

Edel, Abraham. 1955. *Ethical Judgment.* Glenco, Ill.: Free Press.

———. 1963. *Method in Ethical Theory.* London: Routledge & Kegan Paul.

Edel, May M., and Abraham Edel. 1959. *Anthropology and Ethics.* Springfield, Ill: Charles C. Thomas.

Emerson, Ralph Waldo. 1981. *Nature,* in Carl Bode, ed., 1981, 7–50.

———. 1981. "The Poet." In Carl Bode, ed., 1981, 241–265.

———. 1981. "Self-Relience." In Carl Bode, ed., 1981, 138-164.

———. 1981. "The Transcendentalist." In Carl Bode, ed., 1981, 92–110.

Fairfield, Roy P., ed. 1961. *The Federalist Papers.* Garden City, N.Y.: Doubleday.

Farber, Marvin. 1959. *Naturalism and Subjectivism.* Springfield, Ill.: Charles C. Thomas.

Feibleman, J. K. 1946. *An Introduction to Peirce's Philosophy.* New York: Harper & Bros.

Feuer, Lewis S. 1964. "Meeting the Philosphers." *Survey* (April 1964): 10–23.

Flower, Elizabeth, and Murray G. Murphey. 1977. *A History of Philosophy in America.* 2 vols. New York: Capricorn.

Gallie, W. B. 1952. *Peirce and Pragmatism.* Hammondsworth, Middlesex: Penguin.

Garver, Newton, and Peter H. Hare, eds. 1986. *Naturalism and Rationality.* Buffalo, N.Y.: Prometheus.

Gavin, William J., ed. 1988. *Context Over Foundation: Dewey and Marx.* Boston: D. Reidel.

Goodman, Russell B. 1990. *American Philosophy and the Romantic Tradition.* New York: Cambridge University Press.

Goudge, Thomas A. 1950 *The Thought of C. S. Peirce.* Toronto: University of Toronto Press.

Gray, Christopher B., ed. 1989. *Philosophical Reflections on the United States Constitution.* Lewiston, N.Y.: Edwin Mellen.

Haack, Susan. 1982–1983. "Theories of Knowledge: An Analytic Framework." *Proceedings of the Aristotelian Society* 83: 143–157.

———. 1989. "Rebuilding the Ship While Sailing on the Water." In R. Barrett and R. Gibson, eds., 1989.

———. 1995a. *Evidence and Inquiry.* Oxford: Blackwells.

———. 1995b. "Ocherednye Pokhorony Epistemologii" (Epistemology's Next Funeral). *Voprosy Filosofii,* no. 7: 106–123.

Hegel, G. W. F. 1987. *Logic.* Translated by William Wallace. New York: Oxford University Press.

Holdt, Jacob. 1985. *American Pictures.* Copenhagen: American Pictures Foundation.

Holt, Edwin B., et. al. 1912. *The New Realism.* New York: Macmillin.

Holt, Edwin B., Walter T. Marvin, W. P. Montague, Ralph Barton Perry, Walter B. Pitkin, E. G. Spaulding. 1910. "The Program and First Platform of Six Realists." *The Journal of Philosophy* 7, no. 15: 393–401.

Hook, Sidney. 1927. *The Metaphysics of Pragmatism.* Chicago: Open Court.

———. 1933. *Towards the Understanding of Karl Marx.* New York: John Day.

———. 1934. *The Meaning of Marx: A Symposium.* New York: Farrar & Rinehart.

———. 1936. *From Hegel to Marx.* New York: Reynal & Hitchcock & V. Gollancz.

———. 1949. "Academic Freedom and Communism." *New York Times Magazine,* February 29. Reprinted in John C. Wahlke, ed., 1952, 84–89.

———. 1961. *The Quest for Being.* New York: St. Martin's.

———. 1962. "Amerikanskaya Filosofiya Segodnya" (American Philosophy Today). *Amerika,* no. 68.

James, William. 1956. *The Will to Believe.* New York: Dover.

———. 1970. *The Meaning of Truth.* Ann Arbor: University of Michigan Press.

———. 1971. *Essays in Radical Empiricism and A Pluralistic Universe.* New York: E. P. Dutton.

———. 1981. *Pragmatism.* Indianapolis: Hackett.

Krikorian, Yervant H., ed. 1944a. *Naturalism and the Human Spirit.* New York: Columbia University Press.

Krikorian. Yervant H. 1944b. "A Naturalistic View of Mind." In Yervant H. Krikorian, ed., 1944a, 242–269.

Kuklick, Bruce. 1985. *Josiah Royce: An Intellectual Biography*. Indianapolis: Hackett.

Lachs, John. 1992. "O Pluralizme Chelovecheskoi Prirodii" (On the Pluralism of Human Nature). *Voprosy Filosofii*, no. 10: 103–111.

Lamont, Corliss. 1957. *The Philosophy of Humanism*. New York: Philosophical Library.

———. 1967. *Freedom of Choice Affirmed*. New York: Horizon.

Lamprecht, Sterling Power. 1940. *Empiricism and Natural Knowledge*. Berkeley: University of California Press.

Larrabee, Harold A. 1944. "Naturalism in America." In Yervant H. Krikorian, ed., 1944a, 319–353.

Lewis, C. I. 1929. *Mind and the World Order*. New York: Dover.

———. 1957. *Our Social Inheritance*. Bloomington: Indiana University Press.

———. 1962. *An Analysis of Knowledge and Valuation*. La Salle, Ill.: Open Court.

Lothstein, Arthur. 1979. "From Privacy to Praxis: The Case for John Dewey as a Radical American Philosopher." Ph.D. diss., New York University.

Lowe, Victor. 1941. "The Development of Whitehead's Philosophy." In Paul Arthur Schilpp, ed., 1941, 15–124.

Madison, James. 1976. *Notes of Debates in the Federalist Convention of 1787*. Athens: Ohio University Press.

Manicas, Peter T. 1982. "John Dewey, Anarchism and the Political State." *Transactions of the Charles S. Peirce Society* 18, no. 2: 133–158.

———. 1988. "Philosophy and Politics: An Historical Approach to Marx and Dewey." In William J. Gavin, ed., 1988, 147–175.

Marsoobian, Armen., Kathleen Wallace, and Robert S. Corrington, eds. 1991. *Nature's Perspectives: Prospects for Ordinal Metaphysics*. Albany: State University of New York Press.

McBride, William L. 1988. "Science, Psychology, and Human Values in the Context of Dewey's Critique of Marx." In William J. Gavin, ed., 1988, 37–47.

McClellan, James. 1988. "Logical Pragmatism and Dialectical Materialism" (in Russian). *Filosofskie Nauki*, no. 11: 72–80.

McDermott, John J. ed. 1969. *The Basic Writings of Josiah Royce*. 2 vols. Chicago: University of Chicago Press.

Miller, Perry. 1965. *The Life of the Mind in America*. New York: Harcourt, Brace, Jovanovich.

Murphey, Murray. 1961. *The Development of Peirce's Philosophy*. Cambridge, Mass.: Harvard University Press.

Nagel, Ernest. 1944. "Logic without Ontology." Yervant H. Krikorian, ed., 1944a, 210–241.

———. 1954. *Sovereign Reason*. Glencoe, Ill.: Free Press.

———. 1956. *Logic without Metaphysics*, Glencoe, Ill.: Free Press.

———. 1961. *The Structure of Science*. New York: Harcourt, Brace & World.

Noonan, John T. Jr. 1988. "'Quota of Imps.'" In Merrill D. Peterson and Robert C. Vaughan, eds., 1988, 171–199.

Parrington, Vernon L. 1954. *Main Currents in American Thought.* 3 vols. New York: Harcourt, Brace & World. Russian translation, *Osnovnye Techeniya Amerikanskoi Mysli.* T. 1–3. Moskva, 1962.

Peirce, Charles Sanders. 1931–1958. *Collected Papers of Charles Sanders Peirce.* Vols. 1–6, edited by Charles Hartshorne and Paul Weiss; vols. 7 and 8 edited by Arthur W. Burks. Cambridge, Mass.: Belknap Press of Harvard University Press.

Perry, Ralph Barton. 1912. *Present Philosophical Tendencies.* New York: Longmans, Green.

———. 1964. *Puritanism and Democracy*, New York: Harper & Row.

Peterson, Merrill D., ed. 1975. *The Portable Jefferson.* New York: Penguin.

Peterson, Merrill D., and Robert C. Vaughn, eds. 1988. *The Virginia Statute for Religious Freedom: Its Evolution and Consequences in American History.* New York: Cambridge University Press.

Randall, John Herman Jr. 1946. "Metaphysics: Its Function, Consequence and Criteria." *The Journal of Philosophy* 43, no. 15: 401–412.

———. 1957. "Substance as Process." *The Review of Metaphysics* 10, no. 4: 580–601.

———. 1958a. *Nature and Historical Experience.* New York: Columbia University Press.

———. 1958b. *The Role of Knowledge in Western Religion.* Boston: Starr King.

———. 1960. *Aristotle.* New York: Columbia University Press.

———. 1967. "Metaphysics and Language," *The Review of Metaphysics* 21, no. 4: 591–601.

Rawls, John. 1994. "Teoriya Spravedluvostu—Glava I. Spravedlivost' kak Chestnost'" (The Theory of Justice—Chapter 1. Justic as Fairness). *Voprosy Filosofii*, no. 10: 38–52.

Rescher, Nicholas. 1977. *Methodological Pragmatism.* New York: New York University Press.

Rorty, Richard. 1979. *Philosophy and the Mirror of Nature.* Princeton: Princeton University Press.

———. 1982. *Consequences of Pragmatism.* Minneapolis: University of Minnesota Press.

———. 1994. "Filosofiya i Budushchee" (Philosophy and the Future). *Voprosy Filosofii*, no. 6: 29–34.

Rosenthal, Sandra. 1995. "Eticheskoe Izmerenie Chelovecheskogo Sushchestvovaniya: Pragmaticheskii Pyt Muda za Predelami Absolyutizma i Relyativizma" (The Ethical Measure of Human Life: Mead's Pragmatic Approach to the Limits of Absolutism and Relativism). *Voprosy Filosofii*, no. 5: 137–142.

Royce, Josiah. 1885. *The Religious Aspect of Philosophy*, New York: Houghton, Mifflin.

———. 1892a. "The Implications of Self-Consciousness." *The New World* 1: 289–310.

———. 1892b. *The Spirit of Modern Philosophy*. New York: Houghton, Mifflin.
———. 1899. *The World and the Individual*. New York: Macmillan.
———. 1904. "The Eternal and the Practical." *Philosophical Review* 13: 113–142.
———. 1908. *The Philosophy of Loyalty*. New York: Macmillan.
———. 1913. *The Problem of Christianity*. New York: Macmillan.
———. 1966. "The Two-Fold Nature of Knowledge," edited by Peter Fuss. *Journal of the History of Philosoph* 4: 326–337.
Ryder, John. 1988. "Naturalism, Dialectical Materialism and an Ontology of Constitutive Relations." In William J. Gavin, ed., 1988, 229–254.
———. 1989. "Private Property and the United States Constitution." In Christopher B. Gray, ed., 16–28.
———. 1991a. "Ordinality and Materialism." In Marsoobian et. al. eds., 201–220.
———. 1991b. "Naturalizm, Dialekticheskii Materializm i Ob'ektivnost'" (Naturalism, Dialectical Materialism and Objectivity). *Vestnik Moskovskogo Universiteta*, Philosophy Series, no. 1: 85–90.
———. 1993. "The Use and Abuse of Modernity: Postmodernism and the American Philosophic Tradition." *The Journal of Speculative Philosophy* 7, no. 2: 92–102.
Santayana, George. 1905–1906. *The Life of Reason*, New York: Charles Scribner's Sons.
———. 1925. *Dialogues in Limbo*. New York: Charles Scribner's Sons.
———. 1927–1940. *The Realms of Being*. New York: Charles Scribner's Sons.
———. 1951. *Dominations and Powers*. New York: Charles Scribner's Sons.
———. 1955. *Scepticism and Animal Faith*. New York: Dover.
Scanlon, James P. 1985. *Marxism in the USSR*. Ithaca, N.Y.: Cornell University Press.
Schilpp, Paul Arthur, ed. 1941. *The Philosophy of Alfred North Whitehead*. La Salle, Ill.: Open Court.
Schneider, Herbert W. 1963. *A History of American Philosophy*. New York: Columbia University Press.
———. 1964. *Sources of Contemporary Philosophical Realism in America*. New York: Bobbs-Merrill.
Schwager, Robert S. 1988. "A Constitutional Right to Revolution?" State University of New York—Moscow State University Conference on the U.S. Constitution, State University of New York College at Cortland, January 1988.
Sellars, Roy Wood. 1916. *Critical Realism*. Chicago: Rand-McNally.
———. 1927. "Why Naturalism and not Materialism?" *Philosophical Review* 36: 216–225.
———. 1932. *The Philosophy of Physical Realism*. New York: Macmillan.
———. 1943. "Verification of Categories: Existence and Substance." *Journal of Philosophy* 40: 197–205.
———. 1944–1945. "Reflections on Dialectical Materialism." *Philosophy and Phenomenological Research* 5: 157–179.

———. 1960. "Panpsychism or Evolutionary Naturalism." *Philosophy of Science* 27, no. 4: 329–350.

———. 1962. "Tri Stupeni Materializma" (Three Levels of Materialism). *Voprosy Filosofii* 23, no. 8.

Sellars, Roy Wood, V. J. McGill, and Marvin Farber. 1949. *Philosophy for the Future.* New York: Macmillan.

Singer, Beth J. 1994. "Demokraticheskoe Reshenie Problema Etnicheskogo Mnogoobraziya" (The Democratic Resolution of the Problem of Ethnic Diversity). *Voprosy Filosofii*, no. 6: 89–97.

Skrupskelis, Ignas K. 1969. "Annotated Bibliography of the Published Works of Josiah Royce." In John J. McDermott, ed., 1969, 2:1167–1226.

Thompson, M. 1953. *The Pragmatic Philosophy of C. S. Pierce.* Chicago: University of Chicago Press.

Thoreau, Henry David. 1966. *Anti-Slavery and Reform Papers*, ed. Walter Harding. Montreal: Harvest House.

———. "A Plea for Captain John Brown." In Henry David Thoreau 1966, 42–65.

———. "Civil Disobedience." In Henry David Thoreau 1966, 1–25.

———. "Slavery in Massachusetts." In Henry David Thoreau 1966, 26–41.

———. "Life Without Principle." In Carl Bode, ed., 1975, 631–655.

———. *Walden, or Life in the Woods.* In Carl Bode, ed., 1975, 258–572.

Toulmin, Stephen. 1990. *Cosmopolis.* New York: Free Press.

Trotsky, Leon. 1973. *Their Morals and Ours.* Edited by George Novak. New York: Pathfinder.

Von Hagen, Mark. 1991. "The Stalin Question." *The Nation*, March 25: 382–387.

Wahlke, John C. ed. 1952. *Loyalty in a Democratic State.* Lexington, Mass.: D. C. Heath.

Warren, W. Preston, ed. 1970. *Principles of Emergent Realism: Philosophical Essays by Roy Wood Sellars.* St. Louis: Warren H. Green.

Wiener, Philip. 1949. *Evolution and the Founders of Pragmatism.* Cambridge, Mass.: Harvard University Press.

———. 1967. "A Soviet Philosopher's View of Peirce's Pragmatism." *Transactions of the Charles S. Pierce Society* 3: 3–12.

Wells, Harry. 1954. *Pragmatism: Philosophy of Imperialism.* New York: International Publishers.

West, Cornel. 1989. *The American Evasion of Philosophy.* Madison: University of Wisconsin Press.

White, Morton. 1987. *Philosophy, "The Federalist," and the Constitution.* New York: Oxford University Press.

Whitehead, Alfred North. 1906. "On Mathematical Concepts of the Material World." *Philosophical Transactions, Royal Society of London*, series A, 205: 465–525.

———. 1919. *An Enquiry Concerning the Principles of Natural Knowledge.* Cambridge: Cambridge University Press.

———. 1920. *The Concept of Nature.* Cambridge: Cambridge University Press.

———. 1925. *Science and the Modern World.* New York: Macmillan.

———. 1967. *Adventures of Ideas.* New York: Free Press.

———. 1978. *Process and Reality.* Corrected edition. Edited by David Ray Griffin and Donald W. Sherburne. New York: Free Press.

———. 1990. *Izbrannye Raboty po Filosofii* (Selected Philosophical Works). Moskva: Progress Publishers.

Whitehead, Alfred North, and Bertrand Russell. 1910–1913. *Principia Mathematica,* Cambridge: Cambridge University Press.

Wills, Garry. 1979. *Inventing America.* New York: Vintage.

———. 1982. *Explaining America,* New York: Penguin.

Woodbridge, Frank James Eugene. 1926. *The Realm of Mind: An Essay in Metaphysics.* New York: Columbia University Press.

Zimring, Fred. 1984. "Cold War Compromises: Albert Barnes, John Dewey, and the Federal Bureau of Investigation." *The Pennsylvania Magazine of History and Biography* 108, no. 1: 87–100.

INDEX

John Ryder is professor of philosophy and dean of arts and sciences at the State University of New York at Cortland.